D0765701

Accident

Accident

A Philosophical and Literary History

ROSS HAMILTON

The University of Chicago Press
Chicago and London

Ross Hamilton is associate professor of English at Barnard College.

The University of Chicago Press, Chicago 60637
The University of Chicago Press, Ltd., London
© 2007 by The University of Chicago
All rights reserved. Published 2007
Printed in the United States of America

16 15 14 13 12 11 10 09 08 07   1 2 3 4 5

ISBN-13: 978-0-226-31484-6 (cloth)
ISBN-10: 0-226-31484-7 (cloth)

The University of Chicago Press gratefully acknowledges the generous support of Barnard College toward the publication of this book.

Library of Congress Cataloging-in-Publication Data

Hamilton, Ross, 1964–
    Accident : a philosophical and literary history / Ross Hamilton.
        p. cm.
    Includes bibliographical references and index.
    ISBN-13: 978-0-226-31484-6 (cloth : alk. paper)
    ISBN-10: 0-226-31484-7 (cloth : alk. paper)   1. Aristotle.   2. Accidents
(Philosophy)   3. Substance (Philosophy)   I. Title.
    B491.A24H36 2007
    111'.1—dc22
                                                                            2007014868

CONTENTS

ACKNOWLEDGMENTS

The scope of this book leaves me indebted to many scholars who modeled a level of intellectual commitment that inspired me and urged me forward. I profited from studying with Hubert Damisch, Georges Didi-Huberman, Paul Fry, John Guillory, Geoffrey Hartman, Sarah Kofman, and Clifford Siskin, but I owe John Hollander and Louis Marin special thanks for their intellectual generosity to a young scholar.

In my need for advice in fields farthest from my own specialties, I consulted numerous friends and colleagues and am grateful for their comments on preliminary drafts. Among those whose knowledge made significant contributions to my thoughts I would like to single out Bashir Abu-Manneh, Jonathan Arac, Taylor Carman, Jenny Davidson, Nicolas Dames, David Damrosch, Kathy Eden, Alan Gabbey, Daniel Heller-Roazin, Gerrit Jackson, Colin Jager, Matthew Jones, Christiane Joost-Gaugier, Joel Kaye, Paula Loscocco, Wolfgang Mann, Samuel Moyn, Fred Neuhouser, Robert Pasnau, Peter Platt, Adam Potkay, Anne Lake Prescott, Martin Puchner, Tom Ratkin, James Shapiro, Herb Sloan, Manya Steinkoler, Carl Wennerlind, Corey Wetherington, John Yolton, and the anonymous reviewers.

I would be remiss not to give special thanks to those who not only contributed to the intellectual content of the book but supported me in many ways throughout the process of completing it: my excellent and wise friends Christopher Baswell and Charles Mahoney, my colleagues James Basker, Mary Gordon, Maire Jaanus, David Kastan, and Karl Kroeber, and my iron disciplinarian and favorite critic, Hertha Schulze.

Barnard College and Columbia University have been a congenial place in which to write this book. The college supported my writing through a semester's sabbatical, and Akeel Bilgrami and the Heyman Center for the Humanities provided an exciting interdisciplinary place for the exchange of ideas. I also wish to thank the Gilder Foundation for financial support.

I have benefited from the insight and experience of Alan Thomas at the University of Chicago Press. Randolph Petilos helped to guide me through the publication process, and Erik Carlson provided expert editorial advice. I would also like to thank Christopher Rogers and Bernhard Kendler for their earlier support of my ideas.

This book is dedicated to my parents, Mary and Bert Hamilton, whose lives have been models of scholarship, integrity, and substance.

The Shock of Experience

A car hits Giacometti as he crosses the place des Pyramides, and he experiences a feeling of joy. A glance at a newspaper notice causes Rousseau to collapse on the road to Vincennes under the force of his vision of another universe. Montaigne is knocked from his horse in the Périgord and feels as though his spirit is hovering above his bleeding body. In his garden in Milan, Augustine opens a page in the *Epistles* and senses a divine light flooding his heart as he penetrates the meaning of what he reads.

What do these experiences have in common? Each was surprising and life transforming, but not all correspond to the current notion of accident as an unexpected event. Why would an act of reading be considered accidental? Even posing this question implies the extent to which we have been conditioned to think that accidents involve physical change. For that reason, although we may hesitate to apply the term "accident" to the reading of a text, we readily accept Giacometti's car crash or Montaigne's fall from his horse as accidental events.[1] But for centuries the association with a physical event was only one way of thinking about accident.

Aristotle had formulated a powerful alternative conception. He used the term "accident" (*sumbebekos*) to distinguish the mutable or inessential qualities of a thing from its defining essence or substance. He used the same term to refer to accidental events, so a link between unexpected events and the defining qualities of a person or thing appears at the beginning of the history of accident. Although the association of accident with a state of being seems surprising to us because it is no longer

---

1. The understanding of accident as event informs the most comprehensive study to date of the philosophical bases for the idea, Michael Witmore's discussion of examples from Shakespeare and Bacon in *The Culture of Accidents: Unexpected Knowledges in Early Modern England* (Stanford: Stanford University Press, 2001).

current in our ordinary use of the term, it was a basic premise of Aristotle's system of thought. As he argued in his *Metaphysics,* the question of what constitutes the substantive quality of a thing lies at the heart of any understanding of being. Separating this essential quality from the inessential ones provided a foundation for thinking about existence. Augustine's conversion and Rousseau's illumination involved this second sense of accidents as qualities. Their transforming experiences purged them of qualities inessential to a sudden redefinition of who they were.

This book follows transformations of Aristotle's double understanding of accident up to the present. Only this long time span allows us to grasp the intricacy of the interactions between accident as a quality and accident as an event. While for us Augustine, Montaigne, Rousseau, and Giacometti represent dramatically different perceptions of selfhood in widely different historical contexts, they share a common conceptual inheritance in Aristotle's double sense of accident. In part, the similarities between their accounts reflect the extent to which familiarity with earlier texts conditions the interpretation of experience. But textual palimpsests cannot in themselves explain the process of change that we observe when following the deep history of accident.

Some shifts in this history appear as radical transformations. We might think of the way in which medieval Scholastics turned Aristotle's metaphysical substance into divinity or Renaissance skeptics accentuated the subjective impact of contingent events. Enlightenment empiricists further shifted the conceptual ground by bracketing substance from the sensory data they prized, while the romantics rediscovered substance in the guise of nature. Yet to envision the changing interpretation of accident as a series of historical ruptures would be to oversimplify the evidence provided by literary as well as philosophical texts and to ignore the enduring presence of Aristotle's categorical thought, which manifests itself in unexpected formulations and often in agonistic contexts. Examining the history of accident reveals the extent to which conventional periodization has limited our understanding of the metaphysical aspects of historical change.

Modern critics, especially those influenced by Martin Heidegger's critique of Western metaphysics, deploy traces of Aristotle's notions of substance and accident within theoretical manifestos that express their modernity. Three who display the tensions implicit in the Aristotelian heritage as they engage the question, What is being *now?* are the French theorists Paul Virilio, Michel Foucault, and Alain Badiou. Although their work represents a dialogue among cultural contemporaries, their approaches involve distinctive attributes of contemporary experience, such as changes in technology, the production of knowledge within the sociology of power relationships, and the omnipresence of scientific and mathematical modes of thought. By using such unsettled (and unsettling) contexts of modernity as the bases for contemplating questions of self-understanding, these critics have developed hypotheses that illuminate the central issues of this book and demonstrate the relevance of studying accident over the *longue durée*.

Paul Virilio stands foremost among contemporary critics in his emphasis on the postmodern impact of technology.[2] For him, the innovations of the twentieth century have taken accidental events to extremes, mass-producing them and preparing for what he calls the "integral accident," a continental, multicontinental, or even planetary event that will involve the serial production of catastrophes. He perceives a radical new relationship between accidental events and how people think. In his theory inherent aspects of techno-scientific knowledge, such as cinema, television, and digital simulation, transform Aristotle's accident of substance into what he calls an accident of knowledge. "For Aristotle in his day and for us today," he writes, "if the accident reveals the substance, it is indeed the *accidens*—what happens—which is a kind of analysis, a technoanalysis of what *substat*—lies beneath—all knowledge."[3] Virilio's concern is that exposure to thought technologies induces a voluntary blindness to the implications of events that damages any sense of responsibility for individual actions, and this "love of radical mindlessness" is replacing (or has already replaced) philosophical introspection.

The philosophical crisis that alarms Virilio began to encourage multidisciplinary responses as early as the mid-twentieth century. Historians as well as philosophers questioned how the same data could provide dif-

2. Virilio's works that deal explicitly with violent accident include *The Information Bomb*, trans. Chris Turner (London: Verso, 2000), *A Landscape of Events*, trans. Julie Rose (Cambridge, MA: MIT Press, 2000), and *Unknown Quantity*, trans. Chris Turner (London: Thames and Hudson, 2003), the catalog for the exhibition Museum of Accidents presented at the Fondation Cartier in Paris, 29 November–30 March 2003, which displayed images of natural accidents, such as hurricanes or ice storms, industrial and environmental accidents, wrecks, derailments, and air accidents, and deliberate accidents, such as terrorist bombings.

3. Virilio, *Unknown Quantity*, 24. To make this parallel hold, Virilio appears to be thinking of accident as a quality that inheres in substance. Thus, accidental events may be understood as inherent aspects of techno-scientific knowledge—even though their presence is not inevitable.

ferent or even conflicting explanations in different theoretical contexts.[4] Such questions enlarged investigations into the conditions that affect perception and how people understand themselves as agents and as interpreters of experience. Thus, in the 1970s, as Michel Foucault moved from his studies of the power structures embedded in the history of madness (or of their relation to natural history and biology) toward his transhistorical analysis of sexuality, he proposed that new systems of thought did not fulfill grand historical designs but were formed from successive theories produced by small, unrelated causes.[5] Translation obscures Foucault's distinction between *connaissance* (as the relation between the subject and the object to be known and the rules that govern this relationship) and *savoir* (the conditions within a particular period that allow such an object to be presented to *connaissance*), but it is critical to clarifying his development of two axes of understanding: his archaeological and genealogical models. The "genealogical" model expanded the earlier "archaeological" concept, in which systems of thought succeeded one another chronologically. It offered an understanding of transitions in intellectual history that did not involve concepts of origin, progression, or end. An investigation that combined both ways of regarding evidence—one that was "genealogical in its design and archaeological in its method"—could escape the limitations imposed by historical preconceptions. The ultimate focus of Foucault's hypothesis was what he termed "the historical ontology of ourselves."[6] He elaborated on this idea in an interview: "Three domains of genealogy are possible. First, a historical ontology of ourselves in relation to truth through which we constitute ourselves as subjects of knowledge; second, a historical ontology of ourselves in relation to a field of power through which we constitute ourselves as subjects acting on others; third, a historical ontology in relation to ethics through which we constitute ourselves as moral agents."[7] The genealogical model enabled Foucault

4. For example, Saul A. Kripke, revisiting the so-called cluster theory interpretation of the Aristotelian categories in 1972, asserted: "It really is a nice theory. The only defect I think it has is probably common to all philosophical theories. It's wrong." *Naming and Necessity* (Cambridge, MA: Harvard University Press, 1972), 64. Accepted as shocking and liberating at the time, the tone of Kripke's work remains convincingly "modern."

5. Michel Foucault, "Nietzsche, Genealogy, History," trans. Donald F. Brouchard and Sherry Simon, in *Aesthetics, Method, and Epistemology*, ed. James D. Faubion, trans. Robert Hurley et al. (New York: New Press, 1998), 369–91.

6. Michel Foucault, "What Is Enlightenment?" trans. Catherine Porter, in *Ethics: Subjectivity and Truth*, ed. Paul Rabinow, trans. Robert Hurley et al. (New York: New Press, 1997), 315, 316.

7. Michel Foucault, "On the Genealogy of Ethics: An Overview of Work in Progress," in *Ethics: Subjectivity and Truth*, 262.

to expose the metaphysical assumptions behind systems of thought that condition their possibility.[8] Thus, in his incomplete *History of Sexuality*, he examined the question of being in terms of changing relationships between the self and the body, focusing on how the subject (as the product of external powers) comes to understand itself.

Foucault's student Alain Badiou shifted his focus of inquiry from the self-analytical subject to the nature of experience. His work engages the fundamental significance of the event but with specific attention to subtle problems inherent in interpretation. In his theory, the manner of perceiving an event determines a subject's ontological status. As a consequence, his work is particularly interesting in terms of our analysis of accident because his complex philosophical discourse integrates Aristotle's double frame of reference by treating the problem of determining the nature of events in relation to the search for essence. By asserting that understanding the nature of an event provides a new understanding of being, Badiou reenvisions the relationship between the Aristotelian categories.

Understanding how Badiou reformulated this relation requires a brief survey of the mathematical basis of his work. As an analytical tool, he adopted the set theory invented by Georg Cantor in 1873.[9] Set theory offered him a language he could use to postulate that an event (conceived as a "unit of one" within its situational context or "multiple") can conceptualize the unknowable or indeterminate. In other words, his mathematical ontology enabled him to address the enduring philosophical and theological problem of substance.

In set theory each model has its own language, whose various formulas express certain properties, and all the properties expressed by subsets of this model can be described in this language. To explain historical change, Badiou incorporated the generic set, a mathematical idea invented by Paul Cohen in 1963. In set theory, when a model is seen to possess a new subset that cannot be known by its properties or discerned

---

8. Stuart Elden, "Reading Genealogy as Historical Ontology," in *Foucault and Heidegger: Critical Encounters*, ed. Alan Milchman and Alan Rosenberg (Minneapolis: University of Minnesota Press, 2003), 201.

9. Set theory postulates an assemblage of entities that are not defined in terms of more fundamental concepts yet can be used to define all other mathematical concepts. All citations of *Being and Event* are taken from Oliver Feltham's translation from the original Éditions du Seuil publication of 1988 (London: Continuum, 2003). Feltham and Justin Clemens, the editors and translators of Badiou's *Infinite Thought: Truth and the Return to Philosophy* (London: Continuum, [2003]), provide a useful point of entry to his thought in their introduction by summarizing *Being and Event* and situating his work in relation to poststructuralist theory.

by the language of the model, the new set is not "presented" mathematically. Cohen's innovation consisted in discovering a method for describing such a generic set without betraying its "indiscernability." His solution was to add it to an existing model and thereby form a new set. Because the generic multiple now *belongs* to the new set, it is presented in it: Cohen's theory schematizes a historical situation that has undergone a discernible change. For Badiou, by approximating the result of finite enquiries into the nature of the event, a mathematical idiom of this kind makes it possible to conceptualize historical change.

Badiou uses the French Revolution as a concrete example of the difficulties inherent in the historical "multiple." This event, he writes, forms a unit of one out of everything that makes up France circa 1789–94. A historian might inventory this site in terms of all the traces and facts the period delivers: electors, sansculottes, members of the Convention, Jacobin clubs, soldiers of the draft, English spies, and Vendeans, as well as the price of goods, the guillotine, the massacres, the theater, the *Marseillaise*, and so on. Such a procedure, he believes, merely undoes the event into an infinite number of coexisting gestures, things, and words: listing elements in this way does not constitute a "truth procedure." We can compare these historical elements to the properties expressed in the idiomatic language of a set theory model. For example, the term "revolution" (as a generic set) filters the entire sequence of facts, not only presenting the infinite multiple the entire site contains (the model set of France in 1789–94), but also marking the presentation of itself as the "one" of the infinite multiple.[10]

What is at issue for Badiou is whether an event like the French Revolution belongs to the situation (the model set) as one part of the multiple (which is logically impossible because the situation's various elements belong *to* it) or does *not* belong to the situation (as in the case of the indiscernible subset in generic set theory). In that case one might argue that "French Revolution" would be merely a word that presents nothing. Badiou then argues that such an event either ruptures the site's being or forces the situation to reformulate (creating, in other words, a new set to which it "belongs").[11] In that sense, accidental events can be experienced as ruptures that destroy a system (unless they can be explained) or as instruments for the creation of entirely new systems.

10. Badiou, *Being and Event*, 180.
11. Ibid., 183. Badiou's ontological expression of this shift describes the event letting forth "from inconsistent being and the interrupted count, the incandescent non-being of an existence." This summary necessarily reduces both the mathematical and the philosophical content imbedded in Badiou's dense argument.

On the basis of his analysis of the event, Badiou also reconfigures the poststructuralist problem of agency. Foucault had postulated that the subject must resist power by the aesthetic project of self-authoring. Badiou counters by maintaining that subjectivization involves a long, active transformation through which human beings not only recognize an event that disrupts the situation in which they find themselves—a situation that cannot be understood in terms of existing knowledge—but proceed to act faithfully within that recognition. Striving to address the set newly presented within the multiple turns subjects into agents of change. In effect, it makes them modern.

Similarities between these three examples suggest the extent to which even highly original critics are conditioned by historical situations. In each case, we observe a determined effort to stand outside the object of examination and the intellectual traditions that are perceived as limited or even outworn modes of understanding its essential nature. Yet the dissatisfaction that stimulates a desire to "modernize" the existing perception of the past remains intimately bound up with an intellectual inheritance that determines the range of available concepts. Beneath Badiou's rejection of data compilation as "truth" lies the troubled inheritance of Enlightenment empiricism as well as the urgent complexity of new historical practice. Beneath Virilio's diatribes against the mindlessness imposed by enslavement to new technology lies a quest to comprehend the formation of ideas that stretches from Descartes to Derrida. In the sense that this study excavates conceptual layers back to Aristotelian bedrock, it partakes of this quest, yet it cannot escape doing so in the manner of a "modern" who is aware not only of the pitfalls attached to questions of intertextuality but also of the historical implications of Foucault's archaeological and genealogical premises.

In a series of essays compiled under the title of *Historical Ontology*, Ian Hacking deployed a specifically linguistic method of resisting the expansion of historical data as an end in itself. His "analysis of words in their sites" simultaneously acknowledged his pursuit of Foucault's goal of refining the interrelation between *connaissance* and *savoir* and Badiou's recognition of the centrality of language in any attempt to understand either being or events. As a historian of science, Hacking used the study of the brain to demonstrate how a "sentence" considered valid at one point in time might become impossible at another. "The kinds of things to be said about the brain in 1780," he noted, "are not the kinds of things to be said a quarter-century later. That is not because we have different beliefs about brains, but because 'brain' denotes a new kind of object in the later discourse, and occurs in different sorts of sentences." In other words, mental functions that had been abstracted from the physical matter of the brain were now understood to reside within it.[12]

One of the chief investigative tools used in this book applies a version of Hacking's analysis of words in their sites. For example, substituting the word "accident" for "brain" in his example reveals a comparable mutation of meaning near the end of the eighteenth century: Rousseau's concept of accident as a gamble with personal identity becomes Wordsworth's identification of accident as a sign of poetic election. The difference is subtle yet far reaching. Moreover, "small, unrelated causes" associated with subjects that were also undergoing conceptual shifts—such as the development of mathematical attempts to contain uncertainty that resulted in statistical theory or the exploration of the operation of the nervous system in the formation of thoughts and feelings—appear implicated in this change. This book will argue that similar mutations (associable with similar shifts in knowledge bases) occur throughout the history of accident.

Although Aristotle's ontological categories opposed substance to accident, over time what we might describe as coordination, symbiosis, or even commingling of his terms blurred or superseded their opposition. Encoded in the accident experience, following it like a shadow, are reformulations of accidental qualities. As a result, moments of conceptual shift function less as breaks than as hinges between one mode of perception and another. Our general lack of familiarity with the concept of accidental qualities, accompanied by the strength of our contemporary association of accident with events that dislocate or rupture circumstances, makes this kind of conceptual enchainment appear counterintuitive, but I will argue that my examples demonstrate it in three important ways:

> A symbiotic relationship exists between accidental qualities and accidental events.
>
> The notion of identity interacts as much with the understanding of accidental qualities as with the understanding of accidental events.

12. Ian Hacking, *Historical Ontology* (Cambridge, MA: Harvard University Press, 2002), 77. Hacking's developmental histories, *Emergence of Probability: A Philosophical Study of Early Ideas about Probability, Induction and Statistical Inference* (Cambridge: Cambridge University Press, 1984) and *The Taming of Chance* (Cambridge: Cambridge University Press, 1990), influenced early versions of this study, although, in my judgment, the evidence does not sustain a developmental hypothesis.

The value of substance relative to the value of accident serves as a marker
in the cultural identification of what it means to be "modern."

Variations occur within each of these factors, but the presence or absence
of any factor also varies. Moreover, the nature of interdependence varies
across historical time, and contemporary examples do not necessarily ex-
hibit the same variations. To preserve as many nuances as possible, I adopted a version of Foucault's double axes of genealogy and archaeology,
using axial criteria to determine the selection of texts as well as in the
process of analysis. Thus, the following chapters emphasize texts capable
of presenting an interaction between accidental qualities and accidental events (especially in the areas of autobiography and the novel). But
each example also addresses the question of identity within an ontological framework whether or not a given text explicitly uses an ontological
vocabulary.

The decision to allow cinematic examples to dominate the final chapter may appear unexpected or even unjustified, so this choice requires
additional explanation. On the one hand, it gestures toward the technological shift in knowledge that alarms Virilio. Certainly strong arguments can be made that digitalization represents a change in knowledge
production analogous to that of print culture in the eighteenth century.
We also see connections to the broader problem of concept formation
and transmission. The visual "texts" that appear at intervals throughout
the following chapters are intended to address what appear to be diverse
functions of image making in relation to language. By the nineteenth
century, the synthetic grasp of art, philosophy, and literature exemplified
by Raphael's Vatican frescoes had given way to a detachment of idea from
language that was crystallized in the work of the impressionists and the
symbolists. And the innovative absorption of the pictorial potential of
photography found in the work of Degas anticipated expressive characteristics of form that would become elements within the new grammar
of cinema. While the scope of my project precludes a detailed analysis
of how profoundly both language and sight depend on ideological constructs, the interplay between accidental qualities and ways of perceiving
or conceiving the world suggests that contemporary technology may be
creating a new "model set" whose language will privilege visual form.

The difficulty of selecting valid subject matter is symptomatic of the
interpretive problem Badiou identified in *Being and Event*. What mode of
analysis permits us to determine whether an event belongs to a situation
or not? Cohen's generic set theory provided a tool by shifting the anomaly

into a new context. Assembling what might be viewed as a "mess" of texts is designed to accomplish a similar purpose. It dramatizes the extent to which traditional markers for historical change fail to register the way a given text legitimizes or delegitimizes them. Moreover, it shows that the direction of innovation or revision does not necessarily reflect how stimuli were perceived at the time. Although my discussion accentuates the contingent ambiguity imposed on the book's method, I would argue that centering my discussion on the interplay between qualities and events has allowed me to replace an impressionistic view of conceptual motility with a stroboscopic one more capable of capturing counterintuitive aspects of the phenomena.

We might compare the result to the sequential images Eadweard Muybridge achieved when he set up threads that a horse would trip as it ran past a series of twelve cameras: phenomena invisible to the naked eye suddenly presented themselves for analysis. The aesthetic impact of his images could not match that of the running horses Degas painted at the race track, but his photographic technique delivered information never before available. Freezing movement in time showed that the horse tucks its hooves under its body at the moment when all four feet leave the ground. I offer the reader a comparable series of images that allow us to examine the gait of a moving thought.

CHAPTER ONE

Accidental Origins:
Defining Accidental Qualities and Events

I. Substance and Accident

Aristotle's world consisted of distinct kinds of things that were distinguished from one another by differences in structure and patterns of behavior. The ten categories he established as he sought to comprehend this world mark the starting point of the history of accident. Nine of them denote qualities he termed "accidental." They earned that classification because he considered them inessential to the first quality, the essence or substance of a thing. Yet because his system required all ten categories, his formulation established a lasting interdependence between the two concepts. To understand his notion of accident, therefore, we must first understand what he meant by "substance."

Aristotle's word for substance is *ousia*, an abstract noun from the verb *to be*, and in *Metaphysics* 7 he explained that "the question which, both now and of old, has always been raised, and always been the subject of doubt, viz., what being is, is just the question, what is substance?"[1] As he admitted, however, the word refers to many different things, and he listed what earlier philosophers thought to be substances, namely, animals and plants, "natural bodies," such as air, fire, earth, and water, and the physical universe and its parts, the stars, the moon, and the sun (7.2).[2] His own system proposed to reveal the fundamental substance of

---

1. Aristotle, *Metaphysics*, 7.1.1028b2–5, in *The Complete Works of Aristotle*, ed. Jonathan Barnes, 2 vols. (Princeton: Princeton University Press, 1995). All further translations of Aristotle's works are from this edition.

2. What we know of earlier theories derives primarily from Aristotle's own writings. In general, he considered earlier theories insufficiently rigorous. Although he shared the belief that water, fire, air, and earth were primary substances that composed all matter, he

any thing by classifying the evidence of the senses. A changeable quality, such as the "accident" of whiteness, was predicated on the prior existence of some concrete thing that could lose or gain its coloring. Thus, in contrast to Plato, who might call a thing "white" by virtue of its participation in the prior abstract form of Whiteness, Aristotle focused on observable qualities.

We may use Socrates, one of Aristotle's favorite examples, as a figure to explicate his categories: Socrates as substance (Socrates is a philosopher); quantity (his height); quality (his dark complexion); relation (single); place (Athens); time (today); position (standing); state (holding a book); activity (speaking); and passivity (being asked a question). Substance appears first in this list because substances are primary. All the other categories depend upon that essence. The defining "substance" of Socrates—what makes him the thing he is—is his ability to reason. Although substance is unchanging and the categories themselves are fixed by the system, everything belonging within any of the other nine categories—those Aristotle denominated "accidental"—is mutable. For example, if we suppose that on a previous day Socrates had been sitting with a group of people in Aegina and writing on a tablet, the qualities of place, relation, time, position, or state would differ, but he would remain the same substance.

Mutability explains why the accidental qualities occupy a secondary position in Aristotle's categorical system in relation to the enduring essence of a thing. However, just as he defined accidents as inessential with respect to substance, he defined substance in opposition to accident. Accidents must inhere in some thing—Socrates' action or hair color requires his existence—but substances cannot be predicated on any other thing—Socrates can never be an attribute of Alexander or Plato. "That which is

---

did not limit his understanding of substance to these four things. He countered what now appears to be the prescient materialism of Democritus and the atomists, who envisioned all things made up of microscopic corpuscles generated at random, by arguing that matter has function. He rejected the Pythagoreans' mathematical understanding of substances because in his view numbers presupposed experience with things. He was fully aware that this difficult problem fostered a variety of premises: "Some do not think there is anything substantial besides sensible things, but others think there are eternal substances which are more in number and more real, e.g. Plato posited two kinds of substance—the Forms and the objects of mathematics—as well as a third kind, viz. the substance of sensible bodies" (*Metaphysics* 7.2.1028b18–21). Wolfgang-Ranier Mann, *The Discovery of Things: Aristotle's Categories and Their Context* (Princeton: Princeton University Press, 2000), argues for the revolutionary nature of Aristotle's claim for things as a reflection of his engagement with earlier Greek philosophy.

called substance most strictly, primarily, and most of all," he wrote in the *Categories*, "is that which is neither said of a subject nor in a subject" (5.2a12–14).[3]

The long and complex history of Aristotelian studies indicates the difficulty of establishing with clarity or certainty whether a given quality represents the substance of a thing or merely one of its inessentials. Determining the substance of even a simple object, such as a table, raises issues about the material from which it is made as well as the origin of its essential nature. Presumably a table formed of a specific piece of maple might have been formed from another piece of maple, a different kind of wood, or even from another material, such as stone. In that case, some undetermined quality of "tableness" would seem to be the table's essential property. Conversely, if the piece of maple had been formed into something other than the table, that particular table could not exist.[4] The question of how to distinguish an essential property from an accidental one becomes even more difficult if the thing is alive, for by definition a living being cannot be fixed in time.

To address the problem of change or transformation, Aristotle proposed that a quality that is neither a common occurrence nor necessary to the existence of some thing over time should be called accidental: "Since, among things which are, some are always in the same state and are of necessity (not necessity in the sense of compulsion but that which means the impossibility of being otherwise), and some are not of necessity nor always, but for the most part, this is the principle and this the cause of the existence of the accidental; for that which is neither always nor for the most part, we call accidental."[5] This explanation defines accident in

3. Aristotle does not use the word "accident" in the *Categories*, although it appears in the *Physics* and the *Metaphysics*. Michael Frede, *Essays in Ancient Philosophy* (Minneapolis: University of Minnesota Press, 1987), chap. 3, "Categories in Aristotle," notes that the first term in the list of categories translates literally as "what it is" but usually is interpreted as "substance." See also Richard Tierney, "On the Senses of '*Symbebekos*' in Aristotle," *Oxford Studies in Ancient Philosophy* 21 (2001): 61–82.

4. Saul A. Kripke, *Naming and Necessity* (Cambridge, MA: Harvard University Press, 1972), 114–15, argues this example in a note.

5. Aristotle *Metaphysics* 6.2.1026b28–32. The *Metaphysics* contains Aristotle's most sustained elaboration of the idea of accident. Among the many discussions of his distinction between substance and accident in the *Metaphysics*, see especially Richard Sorabji, *Necessity, Cause, and Blame: Perspectives on Aristotle's Theory* (Ithaca: Cornell University Press, 1980), esp. chap. 1; Robert Heinaman, "Aristotle on Accidents," *Journal of the History of Philosophy* 23, no. 3 (July 1985): 311–24; and Alan Code, "Aristotle: Essence and Accident," in *Philosophical Grounds of Rationality*, ed. R. Grandy and R. Warner (Oxford: Clarendon Press, 1986), 411–39. Michael Wedin, *Aristotle's Theory of Substance: The Categories and Metaphysics Zeta*

accord with the state of a thing at a particular time. His first example takes the common human interest in the weather and defines the accidental as the unusual. A quality that experience might lead us to define as improbable, like the occurrence of a record-breaking cold spell during the "dog days" of late summer, he would call an accident. On the other hand, a heat wave at that time of year would not be called accidental because the weather in August is usually warm. He extrapolates from the effects of the sunny Mediterranean climate to assert that since men are always and for the most part tanned, a pale skin is accidental (6.2.1026b33–37). In a cloudy climate, a tan would be accidental for the same reason. As relative qualities, then, accidents acknowledge the complexity of sensory experience, but they also require an assessment of the probability that a particular experience will or will not occur. They demand interpretation.

Aristotle used his system of categories to order the continual flow of information provided by the senses. Substance provided stability by allowing a thing to remain itself within changing circumstances. It created a *reidentifiable subject of change*.[6] In our simple example of the wooden table, substance would allow it to remain the same object even if its legs or top were replaced. To explain how this could be so, he postulated the existence of what was, in effect, the substance of all substances. Of the possible candidates for this function that suggested themselves, he chose a combination of form and matter.[7]

Neither matter nor form is complete in itself, but in combination they constitute a material substance. Prime matter provides the "stuff," and substantial form provides the common ground for the thing's defining properties. Form allows it to be the kind of thing it is—a human being, for example, rather than a horse or a dog—and to possess the powers of its kind.[8] (We must be careful here not to confuse "form" with specific appearance: Socrates' human form distinguishes him from other

---

(Oxford: Oxford University Press, 2000), provides a "compatibilist" reconciliation of the *Categories* and the *Metaphysics* that references the principle "incompatibilist" arguments.

6. J. L. Ackrill, *Aristotle the Philosopher* (Oxford: Oxford University Press, 1981), 120.

7. Characteristically, Aristotle's answers to this question have become the focus of continuing debate. See Wedin, *Aristotle's Theory of Substance*; and the lengthy introduction to Michael Frede and David Charles, *Aristotle's Metaphysics Lambda: Symposium Aristotelicum* (Oxford: Oxford University Press, 2000), for the two principal views on this issue.

8. This formulation did not, of course, prove satisfying. As the title of *Naming and Necessity* suggests, Kripke explores the question of identity in terms of substance and accident across "all possible worlds," asking, in effect, whether Socrates would have been the same entity if he had not become a philosopher, had lived in China rather than Greece, or were teaching in a public school today.

animals, but what distinguishes him from other men is his substance.) Aristotelians assumed that the destruction of substantial form would destroy the kind of thing the thing is. In that sense it corresponded to essence or substance, a link that fostered misunderstandings on the part of later philosophers. However, substantial form could not be considered identical to substance, because it was not complete in itself (in the sense that it required matter in order to be the form of something). Moreover, destroying a thing's form would not destroy its being.

In the *Categories*, Aristotle made the important general point that substance (as this composite of form and matter) had the capacity to receive various or even contradictory qualities. Because accidents by definition are both mutable and extrinsic to substance, they may alter at a specific moment (as when Socrates sits down) or over time (as when he becomes hot in the sun but cools off in the shade or when he grows old). To further complicate this concept, substances themselves may be transformed (as when Socrates dies). In contrast to accidental change, which alters only the perceptible qualities that depend on substance, substantial change transforms one substance into another. Rather than claiming that accidents cause substantial change (as our connotation of cause and effect may lead us to suppose), Aristotle argued that substantial change enables apparent change: "In the case of substances it is by themselves changing that they are able to receive contraries. For what has become cold instead of hot, or dark instead of pale, or good instead of bad, has changed (has altered); similarly in other cases too it is by itself undergoing change that each thing is able to receive contraries" (*Categories*, 5.4a30–34).

Aristotle's distinction between kinds of change appears in the example of a plant, which germinates, grows, flowers, and dies. Each stage in the temporal process alters the physical qualities of the plant, but its substance remains unchanged. Causes of change reside in the potential of the substance to receive a particular kind of action from the agent, as when a seed of the plant sprouts under the action of sun and rain. The plant's form is not imposed on it by this action; it is inherent in the passive seed. This inherent potentiality binds different natural kinds together as species or genera. Although a specific plant may or may not follow the stages of development typical of its kind, it is the nature of a maple tree to self-seed just as it is the nature of Socrates to reason.

Things come to be in different ways, Aristotle wrote in the *Physics*, "by change of shape, as a statue; by addition, as things which grow; by taking away, as the Hermes from stone; by putting together, as a house" (1.7.190a3–8). Only when such changes take place unexpectedly or contrary to normal expectations would he classify the result as accidental. One of his examples of such an accidental change, when the arm of a marble statue breaks off, accords with our contemporary sense of what an accident is. Others, such as when a statue is dressed in ceremonial robes, a growth deforms the appearance typical of a plant, or the dimensions of a house are measured incorrectly, appear counterintuitive, unrelated to our notion of accident as a purely physical rupture. The fact that Aristotle viewed all these examples as changes in quality profoundly influenced future interpretations of his thought.

II. Accidental Events

Sumbebekos, the word Aristotle used to denote the accidental or unexpected qualities of a thing, is the same word he used to define events that occur unexpectedly: "We call an accident that which attaches to something and can be truly asserted, but neither of necessity nor usually, e.g. if one in digging a hole for a plant found treasure. This—the finding of treasure— happens by accident to the man who digs the hole; for neither does the one come of necessity from the other, or after the other nor, if a man plants, does he usually find treasure" (*Metaphysics,* 5.30.1025a14–16). Although later philosophers treated accidental events as distinct from accidental qualities, we recognize the logic for linking the two. If we remember that Aristotle addressed the problem of change with reference to the state of a thing at a particular time, we can see the relation between the inherent mutability of an accidental quality and the temporal shift in circumstances implicit in an accidental event. Thus, changes in quality imply an occurrence or an act taking place in time, such as getting a tan, standing up, reading, or speaking, while changes in circumstances have the power to alter accidental qualities.[9]

In the example of the man finding buried treasure, determining whether or not to call the event an accident involves interpreting the relation between intent and outcome. No matter how thrilling or significant the discovery of treasure may be, it remains accidental to the intended

9. To alleviate ambiguity, Terence Irwin advocated translating *sumbebekos* as "coincident": "Coincident, symbebe/kos. The term (often translated as 'accident') is derived from sumbainein, 'come about together,' which often just means 'happen' or 'turn out.' Sumbebe/kota include many things that are not, in the ordinary sense, accidents or coincidences." Aristotle, *Nicomachean Ethics,* ed. Terence Irwin, 2nd ed. (Indianapolis: Hackett, 1999), 320. See also the entry for *sumbainein* in Hermann Bonitz, *Index Aristotelicus,* 2nd ed. (Graz: Akademische Druck, 1955).

purpose of digging a hole for a plant. A logical chain of events could explain why the treasure was buried in a particular spot or why the person decided to put a plant precisely there, but for Aristotle, no causal connection links these two events. As a result, he defines an accidental event not merely as an exceptional, rare, or unlikely occurrence—what happens "not for the most part"—but adds the further qualification that the outcome must differ from the one intended. Therefore, just as subtle distinctions define the nature of the relationships among inessential qualities, his definition of the accidental event is predicated on an interpretive analysis of the purpose for which the act was undertaken.

Not all events are done "for the sake of something," but when they are, Aristotle separated those caused directly (in the sense that a deliberate action results in the expected outcome) from those that occur as the result of incidental causes (in which an action undertaken to achieve one purpose results in a different, yet relevant, outcome). Unexpected outcomes resulting from intentional actions can be ascribed to chance (*tuché*).[10] He gave the example of a chance encounter in a marketplace:

> A man is engaged in collecting subscriptions for a feast. He would have gone to such and such a place for the purpose of getting the money, if he had known. He actually went there for another purpose, and it was only accidentally that he got his money by going there; and this was not due to the fact that he went there as a rule or necessarily, nor is the end effected (getting the money) a cause present in himself—it belongs to a class of things that are objects of choice and the result of thought. It is when these conditions are satisfied that the man is said to have gone by chance. If he had chosen and gone for the sake of this—if he always or normally went there when he was collecting payments—he would not be said to have gone by chance. (*Physics*, 2.5.196b34–197a5)

The man did not go to the market because he wanted the money, and Aristotle argued that "the causes of the man's coming and getting the money (when he did not come for the sake of that) are innumerable. He may have wished to see somebody or been following somebody or avoiding somebody, or may have gone to see a spectacle" (*Physics*, 2.5.197a17–19). In

---

10. Although Aristotle also treated chance events and misfortune resulting from errors in judgment or action in the *Rhetoric* (1.10.1369a32–34) and the *Poetics* (24.1460a27–1460b5), these texts did not reappear in Europe until the mid-sixteenth century. For a discussion of accident and probability in these texts see Kathy Eden, *Poetic and Legal Fiction in the Aristotelian Tradition* (Princeton: Princeton University Press, 1986), esp. 25–61.

other words, because chance applies only to outcomes linked to actions chosen and performed with a specific purpose in mind, the term requires a clear understanding of initial intent. To counter those who might argue that "nothing happens by chance," he introduced an interpretive notion of causation. An observer might interpret an action as having a certain purpose, but that interpretation could be false. In the marketplace example, interpreting the purpose of the man's trip as an attempt to collect subscriptions would be a false conclusion.[11]

Aristotle established a continuum of chance causes analogous to the continuum of accidental qualities that he established in his discussion of substance. For example, he reasoned that house-building capabilities are the direct cause of a house, while any attributes of the house builder, such as being pale or musical, are incidental to it (*Physics*, 2.5.196b24–29). From this comparison, he concluded that chance bears the same relation to outcome that an inessential quality bears to substance and thus can never be considered a direct cause, only an incidental one. In his *Metaphysics*, he restated this relationship in an example in which a man arrives at Aegina not because he intended to go there but because he was carried out of his way by a storm or captured by pirates. An external agent interrupted the intended outcome of the event. "The accident has happened or exists,—not in virtue of itself," he wrote, "but of something else; for the *storm* was the cause of his coming to a place for which he was not sailing, and this was Aegina" (5.30.1025a25–29). The fact that the man ends up on Aegina is accidental because chance brought him there when he intended to go somewhere else, but chance enters through the direct act of the storm or the pirates.

Just as intended events result from causes that are obvious or willed, Aristotle argued that chance events (because they involve thought and choice) also have logical causes. However, if a storm frustrates the man's intention to go to somewhere other than Aegina, the cause is an inanimate thing. To distinguish an unexpected event that occurs in nature, Aristotle employed a second and wider term, "spontaneity" (*to automaton*). Like chance causes, spontaneous ones require analysis of intent. For example, when a rock rolls from a cliff because of its own weight and hits a man, an observer might interpret the event as intentional—the result of a push by an enemy or a divine intervention—but because the rock's

---

11. Jonathan Lear, *Aristotle: The Desire to Understand* (New York: Cambridge University Press, 1988), 37.

movement simply represents weight seeking its natural place, that interpretation would be wrong (*Physics*, 2.6.197b30–35).

Aristotle recognized that natural events do not occur with unvarying regularity. They may happen in one way for the most part, but sometimes happen in another way, and thus, he identified exceptions to what happens for the most part as accidental. Since he did not admit causeless events into his understanding of the world, he assumed that such events also must have causes. Recognizing that not all of them can be explained scientifically, he conjectured that peculiarities in the matter of the thing (weight in the case of the rock) caused exceptions to occur, and the concept of *to automaton* explained them.

Aristotle asserted that chance necessarily enters the sphere of moral actions when positive results from a momentous accident are considered "good" and negative results are considered "evil": "The terms 'good fortune' and 'ill fortune' are used when either result is of considerable magnitude. Thus one who comes within an ace of some great evil or great good is said to be fortunate or unfortunate. The mind affirms the presence of the attribute, ignoring the hair's breadth of difference. Further, it is with reason that good fortune is regarded as unstable; for chance is unstable, as none of the things which result from it can hold always or for the most part" (*Physics*, 2.5.197a25–32). In the *Poetics*, Aristotle clarified the idea of moral capability in his example of the fall of a bronze statue representing the murdered king Mitys. Placed in the town square at Argos, the statue fell on the murderer while he was standing among the onlookers during a public spectacle. According to Aristotle, if the statue fell because of its own weight or as the result of a structural defect in its form, witnesses who interpreted the event as an act of retribution would be wrong. Yet because the bronze statue takes the form of Mitys and the victim is his murderer, the concept of *to automaton* intersects with the idea of intention embodied in *tuché*. More powerfully than a falling rock or a storm-driven ship, this event seems to imply a moral force: punishment by divine judgment or vengeance exacted by the spirit of Mitys. Aristotle acknowledged that an event of that kind could seem marvelous. Because such circumstances allow for a significant expansion of the "inessential," they create the possibility that an accidental event may be perceived as "not without a meaning" (9.1452a1–10).

In fact, by claiming that a knowing spectator might interpret the statue's fall as an act of retribution, Aristotle suggested that any accident, perceived in its proper context, may possess interpretive consequences. Just as an interpreter of the exchange of money between the men who met in the marketplace must know their initial intentions in order to determine whether to call the event an accident, the observer of a seemingly spontaneous natural event must know what acts preceded it in order to perceive its implication. For those having this knowledge, however, the accident of the falling statue invites moral interpretation. Assigning "meaning" to such an event generates an implicit tension between a philosophical understanding, which would dismiss the fall as an accident and therefore inessential, and a narrative account, which might posit agency behind the fall. Although Aristotle emphasized the psychological effect of perceiving evidence of design where it seems unwarranted, in the *Poetics* he recognized that a mistaken interpretation, such as attributing moral judgment to a chance event, constitutes the action of some of the best-constructed tragedies.[12]

III. Plotting Accident

In the *Poetics*, Aristotle ascribed primary importance to the combination of events that make up a tragic plot: "The most important of the six [parts of every tragedy] is the combination of the incidents of the story. Tragedy is essentially an imitation not of persons but of action and life. All human happiness or misery takes the form of action; the end for which we live is a certain kind of activity, not a quality. Character gives us qualities, but it is in our actions that we are happy or the reverse. In a play accordingly they do not act in order to portray the characters; they include the characters for the sake of the action. So that it is the action in it, i.e. its plot, that is the end and purpose of the tragedy; and the end is everywhere the chief thing" (6.1450a15–23). Here Aristotle distinguished between *qualities*, which he associated with the characters in the play, and *incidents*, which he believed provide the means by which tragedy fulfills its purpose as an imitation of action and life. This distinction reminds us of the nuances in his concept of accident when he applied the term to living things in which change occurs over time or when intention must

---

12. For a recent argument for the interpretive value of reading the *Poetics* in terms of the *Metaphysics*, see Martha Husain, *Ontology and the Art of Tragedy: An Approach to Aristotle's Poetics* (Albany: State University of New York Press, 2002), esp. chap. 1. Aristotle's rhetorical theory has a bearing on the discussion of both character development and psychological interpretation. A thorough analysis of this topic would constitute a complex but valuable addition to the understanding of accident and probability.

be taken into account. By identifying a "combination of the incidents" as the central element in tragedy, he opened the way for a series of related events (whether accidental or intended) to acquire additional relevance within his literary theory.

In the *Poetics* Aristotle began by comparing history, as a record of singular events that happened at a particular time or place, to poetry, as a presentation of universals, that is, acts which a person possessed of particular qualities will probably or necessarily say or do. This description of universals suggests that a historian could present an accident while a poet could not. However, Aristotle assigned unexpected events a significant role in arousing pity and fear in the audience:[13] "Tragedy, however, is an imitation not only of a complete action, but also of incidents arousing pity and fear. Such incidents have the very greatest effect on the mind when they occur unexpectedly and at the same time in consequence of one another; there is more of the marvellous in them then than if they happened of themselves or by mere chance" (9.1452a2–6). This passage offers a greatly expanded role for accident. For the tragedy to achieve its goal of cathartic experience, shocking or surprising events become essential components of dramatic art. In this sense, the actions that make up a tragic plot form a series of unexpected occurrences designed to compel the audience to perceive causal relationships between them. Of course, the spectators of a Greek tragedy possessed the prior knowledge required for accurate interpretation. What moved them was partly seeing the seemingly accidental event turn out to be necessary and partly seeing how grasping the same realization affected the characters. In other words, by fostering interpretation, Aristotle imbued the literary mode of the accident with significance.

The central example Aristotle used in the *Poetics*, the *Oedipus Rex* of Sophocles, presents accident in many guises: the herdsman saves the infant prince from his intended death by exposure, Oedipus kills Laius at the crossroads, and answering the riddle of the Sphinx leads him to marry his mother. We can define these events as accidental within the world of the story because the characters' interpretation of them as chance events deflects the outcome. However, within the structure of the tragedy, these

---

13. For a related attempt to explain the tension, especially in *Poetics* 9, between Aristotle's preference for "depicting events undisturbed by accidents" while he eschews the "obvious and the forseeable" event, see Dorothea Frede, "Necessity, Chance, and 'What Happens for the Most Part' in Aristotle's *Poetics*," in *Essays on Aristotle's Poetics*, ed. Amélie Oksenberg Rorty (Princeton: Princeton University Press, 1992), 197–219.

events must appear probable or even necessary in order to produce the outcome intended by the playwright, which is new knowledge for both the characters within the play and the audience.

Aristotle used the example of the Messenger who intends to gladden Oedipus and remove his fears about his mother by revealing the secret of his birth to illustrate this reversal of fortune (11.1452a22–26). The finest action of tragedy, he asserted, employs the device of an unintended yet plausible outcome to initiate new knowledge: "A discovery is, as the very word implies, a change from ignorance to knowledge, and thus to either love or hate. . . . The finest form of discovery is one attended by reversal, like that which goes with the discovery in *Oedipus*" (11.1452a30–34). On one level, therefore, we might say that the plot of *Oedipus Rex* inverts the discovery of buried treasure. Hoping to save his city from the plague, Oedipus digs into his past, but the outcome is not what he expects. Moreover, discovering the real import of his actions alters his qualities. No longer the king, husband, or son he once was, he exchanges his ability to see the material world for another kind of knowledge.

The drama permits the audience to observe his process of discovery so that they may participate in a discovery of their own: the interpretation of the tragic fall of Oedipus. To achieve this goal, the playwright must present narrative accidents as probable or necessary events and purge them of ambiguity or chance in order to reach the heights of his art. In other words, although accidents receive the lowest priority in Aristotle's theoretical and logical treatises, in the *Poetics* he conceives of tragedy as composed of these very accidents. His fundamental reappraisal of the psychological value of chance events redefines the literary status of accident.[14]

IV. Who Is Oedipus?

In *Oedipus Rex*, the nature of being lies at the heart of the tragedy. The action of the play turns on a search for identity, but that search is intimately linked to a reinterpretation of actions that initially appear to reach their desired goals. Since Oedipus defines himself in terms of his accomplishments, he is forced to acknowledge the mutability of what he once understood as his defining qualities. In other words, the interaction between

---

14. For another explication of the place of the "persuasive impossibility" (Eden, *Poetic and Legal Fiction*, 37) in the larger context of Aristotle's poetic theory, see Stephen Halliwell, *Aristotle's "Poetics"* (Chicago: University of Chicago Press, 1998), 74–78.

the two meanings of *sumbebekos* (as accidental quality and accidental event) propels the dramatic action.

To resolve the famous riddle of the Sphinx—the self-defining prelude to the action of the play—Oedipus drew on his own understanding to link the baby (moving on four legs), the grown man (on two), and the old man with his cane (on three) as a single entity, "man." As he announces at the beginning of the play, "I the ignorant Oedipus, it was. I that found the answer in my mother-wit, untaught by any birds." [15] Yet the audience will discover that his identity as the successful riddler is no more definitive than his identity as a maimed man (given the name of "swollen-foot" from the wound he received when he was exposed as an infant and then blinded by his own hand in the horror of self-recognition at the end of the play). Accidental events have made him by turns a patricide, an incestuous son, the ruler of Thebes, and ultimately an outcast. [16]

For Aristotle, the question Who is Oedipus?—like the question What is being?—would be a question of what substance could allow the character to perform all the actions of this tragedy. His ideas about form provide an answer. Aristotle equated the soul (*psuché*) with the form of the body, which enabled its material substance to fulfill its essential functions. [17] In *On the Soul,* he compared the relation of body and soul (that is, the matter and form of a human being) to the relation between wax and the shape it might take: "That is why we can dismiss as unnecessary the question whether the soul and the body are one: it is as though we were to ask whether the wax and its shape are one, or generally the matter of a thing and that of which it is the matter. Unity has many senses . . . but the proper one is that of actuality" (2.1.412b5–9). Aristotle premised his notion of the individual on similarity of form and difference of matter. The traditional view of his thought claims that individuals of the same

---

15. Sophocles, *King Oedipus,* in William Butler Yeats's translation, reprinted in *Greek Plays in Modern Translation,* ed. Dudley Fitts (New York: Dial, 1949), 356–57. All citations are of this edition.

16. Alex Woloch, *The One vs. the Many: Minor Characters in the Space of the Protagonist in the Novel* (Princeton: Princeton University Press, 2003), 323–25, notes that being the only person who understands the changing condition of man's consciousness is what enables Oedipus to solve the riddle of the Sphinx, yet his ignorance of his own parentage is what compels him to self-knowledge and thus self-creation.

17. *Psuché* (from which "psychology" and other terms derive) is usually translated as "soul," but Jonathan Barnes translates it as "animator" in *Aristotle* (Oxford: Oxford University Press, 2000), 185. Aristotle's assertion that the soul dies with the body posed doctrinal problems for later Christian interpreters.

species are distinct from each other on account of their differing matter. This view assumes that he would recognize that each candle in a matching series is composed of an individual unit of wax or that while Oedipus and Laius share the form of man, as individuals they possess separate matter.[18]

Although the definition of substance is Aristotle's closest analogy to what we might understand as the "self," it is not clear how he understood the substance of an individual man in everyday circumstances—the Socrates sitting, standing, lecturing, tanning himself in the marketplace—in relation to his concept of substance as the theoretical entity that underlies all accidental qualities. His typical example of Socrates as a philosopher suggests a definition that rests on the individual's position in society or on the performance of a function (such as the house builder, whose function of building provides another favorite example). Thus, Oedipus might be defined as a king, but this definition would not articulate his individuality in the modern sense of the term, nor would it unify his character across the entire narrative. What is clear is that at his birth the oracle defines him as a man who murders his father and marries his mother. No action by his father, mother, or himself can prevent him from performing these preordained functions. Indeed, all the choices made by the characters simply ensure that he will fulfill that definition.

At the opening of *Oedipus Rex*, Oedipus voices the notion of substance as a controlling or animating aspect of his nature when he says, "How can I, being the man I am, being King Oedipus, do other than all I know?" The Priest's response acknowledges his royal substance: "Oedipus, King, not God but foremost of living men, seeing that when you first came to this town of Thebes you freed us from that harsh singer, the riddling Sphinx, we beseech you, all we suppliants, to find some help; whether you find it by your power as a man, or because, being near the Gods, a God has whispered you. Uplift our State; think upon your fame; your coming brought us luck, be lucky to us still." (349). His speech also dem-

---

18. This notion of differing matter would be used during the medieval period to argue for the necessity of the resurrection of the body. One of the most complex current questions in Aristotelian studies is the principle of individuation. In addition to the traditional view described here, which was adopted by the Scholastic theologians, Michael Frede (*Essays in Ancient Philosophy*, 49–71), among others, has claimed that individuals of the same species have different forms which account for their differing from one another or that individuals of the same species are things in their own right and neither matter nor form can serve as a principle of individuation. See, for example, Myles Burnyeat, *A Map of Metaphysics Zeta* (Pittsburgh: Mathesis Publications, 2001).

onstrates the dramatic impact of any moral interpretation of unintended outcomes. As one of the internal observers of events, he interprets the actions of Oedipus as fortunate on the basis of his partial understanding of prior circumstances. Like Oedipus himself, the Priest knows only the actions and events that allowed Oedipus to become king, not those of his origin. The encounter of Laius and Oedipus at the crossroads meets Aristotle's definition of a chance event. Its unintended outcome is patricide and the double crime of the destruction of the family. Likewise, solving the riddle set by the Sphinx may be regarded as accidental because the action achieves the intended result of saving Thebes and making Oedipus king but leads unintentionally to incest and the punitive plague. Initially, Oedipus believes himself to be uniquely fortunate: "I think myself the child of Good Luck, and that the years are my foster-brothers. Sometimes they have set me up, and sometimes thrown me down, but he that has Good Luck for mother can suffer no dishonor. That is my origin, nothing can change it." (373). But his true mother is Jocasta, and his social dishonor will be complete at the ending of the tragedy.

The central irony of the play rests not only on the unintended outcome of choices, but on misinterpretation of events. However, it is the qualities of the characters that compel them to act as they do. In that sense, Oedipus's "self" directs the action. If he had not been proud, he would not have fought with a stranger at the crossroads; if he were not intelligent, he could not have answered the riddle of the Sphinx; if he had not possessed integrity, he would not have sought an explanation for the plague. We can recognize in this example the connection between Aristotle's explanation of the poetic function of character and his explanation of plot: characters act in accordance with particular qualities while the plot integrates their acts into the narrative structure. The character and the plot of *Oedipus Rex* enact Aristotle's double definition of accident.

V. Transcendent Reality

Although we have become accustomed to seeing a dramatic change between classical and Christian thought, from the perspective of substance and accident, the differences appear less divisive.[19] On the one hand, the

19. Eric Auerbach's close readings in *Mimesis: The Representation of Reality in Western Literature*, trans. Willard R. Trask (Princeton: Princeton University Press, 1953), which juxtapose the present-oriented, physical conception of character he finds in Homer to the opaque, transformative, and spiritually complex characters of biblical narrative, exemplify this tradition. For him, sensory appearance, as the dominant classical view, and meaning,

search for self-knowledge and self-discipline continued within the traditions of the spiritual exercise. However, such striving began to find its
goal outside the boundaries of the individual. Plotinus (205?–270?) represents a particularly productive example of both the conservative and
innovative aspects of this process.

An effort to reconcile Aristotle's empirical philosophy with Platonic
idealism extended across the entire period, as access to texts (and the capacity to translate them) affected the interpretation of his central concepts. For Plotinus, the goal of defending Plato and living in accord with
Platonic teachings was conditioned by his conviction that Aristotle's critique of Plato was based on an accurate knowledge of his work. As a result, he not only read Aristotle assiduously but also adopted his terminology for his own arguments.[20] Although he did not consider himself an
innovator, his manipulation of the concept of substance lifted its relationship to accident into a new spiritual and moral plane.

Like Aristotle, Plotinus aspired to create a philosophical system for
describing reality that would be completely clear and intelligible. He believed that he could explain the multiplicity of things (and also the multiplicity of basic principles that inform them) only through a unifying
principle that superseded them all. Otherwise their combinations would
be inexplicable, and he found such randomness intellectually intolerable.
Accordingly, he proposed a system composed of an ascending order of
being with matter occupying the lowest level. At the highest level was an
irreducibly simple essence that was not a specific thing but was capable of

---

as the dominant Christian view, offer antagonistic perceptions of reality. In recent criticism
change is perceived less in terms of oppositions than as fusion of conceptual functions. For
example, discussing his unfinished *History of Sexuality* in an interview published in "On
the Genealogy of Ethics: An Overview of Work in Progress," in *Ethics: Subjectivity and Truth*,
ed. Paul Rabinow, trans. Robert Hurley et al. (New York: New Press, 1997), 255, Michel
Foucault analyzed the shift from classical to Christian culture in terms of the concept of
epimeleia heautou (care of the self). When Christianity adopted the classical practice of contemplative self-knowledge and transformed it into *epimeleia tonallon* (the care of others),
it became the pastor's job. Thus, the classical process of self-definition lost a large part of
its autonomy by being channeled through the pastoral institution of the care of souls. For
Foucault, therefore, the Renaissance culture of the self does not represent the reappearance
of something lost during the medieval period as much as a reaffirmation of a displaced
function. Arnold I. Davidson, "Ethics as Ascetics: Foucault, the History of Ethics, and Ancient Thought," in *Foucault and the Writing of History*, ed. Jan Ellen Goldstein (Oxford: Basil
Blackwell, 1994), analyzes Foucault's work on "care of the self" in relation to contemporary
historical theory.

20. The commentary of Alexander of Aphrodisias (early third century) supported Plotinus's perception that Aristotle regarded himself as an opponent of Plato on many topics.
Porphyry's life of Plotinus affirms that he was thoroughly familiar with the *Metaphysics*.

being present in all things. He named this essence the One.[21] As the first principle in his hierarchical system, it has the power to produce mind and, through mind, the soul. The union of the One with mind explains man's contemplative essence, but the matter that composes bodies and permits their sensory existence lacks the capacity of understanding that derives from mind. The soul, then, provides the desires that animate a living being. In this formulation, aspects of Aristotle's concept that sensory accidents are predicated on substance commingle with Plato's concept of Forms.[22]

The ineffable nature of the One in this system reconstructs the distinction between primary and secondary qualities in Aristotle's analytical classification. Plotinus did not abandon the possibility that self-knowledge and the exercise of will could direct moral action, but by broaching the idea that substance must be spiritual rather than physical, he suffused Aristotle's definition of the rational substance of a human being with new levels of emotion.

Breaking the links to matter, which Plotinus regarded as evil, enables man to reconnect the empirical self—the agent of his moral actions—with the ideal, contemplative self. Man's deepest inner compulsion, he believed, consists of his desire to realize his potential divinity by fusing with the One.[23] In the sixth Ennead, he expressed the movement upward toward this mystical union in terms that recall the relation between substance and accident: "Thus the Supreme as containing no otherness is ever present with us; we with it when we put otherness away. It is not that the Supreme reaches out to us seeking our communion; we reach towards the Supreme; it is we that become present."[24] Elsewhere, he compares the process of becoming "present" by acquiring self-knowledge to the

21. See John Peter Kenney, *Mystical Monotheism: A Study in Ancient Platonic Theology* (Providence: Brown University Press; Hanover: University Press of New England, 1991), 144.

22. The uniqueness and simplicity of the One posed a problem that haunted the notion of substance into the eighteenth century. See R. James Hankinson, *Cause and Explanation in Ancient Greek Thought* (Oxford: Clarendon Press, 1998), 414.

23. For a discussion of the spiritual exercises whose essential psychic content was "the feeling of belonging to a Whole," see Pierre Hadot, *Philosophy as a Way of Life: Spiritual Exercises from Socrates to Foucault*, trans. Michael Chase, ed. Arnold I. Davidson (Oxford: Basil Blackwell, 1995). Plotinus conceived of a "world soul" (generated by the One through mind) in addition to the individual soul, a concept of *psuché* conceptually distinct from any modern sense of self. The figure of the sage or wise man, whose way of life reflects this spiritual striving, mediates between the notion of an individual understood as having specific roles within the social framework of a group and the supernatural force represented by *psuché*.

24. Plotinus, *The Enneads*, trans. Stephen MacKenna, ed. B. S. Page, 2nd ed. (London: Faber and Faber, 1957), 6.9.8. All citations are taken from this text.

creation or polishing of a statue. Man purifies himself not by adding qualities, as a painter might add colors to an image, but by removing what is
inessential in order to reveal the substantive inner beauty (1.6.9).

Somewhat surprisingly, the terms Plotinus used to describe this mystical union are tactile. Some signify activity—the giving of the self; others
express a more passive connotation of enthusiasm or rapture. Although
he rarely employs the term *ekstasis*, which carries the meaning of "going
forth from the self" (rather than the sense of "ecstasy" that it acquired
from the Christian mystics), the emotional intensity of the experience
is unmistakable:[25] "And one that shall know this vision—with what passion of love shall he not be seized, with what pang of desire, what longing
to be molten into one with This, what wondering delight! If he that has
never seen this Being must hunger for It as for all his welfare, he that has
known must love and reverence It as the very Beauty; he will be flooded
with awe and gladness, stricken by a salutary terror; he loves with a veri-
table love, with sharp desire; all other loves than this he must despise,
and disdain all that once seemed fair" (1.6.7). Porphyry's narrative of his
teacher's life begins by accentuating a tension between the physical and
spiritual attributes of the man. "Plotinus, the philosopher our contemporary," he wrote, "seemed ashamed of being in the body."[26] Immediately following this arresting statement, he tells how a portrait painter
was forced to resort to a ruse in order to capture a likeness of Plotinus
and gives an account of his personal habits (such as the fact that he did
not bathe but enjoyed a daily massage), his medical condition, and finally a detailed secondhand report of his illness and death. This emphasis on physical details confers on the narrative a double point of view: it
functions both as a demonstration and as a record. Evidence from other
sources confirms the tension between spiritual striving and engagement
in ordinary life that characterized Plotinus.[27] And because Porphyry pres-

25. For a discussion of terminology, see *Enneads*, introduction to the second edition, by
Paul Henry, xlix.

26. Porphyry, "On the Life of Plotinus and the Arrangement of his Work," in *The
Enneads*, 1.

27. For example, according to the praise Plotinus received posthumously from the oracle of Apollo, when he lost his intense concentration ("when your mind thrust out awry"),
the Immortals poured down "a dense shaft of light that your eyes might see from amid the
mournful gloom" (Porphyry, "On the Life of Plotinus," in *The Enneads*, 16). On the other
hand, in contrast to the intense emotion Plotinus experienced during these visions, his
spiritual practice counseled emotional distance from current events: "Murders, death in all
its guises, the reduction and sacking of cities, all must be to us just such a spectacle as the

ents himself as a reluctantly persuaded disciple, companion, and literary executor, he becomes a character in the story.[28]

The way in which individuals respond to circumstances emerges as a theme in Porphyry's account. For example, he tells how an Egyptian visiting in Rome, who happened to be introduced to Plotinus through a mutual friend, wished to display his skills by summoning the philosopher's guiding spirit. However, when a divinity rather than a spirit guide appeared, he exclaimed, "You are singularly graced; the guiding spirit within you is not of the lower degree but a God." Porphyry added that the manifestation so moved the priest's assistant with envy ("or terror") that he strangled the birds he had been holding. Chance determined this occasion, but Porphyry immediately followed the anecdote with the information that Plotinus was stimulated by his preoccupation with his inner presence to write an essay entitled "Our Tutelary Spirit" in which character determines the outcome of an accidental event:

> The Universal circuit is like a breeze, and the voyager, still or stirring, is carried forward by it. He has a hundred varied experiences, fresh sights, changing circumstances, all sorts of events. The vessel itself furnishes incident, tossing as it drives on. And the voyager also acts of himself in vir-

---

changing scenes of a play; all is but the varied incident of a plot, costume on and off, acted grief and lament. . . . All this is the doing of man knowing no more than to live the lower and outer life, and never perceiving that, in his weeping and in his graver doings alike, he is but at play; to handle austere matters austerely is reserved for the thoughtful: the other kind of man is himself a futility" (Plotinus, *The Enneads* 3.2.15).

28. In addition to editing the work of Plotinus, Porphyry composed the *Isagoge*, a commentary on the *Categories* intended to resolve the opposition between Plato and Aristotle. In it, Aristotle became the authority for things perceived by the senses and Plato for those conceived by the mind. As the first book in the syllabus for students of philosophy during late antiquity, the work exercised enormous influence. Porphyry's understanding of Aristotle's concept of separable and inseparable accidents entered into the question of being. He rejected the notion that substances cannot compose other substances, claiming that body and soul are both substances that combine to create a different substance, the living organism. From a Platonic point of view to describe a soul in relation to a body lessens its reality as something independent of the body or of sense perception. Aristotle's influence, therefore, challenged the Platonic understanding of reality as separate from appearances and resulted in a double way of thinking about the soul. Porphyry remained committed to the idea of a chain of relationships culminating in the One as defined by Plotinus. In practice, by asserting that the soul must turn inward to return to the One and become what it essentially is, this position, like the concept of the "going forth of the self," prepared a vocabulary for later Christian concepts. See A. C. Lloyd, "The Later Neoplatonists," in *The Cambridge History of Later Greek and Early Medieval Philosophy*, ed. A. H. Armstrong (Cambridge: Cambridge University Press, 1967), esp. 288–89.

tue of that individuality which he retains because he is on the vessel in his own person and character. Under identical circumstances individuals answer very differently in their movements and desires and acts; hence it comes about that, be the occurrences and conditions of life similar or dissimilar, the result may differ from man to man, as on the other hand a similar result may be produced by dissimilar conditions: this (force of circumstance) it is that constitutes destiny. (3.4.6)

Porphyry's story of the appearance of the guiding divinity presents an emphatic contrast to the claim that Oedipus made for independent reasoning when he opposed Tiresias's oracular reading of signs. In fact, Plotinus did regard things in the natural world as a means to approach an understanding of the ephemeral. "Things here are signs," he wrote. "They show therefore to the wise teachers how the supreme God is known; the instructed priest reading the sign may enter the holy place and make real the vision of the inaccessible" (6.9.11).

In discussing *Oedipus Rex* I argued that accidental qualities and events had assumed increased significance by providing the occasion for interpretation. Plotinus recalibrated that value, not because he disdained reason but because he desired freedom from all material inessentials. Although he appears in Porphyry's account as a mystic who holds himself remote from physical concerns, his life work continued the Greek attempt to explain reality within the tradition of the natural sciences. For the story of substance and accident, therefore, he stands on the cusp of an intellectual transformation.

VI. Augustine's Chance Conversion

The philosophical mysticism of Plotinus differed greatly from the mysticism of the Gospels and after the collapse of the Roman Empire, the text of his *Enneads* disappeared from the Christian West until the fifteenth century. However, the work of Augustine of Hippo (354–430)—the exemplary and influential figure in the confrontation between classical and Christian ideas—transmitted his influence to Thomas Aquinas and through him to large areas of Western thought.

Augustine's autobiography offers one of the earliest examples of the way a character's thoughts express self-understanding through stories.[29]

---

29. Brian Stock, *Augustine the Reader: Meditation, Self-Knowledge, and the Ethics of Interpretation* (Cambridge, MA: Harvard University Press, 1996), 110–11.

Outwardly, his *Confessions* extend the spiritual exercises that formed part of the pedagogical practice of Plotinus. For both thinkers, the purpose of attaining self-knowledge was to achieve an understanding of a higher power beyond human reason and articulated both the conflict between the powerful appeal of the sensible world and the desire for union with a divine principle. What motivated Augustine to write was the value he placed on sharing the process that led him to his Christian faith.

At the age of twenty, Augustine read the Latin translation of the *Categories* of Aristotle, a text revered by contemporary rhetoricians, but he found it intellectually disappointing.[30] In retrospect, he judged that Aristotle's insistence that accidents inhere in substance had blocked him from understanding his true relation to God: "Thinking that absolutely everything that exists is comprehended under the ten categories, I tried to conceive you also, my God, wonderfully simple and immutable, as if you too were a subject of which magnitude and beauty are attributes. I thought them to be in you as if in a subject, as in the case of a physical body, whereas you yourself are your own magnitude and your own beauty. By contrast a body is not great and beautiful by being body; if it were less great or less beautiful, it would nevertheless still be body. My conception of you was a lie, not truth, the figments of my misery, not the permanent solidity of your supreme bliss" (IV.xvi.29).

Augustine reported that he read Aristotle "without an expositor." He differentiated such reading from the process of academic study because it seemed to implant an authoritative text in his mind and heart without his volition. In writing about this experience twelve years later in his *Confessions*, he understood his critical response as the first of a series of experiences involving reading that prepared for his conversion to Christianity. It allowed him to realize that the hermeneutic of the Word could replace Aristotle's method of comparative analysis as well as Porphyry's process of drawing metaphysical significance from exceptional or unexpected events. Throughout the *Confessions*, he minimized descriptions of physical things in favor of descriptions of emotions and thoughts, a focus

---

30. "The book seemed to me an extremely clear statement about substances, such as man, and what are in them, such as a man's shape, what is his quality of stature, how many feet, and his relatedness, for example whose brother he is, or where he is placed, or when he was born, or whether he is standing or sitting, or is wearing shoes or armor, or whether he is active or passive, and the innumerable things which are classified by these nine genera of which I have given some instances, or by the genus of substance itself." Augustine, *Confessions*, trans. Henry Chadwick (Oxford: Oxford University Press, 1992), IV.xvi.28. All further references to the *Confessions* are from this edition.

that underscores his shift from interpreting events or qualities appearing in the natural world to interpreting textual abstractions.

To follow the transformation of accident in Augustine's thought we need to understand not only that he rejected Aristotle but also that he turned away from the Manichees, a heretical and persecuted Christian sect to which he belonged for nine years.[31] Initially, he was attracted to the Manichees because they saw the world as a battle between opposing forces of good and evil, light and dark, or (especially relevant to his own struggles) between soul and body. Like Plotinus, Augustine thought of evil in material terms, and in the *Confessions*, he recounted his delivery from Manichaean beliefs under the influence of Neoplatonic idealism:

> By now my evil and wicked youth was dead. I was becoming a grown man. But the older I became, the more shameful it was that I retained so much vanity as to be unable to think any substance possible other than that which the eyes normally perceive. From the time that I began to learn something of your wisdom, I did not conceive of you, God, in the shape of the human body. I always shunned this, and was glad when I found the same concept in the faith of our spiritual mother, your Catholic Church. But how otherwise to conceive of you I could not see. I a mere man, and a man with profound defects, was trying to think of you the supreme, sole and true God. With all my heart I believed you to be incorruptible, immune from injury, and unchangeable. (VII.i.1)

Rather than interpreting the world as a Manichaean struggle, Augustine began to envision a hierarchically structured world with God, as the One, at the top. Neoplatonism helped him recognize, first, that God is not a body, and, second, that the philosophical notion of a chain of being might permit his soul to rise to God if it were not dragged down by the demands of his body.[32]

31. The followers of the sect's founder, Mani, "the Apostle of Jesus Christ," spread aggressively from Mesopotamia into the Christian Roman world, arriving in Carthage in 296. Manichaean missionaries were the Elect, who denied the Old Testament because they refused to allow any material existence to divinity, as when God walked in the shade of the Garden of Eden.

32. Even in passages of the *Confessions* most directly inspired by Plotinus, the distance between classical and Christian mysticism is perceptible. For example, Plotinus ultimately released the practitioner from reliance on spiritual guidance, while Augustine accentuated the divine grace that stimulates the inward examination leading to self-knowledge.

Augustine derived a major source of new insight from Saint Ambrose, whose allegorical sermons helped free him from his dependence on the material world and prepared him to interpret the chance reading that converted him to Christianity. The preaching of Ambrose encouraged him to compare the distinction between the spirit and the letter that he had encountered in reading the epistles of Paul to the distinction between inner and outer self. Awareness of the potential interpenetration of text and self enabled him to understand how a piece of writing could mediate reality by transforming thoughts into words. Thus, a devout reader might possess an inward understanding of a story before being able to translate it into action. This perception confirmed for him the Platonic value of reality beyond representation, but it also linked mental representation to an exegetical and interpretive process that enabled him to build the new self he so desired.

Ambrose read silently, contrary to his contemporaries' usual practice of reading aloud, and when Augustine observed him decoding the written signs in silence, he understood the practice as a spiritual exercise that directed attention to the inner life. Mastery of silent reading signified the reader's ability to seek the sense of the text in his heart. In his visceral need to take God into his soul, he applied this new way of reading to the narrative of the Bible, and especially the New Testament, which contained "the face of this devotion, tears of confession, your sacrifice, a troubled spirit, a contrite and humble spirit" (VII.xxi.27).

Augustine claimed that the story of the Passion distinguished Christian thought from Platonic philosophy. A passage in which he clearly recalled the spiritual ascent Plotinus described in the final pages of the *Enneads* demonstrates this difference. In it he recounted an experience that took place one evening during a conversation with his mother, Monica, as the story of a "going forth of the self":

> The conversation led us towards the conclusion that the pleasure of the bodily senses, however delightful in the radiant light of this physical world, is seen by comparison with the life of eternity to be not even worth considering. Our minds were lifted up by an ardent affection towards eternal being itself. Step by step we climbed beyond all corporeal objects and the heaven itself, where sun, moon, and stars shed light on the earth. We ascended even further by internal reflection and dialogue and wonder at your works, and we entered into our own minds. We moved up beyond them so as to attain to the region of inexhaustible abundance where you

feed Israel eternally with truth for food. There life is the wisdom by which all creatures come into being, both things which were and which will be. But wisdom itself is not brought into being but is as it was and always will be. Furthermore, in this wisdom there is no past and future, but only being, since it is eternal. For to exist in the past or in the future is no property of the eternal. And while we talked and panted after it, we touched it in some small degree by a moment of total concentration of the heart. And we sighed and left behind us "the firstfruits of the Spirit" [Rom. 8: 23] bound to that higher world, as we returned to the noise of our human speech where a sentence has both a beginning and an ending. But what is to be compared with your word, Lord of our lives? It dwells in you without growing old and gives renewal to all things. (IX.x.24)

Augustine was remembering a significant moment in his *bios* (literally "course of a lifetime"), but his language evokes the extent to which memory appears as the source of the inner light of self-knowledge. As a repository of the deep understanding needed for exegesis, memory resolved the problem of how as a Manichaean he could have been aware of his soul yet mistaken about its nature. He recognized that memory was specific to each individual and that its contents admitted multiple interpretations, but he ascribed to it a shaping power. Far from functioning merely for mechanical retrieval, memory's capacity to bridge time and space served as what he called the "embrace of my inner man, where my soul is floodlit by light which space cannot contain, where there is sound that time cannot seize, where there is a perfume which no breeze disperses, where there is a taste for food no amount of eating can lessen, and where there is a bond of union that no satiety can part" (X.vi.8). It enabled him to "remember God."

Initially, Augustine implied that memories were static and remained unchanged, like archaeological deposits laid down in layers. Gradually, however, he modulated this image to include the idea that over time new configurations of memories evoke new shapes of the self. The verb he used to describe this weaving of changing temporal patterns is *contexo*. Its connotations of context and text hark back to the importance of the Word and the interpretation of texts, but they also suggest the continuity in his life story. In this new formulation, memory allowed him to be the same person in his youth, maturity, and old age. Although the past no longer exists, memory returns it to a potent kind of reality in the present. The way in which he grounded this concept in the principle of being echoes Aristotle's argument that substance provides an enduring ground for mutable accidents.[33]

Just as Aristotle provided the conceptual dualism of substance and accident and the definitions of accidental qualities and accidental events that form the basis for my study, Augustine provided a model for the narrative of the self-defining accident. The conversion scene he recounted in the *Confessions* established the preconditions that apply to such events while revealing components of his distinctive interpretive attitude. Attending closely to all aspects of his narration of this experience allows us to lay down a conceptual baseline against which to compare the responses of later authors.

Aristotle's definition of accidents as unusual or unexpected events makes the conversion experience qualify as accidental in the classical sense, and the actions that compose the experience appear random in themselves. Augustine hears an unseen person chanting a phrase he interprets as a command to read ("tolle, lege"); he chances on a text from the Epistle of Paul which he happened to leave lying on the table. His conviction that the outcome was intended (and thus no longer "accidental" in the Aristotelian sense of the term) carries profound interpretive import.

The narrative presents a complex structure based on the sudden and unanticipated effects of reading, but Neoplatonic models of the "going forth of the self" also lay behind Augustine's experience. Moreover, he had in Saul's conversion on the road to Damascus a powerful Christian model by which to interpret what happened to him. The book of Acts recounts no fewer than three times (9:1–19, 22:5–16, 26:12–18) how Saul, "breathing out threatenings and slaughter against the disciples of the Lord," rode toward Damascus:

> And as he journeyed, he came near Damascus: and suddenly there shined round him a light from heaven: And he fell to earth, and heard a voice saying unto him, Saul, Saul, why persecutest thou me? And he said, Who art thou, Lord? And the Lord said, I am Jesus whom thou persecutest: it is hard for thee to kick against the pricks. And he trembling and astonished said, Lord, what wilt thou have me to do? And the Lord said unto him,

33. This discussion as well as later comments on the role of memory in Augustine's text is indebted to the analysis of the *Confessions* by James Olney, *Memory and Narrative: The Weave of Life-Writing* (Chicago: University of Chicago Press, 1998), esp. 26ff.

Arise, and go into the city, and it shall be told thee what thou must do. And the men which journeyed with him stood speechless, hearing a voice, but seeing no man. And Saul arose from the earth; and when his eyes were opened, he saw no man: but they led him by the hand, and brought him into Damascus.[34]

In Damascus, the devout Ananias tells Saul that he is the Lord's "chosen vessel," and "immediately there fell from his eyes as it had been scales: and he received sight forthwith, and arose, and was baptized" (Acts 9:9, 15, 18). He becomes Paul, warrior for God's word.

In the *Confessions,* Augustine was waiting impatiently for God to reveal himself as he did to Saul, and the absence of illumination made him profoundly unhappy. He longed for a comparable experience—to hear God's voice and become another man. On the day of his conversion, at the end of August 386, he was in the garden of his mother's house in Milan, pouring out his distress to his friend Alypius. "What is wrong with us?" he asked. "Uneducated people are rising up and capturing heaven [Matt. 11:12], and we with our high culture without any heart—see where we roll in the mud of flesh and blood. Is it because they are ahead of us that we are ashamed to follow?" (VIII.viii.19). Unable to communicate his longing, he retired to a more secluded part of the garden and threw himself on the ground beneath a fig tree: "As I was . . . weeping in the bitter agony of my heart, suddenly I heard a voice from the nearby house chanting as if it might be a boy or a girl (I know not which), saying and repeating over and over again, 'Pick up and read, pick up and read.' At once my countenance changed, and I began to think intently whether there might be some sort of children's game in which such a chant is used. But I could not remember having heard of one. I checked the flood of tears and stood up. I interpreted it solely as a divine command to me to open the book and read the first chapter I might find" (VIII.xii.29). Two factors preceded this event: consciousness of strongly felt personal circumstances and awareness of the outcome of a comparable situation. These preconditions intensified his response. Significantly, in this powerful and influential account, God does not speak directly to Augustine or appear in a beam of light; he is made manifest through a series of accidental events. Hearing a song startles Augustine from his tears. His first impulse is to reason away the strange words as part of a child's game, but because he cannot explain them in that way, he interprets them as the awaited sign. Spoken

34. Acts 9:1, 3–8 (King James Version).

by a disembodied voice, the mysterious words signify an angelic presence conveying a divine command.[35]

Apart from his strong desire to experience such a revelation, Augustine's concept of the human mind provided an intellectual basis for this interpretation. He understood the mind in Trinitarian terms, as three attributes of a single unity (memory, understanding, and will). For him, this triadic form affirmed the correlation of mind to the divine, allowing the inner presence of God to guide human thought. Because the whole being is what remembers, the contest between memory and forgetting also becomes a contest of will against will. When the Stoics introduced the notion of individual moral choice into Plato's idea of the will, they made it independent of knowledge. Thus, Augustine could postulate—against the repeated supposition of Socrates in the dialogues that everyone loves the good and is drawn to evil only through ignorance—that human beings are capable of radically different moral dispositions. His physical actions in the garden expressed the control his will exercised over his body. What he could not control was his mind. This perception of powerlessness, of involuntary thoughts and actions, accentuates the "accidental" aspect of his response to the experience, but he also inserted a discussion of will into his narrative of the events. This discussion clarified the nature of the struggle he had been experiencing, but it also asserted the role grace must play in healing the will.[36]

Augustine's response to the mysterious words also expressed the context of the time and provides a suggestive link between texts as visible signs and the interpretation of accidents. He drew on a model for interpreting texts in which Virgil's words read at random were assigned a prophetic authority. Known as the *sortes Virgilianaes*, the practice employed lines encountered on opening the *Aeneid* at random.[37] Given Augustine's

---

35. According to Pierre Courcelle, *Recherches sur les "Confessions" de saint Augustin* (Paris: De Boccard, 1950), 190, Augustine's earliest narrations of the experience were not precise repetitions of the final text. For example, he did not include the remarkable "tolle, lege" aspect of the experience, nor did he recall it afterward.

36. Charles Taylor, *Sources of the Self: The Making of the Modern Identity* (Cambridge, MA: Harvard University Press, 1989), 138.

37. Augustine's use of the *sortes* also underlines the importance of astrological prediction in Roman society, where Fortune was worshipped as a goddess. For example, in 111 BC a temple dedicated to Fortuna huiusce diei, the Goddess of Fortune of the Present Day, was erected near the Forum and the reading of entrails and supernatural signs was an established practice. The role of fortune and the interpretation of chance events are important themes debated in the *Confessions*. Augustine discussed their validity with his friend Vindicianus, who argued that "chance" is not the purely random source of a correct astrological prediction, but a name that men ascribe to an unknown cause (IV.iii.5). His lesson that the desire

obsession with Virgil (for example, when he famously wept for Dido and in the many parallels from the story of Aeneas to his own physical and spiritual journey), his use of this topos represents another instance of submerged memory.[38] When he hurried back to the book he had left with Alypius, a second seemingly random act completed his conversion. He opened it to a chapter in the Pauline epistles:

> I seized it, opened it and in silence read the first passage on which my eyes lit: "Not in riots and drunken parties, not in eroticism and indecencies, not in strife and rivalry, but put on the Lord Jesus Christ and make no provision for the flesh in its lusts" [Rom. 13:13–14].
>
> I neither wished nor needed to read further. At once, with the last words of this sentence, it was as if a light of relief from all anxiety flooded into my heart. All the shadows of doubt were dispelled. (VIII.xii.29)

He read in the contemplative silence understood to imprint a text on the heart and the passage he read with such high expectations instructed him to turn away from his body, with its mutability and accidents. He interpreted this text as a divine response to the problem that tormented him most deeply. Prepared by his intense desire for change and familiar with the use of texts for casting lots as well as with biblical hermeneutics, he invested two apparently accidental signs—the command to read and the text itself—with transforming personal significance.

Augustine was prepared to ascribe the utmost importance to a textual sign by what we might call the textualized quality of his thought. His rhetorical training fostered his intense engagement with biblical texts, and the richness of his associations with past reading is evident in the dense pattern of quotation woven into the language of the *Confessions*. The kind of reader, thinker, and teacher he was had created the context for his transformative experience (which a modern view would consider less "accidental" precisely for that reason).

---

to interpret may be implanted for higher purposes that are not always understood provided the underlying logic behind Augustine's interpretation of chance in his conversion.

38. He wept for Dido in *Confessions* I.xiii. See also Augustine's repeated use of conspicuously Virgilian nautical metaphors to describe his own psychological journey, e.g., "to commit to the waves" (I.xi.18), "you infernal rivers, the sons of men are thrown into you" (I.xvi.26), "the whirlpool of shame into which 'I was cast out of your sight'" (I.xix.30), "sweeping through the precipitious rocks and desire to submerge me in a whirlpool of vice" (II.ii.2), and "nothing kept me from an even deeper whirlpool of erotic indulgence" (VI.xvi.26).

Language also provides direct evidence for the self-reflexivity of Augustine's thought. His use of the first person singular should not be confused with the classical sense of the individual distinguished as a member of a group or groups. Rather, it makes him what we might now call a "subject," someone capable of identifying the qualities that make him unique.[39] However, speaking in his own name did not imply any egocentric awareness, for it was intimately bound up with his argument for the existence of God.[40] Certainty of his own existence, which rested on being present to himself (as "I," not objectified as "he"), enabled him to initiate a conceptual hierarchy extending to the divinity. Awareness of the limitations of his own reason led him to realize that something must lie beyond those limits. This way of thinking of the self is intimately connected with his conception that the inner light of understanding offered evidence of God's presence.

Striving to extend the relationship between personal narrative and spiritual understanding was also bound up with Augustine's desire to teach his readers the art of reading for spiritual illumination and how to interpret accidental signs. He maintained that through a variation of typology, providential guidance could reveal the meaning of God's historical design, but only after events had taken place. Therefore, in telling his own story, he first presented the information available to him at the time of his experience and only then constructed the focus and emphasis of the narrative on the basis of the overarching understanding he had achieved through distance in time and interpretation. In other words, his narrative control both expressed a pedagogical model of instruction and revealed an echo of divine intent.

39. Jean-Pierre Vernant, "The Individual within the City-State," in *Mortals and Immortals, Collected Essays*, ed. Froma I. Zeitlin (Princeton: Princeton University Press, 1991), 321. Vernant associated the individual with biography, the subject with autobiography or memoir, and the ego with confessions and diaries. Despite the title of Augustine's work, the element of secrecy and self-consciousness essential to Vernant's definition of "ego" does not appear until the *Confessions* of Rousseau.

40. The work of Pierre Hadot offers an important corrective to the tendency to read the *Confessions* as a psychological statement rather than an intrinsically theological work in which events are symbolic and the "I" continues the "I" that speaks in scriptural narratives. See Arnold Davidson's discussion of Hadot's methods as applied to the *Confessions* in his introduction to Hadot, *Philosophy as a Way of Life*, 15–17, as well as Hadot's own description, 51–52, of Pierre Courcelle's allegorical interpretation of the fig tree and the child's voice in the conversion scene. Within its apparent historicity, the *Confessions* offers a paradigm for all conversions. For example, whether or not Augustine actually wept under a fig tree, his narrative alluded to the conversion of Nathanael after learning that Jesus saw him under a fig tree (John 1:48–50).

Each of the three stories that prepare the reader for Augustine's conversion incorporates interpretation of chance events to mark new stages in spiritual understanding. The first involves his friend Alypius. During Augustine's exposition of text in one of his lectures, Alypius assumed that a chance reference to public games was directed at him and this interpretation temporarily changed his behavior. However, as Augustine realized later, his friend had merely passed from one state of illusion to another. In the second story, Simplicianus, who succeeded Ambrose as bishop of Milan in 397, recounted events in the life of a man learned in classical philosophy who was influenced (and ultimately baptized) by Ambrose. After an internal struggle, the man finally made a public profession of his faith. Augustine recognized a similar ethical conflict in his own gradual movement from philosophical to scriptural study, and this realization convinced him of the certainty of his own belief. In the third story, Ponticianus, a Christian high official from North Africa, appeared unexpectedly at Augustine's home. "By chance he noticed a book on top of a gaming table," Augustine wrote. "He picked it up, opened it, and discovered, much to his astonishment, that it was the apostle Paul" (VIII.vi.14). Sensing Augustine's interest, he told him the conversion experiences of two pagan officials who walked to a rustic woodland retreat where they discovered a codex that revealed that the place was inhabited by Christians. They opened it and read an account of the life of Anthony. Humbled and transported by the knowledge contained in this text, they determined to leave the imperial service to serve God. Remembrances of this account appear in the narrative of Augustine's own conversion.[41]

In Augustine's view, all aspects of the created world participate in God's ideas. Its order reflects his eternal laws and the things within it exist as external expressions of his thoughts. This enables them to be understood as signs imbued with revelatory powers. Just as words arise from silence and return to silence after they are spoken, things proceed from essence to existence and then return to God, and future events that are hidden from sight become accessible to the mind. Augustine's conversion provides a model for the act of reading signs imbued with this hidden meaning. Simultaneously literal and metaphysical, concrete and abstract, it offered his readers the possibility of spiritual renewal within the context of accidental experience.

---

41. Stock, *Augustine the Reader*, 77–102, provides an extended interpretation of the preconversion stories.

Our examination of the accidental event allows us to appreciate the magnitude of the conceptual shift implicit in this way of thinking. In effect, Augustine revalued accident as a Christian sign. First, in form as well as content, his narrative turned a seemingly random series of acts and perceptions into a demonstration of providential intent. Second, his description of the moment of conversion signified that God's word could enter a believer in the guise of an accident. These changes acknowledged the power of accidental events to generate self-definition and radically revised the importance of accident within the Christian tradition.

CHAPTER TWO

Divine Substance: Assimilation of Accident within Christian Theology

I. The Book of Substances and Accidents

As medieval Christianity struggled to absorb Aristotle's system of thought, the terms "substance" and "accident" were profoundly altered.[1] Substance became aligned with soul and the accidental event was subsumed into evidence of providential design. In the thirteenth century, the doctrine of transubstantiation required an interpretation of the accidental qualities of the bread and wine. Thus, Aristotle's categories exerted a powerful presence in two great conceptual syntheses, the *Summa theologiae* of Aquinas and Dante's *Divine Comedy*. Nevertheless, throughout this period, problems caused by translation, fragmentation of texts,

---

1. Aristotle's metaphysical writings reentered Christian Europe from Sicily and especially Spain, where the Reconquista allowed contact with Arab texts that translated and drew heavily on classical philosophy. Especially in Cordoba, where Archbishop Raymond of Sauvetat had set up a kind of translation school, the forced conversion of the Moslems and continued presence of Jews helped transmit Aristotelian philosophy into Christian thought. For a full discussion of the early translators, see Bernard Dod, "Aristoteles Latinus," in *The Cambridge History of Later Medieval Philosophy: From the Rediscovery of Aristotle to the Disintegration of Scholasticism*, ed. Norman Kretzmann, Anthony Kenny, and Jan Pinborg (Cambridge: Cambridge University Press, 1982), 45–79. Fernand Van Steenberghen, *Aristotle in the West: The Origins of Latin Aristotelianism*, trans. Leonard Johnston (Louvain: Nauwelaerts, 1970); and Charles Homer Haskins, *The Renaissance of the Twelfth Century* (Cambridge, MA: Harvard University Press, 1927), esp. 279–303, provide accounts of Aristotle's reception. At first, his metaphysical thought was met with suspicion, but by 1255 his known works formed the core study in the curriculum of the Faculty of Arts. It remained so for centuries. See C. H. Lohr, "The Medieval Interpretation of Aristotle," in *The Cambridge History of Later Medieval Philosophy*, 80–98; and Dominick A. Iorio, *The Aristotelianisms of Renaissance Italy* (Lewiston: Edwin Mellen Press, 1991).

and cultural shifts that occurred over the long passage of time created slippages in terminology.

The architectonics of the *Divine Comedy* reflect a system as complex as the one through which Aristotle sought to comprehend his world. Dante interweaves physiology, political history, secular and religious literary traditions, and a mnemonic psychology, while reaffirming the old categories of substance and accident as ordering concepts. However, his theological conception of man's nature and his place in the world transformed the significance of the Aristotelian categories. The final canto of the *Paradiso*, the summit of Dante's spiritual journey, reveals the magnitude of this change.

As Dante draws near the "living Light" of God, he perceives in its depths a book whose leaves contain the substances and accidents of the world. This image fuses into a single light from which emanate three radiant circles. One circle contains the figure of a man, and Dante struggles to conceive how this image can be united with God.[2] In the final lines of the poem, he grasps the answer in a flash of insight. His vision asserts the relationship of all created things, but expressing this order remains beyond his power.

Nature conceived as a collection of books written and bound by God was an image that originated in medieval sermons and was later adopted as a speculation by mystical philosophers. Bernard Silvestris, for example, envisioned heaven as a book covered with pictures that prefigured all earthly things and also compared man's faculty of understanding to a book. By the thirteenth century, the notion of the book of nature had passed into common usage.[3] Dante adopted this imagery in language that accentuated the unifying power of God's love over all aspects of the world:

> O abounding grace whereby I presumed to fix my look through the Eternal Light so far that all my sight was spent therein.
>
> In its depth I saw ingathered, bound by love in one single volume, that which is dispersed in leaves throughout the universe: substances and accidents and their relations, as though fused together in such a way that what I tell is but a simple light.[4]

---

2. The Trinitarian association between this human image and Christ risen in the flesh invokes the central mystery of the Incarnation.

3. E. R. Curtius *European Literature and the Latin Middle Ages*, trans. Willard Trask (New York: Bollingen, 1953), 319–22, summarizes this tradition.

4. Dante Alighieri, *The Divine Comedy*, trans. Charles S. Singleton (Princeton: Princeton University Press, 1971–75), *Paradiso*, XXXIII.85–90. Citations of the *Paradiso* are taken

Dante records the process that allowed him to experience these relationships as a form of spiritual autobiography. As in Augustine's *Confessions*, the full implications of his changing inner condition emerge over the course of the narrative. Not until the final moments of his journey does the pilgrim "Dante," speaking in the present tense, fuse with the narrator of the poem. The course of his journey refutes his original protest that he is not worthy to be singled out for this experience ("I am not Aeneas, I am not Paul"; *Inferno*, II.32). Refined and corrected, the self he has become receives a vision clearly associated with the flash of light that blinded Saul (*Paradiso*, XXX.46–51): he is a new Paul.[5] We cannot associate this trajectory with an accident, for in the world of the *Divine Comedy* nothing can be accidental to God's design, but we recognize how closely it reflects the link between reading and conversion in the *Confessions*. The final moment, in other words, describes a transforming experience.

We also recognize a schematic pattern of associations underlying the description of this experience similar to the densely allusive style of the *Confessions*. Here, too, biblical motifs blend with ancient allegories, such as the ascent of the soul. The descent into hell also reformulates Augustine's recognition of the spiritual need to descend into the self. Dante shared Augustine's sins of lust and involvement with Neoplatonism, and the *Confessions* also gave him a model for writing about himself for the sake of instructing others.[6] Augustine's use of the *Aeneid* in his account of how he traveled from the temptations of literature to God's book would have been familiar to Dante, who also modeled his journey on that of Aeneas. His sense that what is written must be continuously interpreted and questioned underlies his attempt to reconcile Virgil with Augustine.[7]

Although the moral context of the *Divine Comedy* compelled Dante to take the historical world as seriously as his belief in the relationship between man's nature and the order of grace, allegorical interpretation

---

from this translation; later citations of the *Inferno* are from Allen Mandelbaum's translation (Berkeley: University of California Press, 1980).

5. Prudence Shaw, "*Paradiso* XXX," in *Cambridge Readings in Dante's Comedy*, ed. Kenelm Foster and Patrick Boyde (Cambridge: Cambridge University Press, 1981), 201–2.

6. Robert Hollander, *Allegory in Dante's Commedia* (Princeton: Princeton University Press, 1969), 165n and 241n, notes that John Freccero first demonstrated the link between the wanderings of the flesh and of the spirit in book 7 of the *Confessions* with the opening cantos of the *Inferno*.

7. Guiseppe Mazzotta, *Dante, Poet of the Desert* (Princeton: Princeton University Press, 1979), argues this position at length in his chapter "Vergil and Augustine."

grounded his system of thought.[8] For him, since God can use any event or thing in nature as a sign to point to other things, nothing that happens in this world can be deemed accidental. Thus, his vision in paradise presents existence in the form of a book in which things are as meaningful as words. The presence of the maker of this system as a "Living Light" illuminates Dante's culminating vision. What is literally a moment of insight enables him to "read" his experience.[9]

The assertion that the Word of God can be distinguished from the words of men because it is also a thing with a historical existence lies at the heart of Christian theology: in the Incarnation the Word is made flesh. Some words in the Bible function merely as words (for example, those delivering the moral lesson of a parable); others carry deeper meanings that require interpretation. Exegesis can be viewed as the professional practice of determining which is which. The act of interpretation mediates between the possibilities inherent in the ambiguous structure of language.[10]

Dante repeatedly questions conclusions or withholds dogmatic statements of meaning to subvert the reader's certainty about his intent. For example, in the final lines of the poem he leaves the text of the book of

8. Hollander's *Allegory in Dante's Commedia* summarizes the primary elements in the debate about whether Dante used the "allegory of the poets" or the "allegory of the theologians," that is, whether the *Divine Comedy* should be read metaphorically or according to the multiple senses of medieval exegesis (in which Christian significance could be superimposed anachronistically on the Old Testament text because the work was divinely inspired). In part, he bases his own position on references to the letter to Cangrande, attributed to Dante. In paragraph 5 of the letter, Dante uses a reference to the *Metaphysics* to relate the *Paradiso* to the whole *Commedia* because the existence of this part depends on the first two parts (43–44), and in paragraph 8 the letter describes the subject of the poem as twofold—first literal, then allegorical. The effect, according to Hollander, is to treat the world as a substantial shadow that is the tangible counterpart of a heavenly paradigm (52). Mazzotta, *Dante*, 236, notes that paragraph 29 of the letter argues for metaphoricity: "For there are many things which we see by the intellect for which verbal signs are lacking, which Plato suggests in his books by means of metaphors, for he saw many things by the light of his intellect that he could not express in suitable words." This gloss parallels the statement by Thomas Aquinas that argues for the power of metaphor to duplicate the world of reality on the basis of biblical allegory: "For God provides for all things according to the kind of things they are. Now we are of the kind to reach the world of intelligence through the world of sense, since all our knowledge takes its rise from sensation. Congenially, then, Holy Scripture delivers spiritual things to us beneath metaphors taken from bodily things." Thomas Aquinas, *Summa theologiae*, ed. Thomas Gilby, O.P., 60 vols. (London: Blackfriars; New York: McGraw-Hill, 1964–80), ST Ia.1.9. All citations of the *Summa* are taken from this edition.

9. John Freccero, "Introduction to *Inferno*," in *Cambridge Companion to Dante*, ed. Rachel Jacoff (Cambridge: Cambridge University Press, 1993), 181–87.

10. Freccero, "Introduction to *Inferno*," 186, wittily relates the virtual meaning in this systematic process of construction and deconstruction to Derrida's "archécriture."

nature to the reader's imagination: "Here power failed the lofty phantasy" (*Paradiso*, XXXIII.142). As Augustine had demonstrated in the *Confessions*, the faculties of an individual reader determine the impact of the text.[11]

That is not to say that by making the text a fluid field of interpretation Dante abandons conceptual security. The final words reaffirm the power of divine love, which orders the individual's desire and will as easily as it revolves the sun and the other stars in the even movement of a wheel (*Paradiso*, XXXIII.143–45).[12] His image alludes to the three perfect circles of the Trinity, but at the same time, it implies a contrast with the popular notion of the wheel of Fortune. In the material world, as Fortune turns her wheel, unexplained contingencies raise up a man or cast him down. Such accidents have no power within the divine order since they are truly inessential to the state of grace.

At least two concepts present in this passage reflect the *Summa theologiae* of Thomas Aquinas: the perfection of God (I.q.4.a.2) and the desire of the intellect (whose delight is accidental to the essence of happiness) to attain the joy of truth (I–II.q.3.a.4). The idea of the circle as an emblem of perfection appears in his *Of Divine Names*.[13] However, the notion of the unmoved mover derives from Aristotle, whose works Dante studied with guidance from the commentaries of Aquinas. This chain of influence is evident in the accord between Dante's understanding of divine substance in the final lines of the poem and a speech he gave to Aquinas:

> That which dies not and that which can die are naught but the splendor of that Idea which in His love our Sire begets; for that living light which so streams from its Lucent Source that It is not disunited from It, nor from the Love which is intwined with them, does of Its own goodness collect Its rays, as though reflected, in nine subsistences, Itself eternally remaining One. Thence It descends to the ultimate potentialities, downward from act to act becoming such that finally it makes but brief contingencies; and these contingencies I understand to be the generated things which the moving heavens produce with seed and without it. The wax of these and that

11. Mazzotta, *Dante*, 270, believes the *Divine Comedy* confronts the reader with the possibility of two opposed readings (literal and figurative) which neither deconstruct nor cancel each other out but are simultaneously present and always referential. To illustrate this point, he provides a long, close reading of the role of memory and forgetting in *Paradiso* XXXIII that is of particular interest with respect to the notion of the formation of the self.

12. The original text reads, "ma già volgeva il mio disio e '1 velle, / sì come rota ch'igualmente è mossa, / l'amor che move il sole e l'altre stele."

13. Noted in Singleton's commentary to lines 577 and 587–90.

which moulds it are not always in the same condition, and therefore under the ideal stamp it then shines now more, now less; hence it comes that one same plant, in respect to species, fruits better or worse, and that you are born with diverse dispositions. If the wax were exactly worked, and the heavens were at the height of their power, the light of the whole seal would be apparent. But nature always gives it defectively, working like the artist who in the practice of his art has a hand that trembles. (*Paradiso*, XIII.52–78)

This passage testifies to the continuing presence of the ten Aristotelian categories and to the distinction between qualities inherent in a thing and the accidents that signal diversity. Equally apparent, however, is the sense of God's creative power. Dante seemed particularly respectful of the way Aquinas could apply reason to questions that required moral judgment. For Dante, the correct faith and love of God required the combined action of mind and heart, and he supported his positions by appeals to the moral intelligence of Aquinas.[14]

II. Human Nature

Dante's respect for the moral judgment shown by Aquinas accentuates the double importance of the *Summa theologiae* in the study of accident. First, the authority of Aquinas's synthesis, especially as transmitted within Scholastic philosophy, served as a point of reference for concepts of substance and accident into the seventeenth century. Second, his understanding of the relation between accident and moral judgment, an original contribution in his thought, set in motion a complex yet conceptually fragile notion of identity.

Aquinas believed that people could perfect themselves through the virtues, but in order to allow for this possibility, his moral theory needed to demonstrate that under certain circumstances reasoning or persuasion can condition the passions that impel action. Analyzing the functions of the passions in terms of a process of sensory perception, imagination, and judgment allowed the possibility of intellectual control.[15]

14. See Kenelm Foster, *The Two Dantes and Other Studies* (Berkeley: University of California Press, 1977), 61–63; and Christopher Ryan, "The Theology of Dante," in Jacoff, *Cambridge Companion to Dante*, 151. Aquinas was canonized two years after Dante's death.

15. Recent scholars compare the information provided by the passions to the inputs studied by contemporary cognitive science. See Peter King, "Aquinas on the Passions," in *Aquinas's Moral Theory: Essays in Honor of Norman Kretzmann*, ed. Scott MacDonald and Eleonore Stump (Ithaca: Cornell University Press, 1999), 131–32. King asserts that by

To grasp how Aquinas conceived of this reasoning process, we need to consider his notions of both accidental events and accidental qualities. Events offer a more accessible entry into his argument. Aquinas understood that an action might have both an external and an internal cause; that is, it might reflect some combination of perceptions regarding the circumstances, imagined possibilities or options, and well or poorly reasoned judgments about what choice to make. As a result, external circumstances not only affect the passions; they also may affect the will, the agent believed to prompt the passions to operate. For example, a man might choose to perform some harmful act that he would not perform voluntarily under normal circumstances in order to avoid a greater harm he fears will occur if he does not act in this way.[16]

Unexpected events or coincidences can interrupt an action or change the possibilities for response. For example, if the person who found the buried treasure in Aristotle's example were a slave planting on his rich master's estate, his amazement might be the same as that of a free man, but his status would affect whether or not he revealed what he found. For Aquinas, then, the moral virtues are subject to fortune. Because the happiness that derives from a fortuitous event is possible only for a rational agent, and happiness results from acting well, he argued that fortune depends on actions capable of preventing or encouraging moral judgment (*In Phys.*, 2.10.229).

In this view, circumstances determine the connection between what the passion and the will direct, the means of acting, and the outcome. A simple feature of a situation that carries no moral value (such as whether the day is warm or cool) is inessential because it lies outside the act's substance. According to Aquinas, such simple accidents cannot affect the goodness of the act. However, altering the circumstances that surround the action creates new levels of difficulty in making moral choices about what ends to pursue. (In my earlier example, after casting off his load, the captain of a foundering ship might still have to decide who would stay aboard until the end.) For Aquinas, if the will responds to these changed circumstances by recognizing that what is good in some circumstances may be less good in others, this moral conflict can be resolved. The moral virtues aid in this reasoning process. Thus, by distinguishing whether something occurs of

---

maintaining a high level of abstraction, Aquinas produced a psychology of mind superior to that of Descartes. This whole collection of essays reflects a movement to reestablish the sophistication and relevance of Aquinas's thought.

16. King (ibid., 124–25) gives the example of a captain voluntarily casting his cargo overboard in order to prevent his ship from foundering. The notion of "passion" should be understood to exceed rational belief.

necessity or for the most part (to use Aristotle's explanation of accident), a prudent person can evaluate the degree of probability that some contingent circumstance might influence an expected outcome.[17]

Throughout his treatment of chance events, Aquinas emphasized the role of reason in interpreting circumstances in order to determine a morally justifiable outcome, but for him, the role played by fortune did not conflict with the power of divine providence. God's knowledge transcends time so all things are simultaneously present to him, and events occur when, where, and by necessity, contingency, or chance as he has willed them to occur.[18] Aquinas adapted the example of discovering treasure to argue this idea:

17. John Bowlin, *Contingency and Fortune in Aquinas's Ethics* (Cambridge: Cambridge University Press, 1999), 68–74, provides examples of how such determinations may proceed.

18. Dante made Fortune one of the "Intelligences," angelic creatures ordained as ministers and guides of the heavenly spheres. "Your knowledge cannot stand against her force," Virgil declares. "For she forsees and judges and maintains her kingdom as the other gods do theirs. The changes that she brings are without respite: it is necessity that makes her swift; and for this reason, men change state so often. She is the one so frequently maligned even by those who should give praise to her—they blame her wrongfully with words of scorn" (*Inferno*, VII.85–93).

In *The Consolation of Philosophy*, Boethius must accept the turning of Fortune's wheel as emblematic of a world that is always in flux and thus as an explanation not only of his fall from power, but also of suffering and even death. When he questions Lady Philosophy about events that are commonly called "chance or accidental," she accentuates the distinction between accident as a quality and accident as an event by calling the accidental event *casus* and *fortuitum* (i.e., chance or fortuitousness)—*casus* itself deriving from the verb *cadere* (to fall)—rather than employing the Latin *accidere* (to happen). and she transforms Aristotle's familiar accident of finding buried treasure into a Christian sign: "Whenever something is done for some purpose, and for certain reasons something other than what was intended happens, it is called chance. For example, if someone began to dig the ground in order to cultivate a field and found a cache of buried gold. This is believed to have happened fortuitously, but it does not happen as a result of nothing; it has its own causes, the unforeseen and unexpected conjunction of which have clearly effected the chance event. If the cultivator of the field had not been digging, and if the depositor had not buried his money at that point, the gold would not have been found. These, therefore, are the causes of the fortuitous harvest. It is the result of the conjunction of opposite causes, and not the intention of the doers. Neither the man who buried the gold, nor the man who was tilling the field intended the discovery of the money, but, as I said, it happens as a result of the coincidence that the one began to dig where the other had buried. We may therefore define chance as an unexpected event due to the conjunction of its causes with action which is done for some purpose. The conjunction and coincidence of the causes is effected by that order which proceeds by the inescapable nexus of causation, descending from the fount of Providence and ordering all things in their own time and place" (*The Consolation of Philosophy*, trans. V. E. Watts [New York: Penguin, 1969, rev. ed., 1999], V.i.117.

In his commentary on Aristotle's *On Interpretation*, Aquinas invoked Boethius's image

We must say that what happens on earth accidentally, either in nature or in human affairs, is derived from a pre-ordaining cause, namely divine Providence.

For nothing prevents what exists accidentally being taken as a unity by the mind; otherwise the mind could not formulate the proposition, *The man digging a grave discovered treasure.* And just as the mind can apprehend this, so it can bring it about; just as someone knowing where a hidden treasure was might prompt a peasant, who did not know, to dig a grave in that place. Thus nothing stops what happens on earth accidentally from being derived from some ordering cause operating through the mind, and especially the divine Mind. For God alone can change the will, as shown above. Consequently, the ordering of human actions (whose source is the will) must be ascribed to God alone. (I.q.116.a.1)

Although the *Summa theologiae* is not commonly conceived by non-specialists as a pedagogical work, it did serve an educational function, possibly for Dominican students engaged in pastoral work or preparing for such work. The study of moral theology would have been particularly useful for such students, so the *Summa* placed practical concerns within its theological context.[19] Yet the sophistication of the work and the fact that it summarizes his thought on the most controversial and compelling issues of the day implies that it may have been directed at advanced students.[20] Whatever the intended audience, the broad plan represents a project to understand God and because his creative activities are an important aspect of that understanding, Aquinas focused on the human beings

---

of God controlling all things from a timeless citadel high above the mutable world of cause and effect: "But God is wholly outside the order of time, standing, as it were, in the high citadel of eternity, which is all at one time. The whole course of time is subject to eternity in one simple glance. So at one glance he sees everything that is done in the course of time; he sees everything as it is in itself, not as if it were future relative to his view. It is only future in the ordering of its causes. (Though God does see that ordering of causes.) In a wholly eternal way he sees everything that is the case at any time, just as the human eye sees the sitting down of Socrates as it is in itself, not in its causes" (*In Perihermeneias,* in *The Philosophy of Thomas Aquinas,* trans. and ed. Christopher Martin [London: Routledge, 1988], 44). On the conceptual relation between *Boethius and Aquinas* see R. McInerny, *Boethius and Aquinas* (Washington: Catholic University of America Press, 1990).

19. See the influential presentation of this theory in Leonard E. Boyle, *The Setting of the "Summa Theologiae" of Saint Thomas* (Toronto: Pontifical Institute of Mediaeval Studies, 1982).

20. John I. Jankins, *Knowledge and Faith in Thomas Aquinas* (Cambridge: Cambridge University Press, 1997), proposes this view.

created in his image. Virtue became a topic of special relevance for him within his investigation into the ultimate causes of being: "Theology's distinctive investigation is concerned solely with the intellectual powers and the appetites, since that is where the virtues are located" (I.q.78.pr).

The initial question Aquinas posed in his study of human nature ("What is a human being?") is linked to Aristotle's initial question, "What is being?" Aristotle's answer, of course, was substance, but Aquinas, who believed that being is present in nature only in God, revised that answer in significant ways. His faith required another conception both of sensible things and of what constitutes actuality. The answer he proposed shares the Aristotelian belief that what gives life is the *anima*. We retain this meaning when we say Socrates is "animated," that is, he is full of life, both literally and figuratively. But Aristotle's assumption that the body was composed of substances like fire, earth, or water accentuated its materiality. Even his doctrine of prime matter, which he had developed to explain how Socrates might undergo substantial change and still remain Socrates, could not explain how he came to be or the existence of his soul. This idea, of course, was central to medieval thought.

Aquinas viewed early ideas about the materiality of things as the cause of the greatest confusion about human nature, and he sought a more fundamental answer to the question of being, one compatible with the Christian doctrine of creation. For him, the form God gave to matter was the ultimate cause of life, and thus, he equated form with soul. He agreed with Aristotle's conception of substance as a single thing, so he could not accept a division of matter (body) and form (soul) although he distinguished them from one another even at the most basic level of prime matter. To resolve this problem, he proposed that prime matter be understood as a power to become something actual, a thing's existence. Matter and form were simply different ways of describing this fundamental actuality. Since nothing can cause its own existence, the change from potentiality to actuality must come from God.

Unfortunately, the importance of form in Aquinas's thought does not make it particularly easy to grasp his subtle distinctions in the use of terms. Aristotle would have expressed his understanding of the human being as a composite of *anima* with body (that is, flesh and bones) by saying that its essence was a composite of substantial form and common matter. He did not consider this relationship a question of identity as we would understand it today. Rather, he proposed that it is Socrates' substantial form that provides the internal cause of the accidental properties that give him his particular appearance and qualities (his height, weight, skin color, standing, sitting, philosophizing, etc.). In other words, substantial form both animates him and explains who Socrates is.[21]

The creative role Aquinas gave to providence did not completely resolve the problem of substantial change. Aristotle's distinction between substance and accident acquired a personal meaning when people faced events that involved more drastic physical changes than sitting or standing. If Socrates contracted a fever, he might recover, so that kind of change still could be explained within the notion of accidental qualities. If he died, however, a change in substance would occur: he would lose his body. In the example of the accident of becoming feverish, the change does not affect Socrates' material substance—the composite of soul and body animated by substantial form. A change in *both* form and matter, however, constitutes a substantial change. From this point of view, Socrates' accidental fever could lead to substantial change, as illness may lead to death.[22]

All that *anima* meant for Aristotle or soul for Aquinas was the difference between an animate and an inanimate substance. However, because being alive is not an accidental quality of a human being, Aquinas could say that the soul made it be the thing it was by providing its existence. He added the important proviso that as a substantial form, the soul perfects the parts as well as the whole: "It is obvious that not every principle of vital activity is a soul. Otherwise the eye would be a soul, since it is a principle of sight; and so with the other organs of the soul. What we call the soul is the root principle of life. Now though something corporeal can be some sort of principle of life, as the heart is for animals, never the less a body cannot be the root principle of life" (I.q.75.a.1.c). In this view, a hand

---

21. Robert Pasnau, *Thomas Aquinas on Human Nature: A Philosophical Study of "Summa theologiae" Ia 75–89* (Cambridge: Cambridge University Press, 2002), offers what he declares is a somewhat controversial study of Thomist thought on these intricate matters. The various aspects of my account scarcely do justice to Pasnau's overall argument (or the subtleties involved in the mind-body problem itself). See also his "Form, Substance, and Mechanism," *Philosophical Review* 113, no. 1 (January 2004): 34–39. Other valuable discussions include Anthony Kenny, *Aquinas on Being* (Oxford: Clarendon Press, 2002); and Leo J. Elders, *The Metaphysics of Being of St. Thomas Aquinas in a Historical Perspective* (Leiden: E. J. Brill, 1993), 239–68. See also Joseph Bobik, *Aquinas on Matter and Form and the Elements* (Notre Dame: University of Notre Dame Press, 1998), 199–207.

22. Aquinas would say that Socrates would cease to exist at death (even though his soul would continue to exist) and the resurrection would allow him to come back to life. In one sense, it would be possible to say that the pagan Augustine ceased to exist with his conversion or the lovesick Dante was subsumed into an author inspired by divine love, yet it still seemed appropriate to say that in substance they remained the same. Gareth B. Matthews explores the intricacies of Aristotle's understanding of "same" in "Accidental Unities," in *Language and Logos: Studies in Ancient Greek Philosophy Presented to G. E. L. Owen*, ed. Malcolm Schofield and Martha Craven Nussbaum (Cambridge: Cambridge University Press, 1982), 223–40.

cannot function apart from the body because a detached hand cannot be what it is essential for a hand to be. From the perspective of one of its parts, therefore, the body has a fundamental unity. For Aquinas, the criterion of perfectibility supported the idea that living substances enjoy a fundamental unity of matter and form. The soul can be bound to the body, yet exist independently of it because actuality is the unifying element in being.[23]

Aquinas shared Aristotle's emphasis on the primacy of sensory perception of accidental qualities (colors, shapes, smells, and so on), but he recognized that the senses cannot fathom substantial forms. They can be known through the conceptualizing function of judgment, but even this understanding is limited.[24] By abstracting from individual sensory experiences, the intellect can grasp what makes Socrates human, but it cannot determine what makes him Socrates or distinguish him from Plato or Sophocles without the aid of the senses and the imagination.[25] Although nothing in the content of a thought makes it belong to one individual more than to another, one result of the universalizing function of intellect is to link thought to the mental images available within a person's repertoire of concepts. The capacity to acquire concepts, such as the moral virtues, and to employ them, allows human nature to attain happiness by pursuing the goal of good actions.

The relation Aquinas postulated between the soul and the body held for other form and matter composites. He could apply it to a number of examples, such as the creation of a statue from the alloy of bronze that Aristotle used in his *Metaphysics*, to explain the shift from one substance to another. This concept of substantive change, which united matter and spirit

23. See Pasnau, *Thomas Aquinas on Human Nature*, esp. 83ff. The Christian insistence on the immortality of the soul pressured Aquinas's reading of Aristotle's metaphysical texts. Much of the resistance to the return of Aristotle's thought stemmed from the argument that he was unable to recognize the soul's immortality.

24. Aquinas also argued for the immateriality of the intellect in terms of potentiality and change. Unlike a material being that must lose an existing quality in order to receive another (that is, losing whiteness as it tans), intellect has the potential to be altered by thoughts and concepts without losing anything.

25. Anthony Kenny, "Body, Soul, and Intellect in Aquinas," in *Essays on the Aristotelian Tradition* (Oxford: Clarendon Press, 2001), 85–86, provides an account of the operation of the intellect as well as a cautionary analysis of the illusory nature of "self," a concept that he argues Aquinas did well to avoid. Even the more limited concept of self-knowledge presents difficulties for Aquinas in his view. Since the intellect understands by abstracting ideas from matter, what is abstracted is universal, so it cannot directly know anything that is not universal. Aquinas solved this problem for other individuals in terms of the sensory context of thought, but Kenny considers his argument weakened by his theory of the imagination as an inner (and sometimes seemingly physical) sense.

in an indivisible actuality, gave critical support to the doctrine of transubstantiation that informed the Eucharistic first sacrament of the Catholic Church and served as an essential component in its expanding power.

III. Transubstantiation

During the thirteenth century, the church made a concerted effort to ritualize the sacrament of the Eucharist. Liturgical practices sprang up around the sacrament—perpetual light, ritual actions, vestments, bells—all designed to render the presence of God in the church tangible through this miracle. Recognition of the power of the Eucharist appeared in the first article of the Fourth Lateran Council decree of 1215, which secured the link between the Eucharist and the Roman church in the wake of the Albigensian heresy. Since the council asserted that only a priest sanctioned by Rome could administer the sacrament, salvation depended upon a clerical class administering a divine gift.

The Eucharist became a potent symbol not only within the collective religious life but also within the lives of individuals.[26] Transubstantiation allowed the question of the relation of substance to accident to enter into the way people understood their moral being. For Catholics, Christ's word becomes material in this sacrament, and what the believers consume quite literally fills them with faith. Through the power of divine providence the believer participates directly, not symbolically, in the eating of the Last Supper, and this miracle takes place simultaneously across Christendom. The sacrament of the Eucharist is not limited by time or place, but pulls the believer from the material world of time, change, and corruption to an immanent space of substance. As an idiom for articulating human needs, a language of social relations and cosmic order, and a means of giving expression to penitential remorse, it achieves a literal interpenetration of human and divine.[27]

When Aquinas used Aristotle's understanding of substance and acci-

---

26. Theorization of various models of change signified in transubstantiation. Theologians gradually rejected the notion that physical growth represented a mysterious expansion of physical stuff in favor of ideas of digestive transformation, while tales of metamorphosis popular in antiquity were revived and natural philosophers began to study alchemy. Caroline Walker Bynum, *Metamorphosis and Identity* (New York: Zone Books, 2001), 104–5, links the Eucharist to monstrous human and animal transformations.

27. See John Bossy, "The Mass as a Social Institution, 1200–1700," *Past and Present* 100 (1983): 29–61; and Miri Rubin, *Corpus Christi: The Eucharist in Late Medieval Culture* (New York: Cambridge University Press, 1991). Rubin, 185–96, discusses the attribution of the Corpus Christi liturgy to Aquinas, whose Eucharistic doctrine finds close parallels in the lauds.

dent to explain the miracle of transubstantiation, he placed accident at the heart of a pervasive cultural system of critical importance throughout the Middle Ages. His exposition of the doctrine represented the culmination of the *Summa* and a critical document in the understanding of accident.[28] In question 75 of part 3, Aquinas countered the hypothesis that the substance of the bread and wine remains in the sacrament after the consecration by asserting that to believe that the bread remains is to deny the truth of Christ's declaration "This is my Body." Only the change of the substance of bread into God's substance permits Christ's body to appear in the sacrament. Rather than allowing for the annihilation of the substances of bread and wine, he insisted that they are transformed:

> The underlying material constituents, into which mixed bodily natures can be resolved, are the four elements. There is no question of a resolution into primal matter, leaving it without any form at all, because primal matter cannot be without form. Now, since after the consecration nothing remains under the sacramental appearances but the body and the blood, we shall have to say that the elements into which the substance of the bread and wine has been resolved have departed, and this by local motion. But our senses would have perceived this. And, again, the substance of the bread or wine remain until the last instant of the consecration. In the last instant of the consecration we already have the substance of the body or of the blood of Christ, just as in the last instant of generation the new form is present. (III.q.75.a.3.c)

In other words, in the act of consecration, the body and blood of Christ replace the bread and wine. At no time do the substances lack form, for God's substance exists outside the limits of time and space and transub-

---

28. Aquinas layered his argument with references to the work of early theologians who insisted on the truth of the Eucharist. In the *sed contra* of 3a. 75, 1, for example, he wrote: "Hilary says [*De Trinitate*, VIII, 15] *there is no room for doubt about the reality of the body and blood of Christ. Our Lord taught and our faith accepts that his flesh is really our food and his blood is really our drink.* And Ambrose says [*De Sacramentis*, VI, 1] *just as our Lord Jesus Christ is the real son of God, so the real flesh of Christ is what we receive, and his blood is really our drink.*" Aquinas did not mention the heretical theologians who rejected the notion of real presence, among them Berengar, who was forced to sign in Rome in 1059 a formula that "the bread and wine placed on the altar are, after consecration, not only a sacrament, but also the true body and blood of our lord Jesus Christ. . . . [They] are sensible, not only sacramentally but in truth, handled and broken by the hands of the priests and crushed by the teeth of the faithful." Jaroslav Pelikan, *The Christian Tradition: A History of the Development of Doctrine*, vol. 4 (Chicago: University of Chicago Press, 1984), 199.

stantiation takes place within an instant. After the consecration, all that remains of the bread and wine is accidents.[29] In Aristotle's understanding of separable versus inseparable accidents, he drew a loose connection between an object and certain of its features. For example, he implied that if Socrates were walking on the right-hand side of Praxiteles and then shifted to walking on his left, he would be completely unchanged. However, he drew a tighter connection between an object and other qualities. For example, Socrates must be male. The standard view of what happened in transubstantiation demanded that a loose connection apply to *all* qualities of the bread and wine. To support the doctrine of the Eucharist, therefore, Aquinas had to make the accidental qualities more accidental.

According to Aristotle, accidents could not exist without a substance, yet because God's power is the first cause and prior to the power of the bread's substance, Aquinas asserted that this power permits accidents to remain. Therefore, after consecration, the senses that perceive the visual accidents of bread and wine are not deceived, since these accidents are truly present. Faith, rather than the senses, enables the intellect to recognize that the consecrated host is truly the substance of Christ's body. He argued:

> It is obvious to our senses that, after the consecration, all the accidents of the bread and wine remain. Divine providence very wisely arranged for this. First of all, men have not the custom of eating human flesh and drinking human blood; indeed, the thought revolts them. And so the flesh and blood of Christ are given to us to be taken under the appearances of things in common human use, namely bread and wine.
>
> Secondly, lest this sacrament should be an object of contempt for un believers, if we were to eat our Lord under his human appearances.
>
> Thirdly, in taking the body and blood of our Lord in their invisible presence, we increase the merit of our faith. (III.q.75.a.5.c)

---

29. The notion of accident without a substance allows for the possibility of accidents in and of themselves—and confers the possibility of a substantiality on accidents—an objection that was first raised by a participant at the quodlibetal disputation of Christmas 1257, when Aquinas was first teaching as a master in theology at Paris. The objection stated that since after Eucharistic transubstantiation the accidents of the bread and wine remain without their substances, it follows that the accidents themselves will be substances, since the definition of a substance is a "being in itself." In his reply, Aquinas rejected the description of substance as "that which exists in itself" and accident as "that which inheres in something else." Through divine power an accident does not exist in a subject; therefore, it still does not meet the definition of a substance. See John F. Wippel, *The Metaphysical Thought of Thomas Aquinas* (Washington, DC: Catholic University of America Press, 2000), 225–37.

It is a fascinating moment. The believer cannot deny eating Christ's living flesh, yet the horror of cannibalism requires that this flesh be perceived as bread and wine.[30]

The cultural power of the idea of transubstantiation within a medieval cosmology of sin, punishment, and redemption appears in cantos XXXII–XXXIII of Dante's *Inferno* when he encounters first the figure of Ugolino gnawing the head of the man who betrayed him and then, at the nadir of his descent, Lucifer perpetually devouring the bodies of a trinity of traitors. These passages allow us to recognize the extent to which Aristotle's ontological system had become part of literary consciousness.[31]

In Dante's cosmology, the highest degree of spirituality (the zone of the "living Light") represents the farthest remove from matter, while in the ninth circle of hell the gravity of the sinful state has drawn all weight to the furthest depths, where everything has frozen solid. The bodies of the traitors condemned here are frozen in a lake that has "lost the look of water and seemed glass" (XXXII.24), undergoing not a substantial change but a change in accidental qualities that signifies the cold-blooded nature of betrayal. Blind to Christ's substance, they are relegated to an icy region that mirrors their sin. In a sense, therefore, Dante suggests that when an unrepentant sinner dies, what remains is material accidents of the body. For such lost souls, what were mutable accidents of the flesh become immutable prisons of identity.

Dante encounters the most extreme form of treachery when he discovers Ugolino, a member of a leading Ghibelline family of Pisa who

30. Rachel Jacoff, "The Body in the *Commedia*," in *Sparks and Seeds: Medieval Literature and Its Afterlife: Essays in Honor of John Freccero*, Binghamton Medieval and Early Modern Studies 2, ed. Dana E. Stewart and Alison Cornish (Turnhout: Brepols, 2000), 120–21, notes a comparable distaste for the idea of the resurrection of the body, quoting Augustine ("Do not shudder at the resurrection of the body. See its good aspects, forget the evil"). Questions of the form the resurrected body will take included the possibility that it might have been eaten not only by animals, but by cannibals. Caroline Walker Bynum, *The Resurrection of the Body* (New York: Columbia University Press, 1995), esp. 103–11, discusses what she calls the "cannibalism libel," as a threat to the doctrine of the resurrection. The deep concern for material continuity evoked an increasingly literal and materialist vocabulary.

31. Rachel Jacoff, "The Hermeneutics of Hunger," in *Speaking Images: Essays in Honor of V. A. Kolve*, ed. Robert F. Yeager and Charlotte C. Morse (Asheville, NC: Pegasus, 2001), 95–110, surveys the extensive literature surrounding the most contoversial line in the Ugolino episode ("then fasting had more power than grief"; *Inferno*, XXX.75), bringing evidence from theological and iconographic sources to support her argument that his primary sin was his inability to comfort or care for his innocent sons, who were imprisoned with him. As she points out, a pathetic interpretation of this aspect of Ugolino's story was developed in Chaucer's "The Monk's Tale" and passed into numerous eighteenth- and nineteenth-century retellings, all of which, she believes, misunderstood the episode by decontextualizing it.

defected to the Guelphs but later plotted against them with the Pisan Ghibelline leader Archbishop Ruggieri. Ruggieri betrayed him and imprisoned Ugolino and his sons to starve to death. The shades of the two men are frozen together in one hole, and Ugolino digs his teeth into Ruggeri's nape "as bread is devoured for hunger" (XXXII.124–29). By calling his act "bestial" (133), Dante signals metaphorically that the man has sacrificed his human nature. However, he also indicates that the action is a sign of hatred ("per sì bestial segno/ odio"; 133–34), which suggests that it carries additional meaning. As Aquinas says of biblical exegesis, events read in context and with the tradition of faith receive their extraordinary meaning not only by God's ordering of the narrative sequence but by his guidance in the writing.[32] Allegorical aspects of this scene offer evidence of Dante's assumption of exegetical practice.[33]

When Ugolino gives his version of events, he reveals that his sin lay not only in his double treachery but also in a veiled cannibalism:

> Out of my grief, I bit at both my hands;
> and they [his sons], who thought I'd done that out of hunger,
> immediately rose and told me: "Father,
>> it would be far less painful for us if
> you ate of us; for you clothed us in this
> sad flesh—it is for you to strip it off."
>
> (XXXIII.58–63)

Ugolino's sons diagnose their father's act as an expression of hunger, and they offer him their bodies. The father, obsessed with the material accidents of the body, cannot recognize the Eucharistic symbols in their offer, and he takes their words literally: "'And after they were dead, I called them for / two days; then fasting had more force then grief'" (XXXIII.74–76).

During a period in which the veneration of the Eucharist was spreading, the sacrifice of Ugolino's sons provided a Eucharistic subtext for this scene. Initially, Dante compared Ugolino gnawing the skull of Ruggieri

---

32. Robert Durling, "Deceit and Digestion in the Belly of Hell," *Allegory and Representation: Selected Papers from the English Institute, 1979–80*, ed. Stephen Greenblatt (Baltimore: Johns Hopkins University Press, 1981), 63, notes that in the typological structure of the poem, progress prefigures descent into materiality and literalism, during which the figures who represent the various appetites become increasingly substantial.

33. Mark D. Jordan, *Ordering Wisdom: The Hierarchy of Philosophical Discourses in Aquinas* (Notre Dame: University of Notre Dame Press, 1986), 29–32.

to someone hungrily chewing bread. He made three literary additions to this act—the reference to the sons offering to sacrifice themselves, one son's dying cry, "Father, why do you not help me?" (69), and the allusion to the unspeakable crime of cannibalism.[34] Ugolino's punishment parodies the Last Supper.

The pattern of references Dante presents to the reader resonates within the conventions of scriptural narrative. Associations with the Last Supper, with the sacrifice of Isaac, and with the Eucharistic sacrament permit an understanding of Ugolino's story not only in terms of his sin as a betrayer of his city and his family, but also as an example of the inversion of Christian values. Just as Dante's vision in paradise fused the world into an immaterial and luminous love of God, the sinners in hell are immobilized prisoners of the material accidents of the flesh. What he suggested—and this text is no more explicit in its expression than the description of his comprehension of the heavenly vision—was a cannibalistic inversion of the meaning of the sacraments. The traitor's mortal sin is analogous to that of an unbeliever consuming the sacramental wafer without desiring Christ's spirit. Such an act, devoid of spiritual transformation, would indeed represent the most profound form of betrayal, that of Christ's own substance.

Ugolino's punishment prepares us for the figure of Lucifer eternally devouring Brutus, Cassius, and Judas Iscariot.[35] In the ultimate parody of Eucharistic cannibalism, the bodies of these traitors become hosts in an endless inversion of the sacrament carried out by the fallen angel. Their punishment literally embodies their sins, transforming the substance of the betrayers into the vilest form of excremental matter and that of the angel who attempted to usurp God's divinity into a triple-headed monster.

If exegesis reads words as signs pointing to deeper understanding, the sacramental bread and wine are also to be read as signs. Perfect faith al-

---

34. For a Christological reading see Marianne Shapiro, "An Old French Source for Ugolino?" *Dante Studies* 92 (1974): 129–48. See also Ronald B. Herzman, "Cannibalism and Communion in Inferno XXXIII," *Dante Studies* 98 (1980): 53–78; John Freccero, "Bestial Sign and Bread of Angels: Inferno 32–34," *Yale Italian Studies* 1, no. 1 (Winter 1979): 152–66; and Maggie Kilgour, *From Communion to Cannibalism* (Princeton: Princeton University Press, 1990).

35. Jacoff, "Hermeneutics of Hunger," 102–3, notes that the Hellmouth was a ubiquitous visual image. Thirteenth- and fourteenth-century Italian representations of the Last Judgment substituted the mouth (or mouths) of Satan for the Hellmouth. Giotto's *Last Judgment* in the Arena Chapel portrays Satan both eating and defecating.

lows the believer to accept the bread as accidental to the substance that is Christ's body and truly take in his spirit. Concentrating on matter rather than spirit would turn Christ's substance into something basely material and indicate the heavier, sinful nature of the participant. Through a reasoned Aristotelian explication of the Eucharist, Aquinas prepared the believer to recognize God's substance beneath the accidents of the bread (keeping the etymology of "substance" as that which lies under). Because proper understanding of accidental qualities was necessary to avoid sacrilege, the interpretation of accident became a site of moral self-definition. Just as belief in providential design increased recognition of the potential significance of the accidental event, the profound implications of transubstantiation gave increased conceptual force to accidental qualities.

IV. The Library of Thought

The intellectualized and architectonic pattern of thinking that characterized the structure of the *Summa* exerted a pervasive influence on education throughout the thirteenth, fourteenth, and fifteenth centuries. Stimulated by the standardization of the university curriculum and the dominance of Aristotelian ideas, the methods practiced in the schools retained their importance as a basis for organizing academic study (and traces still remain in current university practices). Attempts on the part of followers of Aquinas to identify a common core for the teaching of philosophy led to an emphasis on the doctrine of substance and accident. This doctrine served as a focus of later Scholasticism and the detailed hierarchical structure of statement and rebuttal that characterized the way in which the Scholastics articulated an argument became a hallmark of the period.[36]

Two centuries after Dante's masterly architectonic vision, the continuing power of the Scholastic synthesis of Aristotle's philosophy appeared in a visual summary of contemporary thought, Raphael's great frescoes in the Stanza della Segnatura of the Vatican. Here, in the room that served as the papal library, a complex iconographic program organized around

---

36. Erwin Panofsky, *Gothic Architecture and Scholasticism* (New York: Meridian, 1957). His classic treatise argued the impact of this method on the way the great cathedrals were conceived, but the principle also can be applied to literature—for example, in the dramatic cycles based on the Passion performed into the sixteenth century in France.

the sacrament of the Eucharist asserted not only papal power but the power of the Scholastic tradition as understood at the height of the Italian Renaissance.

From a central crest containing the arms of Pope Julius II, the ceiling of the room divides into four areas, each dominated by a roundel containing an allegorical female figure looking down onto a fresco that represents her thought. Beneath the figure of Theology, the great defenders of the church appear on either side of a monstrance that contains the Eucharist, in the fresco we now call, after Vasari, the *Disputa* (fig. 1). Across the room from Theology, below the figure of Philosophia, another fresco depicts the School of Athens (fig. 2). Here Plato and Aristotle stand surrounded by the great philosophers of classical antiquity. Raphael's celebrated Stanza testifies to the long life of the Scholastic fusion of philosophy and theology.

In Raphael's fresco, the emerald lawn where Dante placed his "philosophic family" in canto 4 of the *Inferno* has become an immense temple open to the sky that stretches to infinity.[37] The philosophers have been taken from limbo and placed within an architectural space that seems to exist between a vision of a classical temple (whose vaulting is reminiscent of the Baths of Caracalla with statues of Athena and Apollo decorating the walls) and a Christian cathedral (whose design represents Bramante's plan for the new Saint Peter's). Yet we recognize that in contrast to Dante's description, Aristotle no longer stands above the others as "the master of the men who know," but shares an equal position with his teacher Plato. Plato steps forward and points upward, emphasizing the idealist and transcendent aims of his philosophy as well as the heavenly bodies he discusses in his *Timaeus*, which he holds in his hand. He looks to the younger Aristotle, who returns his gaze. One of Aristotle's hands gestures forcibly downward, suggesting his interest in

---

37. Dante placed Aristotle highest among the pagan philosophers in the circle of hell reserved for the souls of worthy heathens: "When I raised my eyes a little higher, / I saw the master of the men who know, / seated in philosophic family. / There all look up to him, all do him honor: / there I beheld both Socrates and Plato, / closest to him, in front of all the rest; / Democritus, who ascribes the world to chance, / Diogenes, Empedocles, and Zeno, / and Thales, Anaxagoras, Heraclitus; / I saw the good collector of medicinals, / I mean Dioscorides; and I saw Orpheus, / and Tully, Linus, moral Seneca; / and Euclid the geometer, and Ptolemy, / Hippocrates and Galen, Avicenna, / Averroës, of the great Commentary" (*Inferno*, IV.130–43). In the Stanza, Dante himself appears among the figures surrounding the Eucharist as well as standing with Homer and Virgil in the fresco that depicts Poetry on one of the smaller side walls.

1. Raphael (Raffaello Sanzio), *Disputa* (ca. 1509). Fresco. Stanza della Segnatura,
Vatican Palace. Vatican. (Photograph © Scala / Art Resource, New York.)

earthly questions, such as those discussed in the *Ethics*, which he holds in
his other hand. Raphael arranges other philosophers roughly divided between Platonists and Aristotelians on the steps and the floor below them.
It is an astonishing visual synthesis of contemporary knowledge of classical philosophy.

Plato's position as Aristotle's equal in this interpretation is linked to
the rise of Neoplatonism. One central figure of this late fifteenth-century
revival was Pico della Mirandola, who argued for the philosophical
equivalency of Plato and Aristotle in his *De ente et uno*.[38] The long-haired
young man dressed in white placed between Pythagoras and Anaxi-
mander may be Pico. He is the only figure in the fresco looking directly

38. Translated by Victor M. Hamm as Pico della Mirandola, *Of Being and Unity* (Milwaukee: Marquette University Press, 1943). On the historical context of *Of Being and Unity*, see
Raymond Klibansky, "Plato's *Parmenides* in the Middle Ages and the Renaissance," *Mediaeval and Renaissance Studies* 1 (1941–43): 281–330.

2. Raphael (Raffaello Sanzio), *School of Athens* (ca. 1510–1512). Fresco. Stanza della Segnatura, Vatican Palace, Vatican. (Photograph © Erich Lessing / Art Resource, New York.)

at the spectator, implicitly encouraging viewers to enter the synthetic totality of thought presented in the scene. Significantly, the same figure appears directly across the room in the *Disputa*, dressed now in a blue robe over his toga (the white and blue symbolic of the Virgin) and pointing to the Eucharist—the compositional center of this fresco and indeed of the Stanza itself.[39] As a figure who crosses between philosophy and theology (and we know that Pico professed the significance of transubstantiation), he emphasizes the relation between classical reason and faith.

The *Disputa* is generally regarded to have been painted first, dating from 1509, and it provides the key to the iconography of the other frescoes.[40] The scene shows an idealized council of the church, in which both

39. Christiane Joost-Gaugier identifies the young man as Pico. See *Raphael's Stanza della Segnatura: Meaning and Invention* (Cambridge: Cambridge University Press, 2002), 77–78, 94–95.

40. Giorgio Vasari, *Lives of the Most Eminent Painters Sculptors and Architects,* trans. Gaston du C. de Vere (New York: Knopf, 1996), 720, named this fresco *La Disputa* because he interpreted the convocation as a formal "disputation about the Host [*l'ostia*]." He identified

divine and mortal members gather to approve the doctrine of transubstantiation. At the same time, it represents a symbolic celebration of the Mass with the monstrance holding the consecrated wafer as the central focus of attention for the council just as the Eucharist is the central object of the Mass.[41]

Transubstantiation provided a conceptual basis for the composition. At the top of the fresco, God the father, surrounded by cherubim and angels that melt into a bank of cloud, blesses with his right hand and holds an orb symbolizing his authority in his left. Below him, a gloriole encircles the resurrected Christ, his wounded hands outstretched. Below the figure of Christ the Holy Spirit appears as a dove. On either side of the Trinity, a bank of clouds separates the twelve ascended saints of the church from the theologians grouped on the steps on either side of the altar. The Trinity forms the vertical axis of this compositional cross.[42] Silhouetted against the sky, directly below the Trinity and across the room from Plato and Aristotle, the Eucharist, the living body of Christ on earth, links the material and spiritual worlds. The golden circle around the monstrance is repeated in the aureoles that enclose the Holy Spirit and Christ's resurrected body. These repeated circular shapes and changes in size formally link the host to the visualization of Christ.

The representation of the monstrance expresses a sophisticated understanding of the role of substance and accident in transubstantiation.

---

the urgency of the debate as evidenced in Raphael's depictions of the particular disputants: "Even more art and genius did he display in the holy Christian Doctors, in whose features, while they make disputation throughout the scene [*a due disputando per la storia*] in groups of six or three or two, there may be seen this kind of eagerness and distress in seeking to find the truth of that which is in question [*faccendone segno col disputar*], revealing this by gesticulating with their hands, making various movements of their persons, turning their ears to listen, knitting their brows, and expressing astonishment in many different ways, all truly well varied and appropriate."

41. Sydney Freedberg, *Painting of the High Renaissance in Rome and Florence* (Cambridge, MA: Harvard University Press, 1961), 1:118. The centrality of the doctrine of transubstantiation also appears in the subject of the adjoining Stanza d'Eliodoro, painted in 1511–14. On one of its walls Raphael depicted a miracle that had taken place during a mass celebrated at Bolsena in 1265, when the blood of Christ poured from the host at the moment of consecration.

42. Nearest the altar are the four Doctors of the Church, each identified by his books: on the left, Saint Jerome with his own *Epistolae* and his *Biblia* and Saint Gregory with his *Moralia*; on the right, Saint Augustine with his *De Civitate Dei* and Saint Ambrose, whose work is not entitled. On the right, we have Saint Thomas Aquinas, Saint Bonaventure, Pope Innocent III, Pope Sixtus IV, and Dante. Julius II, prime supporter of the doctrine of transubstantiation, looks toward the Eucharist. Richly dressed in his papal robes, he reaches out as if to cup the Eucharist in a gesture of adoration and control.

Enclosing the material accidents of the consecrated host, it appears to en-close nothing. Barely visible against a covering of light cloud, the wafer seems to blend into the sky and disappear. Raphael gave visual form not to the host but to the substance of the Trinity. In other words, the mate-rial accidents vanish, while the conceptual divinity is made manifest. By depicting this reversal of the material and immaterial, seen and unseen, the fresco visually demonstrates that the believer must accept by faith the doctrine of the Eucharistic transformation of bread and wine into the body and blood of Christ.

As the vanishing point of the perspective, the monstrance enables the composition to convey the way in which God's living substance contains all time and all space. Despite its small size, its significance dominates the scene. The setting dissolves any concrete material architecture. Al-though critics have taken the base of a column represented in the fresco to be the base of the new Saint Peter's, in the world of the *Disputa* the mir-acle of transubstantiation supersedes a physical context. The sweeping semicircle formed by the arrangement of the members of the council and the higher, smaller semicircle of angels and seraphim imply a spiritual architecture. Shaped like the apsidal half dome of a church, this virtual structure replaces the substance of stone architecture with a more perfect spiritual analog.[43]

In contrast, *The School of Athens* takes place in a great temple that is simultaneously a monument from the pagan past and a monument to the future, Donato Bramante's design for the "Cathedral of the World" that was to be built by Julius II. The temple's vast scale provides space for representatives of all rational thought so that it serves as a memory chamber for philosophies. A series of vaulted ceilings extend the painted space toward the limitless sky. The first arch opens onto another, reveal-ing patches of bluer sky and surmounted by a triple window showing a deeper shade of blue. This triple window is the architectonic manifesta-tion of the Trinity across the room, a prefiguration of the revealed truth of Christianity concealed from pagan philosophers. In the *Disputa* the Trin-ity is visible, but in the material world of *The School*, it becomes immate-rial, suggested only in the dual unity of sky and cloud of the same color as the accidents of the consecrated host across the room. We recognize in the impalpable wafer the infinite space and time of the room itself. The power of the Eucharist and its ritual reenactment of the Last Supper en-able the body of Christ to appear across time and space.

43. Freedberg, *Painting of the High Renaissance*, 118–19.

The room's ontologically charged architecture declares that the systems of thought represented in *The School of Athens* must travel from philosophy to theology in order to achieve true knowledge of the substance of God. The design of the Stanza knits up classical and Christian time—from Plato and Aristotle to Julius II. By bringing these figures together in one room, the frescoes assert that metaphysics can lead man toward knowledge of immutable substances, taking him as close as he can come without the truth of theology. Raphael has solved the formal problem of representing the immaterial through his use of light, which dematerializes the physical presence of the host, and he has used spatial composition to suppress both historical and conceptual discontinuities. His work as an ordering intelligence is analogous to Dante's control over the narrative structure of the *Commedia*: it provides an overarching interpretive perspective that subsumes all material accidents to God's providential design. This synchronic vision expresses the faith that lies at the center of the Eucharist, the sacrament that enables the believer to see what the philosopher cannot: the living body of Christ.

The importance of reading that we recognized in both Dante's image of the book of substances and accidents as well as in the narrative of Augustine's conversion finds echoes in the purpose of the room. The Stanza was designed to serve as the private library of Julius II. Its contents were arranged according to the division of knowledge into the faculties of philosophy and theology, law, and poetry that structured the university, and his books were placed on shelves in accordance with the subject of each fresco.[44] The spatial links between the frescoes imply these intellectual correspondences: theology and philosophy represent complementary avenues to truth, one by faith, the other by reason, while the inspiration derived from poetry and the arts complements the deliberation required by law. In this way, the different disciplines form a balanced unity of intellectual and spiritual qualities to structure an ideal library of human thought.[45]

44. Later the room served as a meeting place for the papal tribunal, where the pope affixed his signature to doctrinal law, thereby giving the room its name, Room of the Signature.

45. The number 4, taken by both Plato and Aristotle as the number of primary substances and humors, was also considered by the Pythagoreans to be the first number to produce a solid figure. Indeed, Raphael painted between the roundels and rectangles of the ceiling the four primary substances (fire, air, earth, and water) and their mythological partners derived from Livy. (See Edgar Wind, "The Four Elements in Raphael's Stanza," *Journal of the Warburg and Courtauld Institutes* 2 [1938–39]: 75–79.) The interrelation between these four "faculties" indicates how the room was designed to represent a world. On the number 4 in its Pythagorean guise (the "tetractys"), see S. K. Heninger, Jr., *Touches of Sweet Harmony: Pythagorean Cosmology and Renaissance Poetics* (San Marino, CA: Huntington Library, 1974),

If we remember how Aquinas asserted that the intellect worked to form moral interpretations, we can appreciate how the iconographic elements in the frescoes carry meaning. They do so only within the terms of cultural memory and can be fully understood only when they are considered in combination. Thus, the relation between the books in Julius's library, the painted figures of the philosophers, and the architecture suggests the sort of mnemonic space associated with classical and contemporary memory theory.[46] Most simply, *The School of Athens* serves to remind the viewer of the body of thought contained in the volumes that once filled the shelves below. However, just as classical systems of artificial memory invoked a series of remembered rooms in which to place a particular sequence of thoughts, the endless architectural spaces connoted by the arches of *The School of Athens* project a limitless cultural memory. In that sense, the Stanza memorializes the triumph of the Scholastic project, the great fusion of classical philosophy within Christian theology.

The complex architectonic representations of substance and accident in *The School* and the *Disputa* transform our understanding of the nature of the books contained within the library. On the one hand, we recognize transubstantiation as a description of the way in which the immaterial word of God can be contained in the material books. On the other hand, the act of reading the classical philosophers also involved a form of transubstantiation. Transmuted into theological understanding, Aristotle's concept of substance has become divine.

As the place where the papal librarian could rule on disputes in philosophy, and heresy could be stamped out, the Stanza represents an end point to this phase of my history of substance. Through the idea of substance and the celebration of the Eucharist, the Church of Rome asserted its universal power, yet the synthetic vision immortalized in these frescoes proved vulnerable to attack. Within a decade of the Stanza's completion, Luther posted his theses on the doors of the Cathedral of Wittenberg.

---

esp. 71–145. For an overview of Renaissance architectural use of numbers theory to achieve "harmonic proportion," see Rudolf Wittkower, *Architectural Principles in the Age of Humanism,* third ed. (London: Alec Tiranti, 1962), esp. 101–42.

46. Sir Philip Sidney evokes such a space in his *Defence of Poetry,* ed. J. A. van Dorsten (Oxford: Oxford University Press, 1966), 51: "Even they that have taught the art of memory have showed nothing so apt for it as a certain room divided into many places well and thoroughly known." On the late medieval and early modern retooling of ancient memory theory, see Frances A. Yates, *The Art of Memory* (Chicago: University of Chicago Press, 1966); Mary J. Carruthers, *The Book of Memory: A Study of Memory in Medieval Culture* (Cambridge: Cambridge University Press, 1990); and Janet Coleman, *Ancient and Medieval Memories: Studies in the Reconstruction of the Past* (Cambridge: Cambridge University Press, 1992).

CHAPTER THREE

Skeptical Accidents: Secularization of Accident during the Reformation

I. The Ruling Passion

The Reformation unleashed long and violent struggles both on the battle-field and within the field of ideas, and the conceptual synthesis depicted in the Stanza della Segnatura began to dissolve. Martin Luther's Ninety-five Theses, which he posted in 1517, centered on the abuse of indulgences in relation to the sacrament of penance, but soon he expanded his attack to other sacraments, especially the first sacrament, the Eucharist. Although he rejected the doctrine of transubstantiation as an example of juggling with words by Scholastic theologians, he could not bring himself to reject the miraculous transformation of the bread and wine.[1] His

---

1. In "Letter to the Christians at Strassbourg" (1524), Luther stated: "I confess that if Dr. Karlstadt, or anyone else, could have convinced me five years ago that only bread and wine were in the sacrament he would have done me a great service. At that time I suffered such severe conflicts and inner strife and torment that I would gladly have been delivered from them. I realize that at this point I could best resist the papacy. . . . But I am a captive and cannot free myself. The text is too powerfully present, and will not allow itself to be torn from its meaning by mere verbiage." Trans. and ed. Conrad Bergendoff, in *Luther's Works*, vol. 40, *Church and Ministry II* (Philadelphia: Muhlenberg, 1958), 68. Despite his desire to reject the mystery of real presence as he rejected the system of indulgences and the notion of purgatory upon which it depended, he was caught by the text of the scripture. Christ's words "This is my Body" proved his presence in the bread. However, asserting the primacy of scripture allowed Luther to reject the authority derived from church offices, and his attack took the form of a polemic against the manner in which Scholastic terminology twisted the sense of scriptural texts: "Therefore it is an absurd and unheard-of juggling with words to understand 'bread' to mean 'the form or accidents of bread,' and 'wine' to mean 'the form or accidents of wine.' Why do they not also understand all other things to mean their 'forms or accidents?' And even if this might be done with all other things, it would still not be right to

theory of consubstantiation argued that Christ's body and blood existed alongside the consecrated host, but more radical reformers entirely rejected the presence of Christ's body in the sacrament.[2] Catholic theologians of the Counter-Reformation reaffirmed the doctrine of transubstantiation at the Council of Trent on 11 October 1551, asserting that the material bread was accidental to the substance of Christ's body. The struggle over the status of the Eucharistic bread as accident became one of the most central, violent, and irresolvable problems of early modern thought.[3]

Michel de Montaigne's life exemplifies the pull of conflicting religious affiliations. His mother was half Jewish and his father Catholic. Although he, three brothers, and one sister remained Catholic, one brother and two sisters converted to Protestantism. He was a close friend and supporter of the Protestant leader Henri de Navarre, who became the Catholic Henri IV of France. When he visited Rome, Catholic censors invited him to assist the church with his eloquence, yet late in the seventeenth century, the church proscribed his *Essays*.

Montaigne's first major work, *Apology for Raymond Sebond* (1575–80) grew from the spread of Luther's ideas. It responded to objections to Sebond's *Theologia naturalis*, a late Scholastic text that attempted to prove

---

enfeeble the words of God in this way, and by depriving them of their meaning to cause so much harm. Moreover, the church kept the true faith for more than twelve hundred years, during which time the holy fathers never, at any time or place, mentioned this transubstantiation (a monstrous word and a monstrous idea) until the pseudo philosophy of Aristotle began to make its inroads into the church in these last three hundred years." *A Prelude to the Babylonian Captivity of the Church*, trans. A. T. W. Steinhäuser, rev. Frederick C. Ahrens and Abdel Ross Wentz, in *Luther's Works*, vol. 36, *Word and Sacrament II* (1959), 31.

2. Huldrych Zwingli and other radical reformers attacked Luther's position as an impossible compromise. According to Zwingli, the first error was to presume that Christ's body is in the bread because he says it is. The second error was to presume that the bread remains bread. In other words, taking the text literally makes it impossible to take the bread literally. Rather than existing with Christ's body or transubstantiating, therefore, the Eucharistic bread serves as a remembrance that commemorates Christ's suffering. Zwingli, *Writings*, ed. E. J. Furcha and H. Wayne Pipkin (Allison Park, PA: Pickwick Publications, 1984), 2:233–385. See also G. R. Potter, *Zwingli* (Cambridge: Cambridge University Press, 1976); and W. P. Stephens, *The Theology of Huldrych Zwingli* (Oxford: Clarendon Press, 1986).

3. Euan Cameron writes that the question of the Eucharist "involved more misunderstandings . . . than almost any other issue of the Reformation" (*The European Reformation* [Oxford: Clarendon Press, 1991], 163). On the importance of debates about the Eucharist to the "communal understanding of words and of matter," see also Catherine Gallagher and Stephen Greenblatt, "The Mousetrap," in *Practicing New Historicism* (Chicago: University of Chicago Press, 1997), 136–62, esp. 140–42.

the truth and necessity of Christian doctrine from nature. Montaigne had translated it at the request of his father, who considered the work suited to a time "when the innovations of Luther were beginning to gain favor and to shake our old belief in many places."[4] Later Montaigne learned from a professor of medicine at Toulouse that a text of such erudition and subtlety must have been drawn from the works of Thomas Aquinas, the only scholar "capable of such ideas" (II.12.320–21). In the *Apology,* as throughout his work, Montaigne refused to enter into scholarly disputations or to argue on one side or the other of the theological issues of the day. Instead he focused on the impossibility of reasoning one's way to certainty.

One effect of theological dissension had been to undermine the authority of Scholastic natural philosophy. As a result, all attempts to explore the natural world were polarized. Thus, the Reformation attack on Christ's body made thinking about all substances potentially divisive, pulling theories of the nature of things toward Protestant or Catholic poles. When Montaigne alluded in the *Apology* to the problem of the presence of Christ's body in the Eucharist, the violent potential of theological dissension was only too obvious to him.[5] Rather than engage in metaphysical speculations, he turned the folly of supposedly rational arguments into a meditation on the grammatical follies of the Scholastics and the impossibility of knowing: "Most of the occasions for the troubles of

4. Michel de Montaigne, *The Complete Essays of Montaigne,* trans. Donald Frame (Stanford: Stanford University Press, 1957), II.12.319–20. All further quotations are taken from this translation.

5. Although Montaigne did not mention explicitly the most horrific events of the Wars of Religion, such as the Saint Bartholomew's Day massacre, they color all of part 2 of the *Essays* and form an essential framework for the whole. Judith N. Shklar, *Ordinary Vices* (Cambridge, MA: Harvard University Press, 1984), 240–44, asserts that Montaigne viewed cruelty as the sin from which all others descend, a radical departure from traditional teaching about the deadly sins although it functions as the sin of pride functioned for Aquinas. See also Geraldé Nakam, *Les Essais de Montaigne, miroir et procès de leur temps* (Paris: Honore Champion, 2001), 293ff., on the centrality of cruelty in Montaigne's work and the ways in which he adopted the concept of religious and political conflict as an inner disease from the medical language of contemporary Calvinists although he rejected their theological motive for applying it. "On Physiognomy" addresses the self-destructive aspect of war: "Monstrous war! Other wars act outward; this one acts also against itself, eats and destroys itself by its own venom. It is by nature so malignant and ruinous that it ruins itself together with all the rest, and tears and dismembers itself with rage. We see it more often dissolving of itself than for lack of any necessary thing or through the power of the enemy. All discipline flies from it. It comes to cure sedition and is full of it, would chastise disobedience and sets the example of it; and employed in the defense of the laws, plays the part of a rebel against its own laws" (III.12.796).

the world are grammatical. Our lawsuits spring only from debate over the interpretation of the laws, and most of our wars from the inability to express clearly the conventions and treatises of agreement of princes. How many quarrels, and how important, have been produced in the world by doubt of the meaning of that syllable *Hoc!*" (II.12.392).[6] Why should people die, Montaigne asked, over a linguistic uncertainty? He ascribed much of the responsibility for the violence of the Wars of Religion to intellectuals whose arguments supported sectarian persecutions by clothing uncertainties in the guise of truth and thus fostering intolerance. This passage illustrates how his frame of reference was suffused with earlier systems of thought, but he devoted much of the *Apology* to demonstrating the varied ways in which men had asserted knowledge of the unknowable. Removing the deforming masks of stereotype, prejudice, or rigid certitudes became a primary goal of his *Essays*.

Montaigne's essay "Of Cannibals" illustrates both the lingering vocabulary of earlier theological traditions and the question of moral identity raised by Aquinas. The heart of the essay transposes Eucharistic practice into the practice of cannibalism in the New World.[7] He turns a cannibal prisoner's explanation of the meaning of his captors' intended meal into an ironic commentary on sectarian violence: "I have a song composed by a prisoner which contains this challenge, that they should all come boldly and gather to dine off him, for they will be eating at the same time their own fathers and grandfathers, who have served to feed and nourish his body. 'These muscles,' he says, 'this flesh and these veins are your

---

6. In calling *hoc* "that syllable," Montaigne translated the particular meaning of Christ's phrase from Matthew 26:26. Reformist theologian Cornelius Hoen had circulated a letter in 1521 in which he argued that the word *est* in *hoc est corpus meum* should not be interpreted literally as "is" but rather as *significat*, "signifies." Zwingli also took "is" to mean "signifies" and argued that Christ's use of the phrase "this is my body" was rhetorical rather than literal: "Yet Christ did not say: 'Take, eat, my body is eaten in the bread.' He said, 'This is my body.' How fearful a thing it is to get out of one's depth! If it were I who perverted the words of Christ in that way, surely the axe of judgement would smite me down. The second error is easily perceived, then, and we have only to compare the two and they cancel each other out. For the first maintains that the flesh and blood are present on account of the word 'is.' But if we take that word literally, it destroys the second, which tries to take it literally but still asserts that the bread remains bread. For if the word is taken literally, the bread is not bread but flesh." Zwingli, *On the Lord's Supper: Zwingli and Bullinger*, trans. Rev. G. W. Bromiley (Philadelphia: Westminster, 1953), 176–238, esp. 191–92.

7. See George Hoffmann, "Anatomy of the Mass: Montaigne's 'Cannibals,'" *PMLA* 117, no. 2 (March 2002), 207–21, esp. 212: "The entire essay begins to appear as a ludic inversion of the High Mass, a transposition of eucharistic rites onto cannibalistic ritual to radically defamiliarize the paradoxical sacrifice of god, rather than to god, that lies at the heart of Christian belief."

own, poor fools that you are. You do not recognize that the substance of your ancestors' limbs is still contained in them. Savor them well; you will find in them the taste of your own flesh.'" (I.31.158). The political parody that appears in Dante's vision of Ugolino's cannibalism finds a parallel in this song. By analogy Montaigne transformed the controversy surrounding transubstantiation—the sacramental meal—into a dynamic of self-consumption. As limbs, as veins—the cannibal forefathers survive as material accidents of the body in a cycle that passes from one generation to another. Eating the flesh of another diffuses that person's being into one's own body, but the spiritual significance of the Eucharist has no place in this narrative of endless material transformation.[8]

Although the cannibals roast and eat enemies taken prisoner in battle, they do not do so out of hunger, but as a sign of extreme revenge which transforms their idyllic existence into a constant state of warfare. Lacking the faults of lying or betrayal, they also lack the quality Montaigne prizes most highly, that of clemency. Their society is based so single-mindedly on vengeance that a capacity to fight valiantly and endure capture and death with stoic resolve has become their greatest virtue.

Montaigne saw a parallel bloody-minded ethos among Europeans. For example, he described how the cannibals copy the Portuguese practice of burying prisoners to the waist and shooting them with arrows before hanging them because they think the men who have introduced so many vices into their country are greater masters in every sort of wickedness and thus their form of vengeance must be more painful than their own (I.31.155). He could explicitly (and safely) use the example of the self-destructive culture of the cannibals to suggest that the Wars of Religion had provided the French with a culture in which martial bravery had become equivalent to the savagery of cannibals. "I am not sorry," he wrote, "that we no-

---

8. The idea that cannibals eat their own relatives does not appear in Montaigne's major source materials—accounts by cosmographer André Thevet and Protestant preacher Jean de Léry. His reliance on Léry and conversations with "a simple, crude fellow," a sailor who had lived for ten or twelve years in Brazil, reflects his preference for popular but also contestable sources in which the naïveté of the narrator preserved the account from interpretation. He drew his enthusiasm for the "natural man" of the New World untainted by European civilization from Léry, who expressed his horror at the Saint Bartholomew's Day massacre in a wish to return to his savages. For a discussion of Montaigne's choice of Léry, see Nakam, *Les Essais de Montaigne*, 335–37. David Quint, *Montaigne and the Quality of Mercy: Ethical and Political Themes in the Essais* (Princeton: Princeton University Press, 1998), 160n14, notes that the idea that cannibals eat their relatives does appear in Aquinas (*Summa contra gentiles*, trans. Charles J. O'Neill [Garden City, NY: Doubleday, 1957], 4.80.13). The critical literature on "Of Cannibals" is extensive. In addition to Quint's excellent analysis, see especially Frank Lestringant, *Le Cannibale: Grandeur et décadence* (Paris: Perrin, 1994).

tice the barbarous horror of such acts, but I am heartily sorry that, judging their faults rightly, we should be so blind to our own" (I.31.155).[9]

The men described in Montaigne's anthropological fable can be distinguished from one another only through their conduct in battle, because their cultural ethos compels them all to behave in the same way. Their behavior marks them with a cultural identity and classifies them as cannibals. Accordingly, his analogy to French military aristocrats also objectified them as moral objects.[10] Indeed, despite the frank descriptions of his own tastes and habits, objectification of self-regard characterizes the *Essays*, and his notion of form provided a conceptual language for expressing the unifying power of a moral value.

Montaigne's use of the word *forme* offers a striking example of the intertextuality of ideas involving substance and accident. The Latin word *forma* signified a mold or pattern (derived from the Greek reference to character as the die used to stamp coins) and also as the sort or kind to which individual things belong. As a mode of classification, this etymology recalls the idea of form as the substance of substances that we met in Aristotle and as the soul giving form to the human being in Aquinas. Thus, *forme* carried multiple connotations from the past into Montaigne's innovative expansion of its meaning.

Through the notion of *forme*, Montaigne could equate the character of the denizens of the New World, stamped with their vengeful cannibalism and stoic resolve, with a cast of mind. At the same time, he reframed a way of characterizing a type or species of human being (such as a cannibal or a nobleman) into a notion that could be applied to particularize an individual. He called this cast of mind the "ruling passion" (*forme maistresse*).[11]

The ruling passion represented the most permanent aspect of an individual because it could withstand the impact of circumstances, the

---

9. In "Of Cruelty" (II.27.530) Montaigne records another example of cannibalism. In 1514 George "Sechel" Dozsa, the defeated leader of a Polish peasant uprising, was tortured for three days and made to watch his brother drink his blood. His mental and physical torments climaxed in an enormous cannibalistic festival in which twenty of his favorite captains fed on his body. For Montaigne the fanatical cruelties and cynicism of the Wars of Religion reached a comparable crescendo of depravity.

10. See Jack I. Abecassis, "'Des cannibals' et la logique de la représentation de l'altérité," in *Montaigne et le Nouveau Monde: Actes du Colloque de Paris 18–20 Mai 1992*, ed. Claude Blum, Marie-Luce Demonet, and André Tournon (Saint-Pierre-du-Mont: Éditions InterUniversitaires, 1994), 195–205, on Montaigne's difference from classical moralist historians such as Herodotus and Tacitus and the notion that his own relativism included an aspect of cultural cannibalism.

11. M. A. Screech develops this idea in *Montaigne and Melancholy: The Wisdom of the Essays* (London: Duckworth, 1983), 101–5.

passage of time, or the motility of other desires and it offered a more powerful concept than the Galenic theory that one of the four humors dominated each person. It also secularized the religious connotations that surrounded the Christian idea of the soul. Montaigne's formulation can be compared to the solution that Aquinas proposed when he recast Aristotle's version of the mind-body problem. Like Aquinas, he conceived of an individual particularized not through bodily matter alone, but by the combination of one soul in one body. However, he reversed the Thomist position that the intellect's power of abstraction could enable it to know only the universal, but not itself. "There is no one," he wrote, "who, if he listens to himself, does not discover in himself a pattern all his own, a ruling pattern, which struggles against education and against the tempest of the passions that oppose it" (III.2.615). This idea of distinctive patterning explained the conflicting behavior and judgments he deplored. The *forme maistresse* offered no solution to the problem of empathy or communal understanding. But by postulating that the only example of individuation a man could study was his own, he not only pulled the concept of individuality in a new direction, he established his own method for acquiring self-knowledge.[12]

II. Violent Accident

"Nature has committed herself to make nothing separate that was not different," Montaigne wrote in "Of Experience" (III.13.815). Eggs have long been presented as the most "express example of similarity," he continued, yet even they reveal sufficient marks of difference that an experienced eye (benefiting from the "varied trials art has bred") will not mistake one for another. Likewise, an experienced gamester can distinguish playing cards "simply by seeing them slip through another man's hands." In the development of Montaigne's skeptical empiricism, each observation he made of his habits or his actions represented a pedagogical experience. One result of these lessons of experience is the long catalogs of accidental qualities that occur throughout the *Essays*, so that we know, for example,

---

12. Screech (ibid., 151–52) proposes that this belief accorded with the teaching of the time that every individual bears within himself "the whole form of the human condition." Nevertheless, because one's own form is subject to imperfections or limitations of body and temperament, one must not mistake it for the *maistresse forme* of nature or pass judgments that inevitably reflect these limitations. In Montaigne's view, even great men were contained within the species of man, which allowed him to compare himself to them as different in degree, not in kind.

that he was of less than middling height, had a thickset body and excellent sight, spoke corrupted French, wrote an illegible hand, was better at running than dancing, wrestling, playing tennis, or singing, had a poor memory but an excellent library, recognized neither the many coins currently in circulation nor the implements in his kitchen, and disliked accidents so much that he abandoned himself completely to fortune—simply striving to bear adversity meekly and with patience (II.17).

The question of how one thing (or person) differs from another relates, of course, to the now familiar problem of defining the underlying nature of the human being. To illustrate the difficulty of resolving it, Montaigne took up another example, that of mercury, which was commonly known as quicksilver with reference to the lively motion of which the metal is capable:

> Who has seen children trying to divide a mass of quicksilver into a certain number of parts? The more they press it and knead it and try to constrain it to their will, the more they provoke the independence of this spirited metal; it escapes their skill and keeps dividing and scattering in little particles beyond all reckoning. This is the same; for by subdividing these subtleties [theologians] teach men to increase their doubts; they start us extending and diversifying the difficulties, they lengthen them, they scatter them. By sowing questions and cutting them up, they make the world fructify and teem with uncertainty and quarrels, as the earth is made more fertile the more it is crumbled and deeply plowed. *Learning makes difficulties* [Quintilian]. (III.13.816)

Montaigne's invocation pointed out that the metal's spirit inheres in its matter although it frustrates any attempt to understand its material substance or arrive at "certainty" about the number of its parts.[13] The children who divide the mercury but find that it scatters beyond all control resemble the Reformation theologians whose subdivisions and categories merely demonstrate the uncertainty inherent in any form of understanding. Like quicksilver, substance now names an infinite diversity, a scattering beyond human comprehension. For Montaigne, therefore, substance was neither the potentially knowable (as it was for Aristotle) nor the divine

13. Montaigne's thought reflects the sixteenth-century revival of Democritan atomism, a materialist understanding of the world in which things are made up of an infinite number of unbreakable particles (atoms, from *atomos*, "uncuttable"). Each of these primary substances is in constant motion, and their paths result in an infinite series of prior collisions. Democritus believed the evidence of the senses was unreliable.

(as it was for the Scholastics), but rather a rhetorical term that blocked greater understanding of the multiplicity of experience. From his perspective, the quarrels of the Reformation were exemplary demonstrations of the limits to understanding. If theologians could learn from their experiences (as children do), they would cool the violence of their disputes.

Casting aside the primacy of substance in this way represented a fundamental shift in thought. Leaving questions of absolute truth to theology, skeptics like Montaigne restaged questions of faith and of man's place in the world within the context of a personal language of experience.[14] In that sense, their "new philosophy" operated as a paratheology that pursued the status of substance and accident—terms that continued to signify both philosophically and theologically—in order to interpret a world irreparably fractured by the Reformation. For skeptics, accidental events were of special interest because they were considered ultimately inexplicable.

Montaigne's emphasis on his sensory experiences led to thinking about dying, an experience that cannot be understood before it happens. In "Of Practice" he wrote, "But for dying, which is the greatest task we have to perform, practice cannot help us. A man can, by habit and experience, fortify himself against pain, shame, indigence, and such other accidents; but as for death, we can try it only once: we are all apprentices when we come to it" (II.6.267). Once again, he argued that abstract philosophizing over the unknowable must give way to empirical analysis, and he singled out violent accident as an event that allows the victim to come close to death. His own fall from his horse brought him to the

14. In 1562 the rediscovery and publication of the *Hypotyposes* (usually translated as *Outlines of Pyrrhonism*) of Sextus Empiricus sparked a revival of skepticism that came to be known as the "new philosophy." Sextus was a late member of the school of Pyrrho of Elis (ca. 365–275 BC), a post-Socratic who argued that all knowledge is subject to doubt and asserted that skeptics, lacking proofs concerning the objective existence of things, should avoid taking active positions and therefore conform to local religious customs. This argument resonated among both Catholic and Protestant intellectuals because it seemed to argue for the possibility of religious tolerance. Yet if Catholic intellectuals, such as Montaigne, initially invoked skepticism to quell the extremes of reformist thought, it also could be marshaled against the increasingly dogmatic Catholic theology that emerged after the Council of Trent (Richard H. Popkin, *The History of Skepticism from Savonarola to Bayle*, rev. ed. [Oxford: Oxford University Press, 2003], 17–43). For a general history of the new philosophy see Allen G. Debus, *Man and Nature in the Renaissance* (Cambridge: Cambridge University Press, 1978). Amos Funkenstein sees new philosophy as "a secular theology of sorts" both in the sense that it was "conceived by laymen for laymen" and because "it was oriented toward the world, *ad seculum*" (*Theology and the Scientific Imagination: from the Middle Ages to the Seventeenth Century* [Princeton: Princeton University Press, 1986], 3).

limits of skeptical knowledge of death when he experienced a physical separation between his body and his *anima:*

> During our third civil war, or the second (I do not quite remember which), I went riding one day about a league from my house, which is situated at the very hub of all the turmoil of the civil wars of France. Thinking myself perfectly safe, and so near my home that I needed no better equipage, I took a very easy but not very strong horse. On my return, when a sudden occasion came up for me to use this horse for a service to which it was not accustomed, one of my men, big and strong, riding a powerful work horse who had a desperately hard mouth and was moreover fresh and vigorous—this man, in order to show his daring and get ahead of his companions, spurred his horse at full speed up the path behind me, came down like a colossus on the little man and little horse, and hit us like a thunderbolt with all his strength and weight, sending us both head over heels. So that there lay the horse bowled over and stunned, and I ten or twelve paces beyond, dead, stretched on my back, my face all bruised and skinned, my sword, which I had had in my hand, more than ten paces away, my belt in pieces, having no more motion or feeling than a log. It is the only swoon that I have experienced to this day. (II.6.268–69)

Montaigne's fall took place in the physical center of the war scene. Violence surrounded him, but the event itself occurred at a moment of relative safety, and the immediate cause of the accident was banal: the horse of one of his men careened out of control and hit him like a thunderbolt. In that sense, although the context echoed Saul's fall while riding with his henchmen to persecute the Christians, Montaigne retained no memory of the occasion apart from his feeling of security. The event lacked either the agitated state of mind that prepared Augustine for his life-transforming experience or any external sign to anticipate the significance of what would happen. Nevertheless, Montaigne recorded his sensations after his fall in great detail. First, he described his body like a "log," inanimate, without *anima*.[15] His comrades, believing him dead, took him back to his house. Only after traveling for two hours did he begin to move and breathe, and several times on the journey they paused to let him vomit blood. He felt his life hanging at the tip of his lips and he closed his eyes

---

15. The earlier phrase "hit me like a thunderbolt" and the translation "log" obscure the connotations of *foudroyer* (as either to thunder or lighten) and *souche* (literally a stump with roots) that tighten the biblical links to Saul as well as to the tree of Jesse.

to "help push it out" and took pleasure in "growing languid and letting myself go" (II.6.269). In other words, experimenting with the limits of his sensation allowed him to practice how to die.[16]

In the *Apology* (II.12.324) Montaigne showed his knowledge of contemporary theological interpretations of Paul's wish to be "loosened asunder" as a desire to deliver the soul from the body in order to realize the promises of beatitude.[17] However, the language he used to describe his fall did not connote an ecstatic vision. Rather, the pleasurable sensations he experienced offered an antidote to the fear of death (and thus by extension to the surrounding threat of theological violence as well as to the disputed understanding of conditions pertaining to the afterlife). It is, he asserted, "the approaches that we have to fear."

Not only did Montaigne's fall represent accident in the sense of an intersection of causations, his description also accentuated details that qualify in Aristotelian terms as qualities accidental to the substance of an individual. He recounted his quantity (a little man on a little horse), quality (bruised), relation (ten or twelve paces from his horse), place (a league from his house), time (during civil war), position (splayed out), possession (his fallen sword), action (lying like a log), being acted upon (being picked up by the bystanders).[18] His essence had escaped his body, and these physical details were what remained in his awareness. The deeply ingrained notion of the accidental quality—which still structured his method of self-analysis—testifies to the omnipresence of Aristotelian concepts within the Renaissance vision of the world.

As Montaigne returned to consciousness, he experienced a sudden re-

---

16. Jean Starobinski, *Montaigne in Motion*, trans. Arthur Goldhammer (Chicago: University of Chicago Press, 1985), 223–26, offers an excellent analysis of a passage from "Of Presumption" that demonstrates the relation between the energy implicit in Montaigne's syntax and the active pleasure he derives from turning his vision inward. He points out that when Montaigne celebrates the way in which his opinions boldly condemn his inadequacy, the word he chooses (*insuffisance*) derives from the Latin *sufficere*, meaning "to give support or prop up." The significance is not only experiential, in the sense that he claims nothing beyond his constant enthusiasm, but also ontological, in the early sense of substance as that which stands under. The passage concludes with the phrase "I roll about myself." Starobinski reads this expression as evidence that the "suspended ego is susceptible to the actions of the body," which serves Montaigne as the "agent, instrument, theater, and purpose of the action."

17. Philippians 1:23.

18. Starobinski, *Montaigne in Motion*, 167ff., points out an analogous pattern of reliance on medical terms despite Montaigne's attack on the dubious authority assumed by physicians. He finds, for example, that the plan of "Of Practice" replicates the order of the six nonnatural causes established by Ambroise Paré: atmosphere/air, food and drink, work, or exercise and rest, sleeping and waking, excrement and retention, perturbations of soul.

turn of bodily pain that lasted for several days and continued even as he
wrote his account of the experience. This pain remained as the body's
"memory" of its sudden and shocking fall. But he struggled to recapture
the cause of his accident in explicit detail, and when he succeeded, he experienced the final return of his memory as a second shocking event: "But
a long time after, and the next day, when my memory came to open up
and picture to me the state I had been in at the instant I had perceived that
horse bearing down on me (for I had seen him at my heels and thought I
was a dead man, but that thought had been so sudden that I had no time
to be afraid), it seemed to me that a flash of lightning was striking my soul
with a violent shock, and that I was coming back from the other world"
(II.12.272). At the moment he recaptured his experience clearly, he realized that something astonishing had happened to him. His "self," in the
sense of his intellect or spirit, had been shocked out of his body. Just as
Aristotle asserts that Socrates loses his *psuché* when he dies and ceases to
be Socrates, Montaigne had lost his *anima*. His attempts to remember the
moment that caused his fall were attempts to reunite spirit and matter,
to regain his substance. When he achieved this goal through the opening up of his memory, he experienced a fresh and equally violent shock.
Now, the words he used to describe this reunion of spirit with matter *do*
allude to a conversion. In effect, what was no longer Montaigne (the self
suspended in the moment of his fall) had become Montaigne once more.

Montaigne's response to his accident was not to exploit or interpret it as
a transforming event. He responded just as one might expect from the way
in which he characterized his temperament in his catalog of qualities in
"Of Presumption": he remained passive. In that sense, he resigned himself
to God's agency, and we can compare this reaction, for example, to the way
in which Luther recognized that justification by faith involved a degree of
passivity with regard to actions performed in the world. The second shock,
however, created a different understanding. By willing the reunion of spirit
and matter, he had become the creator of his being. He spoke of a comparable activity of self-definition in "Of Husbanding Your Will," in which—
thinking of the turmoil of the wars and the cruel behavior practiced by his
contemporaries—he argued that individuals are free to choose or control
their relation to the culture and customs of their time. He believed that he
had been able to accomplish this task: "By long usage this form of mine
has turned into substance, and fortune into nature" (III.10.773). We recognize how closely this sociosecular understanding applies to his sudden
realization of the significance of his accident. His reflective processing of

the event allowed him to conceive of his *forme maistresse* as a human accomplishment, a creative work belonging entirely to himself.[19]

Within the limits of the vocabulary of concepts available to him, Montaigne struggled to describe the motion of consciousness, the actuality of a transition from death to life.[20] We can see how his analysis of his accident created a conceptual space beyond skeptical knowledge that would come to be known as the unconscious. Yet Montaigne's accident cannot signify psychologically because its meaning remains interwoven with the theological wars and the new philosophy of the sixteenth century. In later centuries accident will wander and become a secular and psychological phenomenon, but this first literary accident remains a profoundly paratheological experience.

III. The Matter of Philosophy

Introspection, which functions as a central marker of modern subjectivity, appears in Montaigne's *Essays* as a protective response to theological conflict and an application of skeptical philosophy to the problem of understanding human nature. At the end of the century, Hamlet's soliloquies demonstrate a comparable interiority within the bounds of dra-

19. Anthony J. Cascardi, *The Subject of Modernity* (Cambridge: Cambridge University Press, 1992), 64–65, argues against this perception of Starobinski's (*Montaigne in Motion*, 217). He believes that no self-conscious, appropriative subject governs the *Essays* and that Montaigne has difficulty imagining any stable future context for the self. The "formlessness" of his writing and the errant nature of the self whose "passing" is portrayed constitute an inherited source of questions to which the modern subject provides a critical response. For Cascardi, the subject comes to imagine itself standing outside history in order to govern a detotalized world, and its experience is shaped by a series of related splits between fact and theory, reason and desire, and value and rule. These antinomies remain unacknowledged by thinkers on both sides of the debate over modernity and postmodernism. In the larger context of substance and accident, however, Starobinski's reading appears to capture the way in which Montaigne's perception transforms earlier understanding without being completely divorced from it.

20. The act of writing that played such a vital role in his study of himself assumed its importance not by design but through a gradual and unpremeditated evolution of his desire to memorialize Étienne de La Boétie by publishing the only texts that survived the death of his friend. In assuming a presumably temporary identity as an author, whose goal was to preserve the writerly identity of another, he came to understand and thereby memorialize himself. He stands outside himself as an object for contemplation. "Painting myself for others," he wrote in "Of Giving the Lie," "I have painted my inward self with colors clearer than my original ones. I have no more made my book than my book has made me—a book consubstantial with its author, concerned with my own self, an integral part of my life." (II.18.504).

matic fiction. They owe their form to the tradition of the spiritual exercise and the defeat of hubris through self-understanding inherent in classical drama, but they also respond to the character's position within a corrupted environment.[21] The tragic outcome offers a critique of skepticism, which proves powerless to avert substantial changes in body or in mind.

The action of the play traces Hamlet's transformation from philosopher-prince into the vehicle of the Ghost's revenge. In that process the soliloquies invert the function of the premodern spiritual exercise as a mode of elevating the soul through meditation that we encountered in the work of Plotinus. Instead, they resemble the process of interrogation of circumstances that led King Oedipus to a tragic revision of self-understanding. At the level of textual references, the soliloquies present philosophical set pieces that allude to substance and accident in a kind of learned jargon that Hamlet and Horatio would have acquired during their studies in Wittenberg. At a more profound level, however, they question the nature of being and provide a metaphysical basis for the play's central questions of agency, the relation between soul and body, and of the individual will to the divine order.

Hamlet begins with an uneasy question, "Who's there?"[22] Although it is the watchmen who appear on the scene, the object of their shared anxiety is the Ghost, or—in the words of Marcellus—a "thing." The question

21. An immense literature engages the topic of the Renaissance subject in terms of the roles that society asks the individual to play or the role-playing implicit in theatrical representation. John Guillory, " 'To Please the Wiser Sort': Violence and Philosophy in Hamlet," in *Historicism, Psychoanalysis, and Early Modern Culture*, ed. Carla Mazzio and Trevor Douglas (New York: Routledge, 2000), 87–89, discusses Hamlet's performance of Montaigne's philosophy. Michael Witmore's *The Culture of Accidents: Unexpected Knowledges in Early Modern England* (Stanford: Stanford University Press, 2001) constructs his analysis of accidents in *Hamlet* within the theatrical manipulation of "regard." His work is indebted to that of Stephen Greenblatt, whose influential studies of the Renaissance subject (from *Renaissance Self-Fashioning* [Chicago: University of Chicago Press, 1980] to *Hamlet in Purgatory* [Princeton: Princeton University Press, 2001]) use the theater as a model for the determination of social roles and the contingency that surrounds role-playing. Katharine Eisaman Maus, *Inwardness and the Theater in the English Renaissance* (Chicago: University of Chicago Press, 1995), provides a helpful summary of theoretical interventions about the nature of the subject up to 1995. For her, the new historical desire to separate the Renaissance subject from the Enlightenment individual obscures the origin of the inner self she ascribes to the disjoint between representation and self in Renaissance theater. Paul Cefalu, *Moral Identity in Early Modern English Literature* (Cambridge: Cambridge University Press, 2004), treats the topic in the sixteenth and seventeenth centuries (although not in Shakespeare).

22. William Shakespeare, *Hamlet*, ed. Harold Jenkins (London: Routledge, 1990), 1.1.1. All further citations are from this edition (following also its scene divisions and line numberings).

of the Ghost goes to the heart of the problem of defining the nature of things. By consistently referring to the figure as "it," the watchers' vocabulary moves the definition of the true nature of their experience into the context of contemporary questions concerning the relation between body and spirit after death.

Religious controversy at work during *Hamlet*'s composition allows an additional reading of the play in terms of Protestant and Catholic beliefs. The difficulty of interpreting the appearance of the Ghost bears directly on the question of the afterlife. Protestants rejected the Catholic doctrine of purgatory, so the Ghost must either represent the spirit of Old Hamlet confined to purgatory, and hence be understood as a Catholic apparition, or it must be a devil sent from hell that has usurped Old Hamlet's form. If Hamlet believed the Ghost to be the spirit of his dead father, filial devotion would urge him to revenge his murder. But if he believed the Ghost to be a devil assuming his father's shape, a murderous response to its accusation of Claudius would be damning. An immaterial spirit condemned to walk the night because of unabsolved sins committed on earth could not counsel the sin of murder; such counsel could come only from a spirit consigned to hell. To further complicate Hamlet's interpretation, the Ghost's actual words enjoin not revenge but remembrance. Thus, on a symbolic level its command to remember might refer to a Counter-Reformation assertion of the "true" faith. Hamlet's response, however, is instinctively Protestant, for he interprets the Ghost's words as an injunction to perform a kind of mental iconoclasm. He proposes to clear his memory of everything he has learned just as the Reformation cleared all visual images and memorials from the churches.[23]

The skeptical attempt to translate such questions from theology into a philosophical language breaks down with the appearance of the Ghost. Horatio, the play's most skeptical character, recognizes the Ghost as identical in appearance to Old Hamlet, but when he accosts the figure, his sword meets no physical object. "Stay illusion," he calls, making an interpretation based on the evidence of his eyes, his memory of Old Hamlet, and his knowledge that the body of the former king must be decaying in its grave (1.1.127). Yet skepticism cannot vanquish the Ghost. Its appearance represents seemingly incompatible theological traditions, and

---

23. See Keith Thomas regarding "ghosts," in *Religion and the Decline of Magic* (New York: Scribner, 1971), 587–606; Greenblatt, *Hamlet in Purgatory,* chaps. 4 and 5; and Eleanor Prosser, *Hamlet and Revenge* (Stanford: Stanford University Press, 1967), 118–43.

its incitement to revenge reintroduces the violence that skepticism sought to control.

We might compare Montaigne's withdrawal into the tower of his chateau and the process of self-study to Hamlet's absence from Denmark for the sake of his philosophical studies in Wittenberg.[24] His stay at Luther's former university seems to have familiarized him with the language of skeptical materialism. In the soliloquies, Hamlet refers to the uncertainty of human reason, the separation of soul from body, and his disdain for corruptible flesh, but Montaigne could hardly have approved of the use to which he put his learning. Hamlet's goal of inciting bloody-minded action through such spiritual exercises would have seemed highly ironic to the author of the *Essays*. Like the French nobles whom Montaigne compared to the savages of the New World, Hamlet adopts a cast of mind formulated upon an illusory principle of valorous revenge. And like the cannibals, he consumes his *forme maistresse* in the process.

Under the pressure of the changes that result from his father's death and his mother's remarriage, Hamlet forgoes his defining nature not only as the scholar from Wittenberg, but also as the prince of Denmark, the lover of Ophelia, and the courtier who embodied the "glass of fashion and the mould of form" (3.1.156). Forced into a sudden crisis of self-definition, he recognizes that the Ghost's command to revenge his death requires him to distinguish the "baser matter" of his uncle's body and his corrupted spirit from royal authority in order to commit regicide. This translation of an ontological question into the realm of political anxiety allows the play to speak by analogy to Essex's rebellion against Queen Elizabeth just as "Of Cannibalism" allowed Montaigne to engage the Wars of Religion.[25] As the same time, it presents a situation that the contemporary audience could

24. Shakespeare made Laertes a student in Paris, the center of Catholic orthodoxy, a detail that reinforces the embattled context of Reformation disputes. The clearest expression of Hamlet's skeptical training appears in the love letter he wrote to Ophelia before his father's murder. Polonius reads the verse as a typical example of a lover's rhetoric, but the letter displays skepticism's challenge to the Aristotelian notion that the stars and sun are fixed and composed of fire. Hamlet permits Ophelia to call into question the entire Ptolemaic system but not his credibility as an authority on his own feeling. In the context of the play, his behavior and speeches to Ophelia contradict its testimony, making philosophical skepticism a backdrop for emotional ambiguity.

25. Robert Devereaux, Earl of Essex, was appointed lord lieutenant of Ireland in 1599. Unable to deploy the largest and best-equipped Tudor army ever sent to Ireland, in September 1599 he signed an unauthorized truce with the leading Irish rebel, the Earl of Tyrone. Furious, Queen Elizabeth stripped him of his titles. Joined by the Earl of Southampton, Essex then led an abortive raid on the queen in January 1601. He was captured and executed for treason in February.

readily perceive as a challenge to existing definitions of secular identity within the hierarchy of a divinely ordered political system.

Renaissance political theory asserted that the monarch spiritually embodies the realm in his physical body.[26] The emblematic relation between Old Hamlet's two bodies—his smooth form and the health of the kingdom—broke down when Claudius poured the "the leprous distilment" of hebona into his sleeping brother's ear. The poison of fraternal treachery "doth posset / And curd, like eager droppings into milk, / The thin and wholesome blood" and covered his body "Most lazar-like, with vile and loathsome crust" (1.5.68–73). What remained of the royal substance were the vile accidents of the physical body, and because the royal body embodies Denmark, its decay rots the entire kingdom. In that sense, the story the Ghost tells to incite Hamlet to revenge functions as an account of substantial change. The language used to describe the play's motivating crime derives from old theories of substance and accident, and the murderous act inverts the instantaneous transformation that occurs with the blessing of the Eucharistic host. Disbelieving that the substance of kingship is present in Claudius, Hamlet can see in his uncle only gross, material accidents that he regards with disgust.

Even before Hamlet learns how his father was murdered, he frames his unhappiness in the conceptual language of mutable accidents, describing flesh grown sullied (and therefore dirty) or solid (and therefore increasingly material). While the play suggests that his body-hatred is a reaction to his sudden awareness of corrupted sexuality, the clearest expression of it occurs in the speech after the appearance of the Ghost in which Hamlet displays his rejection of Scholastic learning: "What a piece of work is a man, how noble in reason, how infinite in faculties, in form and moving how express and admirable, in action how like an angel, in apprehension how like a god: the beauty of the world, the paragon of animals—and yet, to me, what is this quintessence of dust? Man delights not me—nor woman neither" (2.2.303–309).

Hamlet's demonstration of man as "the paragon of animals" concludes by reducing Aristotle's incorruptible and immaterial fifth essence (that signifies the soul) to a "quintessence of dust" and joining it to sin, corruption, and decay.[27] This espousal of a violent materialism has been as-

26. This medieval doctrine of kingship is explicated by Ernst H. Kantorowicz, *The King's Two Bodies* (Princeton: Princeton University Press, 1957). See also Debora Shuger, *Habits of Thought in the English Renaissance: Religion, Politics, and the Dominant Culture* (Berkeley: University of California Press, 1990).

27. John Guillory, "'To Please the Wiser Sort,'" 82–109.

sociated with his misanthropy or his even more celebrated misogyny, but the philosophical subtext of the play expresses a more general revulsion against the body that reaches a high point after the murder of Polonius. Hamlet plays verbally with the notion that the action of Claudius has corrupted the royal body first when his former companions, Rosencrantz and Guildenstern, attempt to learn what has become of the body of Polonius (4.3.25–30) and again when Claudius asks the same question.

KING: Now, Hamlet, where's Polonius?

HAM.: At supper.

KING: At supper? Where?

HAM.: Not where he eats, but where a is eaten. A certain convocation of politic worms are e'en at him. Your worm is your only emperor for diet: we fat all creatures else to fat us, and we fat ourselves for maggots. Your fat king and your lean beggar is but variable service—two dishes, but to one table. That's the end.

KING: Alas, alas!

HAM.: A man may fish with the worm that hath eat of a king, and eat of the fish that hath fed of that worm.

KING: What dost thou mean by this?

HAM.: Nothing but to show you how a king may go a progress through the guts of a beggar. (4.3.16–31)

Even spoken in macabre playfulness, Hamlet's radical argument that because all bodies can be reduced to matter, he can trace the progress of a king through the guts of a beggar, emphasizes the violence of his materialism, which renders king and beggar equal as matter. Claudius responds, "Alas, alas"—less in dismay at this fresh evidence of Hamlet's madness than in pain as his nephew's thrust hits its mark. Hamlet has committed an act of philosophical violence against his royal body.[28]

---

28. Hamlet's reference to a convocation of politic worms that makes the body of Polonius their diet puns on the Diet of Worms—where the Catholic Church repudiated Lutheran belief in consubstantiation and affirmed the doctrine of transubstantiation. In this comparison, the place where Polonius is eaten is the tomb, but Hamlet's words also allude to the act in which Christ's body is consumed by the faithful: the endless Last Supper of the Eucharist. Therefore, his joking represents a sardonic and strongly Protestant revisioning of transubstantiation. However, in rejecting one central doctrine of Catholic belief, his materialist stance necessarily diminishes support of the Catholic understanding of purgatory represented by the spirit of Old Hamlet. And by implication, it casts doubt on the validity of the Ghost's transmission of his father's memory and the fatal command that appointed Hamlet to commit regicide. Greenblatt, *Hamlet in Purgatory*, 240.

In the graveyard scene, Hamlet's speech about Alexander employs an example also found Montaigne's essay "Of Cruelty." "The religion of our ancient Gauls," Montaigne wrote, "held that souls, being eternal, never ceased moving and changing places from one body to another. Moreover, their religion combined with this fancy some consideration of divine justice; for according to the behavior of the soul while it had been in Alexander's body, they said that God ordained it for another body to inhabit, more or less disagreeable, and conforming to its condition" (II.11.316–17). Shakespeare intensified Montaigne's thought by turning Alexander's dust into matter to stop a bunghole. This skeptical topos presents both significations of accident. As a quality detached from substance, the dirt that once embodied Alexander travels through time in a series of events that lie beyond human control or prediction.[29]

IV. Accidental Judgments

In Hamlet's famous invocation of being, he contrasts suffering the "slings and arrows of outrageous fortune" to taking "arms against a sea of troubles." This opposition is conventionally interpreted as a reference to suicide, but we also can associate it with Montaigne's deliberations on moral values. The play positions Hamlet in a cultural role analogous to that of the French nobility, and the alternative of taking up arms represents the kind of aggressive behavior Montaigne denigrated in the embattled nobility and sectarian believers. The position of passive acceptance of fortune had served Montaigne well, and he claimed it as a virtue of his own nature. On that ground, we might conjecture that he would have viewed Hamlet's inability to define his own ruling passion as a moral danger. But Shakespeare shifted the parameters of the problem by forcing Hamlet to confront a crisis of self-knowledge. He must answer the question "Who's there?" not only to define the nature of the Ghost but also to know himself.

As a prince and first among the court, Hamlet must become a rebel-

---

29. Not only does Alexander's progress to the bunghole exclude any ordering notion of providential intent, but Hamlet's portrayal of the afterlife of the body as dust also excludes the possibility of purgatory. While his materialist worldview at this point in the play transforms history into an accidental universe in which chance is omnipresent, the theological question of the Ghost's authenticity remains unresolved, and his revulsion against matter imprisons his thought. On the early modern career of "accident" as "event," see also Jacques Lezra, *Unspeakable Subjects: The Genealogy of the Event in Early Modern Europe* (Stanford: Stanford University Press, 1997), especially his introduction.

lious subject in order to kill Claudius; that is, he must abandon his former identity and invent a new one, putting both his body and his soul at
risk. Therefore, he disguises rebellion as suicide, another act prohibited
on both secular and theological grounds. Indeed, we may speculate that
Shakespeare used the degree of Hamlet's intellectual violence to represent the degree to which the character sublimated his physical aggression. Because it is safer to think than to act, Hamlet displaces his desire
for revenge into a philosophical meditation on substance, in the guise of
the now familiar question of being.

When Hamlet unleashes his violence in the cabinet scene, he begins
to actualize his self-transformation. Polonius, misinterpreting the confrontation with Gertrude as a murderous attack, cries out from his hid-
ing place behind the curtain. Although at some level Hamlet must know
that the voice cannot belong to the king, for he left him at his prayers, he
interprets it as the voice of Claudius and thrusts his rapier though the arras. In this sense, the curtain signifies the constraints placed on regicide.
He cannot intentionally kill Claudius, but he can stab an abstracted body
behind a curtain. Yet the curtain also functions ontologically within the
conceptual world of the play. As a theatrical sign, it can be pierced to
wound the king's body as the mousetrap scene wounded his conscience.
As a superficial covering that hides a material body, it is emblematic of
Hamlet's central philosophical problem: determining what lies beneath
surface appearances.

Medieval and Renaissance tropes of allegorical interpretation understood the drawing of a curtain as a sign for revealing truth, and when
Hamlet draws the arras, he discovers what he has become. The arras was
the immediate cause of the accidental death of Polonius because it allowed him to be present in the room, but it also allowed Hamlet to conceive of a liberating misinterpretation. We can interpret its significance
on several levels. On a literal level it reveals the act as an arbitrary and
inessential accident, but in the process it also reveals the violent nature
beneath Hamlet's "seeming" madness and philosophizing. On a more allegorical level, it manifests the problem addressed in skepticism of interpreting uncertain circumstances and signals the disorder to follow. From
this point, all actions lead to unintended outcomes. Thus, the curtain
scene represents the first of the fatal accidents in which the mechanism
of death is hidden, the intended victim escapes, and people misinterpret
the events they see. Decay of spiritual substance charges the world of El-
sinore with a force of misplaced "seeming" that fosters such accidents.

The murder of Polonius unmasks Hamlet as a dangerous and destabilizing force, and Claudius responds by sending him to England. A series of unanticipated circumstances subvert his plan to have him put to death when he arrives: Hamlet's sleepless agitation leads him to discover the death warrant carried by his companions Rosencrantz and Guildenstern. He rewrites it to sentence them in his place, becoming the immediate cause of their deaths and thus advancing another degree toward his self-transformation. Pirates waylay the ship (echoing Aristotle's familiar example of an accidental event that deflects the traveler from his destination), allowing yet another accident to make Hamlet the only person aboard their vessel when it disengages and thus freeing him to return to enact his revenge. These accidents combine to frustrate Claudius's plot, an unintended outcome which in turn becomes the immediate cause of all the accidents that conclude the play.

In Hamlet's "To be or not to be" soliloquy, he alludes to the power of Fortune and his adventures at sea appear to raise his position on the turning wheel of the goddess while casting Claudius down. He interprets them as evidence that a controlling force overpowered his will and pushed him toward his "reckless" act of discovering the death warrant. "In my heart there was a kind of fighting," he tells Horatio (5.2.4–5). If we remember Montaigne's belief that the individual can choose whether to participate in a cultural tradition, we can see that Shakespeare assigned a conventional or premodern quality of belief to his character as a further stage in his transformation. Abandoning skepticism, Hamlet accepts an accidental sign that compels him to believe in "a divinity that shapes our ends, / Rough-hew them how we will" (5.2.10–11).

The divinity that shapes man's ends reveals order within the chaos of events as a sculptor rough-hews an image from his raw material. Hamlet's association suggests that he now believes himself to be formed for the purpose of retribution—like the avenging statue of Mitys. His cruelty toward Ophelia, the murder of Polonius, and the deaths of Rosencrantz and Guildenstern are material weights that give him the destructive power to crush his father's murderer. By implication, the person he has become is no more the author of that action than a fatal falling statue. In fact, Hamlet excuses his murder of Polonius as an accident performed when he was not himself. He tells Laertes that his madness made the death comparable to shooting an arrow over a house and wounding a brother (5.2.226–40). However, both the analogy of the statue and the madman, by absolving him of responsibility, deny his essential humanity. He remains distanced from the moral values with which Montaigne imbued his skeptical philosophy.

Hamlet invokes divine order a second time before his duel with Laertes, when he tells Horatio: "There is special providence in the fall of a sparrow. If it be now, 'tis not to come; if it be not to come, it will be now; if it be not now, yet it will come. The readiness is all" (5.2.215–16). In this passage Hamlet submits to a controlling external force although his allusion to the Calvinist doctrine of special providence appears at odds with his earlier displays of philosophical materialism.[30] But in fact this ambiguity is characteristic of the puzzles of interpretation that haunt the play from the first appearance of the Ghost to the multiplication of accidents that bring the action to its conclusion. The last lines Horatio speaks to Fortinbras reiterate the notion that intentions cannot control outcomes, but none of the terms he uses dignify the dead or render the action heroic:

> So shall you hear
> Of carnal, bloody, and unnatural acts,
> Of accidental judgments, casual slaughters,
> Of deaths put on by cunning and forc'd cause,
> And, in this upshot, purposes mistook
> Fall'n on th'inventor's heads.[31]
>
> (5.2.385–90)

In terms of the action of the play, Hamlet's circumstances resemble those of Oedipus, who also confronted the pollution of his royal house with the power of his will and reason yet could not alter his destiny. However, the nature of the tragic outcome is dissimilar. Although Hamlet accomplishes his revenge, the process reduces his "mould of form" to undifferentiated matter. The end point of his philosophizing is not spiritual illumination but material decay. His personal tragedy lies in this loss of humanizing qualities.

Shakespeare brackets the play's transformation of bodies to dirt within

---

30. "He is also everlasting Governor and Preserver—not only in that he drives the celestial frame . . . but also in that he sustains, nourishes, and cares for, everything he has made, even to the least sparrow." John Calvin, *Institutes of the Christian Religion*, ed. John T. McNeill, trans. Ford Lewis Battles, vol. 1 (London: S. C. M. P., 1961), I.xvi.1.

31. In this passage the second quarto text of Hamlet prints "for no cause" rather than "forc'd cause," a reading that reinforces the accidental aspect. Aristotle's *Poetics* was rediscovered in the sixteenth century, so Shakespeare could have encountered his example of the statue of Mitys, but Horatio's speech opens a space for the type of interpretation that Aristotle deliberately withheld from the fall of an inanimate statue—the belief in providential design that had intensified within Calvinist theology as the doctrine of "special providence."

a web of power whose source remains uncertain. The results are tangible; the cause ambiguous. Just as the Reformation attack on the corruption of the church signaled a revival of religious faith and speculation, the materialist anxiety expressed in this play and the skeptical openness found in the essays of Montaigne create a conceptual space for fresh solutions to the definition of man's relation to his world. Science will occupy this space, setting the stage for an intellectual revolution whose goal will be to account for everything—every sparrow that falls and every grain of sand—through the operation of natural laws. In this empirical world, accidental qualities will become sites of observation that occupy an important place in the generation of new knowledge. But before this can happen, the unanticipated, unexpected event must be disciplined into experimental design. Accident must be subjected to the scientific method.

CHAPTER FOUR

Accidental Experience: Radical Enlightenment and the Science of Accident

I. Thinking Substance

Skepticism could critique claims to absolute truth, but its inability to formulate a satisfying replacement for those beliefs created a climate of uncertainty and proved ineffectual as a defense against continuing violence. In the wake of the Thirty Years' War, a renewed search for intellectual certainty absorbed the attention of mid-seventeenth-century thinkers like Descartes or Spinoza. However, even as they sought to break with the past, they derived their conceptual vocabulary from earlier philosophical traditions. Descartes, whose ambition was to create a system of thought that could withstand criticism from both Aristotelians and skeptics, fully recognized the power of Scholastic training. In the preface to the French edition of his *Principles of Philosophy* (1647), he addressed the extent to which Scholasticism inhibited intellectual development: "Those who have not followed Aristotle have nevertheless been saturated with his opinions in their youth (since these are the only opinions taught in the Schools) and this has so dominated their outlook that they have been unable to arrive at knowledge of true principles."[1] Yet even as he dismissed elements of Scholastic teaching, he could not avoid using concepts inherited from the Scholastic tradition.

Descartes's *Meditations on First Philosophy* (1641) presents an example of his use of multiple resources. Its autobiographical form reflects the tradition of the spiritual exercises advocated in the teachings of Ignatius of

---

1. Preface to the French edition, in *The Philosophical Writings of Descartes*, trans. John Cottingham (Cambridge: Cambridge University Press, 1985), I, 182. Unless otherwise noted, all citations of Descartes's works are from this edition.

Loyola, familiar to him from his Jesuit school days, and demonstrated by Augustine, whose *Confessions* he had encountered in Paris during the 1620s. But he broke from the Ignatian stress on memory and the imaginative use of objects (such as the instruments of Christ's Passion) as aids in meditation that had entered the tradition from the work of Aquinas.[2] Instead, he preferred the method of cleansing the memory of acquired images Augustine had used to purge his own thoughts of the teachings of the Manichees. However, Descartes adopted a conceptual structure shared by both traditions. It consisted of three stages: after purging himself of beliefs grounded in memory and sensory errors, the meditator experiences an illumination that enables him to attain the goal of uniting his will to God. As presented in the *Meditations*, this process constitutes a form of spiritual exercise. Descartes first exhorts the reader to abandon reliance on the senses or even on established mathematical truths.[3] His second meditation produces the illumination of the *cogito*. Only after establishing proof of the *cogito* does he proceed to the third meditation, which presents his argument for God's existence. The fourth meditation addresses the critical function of the will in achieving mental discipline. It not only argues that the will directs the mind to accept perceptions but also shows that willing a judgment about something which the intellect cannot clearly grasp is the cause of error.

Writing in the first person, as Augustine had done, Descartes described all the accidental qualities of the scene ("I am here, sitting by the fire, wearing a winter dressing-gown, holding this piece of paper in my hands"; II.i.19). Just as Augustine had written about himself in order to bring others closer to God, Descartes employed self-analysis to bring the creation of a metaphysical foundation for an altered perception of the nature of the world before the reader in the most vivid way. The "I" in his text stands imaginatively for "you," the person he was inviting to share his discoveries.

To create conviction in the reader's mind, Descartes dramatized the sequence of his thoughts using a mode of questioning loosely based on

2. Gary Hatfield, "Senses and the Fleshless Eye: The Meditations as Cognitive Exercises," in *Essays on Descartes' "Meditations,"* ed. Amélie Oksenberg Rorty (Berkeley: University of California Press, 1986), 48–51. See also Pierre Hadot, *What Is Ancient Philosophy?* trans. Michael Chase (Cambridge, MA: Harvard University Press, 2002), 263–65, which discusses the afterlife of the spiritual exercise into the nineteenth century.

3. Descartes developed a unique geometry designed to play a key role in this process by habituating the practitioner to intuit ideas in a manner that ensured their validity. See Matthew L. Jones, *The Good Life in the Scientific Revolution: Descartes, Pascal, Leibniz, and the Cultivation of Virtue* (Chicago: University of Chicago Press, 2006), 15–53.

the Scholastic mode of disputation that would have been familiar to his audience. Doubts about the reality of the visible world led him to the possibility that everything he experienced (or believed or thought he knew) might be a dream created by an evil demon. Determined to remain fixed on his meditation, he questioned the veracity of all external things, including his body, as well as his former understanding of what a human being was: "What then did I formerly think I was? A man. But what is a man? Shall I say 'a rational animal'? No; for then I should have to inquire what an animal is, what rationality is, and in this way one question would lead me down the slope to other harder ones" (II.ii.26). After expressing and rejecting his doubts, Descartes made a critical discovery: even though he had been forced to doubt the existence of his body, he could not doubt the reality of his process of thinking. His discovery of the primacy of thinking led him to the principle that the self exists as thinking substance: "But what then am I? A thing that thinks. What is that? A thing that doubts, understands, affirms, denies, is willing, is unwilling, and also imagines and has sensory perceptions" (II.ii.28).

Cogito ergo sum provided the axiom from which he would proceed. In opposition to the Aristotelian or Thomist assumption that all knowledge derives from the intellectual act of abstracting sensory particulars, he placed his discovery that everything he sensed appeared first as thought.[4] His intuition that what appears to be a spontaneous visual process of perceiving something is actually an illusion conditioned by mental processes seems surprisingly close to revelations of the twentieth-century science of vision. However, for the history of accident the crucial aspect of the *cogito* lies in its transformation of a man's substance from the observable sphere of a role performed in society (Socrates posing questions in the Agora or Aristotle's anonymous house builder) to the invisible sphere of mental action (Descartes meditating alone in his room).

Merely having a thought, however, did not ensure its certainty. Descartes broke from Aristotle's mode of reasoning by instituting a method for making judgments that would replace voluntary (and possibly erroneous)

---

4. Charles Taylor, *Sources of the Self: The Making of the Modern Identity* (Cambridge, MA: Harvard University Press, 1989), 141, notes that Augustine had pointed out the etymological link between *cogitare* and *cogere* ("to bring together" or "to collect" in the sense of making an order) in a perception that Taylor calls a "proto-cogito." Thoughts, Augustine wrote, "must be rallied and drawn together again, that they may be known; that is to say, they must as it were be collected and gathered together from their dispersions: whence the word 'cogitation' is derived" (*Confessions*, trans. Henry Chadwick [Oxford: Oxford University Press, 1992], X.xi.18).

thoughts. Since for him thoughts derived from external stimuli came involuntarily, the first judgment was to recognize that sense perceptions generate material accidents, like the color yellow or the brightness of a light, and that the way they were experienced could differ from the way they were. Sensory qualities, he believed, were nothing more than impressions in the person experiencing them. Therefore, the words "I seem to see a light" might mean something quite different to a man born blind than to one with normal sight because the words used to express thoughts function as signs, not as proofs of existence. "Why could nature not also have established some sign," he asked, "which would make us have the sensation of light, even if the sign contained nothing in itself which is similar to this sensation?"[5] Only a clear and distinct perception of what our sensations are enables us to pass judgments about their validity.

For Descartes, knowledge with divine import provided grounds for escaping error. God's goodness grounds man's limited certainty. Because he is no deceiver, those things we perceive to be clear and distinct must be true. Descartes retained the Aristotelian notion that the conjoined powers of soul and body are needed to effect sensory perceptions and the emotions that surround and condition them. He postulated that sensations excite the flow of animal spirits in the nerves that over time literally carve out channels in the brain, while the cognitive powers of the soul are required to receive ideas, draw inferences, and critique them. In other words, the capacity to judge the validity of sensory perceptions depends on a combination of three factors: the physical properties of the object, properties inherent in the changing condition of the mind, and the soul's awareness of its own processes. If proof of the *cogito* formed a necessary preamble to Descartes's argument for God's existence, at the same time, the perfection of God made it impossible that the *cogito's* foundation—his sense of his own existence—could be a delusion.[6] Nevertheless, by making human understanding autonomous, he established the power to evaluate experience as a new standard for interpreting the truth and thus prepared a role for scientific observation as a source of knowledge independent of divine revelation.

5. René Descartes, "The World," in *Philosophical Writings*, I, i, 4.

6. Although Descartes's method replicated the process of the spiritual exercise, the illumination of the *cogito* did not depend on grace. The so-called trademark argument of the third meditation was indebted to Boniface and Augustine. Descartes postulated that the cause of the idea of God as the "eternal, infinite, immutable, omniscient, omnipotent and the creator of all things" resided in him because it had been instilled by God as "the mark of the craftsman stamped on the work." In other words, it represented what Montaigne called form.

In the later seventeenth century the dualism of body and soul in Cartesian thought tended to be aligned with Aristotle's matter and substantial form, but this simplification obscured the extent to which matter and form were bound together in Aristotle's notion of substance.[7] For him, substantial form was more a substance than matter because it had the capacity to change while matter possessed only the potential to receive changes, but its combination with matter remained essential. In fact, the Scholastics had required delicate arguments to demonstrate that the human soul was the only substantial form capable of an independent existence.[8] Descartes thought that the Aristotelian concept of substantial form blocked a description of natural change by reducing generation (as a change in substance) to alteration (a change in qualities). He also rejected Aristotle's hypothesis of formless prime matter underlying corporeal substances. Instead, he argued that prime matter could be the material cause of substance if it possessed an accidental form that was essential to its existence. In nature no material substance can exist without quantity, he reasoned, making it the most obvious candidate.[9] Extension is not an accident of bodies but an essential quality. When they cease to extend they cease to exist.[10] Descartes's concept of extension not only occupies the place of the Aristotelian prime matter, it also reorders the relation between substance and accident.

To demonstrate the validity of giving extension such a special status, Descartes chose an example that would have been familiar to Aristotelians, that of wax: "Let us take, for example, this piece of wax. It has just been taken from the honeycomb; it has not yet quite lost the taste of the

---

7. Anthony Kenny, "Aristotle versus Descartes on Sensation," in his *Essays on the Aristotelian Tradition* (Oxford: Clarendon Press, 2001), 102–15, discusses current commentaries, arguing that sensation is a mode of a third entity, neither mind nor body, but the composite human being. He thinks the interaction of soul and body parallels the relation Descartes established of thought to perception and volition. In this view, intellect comprises a broad sense, which includes all cognitive activities of the mind but not the volitional ones, and a narrow sense that distinguishes intellect from imagination and sense. Kenny considers the link between them contingent, because sensation can take place in a soul unattached to a body.

8. Dennis Des Chene, *Physiologia: Natural Philosophy in Late Aristotelian and Cartesian Thought* (Ithaca: Cornell University Press, 1996), 54. His treatment of the ways Descartes manipulated or misconstrued Aristotelian thought illuminates the process of transmission as well as the source texts.

9. Ibid., 81–83. "Only the eye of faith sees that in the Eucharist the body and blood of Christ are present without their quantity" (97). Des Chene notes that transubstantiation was the only theological controversy Descartes engaged.

10. Ibid., 364.

honey; it retains some of the scent of the flowers from which it was gathered; its colour, shape and size are plain to see; it is hard, cold and can be handled without difficulty; if you rap it with your knuckle it makes a sound. In short, it has everything which appears necessary to enable a body to be known as distinctly as possible" (II.ii.30).

His description afforded an empirical and recognizable moment of everyday observation. Yet the accidental qualities of the wax mutated before his eyes, for when he moved it close to the fire, all the material accidents he had just described were burned away: the smell vanished, the color changed, it became liquid and hot, and it no longer made a sound when struck. If he subtracted all the accidentals (that is, the mutable qualities like smell or color) from the wax, he was left with the notion that essentially it was something extended in three dimensions (res extensa). His perceptions of the "piece" of matter that constituted the wax rested, therefore, on the length, breadth, and depth that indicated a geometric figure. Extension gave material substances a precise corporeal reality.

Conceiving of wax as a geometrical figure, rather than a substance that possesses qualities in common with other substances, did not entirely resolve the problem posed by the mutation of its accidental qualities, but Descartes had shifted the basis of his understanding from the object itself (what the intellect conceives, in the Aristotelian formulation) to his new process of analyzing how the intellect acquires conceptions. By casting his argument in the form of meditations, he proposed to accustom the mind to attending to the intellect as a source of knowledge that was independent of the senses. This difference in direction remade Aristotle's substance-accident distinction and grounded Descartes's philosophy in an understanding of the mind.[11]

Descartes distinguished human beings from all other things in the world on the basis of their capacity to perform actions that required thought. Involuntary or spontaneous functions could be performed by

---

11. John P. Carriero, "The Second Meditation and the Essence of the Mind," in Rorty, Essays on Descartes' "Meditations," 214–17. Matthew L. Jones, The Good Life in the Scientific Revolution, 58ff., argues persuasively that rhetorical tradition influenced Descartes's "subjectivist" solution to problems of knowledge in ways that significantly altered the relation between substance and accident. Jones observes that for scholastic philosophers, true definition captured the essential or substantial features of a thing. Merely describing external attributes or metaphorically evoking the thing, as poets or orators did, could never constitute genuine knowledge. When Descartes replaced definitions involving forms, qualities, teleological motions, and efficient causes with detailed descriptions of material structures and matter in motion, he upset this hierarchy of definition and "reduced the essence of things to their accidents, as they had been traditionally understood."

animals or even automata. Therefore, in the Cartesian view, functions that Aristotle had ascribed to the *anima,* including digestion, the beating of the heart, growth, breathing, waking and sleeping, perception of light, sounds, smells, tastes, heat, and other sensations, and even the function of memory, which receives and records sensations and had become associated with the soul in the Christian transformation of terminology, belonged to the body. They were mechanical functions that he could explain as operating like the hydraulic machines made up of cogs, levers, and pumps available within the world of seventeenth-century mechanics.[12]

On this physiological level, Descartes could describe all animals as machines, but he believed that a machine flexible enough to act in every situation as reason enables men to act was a moral impossibility (*Discourse on Method,* V).[13] Even in the eighteenth century, when elaborate automata capable of writing, drawing, and playing music dazzled the public, the mechanical figures were mute. Thus, reason and speech identified human beings. He did allow that machines could walk or sing if those actions

---

12. In his youth Descartes saw mechanical statues in the grottoes of Saint Germain similar to those described by Salomon de Caus in *Les Raisons des forces mouvantes avec diverses machines* (1615). Springs concealed under the floor tiles were activated when the visitor stepped on them, causing hydraulic tubes embedded in the limbs and faces of the figures to move so that Neptune could brandish his trident or a monster spew water in the visitor's face. See his posthumous *Traité de l'homme* (1664), reproduced in Descartes, *Oeuvres complètes,* ed. Charles Adam and Paul Tannery (Paris, 1897–1913), XI.130. He postulated that a comparable hydraulic mechanism allowed the rational soul to activate the body. When it pushes on the pineal gland, fluid animal spirits convey this pressure along the hollow tubes of the nervous system, making the muscles swell and contract. Of course he understood God as the creator of such machines. In the *Discourse on Method* he added that if those familiar with automatons were to compare such machines with the body of any animal, they would recognize the incomparable sophistication of God's mechanical designs (*Philosophical Writings,* I, v, 56). See Peter Dear, "A Mechanical Microcosm: Bodily Passions, Good Manners, and Cartesian Mechanism," in *Science Incarnate: Historical Embodiments of Natural Knowledge,* ed. Christopher Lawrence and Steven Shapin (Chicago: University of Chicago Press, 1998), 58–60. Saul A. Kripke, *Naming and Necessity* (Cambridge, MA: Harvard University Press, 1972), 144, argues that Descartes did not resolve the mind-body problem with his assertion that a mind is distinct from the body since it could exist without the body. The theory that a person is nothing over and above his body in the way that a statue is nothing over and above the matter of which it is composed, he notes, would have to hold that a person exists if and only if his body exists and has a certain additional physical organization. The correspondence between a brain state and a mental state has an obvious element of contingency.

13. Descartes postulated two ways to distinguish a mechanical figure from a human being: "Automatons never answer in word or sign, except by chance, to questions put to them; and secondly, that though their movements are often more regular and certain than those of the wisest men, yet in many things which they would have to do to imitate us, they fail more disastrously than the greatest fools" (letter to Reneri, 1638, in *Philosophical Writings,* III, vi, 40).

occurred without the mind attending to them, but he posited what he called a "rational soul" to carry out functions that required mental attention.[14] Lack of mind or a "rational soul" made the actions of automatons purely involuntary.

The connection between the concept of the body as a mechanical system and the concept of the rational soul controlling all actions that are not involuntary or spontaneous allows us to consider the automaton as a marker of Descartes's understanding of substance and accident. The substance of an automaton consists of nothing other than the quality of extension, and its actions, which result from purely mechanical operations, are accidental events in the Aristotelian sense of *to automaton*. It lacks mind, which Descartes equated with soul as thinking substance.[15] Although the human body is also substantively extension and its involuntary motions also are accidental, it is animated by the mental operations of the soul. While human beings exist, they think.

As we have recognized, Descartes postulated that sensory perceptions depended on an interaction of soul and body. So did the passions. In Descartes's mechanistic system, all emotions are modifications or combinations of six primitive passions (wonder, love, hatred, desire, joy, and sadness). Like Aquinas, he understood mastering these passions to be the goal of wisdom, but he explained their operation in relation to the micro-mechanical theories involving movement through space that he used to explain the physiology of the body.[16] For example, in *The Passions of the Soul* (1649) he recognized that people laugh when they are tickled even

14. Dear, "Mechanical Microcosm," 66–70, argues that the social aspect of Descartes's second qualification (that automata cannot respond to the contingencies of life) permits morality to mediate between the passions of the mind and the mechanistic body.

15. In treating substantial form as substance in the sense of being subsistent, Descartes clearly misunderstood the position accepted by the Scholastics. However, Renaissance Aristotelians (such as Eustachius a Sancto Paulo) had described both substantial form and matter as substances, so it was natural for Descartes to read substantial forms as independent but incomplete in the sense that they do not occur apart, from matter. As a result, his liberal ontology of substances ran together the Scholastic distinction between artifacts and living organisms. His concept of mind did not sustain body as a substantial form would. Mind has causal efficacy only on the pineal gland. See Robert Pasnau, "Form, Substance, and Mechanism," *Philosophical Review* 113, no. 1 (January 2004): 47–54.

16. In his treatises on mechanics, Descartes resolved the problem of how to demonstrate the operation of invisible components with illustrations that exploded views of internal mechanisms or removed surfaces to show hidden parts and he used captions to explain their functions. Dennis Des Chene, *Spirits and Clocks: Machine and Organism in Descartes* (Ithaca: Cornell University Press, 2001), 152. Des Chene compares Descartes's books to machines in which text and illustrations function together to enable the reader to see, imagine, and conceive.

though they receive no pleasure from it. Tickling awakened an "impression of joy and surprise" in their imagination, "which previously made them laugh for the same reason." This emotion caused the lungs to be swollen suddenly and involuntarily by blood sent to them from the heart (I.3.211). He believed the will exercised no more control over these changes in the body than it could over contingent events, but that careful training could modify the effects of changes set in motion when sensory phenomena physically alter the geometry of the brain: "The objects which strike our senses move parts of our brain by means of the nerves, and there make as it were folds, which undo themselves when the object ceases to operate; but afterwards the place where they were made has a tendency to be folded again in the same manner by another object resembling even incompletely the original object" (letter to Chanut, 6 June 1647, III, p. 322). To alter behavior, the operation of the mind must crease new folds into the brain. This practice resembled rote conditioning by association rather than the discipline of spiritual exercise.[17] In Descartes's conception of this process, accidental encounters with external objects create the associations that press these folds in place, and only the memory can erase them. However, this kind of conditioning explained only the involuntary portion of the thought process. Unlike sensory perceptions and the passions, which required the united powers of soul and body, understanding and willing occurred in the soul alone. In *Passions of the Soul*, he envisioned the soul's perception of its own operations free from either the ideas conveyed by the animal spirits or the passions and their more destructive consequences. He called this class of thoughts *émotions intérieures*, for they were excited by the soul as it perceived and judged its own thoughts. When ideas appear clear and distinct, they arouse these intellectual emotions and engage the will to act upon them.[18]

Descartes's theories posited a new understanding of how ideas might

17. Montaigne also used the image of folds to describe the complexity of the mind: "It is a thorny undertaking, and more so than it seems, to follow a movement so wandering as that of our mind, to penetrate the opaque depths of its innermost folds, to pick out and immobilize the innumerable flutterings that agitate it." Michel de Montaigne, "Of Practice," in *The Complete Essays of Montaigne*, trans. Donald Frame (Stanford: Stanford University Press, 1957), II.12.273.

18. For a discussion of the relation between passion and intellect in Descartes's thought see Susan James, *Passion and Action: The Emotions in Seventeenth-Century Philosophy* (Oxford: Clarendon Press, 1997), esp. 196–200. Dear, "Mechanical Microcosm," 71, asserts that the rigid distinction between the passions and reason is rooted in "a mechanistic ontology effectively *defined* by the mind-body distinction" and this ontology is what allows individuals to make personas.

be formed, but despite their novelty, he maintained the subordinate status of accident by restricting it to the material surface of experience. At the same time, however, he shifted the boundary between physical and mental accidents. By removing the animating function from the soul and delivering it to the body, he had reconstructed the idea of what it meant to be alive. In the example of an inanimate material object like the piece of wax, he had equated geometric properties (the *res extensae*) with substantial form, but even when he asserted that the quality of being alive resided in the body, he did not equate the substantial form of a living being with the body's geometric properties. When Aristotle defined the substance of Socrates as his capacity for philosophical reasoning, he did not doubt that Socrates could be found tanning himself in the marketplace. While Descartes would have agreed in defining Socrates' substantial form as mind, he might have added that his tanning himself could be an illusion. In fact, in his first meditation, he could imagine his own body formed of glass or his head of a pumpkin.[19] This radical emphasis on mind in Descartes's philosophy reshuffled the conceptual cards of substance and accident to give associations and other accidents involved in mental processes an increased importance.[20]

Reformulating the accidental qualities in this way also altered the understanding of accidental events in Descartes's system. On the one hand, his belief that mechanical operations determined behavior when the mind was not controlling the body might seem to allow physical accidents less impact. If they merely produced sensations without having the power to affect ingrained behavior, they would be susceptible to all the errors aroused by unclear perception. However, if the soul exercised its capacity to engage in inference and critique, accidental events would provide the occasion for probing how the world worked in order to yield such accidents. Then the impact of an accident had the power to trouble the "thinking substance" and effect conceptual change. In the sense that Cartesian thought shifted accidental events into the plane of rational thought, disrupted the bond between matter and form, and called into question old patterns of causation and generation, it prepared the way for new methods of examining the world and new avenues through which accidental events could illuminate the interpretation of the self.

19. Descartes, *Philosophical Writings*, II, i, 19.
20. Maureen Rozemond, *Descartes's Dualism* (Cambridge, MA: Harvard University Press, 1998), 172.

II. The Science of Accident: Probability, Alchemy, and Universal Law

Cartesian materialism laid the foundation for an understanding of substance and accident within natural laws. This development would make accident, which Aristotle had excluded from scientific understanding (*Metaphysics*, 6.4.1027b18), a subject for scientific investigation. Descartes's method consisted of four steps: first, "never to accept anything as true if I did not have evident knowledge of its truth"; second, "to divide each of the difficulties I examined into as many parts as possible"; third, "to direct my thoughts in an orderly manner" from simplest to most complex; and finally to make general reviews and "enumerations" (*Discourse on Method*, II.29). Yet just as he incorporated principles of classical geometry and the concept of extension into his theory of substantial form, his method demonstrates a debt to the Scholastic practice of articulation, classification, and enumeration within his mental discipline.[21]

One conventional mark for the transformation of knowledge that occured during the seventeenth century relies on measuring the sophistication of mathematical advances. By the end of the sixteenth century, progress was evident not only in better methods of calculation and prediction, but also in theoretical improvements. Theories of probability that resulted from this effort affected the understanding of the accidental events that disrupted expected chains of cause and effect and continued to challenge existing systems of belief in both theology and the sciences.[22] They offered a way to control the impact of accidental circumstances in daily life.

21. Nicholas Jardine, "Epistemology of the Sciences," in *The Cambridge History of Renaissance Philosophy*, ed. Quentin Skinner and Eckhard Kessler (Cambridge: Cambridge University Press, 1988), 711, notes that it is not possible to establish a specific context for Descartes's epistemology of science. Given the current state of research, he believes that it is premature to focus on questions of continuity and impact on the new science. However, his article does trace the substantial changes in classification and subordination of university arts and sciences at the time. Discussions of how to order material occurring within particular disciplines expressed concern not only with teaching but also with how to knit facts and principles together into a body of rational science.

22. According to Ian Hacking, *Emergence of Probability: A Philosophical Study of Early Ideas about Probability, Induction and Statistical Inference* (Cambridge: Cambridge University Press, 1984), 45–46, Descartes had no interest in probability. "Although he had grave qualms about *scientia*," Hacking argues, he employed inductive reasoning from cause to observable effect. Recognizing that "no scholastic would call that 'demonstration,'" Descartes asserted that it would still deserve that term in common speech. "In the waning distinction between

Seventeenth-century probability theorists were influenced by practices that had been well developed during the Renaissance, primarily in order to calibrate degrees of risk and reward in business or evaluate the weight that should be given to a particular witness in a legal proceeding.[23] These principles were dominated by the need for just or equitable solutions to uncertain circumstances, but they were extended by analogy to problems of moral or theological certainty. This double heritage linked probability theory to pragmatic applications, such as gambling, as well as to questions of belief. The work of influential early mathematician-philosophers like Blaise Pascal, Christiaan Huygens, Jakob and Johann Bernoulli, and Gottfried Wilhelm Leibniz incorporated mathematical modes of problem solving, but did so within a theological context. Paratheological applications of probability theory supported the importance of interpreting accidental events within the arena of secular experience by giving them spiritual significance.

Pascal's famous wager exemplifies the theological context of his estimate of probability.[24] He calculates the risk and reward of acting as if God exists, and his reasoning process conveys the flavor of the origin of probability theory in ideas of equitable contracts:

> You have two things to lose: the true and the good; and two things to stake: your reason and your will, your knowledge and your happiness; and your nature has two things to avoid: error and wretchedness. Since you must necessarily choose, your reason is no more affronted by choosing

---

high and low science," Hacking continues, "Descartes firmly opted for the high, and thereby determined the course of his philosophy. It had no room for probability." See also James Franklin, *The Science of Conjecture: Evidence and Probability before Pascal* (Baltimore: Johns Hopkins University Press, 2001), 218–22.

23. For a discussion of the commercial origins of mathematical probability, see Edith Dudley Sylla, "Business Ethics, Commercial Mathematics, and the Origins of Mathematical Probability," in *Oeconomies in the Age of Newton*, ed. Margaret Schabas and Neil DeMarchi (Raleigh: Duke University Press, 2003), 309–37.

24. Joseph Walker's English translation of the *Pensées* appeared in 1688, but a manuscript translation circulated among members of the Royal Society during the mid-1670s. Evidently Pascal did not invent the problem of the wager. A version appeared in the Port Royal *Logique* (1662), although it lacked his gambling analogy. In 1664, however, John Tillotson used probabilities and outcome values in an argument nearly identical to Pascal's in his sermon "On the Wisdom of Being Religious." See Lorraine Daston, *Classical Probability in the Enlightenment* (Princeton: Princeton University Press, 1988), 60–61; and John K. Ryan, "The Wager in Pascal and Others," in *Gambling on God: Essays on Pascal's Wager*, ed. Jeff Jordan (Lanham, MD: Rowman and Littlefield, 1994), 11–19.

one rather than the other. That is one point cleared up. But your happiness? Let us weigh up the gain and the loss involved in calling heads that God exists. Let us assess the two cases: if you win you win everything, if you lose you lose nothing. Do not hesitate then; wager that he does exist. "That is wonderful. Yes, I must wager, but perhaps I am wagering too much." Let us see: since there is an equal chance of gain and loss, if you stood to win only two lives for one you could still wager, but supposing you stood to win three?

You would have to play (since you must necessarily play) and it would be unwise of you, once you are obliged to play, not to risk your life in order to win three lives at a game in which there is an equal chance of losing and winning. But there is an eternity of life and happiness. That being so, even though there were an infinite number of chances, of which only one were in your favour, you would still be right to wager one in order to win two; and you would be acting wrongly, being obliged to play, in refusing to stake one life against three in a game, where out of an infinite number of chances there is one in your favour, if there were an infinity of infinitely happy life to be won.[25]

Pascal removed the argument from a dualism of saved versus damned by developing a much more complex understanding of conditioning factors.[26] The essence of the wager is not the obvious notion that if you are convinced of the necessity of choosing, you choose infinity over nothing, but the idea that you must wager. He makes the absence of proof into the crucial point.[27] The wager demonstrates the way in which mathematical principles (and by extension other scientific discoveries) now appeared

25. Blaise Pascal, *Pensées*, trans. A. J. Krailsheimer (New York: Penguin, 1966; rev. ed., 1995), L418.123. Except where noted, citations refer to this translation.

26. Leslie Armour, *"Infini Rien": Pascal's Wager and the Human Paradox*, Journal of the History of Philosophy Monograph Series (Carbondale: Southern Illinois University Press, 1993), 2–3, argues against Hacking's interpretation of the wager in terms of limited possibilities within a probabilistic frame of reference. Pascal believed in action, so for him, the choices are real: behaving as if God exists will make a better world and it is a way of behaving well because one who accepts the existence of God will treat all people as if they were saved.

27. Alain Badiou, *Being and Event*, trans. Oliver Feltham (London: Continuum, 2003), 220–21. Badoiou's discussion of Pascal assumes a relation between mathematical reasoning and the interpretation of events within the context of the wager. For a succinct analysis of the logical arguments see Ian Hacking, "The Logic of Pascal's Wager," in Jordan, *Gambling on God*, 23–28.

capable of providing far-reaching explanations of phenomena even when it seemed impossible to decide between prospective outcomes or different explanations.

In general, however, Pascal believed that the kind of certainty that Descartes sought with his method was unattainable, and he disagreed with many of Descartes's central ideas, such as his way of proving the existence of God or his conviction that illumination can be obtained without grace. Pascal's position was that all belief rests on a basis of miracle. An experience like Descartes's joyous discovery of the *cogito* and his conviction of its certainty is emblematic of the possibility of believing in truth, but it stands alongside other miracles as a gift from God. In that sense, we can compare the questioning form Descartes used in the *Meditations* to demonstrate the independent reasoning power of the mind to the calculation of probability that Pascal described in the wager. Just as the wager was predicated on a belief in the fundamental necessity of wagering, the *cogito* depended on a belief in the fundamental necessity of thinking. What Pascal questioned, in other words, was not the usefulness of the reasoning process, but Descartes's conviction that he had transformed a possibility into a certainty.

The initial context of the wager involved a game in which two players have agreed to play until one wins three throws. If the game was interrupted, the problem was to calculate how the stake would be divided between them, depending on the various combinations of dice that had been thrown up to that moment. Pascal proposed a numerical solution that theoretically could be extended to infinity. His solution was original (in the sense that he knew no other versions at the time he created it), but it was most remarkable for the implications he drew from it. The solution to the pragmatic problem demonstrated that in principle infinity has a number; nevertheless, that number remained as unknowable as the infinite nature of God. This realization of limitlessness intensified his sense that Descartes had not freed man from spiritual uncertainty.

Pascal believed that the relation of finite to infinite presents a puzzle that undermines claims to knowledge about the world. Despite the enormous recent expansion of mathematical powers, he was convinced that the connection between mathematics and physical reality remained obscure. He began the fragment in which he analyzed the wager with another heart-felt exclamation, "Infini-Rien!" He explains this dichotomy in another lengthy meditation on man's condition. The place man occupies in the universe appears fundamentally insignificant, yet imagination can allow him to grasp nature as "an infinite sphere, whose center is everywhere and circumference nowhere." Positioned at the mean between nothing and infinity, he is "incapable of certain knowledge or absolute ignorance" (L199.72).[28]

In this universe the creation of a person represents an arbitrary act; it is as much the result of chance as a roll of the dice. "Our soul is cast into the body," he wrote, "where it finds number, time, dimensions; it reasons about these things and calls them natural, or necessary, and can believe nothing else" (L418.121). Implicitly, his assertion of arbitrary origin served as a critique of Descartes, for he viewed the premises or axioms that served as starting points for any chain of inferences as arbitrary in the sense that more primitive ideas or terms could always be discovered. Behind the *res cogitans* lies the unknown.[29]

Within this chaos of uncertainty, the notion of the arbitrary served as an intermediary between finite and infinite. Just as Christ acted as an intermediary between man and God, probability performed a mediating role in Pascal's thought. He believed humanity becomes something only through its relation to God. Because human beings have the capacity to express everything (in the sense that the whole of reality lies within potential knowledge), humanity has the possibility to become the vehicle through which God could manifest himself if he chose. Thus, Christ's acts and words, which serve as signs to be interpreted, can be compared to accidental events, which also function as signs for interpretation. Pascal used the terms of the wager to give intellectual structure to what he considered was an irrational refusal to acknowledge this relationship as fundamental to being: to increase the chance of escaping nothingness, a person must do something. He recommended believing in God.

In a series of essays entitled "Three Discourses on the Condition of the Great" (ca. 1660), composed as advice to a young nobleman, Pascal

28. Empedocles is the probable source of the notion of a center which is everywhere and a circumference nowhere. Pascal probably read it in the preface to Montaigne's *Essais* edited by Mlle de Gournay.

29. Pascal's own solution considered this problem in terms of the probability theories he applied in the wager: since certainty is impossible, he sought a procedure that would be most likely to produce a provisionally acceptable degree of certainty. Because mathematics was generally accepted as the most certain secular mode of producing knowledge, the procedure he selected was a geometrical one, demonstrating from terms that require no definition and using those terms as the basis for defining other terms in the manner of Euclid. Armour, "*Infini Rien*," 70–71, assumes (more negatively than Pascal himself) that the idea of man positioned midway between nothing and infinity demonstrates that increased knowledge of the world was accompanied by a fading notion of the self as a continuing, distinct substance.

took up the question of the individual's chance origin. The context is secular, but it carries connotations of his religious thought. His ostensible goal was to demonstrate the accidental source of class entitlement and identity. You have no right to the wealth you possess, he wrote, for your existence depends on ancestral marriages that themselves depended on an infinity of accidental visits, idle talk, and a thousand other chance events. The narrative that he offered for contemplation began with Aristotle's familiar shipwreck image:

> When a man is tossed by a storm onto an unknown island, whose inhabitants were having trouble finding their king who had disappeared; and having a great deal of physical and facial resemblance to this king, he is taken for him, and accepted in this capacity by all of these people. At first he did not know what course to take; but finally he decided to yield himself to his good luck. He received all the homage that they wished to render to him, and allowed himself to be treated as a king.
>
> But, since he could not forget his genuine condition, he bore in mind, at the same time he was receiving these homages, that he was not that king that these people were looking for, and that this kingdom did not belong to him. Thus he had a double conception, the one in which he was playing the part of king, and the other in which he recognized his true state, and that it was only chance that had put him where he was. He hid this second view, and disclosed the other one. It was in terms of the first that he dealt with the populace, and in terms of the second that he dealt with himself.[30]

Pascal used the natural man, the victim of the shipwreck, as a counterpoint for the figure of power signified by the absent king, but implicit in this comparison was the idea that man's natural condition is one of postlapsarian misery. Both the man and the king could be understood as exiles—the man from his homeland and the king from his kingdom of faithful subjects.[31] A theological analogy that Pascal characteristically preserved at the level of implication, since he offered no explanation for the loss of the king, suggests the possibility that the king (God) has

---

30. Blaise Pascal, "Three Discourses on the Condition of the Great," in *Pascal Selections*, trans. and ed. Richard H. Popkin (New York: Scribner/Macmillan, 1989), 74.

31. This analysis reflects the reading provided by Louis Marin, *Portrait of the King*, trans. Martha M. Houle (Minneapolis: University of Minnesota Press, 1988), 217–36.

hidden himself voluntarily and will reveal his true presence only to the elect.[32]

In the narrative, Pascal allegorized the division between the king's social identity as king (embodied in his interactions with his subjects, their homages, the trappings that articulate the portrait of kingship) and his inner identity as a man through the literal division between the body of the shipwrecked man and that of the lost king he happens to resemble. The fusion of the two bodies occurs through a sequence of accidental events—the disappearance of the king before the shipwreck, the chance of landing on this particular unidentified island, the likeness (which is not perfect, so that the subjects make the association voluntarily rather than through force of reason), and the sailor's willingness to conceal his true identity. Altering any of these circumstances would have altered the outcome, for they cannot be controlled by either the man or the individuals who form themselves into a body politic by accepting him as their king. The subjects legitimize the man, for his identity is hidden from them. None of them know that only resemblance makes him the king, yet he cannot forget his double identity. Pascal also hid the man's former life, his port of departure, and his destination from the reader just as he allowed the loss of the king to remain unexplained. The island itself exists only as a void at the center of the narrative—the place of identity that the king has left and the place he has left empty that the man now enters.[33]

Narrative ambiguities of this kind serve as a critique of the notion of

32. After Pascal's intense religious vision of 1654, he carried for the rest of his life, stitched into the lining of his clothes, the record he had written during this experience, as a hidden sign of the fervor of his belief.

33. Marin, *Portrait of the King*, 228–31, pursues the possible Eucharistic implications in this passage. He observes that the man knows he is only the sign of the king, while the subjects' idea of him represents the idea of the king. Because the Apostles knew only the bread, they did not see it as a sign, so Christ could give his sign the name of a thing without tricking them or speaking against the usage of men. For the subjects, the thing (bread) has not become something other than bread (the body of Christ) in becoming a sign (the sacramental bread) because the shipwrecked man has not symbolically covered himself with the face or body of the lost king. Pascal, Marin adds, displays the doctrine of the king's two bodies in a critical fashion in which the man who resembles the (lost) king and is henceforth like the king expresses a transubstantiation of one body into another through the king's attempt to exercise absolute power. The physical body of the king and the politico-mystical body of the King acquire a new meaning: the physical body functions only in the space of the mistake and the political finds its function only in usurpation. An influential expression of the problem of fission implicit in this discussion will appear in Locke's philosophy of personal identity in the following section.

substance. If the sailor holds a conviction of his "true identity," the reader must comprehend the assumed role as another aspect of "truth." Moreover, the "true identity" of the man behind the role of the original king remains unknown. In this context, the accidental qualities obscure rather than reveal the substance or essence of the individual human being. In another context, Pascal envisions the uncertainty of identity extending beyond social relationships to encompass the fundamental problem of the soul and the body:

"What is the self?" . . .

And if someone loves me for my judgment or my memory, do they love me? *Me*, myself? No, for I could lose these qualities without losing myself. Where then is the self, if it is neither in the body nor the soul? And how can one love the body or the soul except for the sake of such qualities, which are not what makes up the self, since they are perishable? Would we love the substance of a person's soul, in the abstract, whatever qualities might be in it? That is not possible, and it would be wrong. Therefore we never love anyone, but only qualities . . . we never love anyone except for borrowed qualities. (L688.217)

By offering this ambiguous narrative, Pascal invited the reader to engage in the interpretation of signs, for he believed that all texts were intrinsically fluid. He recognized, for example, that when Descartes borrowed from Augustine the phrases "Matter is in a state of being naturally and irremediably incapable of thought" and "I think, therefore I am," he was transforming their meaning by projecting his own conceptual framework onto the words. Pascal distinguished "writing a word by chance" (as Augustine did—in the passionate recording of experience which Pascal approved) from reasoned manipulation (as practiced by Descartes—with whom he so frequently disagreed).[34] However, just as Descartes theorized that sensory perception depended on both the qualities possessed by the perceived object and properties of the perceiver's mind, Pascal acknowledged that he projected his own ideas onto his reading. For example, he wrote: "It is not in Montaigne but in myself that I find everything I see [in him]" (L689.218). The accidentality implicit in the interpretation of texts results from the individual nature of the reader as well as shifting

---

34. Blaise Pascal, "The Geometrical Mind and Art of Persuasion," trans. Richard H. Popkin, in *Pascal Selections*, 2:192. On Pascal's reading, see Sara E. Melzer: *Discourses of the Fall: A Study of Pascal's "Pensées"* (Berkeley: University of California Press, 1986), 110–41.

contexts for the content and makes the meaning intended by an author represent only one of the potential meanings available within a text.

This perception allowed Pascal to extend the type of allegorical interpretation practiced with sacred texts to texts of all kinds, but it also created a sense that by its very nature the act of reading was a transformative experience. In this view, words function in relation to the reader as the Eucharistic wafer functions for the believer. The accidental signs of language can be taken in by any literate person, just as an unbeliever may chew and swallow a consecrated wafer. But the spiritual reward of partaking of Christ's spirit (commingling his body and blood with the believer's own) requires the condition of belief, just as assimilation of the ideas contained in a text requires active reading. To the extent that this process can alter both the reader's interpretation of what he reads (which may differ from what the author intended) and the reader's mode of perception, it produces a substantial change. In other words, we might say that in Pascal's description, the act of reading is not a mechanical process but an alchemical one.

Like many conventional notions, the image of the alchemist seeking to transform base metals into silver and gold by arcane manipulations in which the degree of spiritual purification of the practitioner controlled success or failure contains aspects of mythological distortion. The mysterious, bearded figure presiding over a study filled with occult paraphernalia represented the antithesis of rationality for the eighteenth century and the essence of romanticism for the nineteenth, but for natural philosophers of the seventeenth century, the search for the philosopher's stone combined a quest for knowledge about the properties of matter with disciplined investigative practice.

Alchemy did not share the privileged status among the disciplines awarded to physics or astronomy, nor did it require the level of mathematical abstraction chronicled in histories of the scientific revolution, so its role in seventeenth-century thought has been comparatively overlooked. However, evidence preserved in the notebooks of "chymists" such as the American George Starkey demonstrates the use of rational laboratory practices involving quantification of results, experimental controls, reproducibility of results, and a theoretical basis for attempts to understand the nature of material substance.[35]

The problem of interpreting substantial change interested chymists

35. See William R. Newman and Lawrence M. Principe, *Alchemy Tried in the Fire: Starkey, Boyle, and the Fate of Helmontian Chymistry* (Chicago: University of Chicago Press, 2002).

because it involved the transformation of matter. Jan Baptista Van Helmont represents an influential theorist among these practitioners. A contemporary of Descartes, he disagreed with the mechanistic explanation of the body, which assumed that direct contact was needed to effect change. In his mind, superficial physical changes—those a mechanist might measure mathematically—differed from the marriage of substances that occurred as a result of chemical reactions. His approach did not simply oppose mechanism with a form of vitalism (a contemporary theory which ascribed life to the constant motion of minute material corpuscles). Van Helmont wanted to distinguish superficial from substantial change.

Descartes's primary motive for reversing the status of matter relative to form had been to provide greater insight into generation. By virtually identifying matter with extension, he gave it the possibility of an independent existence, allowing it to be understood as a complete substance on which accidental qualities might depend.[36] Although he believed his mechanist theories could explain changes in those qualities, conceiving of matter as substance also supported investigation into how material things came to be or ceased to exist. The goal of alchemy lay precisely in the generation of new material substances. A chymist could not be satisfied merely to realize gold's accidental properties of a yellow color, glittering surface, or specific weight; he wanted to achieve its essence.

Van Helmont defined superficial change as the result of a chymical procedure that dissolved a substance and then recaptured it by distillation. A substantial change occurred when the initial ingredients could not be recovered after the experiment. When the basic substance of water changed from liquid to gas or ice, the changes were merely superficial. Yet when it became a constitutive element of metal, wood, oil, or salts, its substance was profoundly transformed.

Alchemical research advanced the rational understanding of the relation between substance and accidental qualities. Indeed, alchemical experimentation exerted an influence on how people regarded accidental qualities parallel to the impact of probability theory on accidental events. In both disciplines, we see a key shift from attempting to place experiences within the natural world into classificatory boxes—a goal that persisted into the early seventeenth century—to a perception of vastly expanded areas of potential discovery. The figure of Isaac Newton illustrates all aspects of this conceptual energy.

36. Des Chene, *Physiologia*, 97.

The eighteenth century purged the record of Newton's extensive alchemical research as well as the studies of biblical chronology and prophecies that he pursued to the end of his life. Moreover, alchemists frequently used allegorical language and symbols to guard their work, so his manuscripts posed difficulties for later scholars. Nevertheless, it seems evident that he understood his search for the philosopher's stone as complementary to his search for universal laws of nature. After 1666, his research focused on processes that would enable him to comprehend how forces like gravity and magnetism operate across distances. He hypothesized that an invisible and intangible matter (which he identified as ether) effected changes in the bodies it inhabited by working eternally to transform solids into liquids and liquids into solids. For Newton, therefore, alchemy existed as a form of natural philosophy that asserted the presence of nonmaterial agents within nature. The emphasis on Descartes's mechanistic philosophy has masked the spiritual component of late seventeenth-century scientific thought in the traditional history of science. Nevertheless, the scientist whose work realized at least a portion of the Cartesian goal directed an active research program toward affirming the primacy of spirit over matter in the universe.[37]

The original title of Newton's *Principia* was *De motu corporum* (On the movement of bodies), but the work advanced beyond vitalist or mechanist explanations of forces to create a new mathematical theory of celestial and terrestrial movements. His mathematical natural philosophy would have been unthinkable without the shift that had taken place in notions of experimentation. Since Aristotle, universal experience had grounded knowledge statements about nature, but to characterize themselves as credible participants in the search for philosophical knowledge, mathematicians like Pascal claimed to possess a technique that was not constrained to knowledge available through received opinion or authority but could produce new experiences. Newton's achievement in making his "physics" an attempt to comprehend the universe rested on the shoulders of such claims regarding empirical knowledge.[38]

Newton refused to condone the kind of hypothetical reasoning that had led Descartes to his theory that vortices filled the space in the heavens, pushing celestial objects along their orbits. As an experimenter, he

37. Betty Jo Teeter Dobbs, *The Janus Faces of Genius: The Role of Alchemy in Newton's Thought* (Cambridge: Cambridge University Press, 1991).

38. Peter Dear, *Discipline and Experience: The Mathematical Way in the Scientific Revolution* (Chicago: University of Chicago Press, 1995), 245–49.

insisted on the importance of developing precise tests for his hypotheses, and as a mathematician, he was able to work out the mathematical consequences of his assumptions. The power of his proofs demolished Descartes's theory, and by demonstrating the existence of gravity as a universal force obedient to a given mathematical law, he confirmed the belief that the world obeyed universal ordering principles.[39] His ideas were accepted into the university curricula, first at Cambridge, then at Oxford, and attempts also were made to apply, adapt, and extend his principles to other domains.

Even as the image of a great scientific genius formed around Newton, popular opinion resisted and mocked his concepts for a generation. Hogarth's cartoon entitled *Weighing House Inn* (fig. 3), published in 1763, transformed earlier notions of changing fortune into a message of intellectual pride humbled by a fall.[40] Fortuna's turning wheel had not quite disappeared from the scene, for Hogarth punned on the idea of gravity as a magnet that whirled a scientist into the air, passing him through stages of levity until he was transformed into a fool. Despite its raillery, the image captured a latent truth about Newton's thought. Having turned the universe into a kind of celestial clockwork in which the pull of the moon explained the tides and the rotation of the earth around the sun accounted for the seasons, he had made man a particle in motion. In ways Newton could not have predicted, his theories laid the foundation for a purely secular understanding of nature.

The discovery of gravity also transformed the theological notion of falling. If Aristotelian natural philosophy linked man to the universe that

---

39. See Frank Durham and Robert D. Purrington, eds., *Some Truer Method: Reflections on the Heritage of Newton* (New York: Columbia University Press, 1990), esp. chap. 2 on Newton's method and style. The bond between scientific inquiry and theology appears in Newton's own understanding of God: "It is agreed that the supreme God necessarily exists, and by the same necessity he is always and everywhere. It follows that all of him is like himself: he is all eye, all ear, all brain, all arm, all force of sensing, of understanding, and of acting, but in a way not at all human, in a way not at all corporeal, in a way utterly unknown to us. As a blind man has no idea of colors, so we have no idea of the ways in which the most wise God senses and understands all things. He totally lacks any body and corporeal shape, and so he cannot be seen or heard or touched, nor ought he to be worshipped in the form of something corporeal. We have ideas of his attributes, but we certainly do not know what is the substance of any thing" ("General Scholium" of 1713, in *The Principia: Mathematical Principles of Natural Philosophy*, trans. I. Bernard Cohen and Anne Whitman (Berkeley: University of California Press, 1999), 942.

40. William Hogarth, frontispiece of a humorous pamphlet by John Clubbe entitled *Physiognomy* (1763).

3. William Hogarth, frontispiece to John Clubbe, *Physiognomy* (1763). Engraving.
(Photograph © Copyright the Trustees of The British Museum.)

surrounded him, in the Newtonian universe man, like all matter, was being pushed and pulled, a puppet of the principle of gravity. People no longer fell away from God into the sinfulness of the body; they fell toward an earth stripped of moral meaning. The modalities of falling were beautifully encapsulated in the *Metaphysics* when Aristotle defined accident as that which falls from substance. By the end of the eighteenth century, this theory of predication no longer seemed to account for things in nature. All that remained was a memory of the lost relation to substance contained in the experience of accident.

III. "I Know Not What"

Newton presided over London's influential Royal Society for the Advancement of Science for almost twenty-five years, lending his prestige to its focus on exploring the natural world. Formed with the goal of using new knowledge to advance the human condition, the society often claimed to employ the methods of careful observation advocated by Francis Bacon in its communal projects.[41] Investigations into the nature and accuracy of observation were of special interest to its members, but until Newton's mathematical proofs gained wide credibility, confidence in new knowledge depended—in the centuries-old tradition—largely on the personal authority of the investigator rather than on evidence drawn from experimentation.

John Locke became a fellow of the society in 1668 and later served as secretary. In the "Epistle to the Reader," which preceded his *Essay Concerning Human Understanding* (1690), he adopted the persona of an "Under-Labourer" whose task was to clear the ground for "Master Builders" like "the incomparable Mr. Newton," physicians like Robert Boyle and Thomas Sydenham, or mathematicians like Christiaan Huygens, by removing the speech and terms that inhibited the progress of natural philosophy.[42] His figure of the under-laborer reflected the practical world of

41. Bacon had modeled his program for reforming natural philosophy by capturing facts drawn from experience on the system he had used in his project to codify English law. His method reflected his interest in learning how things work and how that knowledge might be put to use. Although he did not employ advanced mathematics or experimentation, he advocated observations undertaken with the deliberate intention of using them to compile new and useful information, and his instructions for replicating what he had seen suggested that such data could be sorted into axioms upon which to develop theories capable of explaining observed facts. His *Novum Organon* (1620) consisted of a series of aphorisms intended to supersede the canon of Aristotelian logical texts that formed the initial subject matter at the university. Michael Witmore, *The Culture of Accidents: Unexpected Knowledges in Early Modern England* (Stanford: Stanford University Press, 2001), 3, identifies the link between accident and experiment in Bacon's work as an end to accident's long marginalization within philosophy: "[Accidents'] power to distract or estrange onlookers from habitual patterns of expectation and attention thus gave them unusual epistemological force in the skeptical context of the seventeenth century."

42. The direct stimulus for Locke's undertaking was a discussion that took place during a meeting of one of the study groups of the Royal Society in which he took an active

experience emphasized in the society's pragmatic ethos, but it also points to the purpose of his work, namely, challenging reliance on authority (whether embodied as argumentation in texts or the credibility of high-born persons) by identifying the methods that lie "under" the substantive acquisition of knowledge.[43]

Locke's *Essay* crystallized the way people were beginning to conceive of human experience. He inverted the traditional primacy of substance over accident. Regarding substance as a concept that lay outside the purview of scientific study, he gave new importance to accidental qualities—as empirically observable facts—and new value to accidental events—as sites of empirical analysis. In that sense, his work occupies a seminal position in the history of accident.

Although Locke imagined a philosophy that would limit the role of substance, his critique misrepresented the sophistication of Scholastic thought. The oversimplifications contained in this influential text dramatically affected the transmission of ideas about substance and accident. One casualty was awareness of the complex interrelation between accidental qualities and accidental events that had developed from Aristotelian theories. My attempt to convey what Locke thought at the time, rather than what later critics have discovered in his work, is not intended to suggest that his contemporaries did not question his ideas. Contemporary religious figures understood his theories as a new and dangerous form of skepticism. Bishop Berkeley, for example, accused him of "bantering with substance" while Dr. Stillingfleet, Bishop of Worces-

---

part. See G. A. J. Rogers, *Locke's Enlightenment: Aspects of the Origin, Nature and Impact of His Philosophy* (Hildesheim: Georg Olms Verlag, 1998). Locke's choice of the term "essay" in his title was significant, for the text emulates Montaigne's attempt to marshal evidence that could produce further understanding. References to Montaigne's work also appear in numerous images or metaphors. Locke's library contained a translation of the *Essays* as well as Pascal's *Pensées*. See Richard Ashcraft, "John Locke's Library: Portrait of an Intellectual," in *A Locke Miscellany*, ed. Jean S. Yolton (Bristol: Thoemmes, 1990), 232. According to Ashcraft, Montaigne's work was popular during the seventeenth century, and half of the libraries he surveyed contained copies. Although the composition of the *Essay* occupied almost two decades, Locke did not intend to produce a work of dogmatic certainty and took care to avoid the notion that his statements were more than probabilities.

43. Locke essentially created an English philosophical discipline (distinct from an amalgam of theology with natural philosophy). At the time, he was known to his contemporaries primarily as a physician, and in this process he drew on his background in medicine and chemistry as well as on practical politics and modes of reasoning that owed more to rhetorical and literary traditions than to the Scholastic dialectic. Comparing his earlier *Two Treatises of Government* with the *Essay* demonstrates a significant stylistic change. See J. R. Milton, "Locke at Oxford," in *Locke's Philosophy: Content and Context*, ed. G. A. J. Rogers, (Oxford: Clarendon Press, 1994), 29–47, esp. 42–47.

ter, said that Locke promoted atheism because he had "almost discarded substance out of the reasonable part of the world." [44]

Locke replied to Stillingfleet that Aristotle's method of certainty depended on a general principle by asserting that knowledge of any instance rests on prior knowledge of the generalization. As he insisted time and again, the word "substance" means nothing beyond "we know not what." [45] Although we may write and talk about substance, he argues, we cannot give it any precise content: substance is essentially a pointer. It provides a conceptual place marker in our attempts to understand the relationships among qualities within our sensory experience. To make any further assertion is merely to confuse words with things in the most egregious manner, feigning knowledge and "making a noise with Sounds." [46] Because the notion evades sensation and therefore reflection, it cannot be understood. Substance lies outside the world of experience.

The syntactical shift Locke made in the crucial phrase ("I know not what") renders the notion of substance inert. Like Descartes he presupposes an external self that knows, yet unlike Descartes he refuses to conjecture what lies beyond empirical observation. In other words, his position reflects the practices employed by the Royal Society. His abrasive inflection of substance as the "I know not what" emerges most clearly in the anecdote of the Indian philosopher:

44. Kenneth Winkler, "Lockean Logic," in *The Philosophy of John Locke: New Perspectives*, ed. Peter Anstey (London: Routledge, 2003), 167ff. See also John Leslie Mackie, "Berkeley's Criticism of 'Material Substance,'" in *Problems from Locke* (Oxford: Clarendon Press, 1976), 72.

45. According to Christopher Martin, ed., *The Philosophy of Thomas Aquinas* (London: Routledge, 1988), 63 and 72, Locke's notion that substance has no accidents—is "I know not what"—represents a degeneration of the Scholastic doctrine of what Aristotle or Aquinas believed. Aquinas, he asserts, would not agree with the empiricist position that when we see what a thing does, we know what it can do or has a tendency to do, because for him the effects of all causes can be obstructed. Empiricism, therefore, is not a more apt explanation of science than his. See also Pasnau, "Form, Substance, and Mechanism," 46ff., who points out that Descartes, Hobbes, and Locke mistook the Scholastic understanding of substantial form in two ways. Their first complaint of needless obscurity can be countered by recognizing that the Scholastics themselves stressed that they had no grasp of what substantial forms actually were and tended to presuppose them as useful only as part of a detailed physical account of the natural world. In their focus on the concrete, later thinkers saw no point in the schematic accounts of Scholastics. The second complaint, that it was unacceptable to treat forms as substances, involved a misconstruction. Because the Scholastics understood substantial form to wield real power over and above the purely corpuscular constitution of a body, they would not have explained form in mechanistic terms or seen form as capable of independent existence apart from matter (except for the rational soul).

46. John Locke, *An Essay Concerning Human Understanding*, ed. Peter H. Nidditch (Oxford: Clarendon Press, 1979), II.xiii.18. All further citations of Locke are from this edition.

They who first ran into the Notion of *Accidents*, as a sort of real Beings, that needed something to inhere in, were forced to find out the word *Substance*, to support them. Had the poor *Indian* Philosopher (who imagined that the Earth also wanted something to bear it up) but thought of this word *Substance*, he needed not to have been at the trouble to find an Elephant to support it, and a Tortoise to support his Elephant: The word *Substance* would have done it effectually. And he that enquired, might have taken it for as good an Answer from an *Indian* Philosopher, That *Substance*, without knowing what it is, is that which supports the Earth, as we take it for a sufficient Answer, and good Doctrine, from our *European* Philosophers, That *Substance* without knowing what it is, is that which supports *Accidents*. So that of *Substance*, we have no *Idea* of what it is, but only a confused, obscure one of what it does. (II.xiii.19)[47]

In imagining the origin of the Aristotelian notion of accident, he made a pun: the thinker both lights on the word accident and "runs" into its materiality, thereby "staging" an accident. Indeed, this passage illustrates Locke's technique of translating arguments based on analogy into narrative.[48] His adopted mythology inverted the notion of substance as that in which accident inheres and argued that these first thinkers needed to invent the word substance to support accidents. In a fascinating way, therefore, he reversed the earlier priority of substance over accident: in his world, people run into accidents as substance disappears.

The doctrine of substance, Locke asserted, is a key element in a belief system that cannot be verified by the senses.[49] Since the Indian philosopher

47. Locke repeated the anecdote of the Indian philosopher in II.xxiii.2: "And if he were demanded, what is it, that that Solidity and Extension inhere in, he would not be in a much better case, than the *Indian* before mentioned, who, saying that the World was supported by a great Elephant, was asked, what the Elephant rested on; to which his answer was, a great Tortoise: But being again pressed to know what gave support to the broad-back'd Tortoise, replied, something, he knew not what."

48. See John J. Richetti, *Philosophical Writing: Locke, Berkeley, Hume* (Cambridge, MA: Harvard University Press, 1983), 70.

49. Despite Locke's scientific background and his close personal relation to Newton and the work of the Royal Society, he favored the older corpuscular theory. Although this hypothesis could not be verified by the senses, he entertained it as the best available interpretative principle with which to posit a link between secondary qualities—which he defined as mutable aspects of things like color or taste that can be experienced through the senses yet not defined by language—and primary qualities like shape or size that can be defined by measurement or in numbers. Nevertheless, he clearly regarded corpuscularism as simply the best explanation available at the time. See I. Bernard Cohen, "A Guide to Newton's

cannot look beneath the world, he relies on scraps of received wisdom that allege that it is supported by an elephant, a tortoise, or by substance. Locke's translation of the Latin *"Inhaerentia and Substantia"* into English as *"Sticking on and Under-propping"* suggested the unstable basis on which the ontological system rests. His dismissive rhetoric dismantled the architecture of Scholastic thought. Substance lies beneath the world where it cannot be seen, rather than belonging—in the philosophical topography of the *Essay*—to the sunlit world of real experience.[50]

Acknowledging the limits of human understanding, in his introduction to the *Essay*, Locke explained the necessity of reorienting the focus of his philosophical inquiry. His analysis of the steps he followed is reminiscent of Descartes's struggle to free himself of preconceptions. For Locke, the primary impediment consisted of extending inquiries beyond the capacities of human reason and promoting disputes incapable of resolution (I.i.7). He used the metaphor of a sailor who can fathom the depths of the ocean only to the known limits of his line and determined to restrict his inquiries to subjects that lay within defined limits. In his topological understanding of philosophical issues, the "boundless Extent" of the ocean

---

Principia," in Newton, *The Principia*, 1–370, 54. James Hill and J. R. Milton, "The Epitome (*Abrégé*) of Locke's Essay," in Anstey, *The Philosophy of John Locke*, 25, counter the assertion that Newton influenced Locke's retreat from explaining the way bodies act on one another by corpuscular theory to the softer position that impulse is the only way we can *conceive* of that action. British and Continental contemporaries already had begun to mix up the ideas of Newton and Locke in 1690, the year the *Essay* first appeared in print, although in it Locke refers only to Newton's earlier achievements in mathematics. See Paul Schuurman, "Willem Jacob 's Gravesande's Philosophical Defence of Newtonian Physics: On the Various Uses of Locke," in Anstey, *The Philosophy of John Locke*, 45–46.

50. See especially Michael Ayers, "Substance and Mode," in *Locke: Epistemology and Ontology*, vol. 2 (London: Routledge, 1991), pt. 1. Ayers argues that Locke, following in the path of Descartes, Gassendi, Boyle, and others, reinterprets and redeploys the terminology and framework of Aristotelian logical and scientific theory, adapting it both to the ontology of mechanism and to his own antidogmatic epistemology. Pasnau, "Form, Substance, and Mechanism," 65–67, 68–69, also notes that by treating the corpuscular hypothesis as a departure from Scholastic understanding of the body, Locke presented substantial form as a species of obscurantism. Nevertheless, his theory of substance approached the Scholastic view that a thing is held together by a single form that is causally responsible for its intrinsic properties and nature. Locke accepted the idea that form gives rise to the accidental properties of an individual, giving it its unity at a time and identity over time, but he rejected the idea that abstract general accounts of species and genera can map the real differences between individual constitutions (forms). For Scholastics, the classification of individuals into species tracked the essences of things, but Locke took these distinctions to be haphazard and fallible groupings based on superficial resemblance and argued that it was impossible to distinguish merely accidental qualities from those belonging to the nature of a thing.

of being (that is, the deep metaphysical questions of substance) lies beyond human powers.

Although Locke repeatedly asserted that a man's knowledge cannot go beyond his experience, he questioned how experience could be translated into knowledge. Royal Society projects depended on precise experimental observation. This need stimulated interest in how received authority conditions understanding and affects the mind's capacity to draw valid conclusions, examine unfamiliar ideas fairly, or escape the conceptual abuses associated with careless or inadequate language. Boyle's *Rules for Occasional Meditation* (1665) had applied the popular seventeenth-century tradition of spiritual meditations to a method of closely observing even the most trivial things encountered in daily life, finding clues to basic truths in the universe while plowing a field, rowing a boat, picking a flower, or walking along a street. Although he did not explicitly generalize from this method to the procedures of science, he saw his method enabling ordinary individuals to do what natural philosophers did. The scope of discovery was limited only by the observer's understanding.[51]

Locke's chapters on probability and the degrees of assent countered the distinction between probable and certain knowledge that still operated in Descartes's thought. Although at this foundational moment he instinctively retained a mental construct (in the form of an analogy) as the vehicle of understanding, his discussion provided the best treatment of epistemic probability available in the eighteenth century. He maintained that the probable and the certain belong to a shared continuum and used a metaphor of distance to suggest how the judgment perceives different degrees of probability: what is merely probable appears dimmer than true knowledge. As he argued in book 2, "The Perception of the Mind, being most aptly explained by Words relating to the Sight, we shall best understand what is meant by *Clear*, and *Obscure* in our *Ideas*, by reflecting on what we call *Clear* and *Obscure* in the Objects of Sight" (II.xxix.2).[52]

51. J. Paul Hunter, *Before Novels: The Cultural Contexts of Eighteenth-Century English Fiction* (New York: W. W. Norton, 1990), 200–201, conjectures that the practice of meditative close observation helped create a new type of reader and writer.

52. Locke's canons for evaluating degrees of certainty were traditional and primarily drawn from earlier rhetorical theory and from theology. The religious controversy of the period distinguished between the testimony of human historians and divine testimony, which Locke argued "comes from one, who cannot err, and will not deceive" (IV.xviii.8). Within this schema, he accepted the equation of certain knowledge with the infallible or eternal (and thus essential or substantial) and probable knowledge with the fallible, uncertain (and thus accidental). Leibnitz criticized Locke for siding with Aristotle in basing prob-

In contrast to the misguided Indian philosopher, Locke posited a new type of thinker—"he that enquires." This model helps us understand how he envisioned the future practice of philosophy. His plainspoken "intelligent American," who would be nonplussed by the tautological nature of Scholastic thought (II.xiii.20), was a great demystifier who interrogated the meaning of words. According to the *Essay,* one of the three categories of human understanding was dialectic. Insisting on the fundamental impossibility of knowing substance and separating words from things turned this traditional art of rhetorical reasoning into a study of signs. For Locke, dialectic became *semeiotike.*[53] It is in the sense of semiotics and narrative that we must read his analysis of the way the mind acquires its initial ideas. He began with the established topos of the blank page:

> Let us then suppose the Mind to be, as we say, white Paper, void of all Characters, without any *Ideas;* How comes it to be furnished? Whence comes it by that vast store, which the busy and boundless Fancy of Man has painted on it, with an almost endless variety? Whence has it all the materials of Reason and Knowledge? To this I answer, in one word, From *Experience:* In that, all our Knowledge is founded; and from that it ultimately derives it self. Our Observation employ'd either about *external, sensible Objects; or about the internal Operations of our Minds, perceived and reflected on by our selves, is that, which supplies our Understandings with all the materials of thinking.* These two are the Fountains of Knowledge, from whence all the Ideas we have, or can naturally have, do spring. (II.i.2)

Locke was interested in the acquisition of experience and its composition into ideas. His reference to "characters" rather than words imprinted on the white page suggests that a level of sensory awareness precedes the formulation of concepts. Moreover, latent in his choice of this term are punning implications that humanize the idea. The formation of individual letters within some kind of group context implied that turning letters into words and words into ideas was analogous to the interaction of characters in a story or drama. In that rhetorical stance, to postulate an idea as

---

ability on authority rather than likelihood. See Douglas Lane Patey, *Probability and Literary Form: Philosophic Theory and Literary Practice in the Augustan Age* (Cambridge: Cambridge University Press, 1984), 23. For a discussion of Locke's theology see Ian Harris, "The Politics of Christianity," in Rogers, *Locke's Philosophy,* 197–215; and Victor Nuovo, "Locke's Christology as a Key to Understanding His Philosophy," in Anstey, *The Philosophy of John Locke,* 129–53.

53. See Hans Aarsleff, *From Locke to Saussure: Essays on the Study of Language and Intellectual History* (Minneapolis: University of Minnesota Press, 1982), 27–28.

void of character would be to see it liberated from conceptual constraints just as an individual "void of character" would exist outside an established social system. Such details show us how the *Essay* not only worked to shift thought away from ontology but also toyed with an emerging vocabulary for self-conception.

The seemingly arbitrary nature of what the mind retains and the way it relates impressions involves not only intentional procedures (such as those involved in Boyle's practice of occasional meditation), but also an endless series of what might be called mental accidents. Without entering into the complexities involved in Locke's theories regarding simple and complex ideas, it is important to note that he defended the receipt of sensory impressions as the first stage in acquiring new knowledge. In book 2, chapter 23, he recounts stages in the development of an idea that are adapted from Aristotle. First, the senses deliver perceptions of accidental qualities such as color or taste; second, the mind notes concurrent or coexisting appearances of such qualities; third, it combines qualities connected to one and the same thing as a single idea under a single name. Stages 1 and 2 consist of accidental events, but stage 3 involves deliberation and presumably intent. However, accidents condition the degree of control exercised at all stages.[54]

Locke's version of the conceptual process abandoned the anatomical imagery chosen by Montaigne and Descartes. He no longer envisioned sensations folded into the brain. They were "written" on the blank page and then ordered—syntactically and narratologically—by reflection.[55] His travel writings demonstrate how meticulously he observed the world around him, but he realized that what one person grasped out of the onslaught of sensory data would not be identical with what another individual perceived. Moreover, ideas were already present in the mind when it received new experiences, and some individuals possess stronger memories for retaining them. Over time, some ideas may fade completely, "leaving no more footsteps or remaining Characters of themselves, than

54. Locke embodied the function of memory in physical images (as a storehouse or a presence room as well the blank page), yet he denied the possibility that ideas can have a material location or even that they must be products of a physiological process. Ideas "are actually no where, but only there is an ability in the Mind, when it will, to revive them again; and as it were paint them anew on it self, though some with more, some with less difficulty; some more lively, and others more obscurely" (II.x.2).

55. Jules David Law, *The Rhetoric of Empiricism: Language and Perception from Locke to I. A. Richards* (Ithaca: Cornell University Press, 1993), 51–92, provides a subtle analysis of this process.

Shadows do flying over Fields of Corn; and the Mind is as void of them, as if they never had been there" (II.x.4). In Locke's narrative imagery, signs survive only when they are recorded on the mind (or printed on a page).[56] All these factors contribute to the endless variations that occur within the operations of the mind.

Associations of writing and reading within the metaphor of the blank page illustrate the degree to which Locke eroded earlier distinctions between external evidence (based on authority or doctrine) and the internal operations (the "natural light") of the mind. He inherited the metaphor of the mind as a page or "slate" from Bacon, who derived it from classical thought.[57] For Bacon, the mind's slate was written over by the accumulated notions of Scholasticism, and he employed the metaphor to describe an epistemological problem of "cloudy" perception.[58] In contrast Locke deployed the metaphor within a developmental narrative to describe the mind awaiting the writing of a variety of formative experiences.

Locke's choice of the literary image of the blank page acknowledged the increasing importance of reading and writing within the developing popular print culture. The evolving relationship with the reading public appears in his "Epistle to the Reader." Here he instructed his public how to adopt an active mode of reading, and his illustrative metaphors presented exercises in inference and analogy to help the reader perform the kind of reflective work that could internalize experience.[59] The tradition of the transformative activity of reading that we have already encountered in Augustine and Pascal might have seemed even more significant to him as the reading audience became larger and reading materials more diverse.[60] However, Locke could not be satisfied with the analogy

56. We meet echoes of this language in the reading of "moving accidents uncharacterd" in Wordsworth's "The Ruined Cottage" when the narrator learns to read the absent character's story in the traces of the past that chance to survive. See chap. 7.

57. For a painstaking history of Locke's metaphors of the mind, see William Walker, *Locke, Literary Criticism, and Philosophy* (Cambridge: Cambridge University Press, 1994), chap. 2, "Substance, Space, Labor and Property."

58. Francis Bacon, *The New Organon*, ed. Lisa Jardine and Michael Silverthorne (Cambridge: Cambridge University Press, 2000), 18, from the "Plan of the Work."

59. Paul de Man, "The Epistemology of Metaphor," *Critical Inquiry* (Autumn 1978): 13–30, reprinted in *On Metaphor*, ed. Sheldon Sacks (Chicago: University of Chicago Press, 1979); and Cathy Caruth, *Empirical Truths and Critical Fictions: Locke, Wordsworth, Kant, Freud* (Baltimore: Johns Hopkins University Press, 1991).

60. Patey, *Probability and Literary Form*, 170–72. In England, particularly after the mid-seventeenth century, the essay form indicated a choice of audience and hence a rhetorical pose rather than strictly a philosophic commitment. Considerations of a genteel and general audience governed its argumentative procedures. Essays of the period redirected

of the blank page, because it implied location. For him, the mind was not a place, but something that existed in an active sense. Therefore, in the "Epistle," his reference to thought as a movement or a path reflected his goal of tracing the mind's ascent from its original imprints to complex mental representations.

Comparing ideas allows the mind to achieve some degree of certainty. But Locke recognized that variations in experience affect the formation of complex ideas just as fundamental (or in some sense substantive) ideas reflect accidental inferences. By identifying deliberation as the third stage in the development of an idea, he had oversimplified this problem. Inference could not produce certainty. It might even confuse complex ideas with simple ones. Therefore, the kind of accidental events that conditioned the receipt of experiences could also affect the processing of an individual's stock of ideas.

We are now in a position to see why the opening paragraph of the "Epistle" invokes a hunter who takes pleasure in hawking after truth. "Every step the mind takes in its Progress towards Knowledge, makes some Discovery," Locke wrote, "which is not only new, but the best too, for the time at least" (p. 6.15). The spatial and temporal image of hawking suggested that "he who inquires" possesses a means to capitalize on unexpected conceptual possibilities and allow previously unsuspected data to enter the mind and be processed. The metaphor of "hawking and hunting" not only emphasized the active, aggressive reading his text required; it offered a figure that stood for the active and aggressive inquiry he believed was necessary in order to achieve philosophical understanding. By accentuating the role of discovery in the formation of new knowledge, he further privileged accidents over what he considered to be a barren notion of substance.

Locke associated the "natural light" that illuminated the mind with the faculty of sight. Therefore, he compared the mental process that enabled the seeker for knowledge to form a basis for understanding with the act of seeing—a sensation whose pleasures must be both directly experienced and concrete: "For the Understanding, like the Eye, judging of

---

applications of rhetoric from a vulgar audience to a learned one and widened the literary devices that were employed. During the following century, the development of the novel led to various experiments designed to establish an appropriate relationship between author and audience as well as to teach the practice of reading the new genre. See Clifford Siskin, *The Work of Writing: Literature and Social Change in Britain, 1700–1830* (Baltimore: Johns Hopkins University Press, 1998), esp. pt. 3, pp. 155–90, "Novelism: Literature in the History of Writing."

Objects, only by its own Sight, cannot but be pleased with what it discovers, having less regret for what has scaped it, because it is unknown. Thus he who has raised himself above the Alms-Basket, and not content to live lazily on scraps of begg'd Opinions, sets his own Thoughts on work, to find and follow Truth, will (whatever he lights on) not miss the Hunter's Satisfactions; every moment of his Pursuit, will reward his Pains with some Delight; and he will have Reason to think his time not ill spent, even when he cannot much boast of any great Acquisition" (p. 6.16-24). In this tissue of metaphor, Locke distinguished between Scholastic and empirical thought as a difference between indolence and labor. His new philosopher, who hunted with a limitless desire to see the world, superseded the blind Scholastic, who lazily relied on scraps of Aristotelian thought. In this sense, sensation and reflection, a temporal process that partakes of the mutable aspects of accident, now supported or "stood under" his notion of the understanding.

Although Locke wanted to replace inelastic verbal formulations with active inquiry, he recognized that human experience could not be separated into moments of saying versus moments of seeing. By implication people cannot process or communicate an experience until they formulate it in language: we say what we see.[61] This argument formalized Pascal's intuition about the fluidity of words as signs. Locke asserted that only the creator of a particular word—an Adam naming an experience like jealousy, inferred from the look on someone's face—possessed the connection between the word and his concept. Interpreting the word in a fresh context already involved potential ambiguities. He perceived that a specific chain of prior experiences conditioned an individual's understanding of a term. Moreover, interpretation of that term affected the reception of subsequent terms and the mode of reflecting upon any fresh experiences.[62] Under these circumstances, language appeared to him as a convenience invented and adopted by isolated individuals in their at-

---

61. Law, *The Rhetoric of Empiricism*, 55–56.

62. Locke applied this objection to deride the Roman Catholic belief in transubstantiation: "How is he prepared easily to swallow, not only against all Probability, but even the clear Evidence of his Senses, the Doctrine of Transubstantiation? This Principle has such influence on his Mind that he will take that to be Flesh, which he sees to be Bread" (IV. xx.10). The Catholic believer who interprets the accidents of the bread in terms of Scholastic notions of substance has learned to value authority over his own experience. Accidents of birth and education have conditioned a doctrinal association with the Eucharistic symbol that cannot be validated in terms of either the logic of probability or direct evidence.

tempt to deal with the variety of minds and the inexhaustible particularity of experiences that exist in the world.[63]

Locke's theory of how the mind acquires understanding brings together the double signification of accident as both quality and event that I separated in the earlier discussion of Aristotle. Interpretation of ambiguous experiences had become a substantive component of the creation of knowledge. In other words, in the formation of concepts, raw materials largely composed of accidental qualities, replaced the Aristotelian notion of enduring and commonly recognizable realities. In addition, Locke asserted that accidents of perception manipulated the concepts available for interpretation. As a result, the process of acquiring understanding was necessarily vulnerable to the impact of accidental events.

Although Locke did not attempt to create the kind of comprehensive system of thought that was the goal of Descartes's philosophy, his work altered the Aristotelian classification of substance and accident that had dominated Western thought for so many centuries. Yet this result cannot be credited to Locke alone. It reflects the broad adoption of the strategy of closely observing mutable phenomena in order to discover the secrets of the natural world. This experiential focus viewed accidental qualities as primary sites of new knowledge, reversing their former subservience to substance and making them essential elements in the construction of scientific hypotheses or proofs. At the same time, the realization that even increasingly sophisticated methods of exploration were limited by the nature of human understanding forced an investigation of mental processes. The result shifted the emphasis of the accidental event as an external or physical occurrence to a cerebral one. By absorbing both of these developments into a way of formulating experience as mental images and signs, Locke accomplished more than clearing the ground for further scientific work; he provided the basis for shifting the study of the human mind into the discipline of psychology and the category of literature.

63. Richetti, *Philosophical Writing,* esp. 99–101.

CHAPTER FIVE

Novel Accidents: Self-Determining Accidents in Print Culture

I. Accidental Associations

Locke referred to the self in two different ways. "Man" corresponded to what he understood to be the biological self, whereas "person" corresponded to a virtual self formed through experience. He conceived of persons as "intelligent Agents capable of a Law, and Happiness and Misery" (II.xxvii.26), formed, in other words, through their experiences of pleasure and pain. Memories and the capacity to reflect upon actions that have been performed offered evidence of sameness over the course of a lifetime.[1] This consciousness engendered a sense of personal identity. Although Locke used his terms inconsistently, his idea of person was innovative. Because what a person remembers can be observed and examined and actions or speeches preserved in memory leave traces in the natural world, his concept created a self that could be analyzed by rational methods.[2]

1. Hobbes influenced Locke's relational view of personal identity by introducing the idea that the organizational structure of a thing rather than its stuff can serve as a criterion of identity. He used the image of a river, which is understood to be the same river even when the water in it flows past. In the same way, a man whose actions and thoughts proceed all from the same beginning of motion will be the same. The importance of this notion was that he used consciousness rather than substance to unite and mark the self, and through Locke it passed into modern personal identity theory. See Robert Pasnau, "Form, Substance, and Mechanism," *Philosophical Review* 113, no. 1 (January 2004): 11.

2. John Yolton, *The Two Intellectual Worlds of John Locke: Man, Person, and Spirits in the "Essay"* (Ithaca: Cornell University Press, 2004), 27–28, notes that for Locke the properties of any individual man could reveal some of the properties of the class of men, but he did not believe human knowledge reached to real essences because they did not show up in qualities that could be observed. Possessing knowledge of essence would be like the knowledge possessed by angels or God. It would change our idea of man, he believed, for even the idea

For Locke, mastery of the self through the exercise of reason was the foundation of individual liberty and knowledge, a perspective that recalls the function of the spiritual exercise. But by internalizing awareness of the past and consciousness of the person's sameness across time as operations of the mind, he shifted the way in which the practice of self-improvement regarded accidental qualities. Rather than denying changeable aspects of behavior in order to realize a substantive moral good, complete submission to divine will, or even the elimination of a purely secular habit, he postulated that the person is constructed through the process of forming accidental associations. By affecting mental perceptions and judgments, accidental events had the power to propel far-reaching shifts in consciousness.

What made Locke's *Essay* paradigmatic was his integration of ethics with new knowledge about the function of the brain. Cartesian mechanists had never been able to agree on the location of the soul as the site of the mental powers that distinguished the human being. The first scientist to posit that the soul was limited to the brain was Thomas Willis, Locke's tutor at Oxford.[3] The persuasive mixture of observation and hypothesis contained in his books stimulated research into how the brain exercised control over the body. No topic in physiology was more important than determining how the nerves could carry out this expanded range of brain functions. Physiologists lacked the tools to prove whether or not the nerves were hollow, and thus able to carry animal spirits, and they did not have any other way to explain the brain's control until the discovery of electricity in the eighteenth century. Nevertheless, their research efforts revolutionized knowledge concerning the brain. Even more important for the history of accident, this work stimulated greater awareness that sensibility—that is, sensations and physiological responses newly understood as intimately bound to mental processes of inference and judgment—had the power to shape knowledge.

---

of a particular, individual man "would be as far different from what it now is, as is his, who knows all the Springs and Wheels, and other contrivances within, of the famous Clock at Strasburg, from that which a gazing Country man has of it, who barely sees the motion of the Hand, and hears the Clock strike, and observes only some of the outward appearances" (III.vi.9).

3. Willis's *Pathology of the Brain* and *Anatomy of the Brain* were published in their English translations in 1681. The works were written during the 1660s and 1670s. George S. Rousseau, *Nervous Acts: Essays on Literature, Culture and Sensibility* (London: Palgrave, 2004), 164–68. While recognizing that it would have been natural for Willis to have exerted an influence on Locke's formative years, Rousseau cautions against making a direct cause-and-effect link between their ideas.

Locke's theory about the process of controlled self-formation capitalized on this new interest in sensibility, but it did not account for the lasting impact of chance experiences. To address this problem, he added a new chapter, "On the Association of Ideas," to the fourth edition of the *Essay*, published in 1700.[4] In it, he conceptualized how chance experiences affected the formation of the mind. Perplexed by the fact that even fair-minded people can be guilty of irrational beliefs that they cannot set aside, he began by introducing an observation concerning the strange beliefs of other men:

> Some of our *Ideas* have a natural Correspondence and Connexion one with another: It is the Office and Excellency of our Reason to trace these, and hold them together in that Union and Correspondence which is founded in their peculiar Beings. Besides this there is another Connexion of *Ideas* wholly owing to Chance or Custom; Ideas that in themselves are not at all of kin, come to be so united in some Mens Minds, that 'tis very hard to separate them, they always keep in company, and the one no sooner at any time comes into the Understanding but its Associate appears with it; and if they are more than two which are thus united, the whole gang always inseparable shew themselves together. (II.xxxiii.5)

Chance associations enter the understanding, bringing a whole gang of unnatural connections into the mind. Uninvited, hidden in the form of new sensations, the invasive and irrational associations can take the mind hostage, posing a powerful threat to the understanding, and their malevolent strength is expressed in the individual's extravagant speech or actions. Locke called these ideas "Prejudice," a "Disease," or "Madness."[5]

---

4. The term "association" gave rise to a version of empiricism known as "associationism," whose principal exponent was David Hartley. See his *Observations on Man, His Frame, His Duty and His Expectations* (London, 1749; facsimile, Delmar, NY: Scholars' Facsimiles and Reprints, 1976); and Howard C. Warren, *A History of Association Psychology from Hartley to Lewes* (New York: Charles Scribner, 1921).

5. Locke's training as a physician and his concern with rhetoric made theories of reading probable signs as an integral part of the process of diagnosis (transmitted through Hippocrates, Galen, and Sextus Empiricus) a natural component of his attempt to interpret irrational behaviors. In the diagnostic process, symptoms that were perceptible to laymen could be converted by trained physicians into signs that revealed hidden medical causes, and these signs of bodily illness were termed accidents. The pattern of reasoning from evident effects to invisible causes through the medium of indicator signs passed from the "low" science of medicine into rhetoric, where it became associated with the interpretation of passions or states of mind visible in facial expressions. Ultimately this tradition laid the groundwork for eighteenth-century physico-theology, in which physicians continued to see

As a trained physician, he proposed to trace them back to their accidental origins and thereby effect a cure.

Accidental connections conflate two temporally distinct ideas, making new experiences signify in relation to an original impression as though chaining them into a press gang. Locke retained a Cartesian interpretation of memory to explain habits of thinking. Chance experiences trigger "Trains of Motion in the Animal Spirits" that continue smoothly in the way they began. By wearing down a smooth path, repetition eventually makes the accidental combination of ideas appear "natural" (II.xxxiii.6).

To demonstrate that many of the antipathies people consider "natural" were the accidental results of "early Impressions," Locke compared the example of a grown man who eats too much honey and afterward cannot bear the idea of it with that of a man who "over dosed" on honey as a child. The second man experiences the same "Dislike and Sickness, and Vomiting" but because he has forgotten the cause, he mistakenly assumes his response is natural rather than the result of the initial "over dose."

In a prescient observation that anticipated the eighteenth-century interest in self-formation through events during childhood, he argued that children can be marked in ways that cannot easily be erased. Because they are so susceptible to lasting impressions, parents and tutors must take more care to prevent accidental connections from forming prejudices (II.xxxiii.8). However, the potentially damaging impact of accidental association is not restricted to childhood impressions. Even in adults, accidents had the power to hurt both body and mind: "A Man has suffered Pain or Sickness in any Place, he saw his Friend die in such a Room; though these have in Nature nothing to do with one another, yet when the *Idea* of the Place occurs to his Mind, it brings (the Impression being once made) that of the Pain and Displeasure with it, he confounds them

---

the effects of the soul on the body and of the body on the soul. Thus, transitory accidental qualities formed the basis for the theory of probable signs. Rhetoricians (and jurists) had classified probable signs by degrees of corroborative certainty according to explicit rules as infallible, certain, or essential versus fallible, probable, or accidental. These rules took account of circumstances that might modify the import of clear signs. Circumstances that modified or altered expectations of natural phenomena became signs in their own right. Thus, in the sense that circumstances were mutable properties that signified essential ones (such as an action's true moral or legal character), they also became accidents. By extension, the notion that a trained physician can interpret physical signs with more skill than a layman can be applied to the reading and writing of texts: an experienced reader possesses greater skill in interpreting the arbitrary signification of words, and an experienced writer can more effectively control the impact of the words used to convey ideas.

in his Mind, and can as little bear the one as the other" (II.xxxiii.12). Only the passage of time can dissipate such associations. For example, the death of a child torments its mother and no rational consolations can ease her pain: "Till time has by disuse separated the sense of that Enjoyment and its loss from the *Idea* of the Child returning to her Memory, all Representations, though never so reasonable, are in vain" (II.xxxiii.13).

These examples present the afterlife of a shocking set of impressions, yet the behavior they represent is neither unreasonable nor improbable, so how should the reader distinguish between an impression that can be used in a formative way and a potentially damaging one? In other words, what is the place of accident, violence, and the irrational within Locke's thought? He responded that when accidental associations created hurt or prejudice, as in the fanatical opposition of one belief to another, he objected to them. The separation between religion and civil law is essential, he argued, because religious truth, like substance, cannot be known. In the anecdote of the Indian philosopher, he had relegated questions linked to substance to the darkness beneath the earth because he associated them with darkness of the mind and sectarian strife. In a sense, his chapter on the association of ideas represented a kind of personal history haunted by past experience that gave his understanding of substance a historical meaning that he expressed in his interpretation of human nature. Like substance, man's essence is the "I know not what." Thus, we can see the *Essay*'s interest in human understanding shifting from ontology toward a tentative exploration of individual psychology.

Groping toward a new model of selfhood in which antisocial aspects of the self might be explained and defused as accidental traits and thus modified by education or controlled by reason, Locke turned away from acknowledging the full power of the accidental. However, he recognized that certain aspects of human nature must be retrained in order to achieve the ordered ideal of the Enlightenment. What he created was a prototherapeutic technique in which accidents signaled experiences—irrational, passionate, moving—whose literary potential awaited exploration in the rise of the novel.

II. A Literal Man

The eighteenth-century explosion of print culture fostered communication of new knowledge and new insight to a broader range of readers. Authors incorporated philosophical theories into essays on social issues, such as Locke's *Some Thoughts Concerning Education* and *Two Treatises of*

Government or his former pupil Shaftesbury's *Characteristics of Men, Manners, Opinion, Times.* Later, hybrid forms, such as Pope's overtly philosophical *Essay on Man,* appeared alongside metaphysical musings, such as Johnson's *Rasselas,* or moralized interpretations of natural catastrophes, such as Defoe's *The Storm.* All of these works were concerned with self-improvement or self-formation. In that sense, they continued the tradition of the spiritual exercise in an increasingly secular guise, whose reductive manifestation in our own time is the self-help manual. Accident rose to prominence as a site of self-transformation, and the mutable nature of accidental qualities responded to the new sense that aspects of personal identity could shift over time. This spread and deepening of accident appears clearly in the sensibilities evinced by the eponymous heroes of *Robinson Crusoe, Tom Jones,* and *Tristram Shandy,* representatives of three distinctly different modes of rendering the interaction between accidental events and accidental qualities within the genre that came to be called the novel.[6]

Print culture reflected one aspect of an unprecedented commercialization of society.[7] Writing became a product, and professional authorship became an economic reality that functioned outside the traditional system

6. The term expresses the period's uncertainty about categorical boundaries. Thus Defoe described his work as a "Allegorick History" ("Preface to Volume III of Robinson Crusoe," in *The Life and Strange Adventures of Robinson Crusoe,* ed. Michael Shinagel [New York: Norton, 1975], 240), while Fielding famously termed *Joseph Andrews* (1742) a "comic Epic-Poem in Prose," in *Joseph Andrews,* ed. Martin C. Battestin (Middletown: Wesleyan University Press, 1967), 4. J. A. Downie, "The Making of the English Novel," *Eighteenth-Century Fiction* 9, no 3 (1997): 249–66; and Michael Seidel, "The Man Who Came to Dinner: Ian Watt and the Theory of Formal Realism," *Eighteenth-Century Fiction* 12, nos. 2–3 (2000): 193–212, provide summaries of competing arguments about the vexed origin of the novel that take into account the classic theories of Ian Watt, Michael McKeon, J. Paul Hunter, John Richetti, and others. I have avoided engaging these questions of generic origin in order to concentrate on transhistorical mutations of the concept of accident apart from issues involved in the shifting formats in which our examples appear.

7. During the formative first half of the century, measures of the book business, such as the number of booksellers or the number of titles published, show a stagnant or even depressed economy. Alvin Kernan, *Samuel Johnson and the Impact of Print* (Princeton: Princeton University Press, 1987), 61, notes that the number of London booksellers declined from 151 to 72 between 1735 and 1763 and that 8,836 titles were printed during the decade ending 1710 compared to 7,605 in the decade ending 1750. What prospered was the new periodical press, and the emerging novel took advantage of this mode of publication. Readers were offered pamphlets and journals, but novels also were published in separate sections that could be purchased more cheaply than a bound volume. Lower prices and the possibility of borrowing books from the new innovation of lending libraries made reading affordable and democratic. The expanded readership included women as well as less affluent or less educated readers.

of patronage. An author's subservience to the patron, however, was replaced by subservience to the reading public. In contrast to the patron, whose tastes were known, or a theater audience, whose responses were vocal and often physical, this new reading public represented a challenge because it was both unfamiliar and abstract. To better understand public taste, an author like Daniel Defoe, who needed to sell his work in order to survive, experimented with elements drawn from a range of earlier forms, including journalism, travel narratives, allegory, autobiography, and romance—forms in which accidents were used to stimulate curiosity and provide amusement.

One of the stated functions of the new journalism was to help readers understand human behavior—their own and that of others. People extended their understanding of their relationships to random events as well as to unexpected or ambiguous actions by comparing a vast range of literary accidents with events in their own lives.[8] They could read and reflect on stories in which characters were hit by the shock of experience. By following the narrative implications of mishaps or coincidences under the guidance of an author, people became more conscious of self-determining acts. And authors were quick to grasp the pedagogical implications of this new relationship to their readers.

Best-selling novels of the period satisfied a hunger on the part of readers for experiences through which to recognize and imagine themselves within the world. Learning to read accidents more subtly and precisely taught them how fictional heroes and heroines succeeded within the new culture of risk and reward. Authors exploited the pedagogical potential of forming a rapport with their readers. The novels of Defoe, Henry Fielding, and Laurence Sterne allow us to trace the ways in which the evolution of the pedagogical function of the early novel fostered the development of individual consciousness through the vicarious pleasure of reading. Defoe initiated this development under the strong influence of both probability theory and empirical projects undertaken by the Royal Society. In *Tom Jones,* Fielding used contingent events to foster moral judgments of character, while in *Tristram Shandy,* Sterne's implied critique of Locke's association of ideas introduced the reading public to a new level of subjective awareness.

---

8. J. Paul Hunter, *Before Novels: The Cultural Contexts of Eighteenth-Century English Fiction* (New York: W. W. Norton, 1990), discusses the new sense of place in chap. 5 and the role of journalism in chaps. 6 and 7.

Throughout the period spanned by these three novels, identity was becoming less reliable as it mutated from earlier theories of self as an elusive yet enduring substance toward the irresistible Lockean model of a self determined by remembered experiences. In interesting ways, the shift away from underlying substance went hand in hand with the rise of print capitalism. For example, a flurry of monetary experiments, including the development of a paper economy, became aligned with notions of imposture and forgery. What had seemed economically solid suddenly inhered only in paper-thin surfaces under conditions described in immaterial terms of smoke, clouds, vapors, apparitions, wind, and moonshine. Within this floating world, people lost their bearings.[9]

In *The Life and Strange Surprising Adventures of Robinson Crusoe* (1719), Defoe developed a complete analysis of the causes and effects implicit in the accident of a shipwreck.[10] He used the first person to replicate a factual account, making Crusoe keep a precise record of his voyage. At "7 Degrees 22 Min. Northern Latitude," a storm drives his ship from its course, and after twelve days and nights, a second storm causes it to founder. Only Crusoe survives the passage from sea to the shore (35). His reflections on his survival record a distinctive awareness of the theories of probability:

9. See Dror Wahrman's provocative study *The Making of the Modern Self: Identity and Culture in Eighteenth-Century England* (New Haven: Yale University Press, 2004).

10. The immediate precursor to the storm in *Robinson Crusoe* was Defoe's collection of first-person accounts by survivors of a storm that struck southern England in November 1703, which he published in 1704 as *The Storm; or, A Collection of the most Remarkable Casualties and Disasters which happen'd in the Late Dreadful Tempest, Both by Sea and Land*. His introduction positioned that work as a superior example of the genre of history (which he believed had been debased by romantic or confabulated storytelling) as well as that of the sermon (which he argued required less devotion to truth because it affected a much more limited audience than a printed book). To validate the truthfulness of his work, he deliberately set out to emulate methods used by members of the Royal Society, who relied on eyewitness accounts for additional information to support their own investigations. Royal Society informants were required to meet standards of observation and to record only what they had seen with their own eyes, including even details that initially might be judged insignificant but could prove important upon later consideration. Defoe supplemented the information he gathered himself with excerpts from the society's *Philosophical Transactions*. See Ilse Vickers, *Defoe and the New Sciences* (Cambridge: Cambridge University Press, 1996), 65–67. His texts included a memorandum by the Dutch zoologist Anthony van Leeuwenhoek, whose first reaction to the storm was to conduct experiments to determine whether the water sprayed against his windows came from the sea or the rain. Defoe's insistence on accuracy, the reliability of his sources, and his self-presentation as an impartial editor, "the Age's Humble Servant," make *The Storm* a central text in the development of objective journalism.

Well, you are in a desolate Condition 'tis true, but pray remember, Where are the rest of you? Did not you come Eleven of you into the Boat, where are the Ten? Why were not they sav'd and you lost? Why were you singled out? Is it better to be here or there, and then I pointed to the Sea? All Evils are to be consider'd with the Good that is in them, and with what worse attends them.

Then it occurr'd to me again, how well I was furnish'd for my Subsistence, and what would have been my Case if it had not happen'd. *Which was an Hundred Thousand to one,* that the Ship floated from the Place where she first struck and was driven so near to the Shore that I had time to get all these Things out of her? (51)

Crusoe takes his presence on the island to be a statistical improbability—and thus an accident in the Aristotelian sense of the unusual or unexpected event—and calculates the odds of his survival. This detail emphasizes the fact that the structure of this tale, which ostensibly transforms an atheist into a believer in God's providence, enacts Pascal's argument that in uncertain circumstances, religious belief is worth the wager.

Defoe used information from his earlier writings to color Crusoe's background. As a tradesman as well as an author, he participated fully in the rampant speculation characteristic of his period. His various business ventures resulted in several stays in debtor's prison, and his writing reflects his awareness of the economic changes taking place at the time. One of the projects he envisioned was a type of comprehensive disaster insurance typically associated with gambling.[11] In fact, he noted that London insurance offices, where people could purchase policies on the lives of celebrities, the outcome of sensational trials, or the success of battles, attracted the same clientele as gambling dens.[12]

11. "All the Contingencies of Life might be fenc'd against by this Method (as Fire is already) as Thieves, Floods by Land, Storms by Sea, Losses of all Sorts, and Death it self, in a manner, by making it up to the Survivor." Defoe, *An Essay on Projects* (London, 1697), in *Social Reform*, vol. 8 of *Political and Economic Writings of Daniel Defoe*, ed. W. R. Owens and P. N. Furbank (London: Pickering and Chatto, 2000), 73.

12. Lorraine Daston, *Classical Probability in the Enlightenment* (Princeton: Princeton University Press, 1988), 165. By the first half of the eighteenth century, an increased understanding of mathematical probability and more widespread collection of data, such as mortality statistics, had begun to affect the interpretation of accidents as manifestations of God's will, but the period also saw the rise of professional insurance companies like Lloyd's of London. See also Mary Poovey, *History of the Modern Fact* (Chicago: University of Chicago Press, 1998). Defoe based his own scheme on mortality data (although he adjusted the figures in accord with his hopes for robust clients), but he did not take account of age in

Another form of gambling, the royal lottery, offered the urban poor a rare monthly chance to improve their circumstances. In 1695 Defoe had become the lottery's manager-trustee and thus was able to observe the impact of pandemic gambling on the poor as well as on the middle class, for whom the emergence of lottery millionaires represented an alarming social imbalance. Gambling became associated with loss of self-control and detachment from the laws of cause and effect and was disparaged as an indulgence befitting a reprehensible aristocracy. In fact, at the beginning of the novel, when Crusoe proposes to enter the African slave trade, his father warns him that only men of desperate or superior fortunes should go abroad in search of adventures. In 1712 Defoe had written *An Essay on the South-Sea Trade,* in which he advocated England's South Sea Company as a way to relieve government debt and as a means to gain a useful foothold in American trade.[13] Spurred by the dream of accessing the riches of the New World, the slave trade and the stock markets that developed in both England and France fueled the greed of speculators.[14] Involvement in the slave trade led to Crusoe's accident, which reduced his property to whatever he was able to obtain by hard work and skill, the accidental qualities that enabled him to survive on the island.

In *Two Treatises of Government,* published in 1689, only two months before he published the *Essay Concerning Human Understanding,* Locke argued

---

determining entrance fees. Thus, despite his awareness of data collection, he seems to have shared the popular distrust of basing risk assessment on mathematical calculations.

13. The Scotsman John Law received authorization from the French regent to open the Banque Générale in Paris in 1716. Its functions were to offer shares and issue banknotes serving as currency. The shares were secured by land, and to discourage shareholders from redeeming them too quickly, Law declared substantial dividends. In 1717, when the holder of the Louisiana concession returned it as payment for an immense fine, Law used this acquisition to support a second stock offering designed to exploit the colony through his newly formed Compagnie d'Occident. The English South Sea Company also issued securities backed by a guaranteed interest payment from the government and a monopoly on the slave trade, acquired in the Peace of Utrecht in 1714.

14. In 1720, one year after the publication of *Robinson Crusoe,* frenzied speculation drove up the price of stock in the South Sea Company from 175 pounds at the end of February to over 1,000 pounds at the end of June. Middle-class investors bought on credit or margin, but the bubble burst, and the stock fell to 135 pounds by the end of September. In 1721, William Hogarth created "an Emblematical Print on the South Sea Scene" that recorded the circumstances of the first stock market crash as a flimsy merry-go-round that whirled speculators in the air. A broken wheel of fortune lay on the ground; the rise and fall of commercial credit had replaced Fortuna's wheel. See also Gary Hentzel, "'An Itch of Gaming': The South Sea Bubble and the Novels of Daniel Defoe," *Eighteenth-Century Life* 17, no. 1 (February 1993): 32–45.

that "every Man has a Property in his own Person." As he would argue later in his analysis of individual consciousness, a person's awareness of acts that have been (or are being) performed confers a self-determination. Possession of this created personal identity amounts to ownership over its intellectual resources, power of action, and value in society.[15] According to the *Two Treatises,* man in the state of nature possesses the freedom to determine his own actions as well as to hold possessions within the bounds of the law of nature. Clearly, Crusoe's slave-trading ambitions contravened this notion of self-possession, but Locke's text implies a link between the right to master land or other possessions and the right over one's own person. To earn this right, he suggests, man must become a rational creature—a person possessing moral consciousness.[16] In that sense, the economic motifs that dominate Crusoe's narrative intersect with the tradition of the spiritual exercise.

Like anyone engaged in a survival struggle, when Crusoe is cast away from the speculative world of capitalism, he becomes preoccupied by necessities. Yet even as the island removes him from the world of commodities and the uncertainties of trade, it gives him the raw materials for prosperity, and Defoe endows his character with relentlessly practical responses colored by his own understanding of contemporary scientific inquiry.[17] What an urban Englishman can buy, Crusoe will make through his reason and labor, but before he acquires such luxuries as his famous folding umbrella, his tobacco pipe, or his country house, his pragmatic outlook encourages him to anticipate and respond to the numerous accidents that await him. "I consider'd from the beginning," he writes, "how

15. John Locke, *Two Treatises of Government,* ed. Peter Laslett (Cambridge: Cambridge University Press, 1960), II.120.

16. Yolton, *The Two Intellectual Worlds of John Locke,* 35.

17. Crusoe's island experience begins in September 1659, the year before the foundation of the Royal Society, and several incidents parallel activities of the society's fellows. For example, on 25 March 1663, a Dr. Wilkins presented an account of the way to plant corn. On March 1, 1665, John Evelyn read a history of bread making and Boyle's gardener provided an account of sowing potatoes (Vickers, *Defoe and the New Sciences,* 110). The language of experiment characterizes Crusoe's meticulous observations and experimental trials that eventually enabled him to replicate on his island the comforts of an aristocratic lifestyle. Defoe appears to be drawing on his earlier plan to produce a history of trade and at various points in the account has Crusoe echo Boyle's comment when he appealed for the creation of such a history in his *Usefulness of Experimental Natural Philosophy* (1663–71): necessity is the mother of invention. For example, "Time and Necessity made me a compleat natural Mechanick soon after" (53) or "I improv'd my self in this time in all the mechanick Exercises which my Necessities put me upon applying my self to" (105).

I would provide for the Accidents that might happen, and for the time that was to come" (51–52).

His language recalls the rhetoric of the spiritual exercise, and insofar as his shipwreck has stripped him of society as well as comforts, it creates a scene appropriate for spiritual growth. Although the chief accident of the shipwreck drives him from his intended destination and enforces upon him a lifestyle suited to contemplation, the plot of the story involves accidents that test his understanding of his circumstances and his manner of living. As a model of the Lockean person, he must compare his past with his present. In one of the central and most interpreted of these accidents, he discovers some stalks of English barley growing near his camp:

> It is impossible to express the Astonishment and Confusion of my Thoughts on this Occasion; I had hitherto acted upon no religious Foundation at all, indeed I had very few Notions of Religion in my Head, or had entertain'd any Sense of any Thing that had befallen me, otherwise than as a Chance, or, as we lightly say, what pleases God; without so much as inquiring into the End of Providence in these Things, or his Order in governing Events in the World: But after I saw Barley grow there, in a Climate which I know was not proper for Corn, and especially that I knew not how it came there, it startl'd me strangely, and I began to suggest, that God had miraculously caus'd this Grain to grow without any Help of Seed sown, and that it was directed purely for my Sustenance, on that wild, miserable Place. (63)

His hypothesis that the grain may be a sign of God's providence wavers when he remembers that he had shaken out a bag of chicken feed in that place. Later the incident triggers a more complex understanding of accident in relation to his own actions: "tho' I ought to have been as thankful for so strange and unforseen Providence, as if it had been miraculous; for it was really the Work of Providence as to me, that should order or appoint, that 10 or 12 Grains of Corn should remain unspoil'd . . . as if it had been dropt from Heaven; as also, that I should throw it out in that particular Place, where it being in the Shade of a high Rock, it sprang up immediately" (63). The accident of the grain demonstrates conflicting interpretations of the accidental sign within Defoe's morality tale. Unredeemed, Crusoe instinctively gives it an empirical reading. The providential explanation remains latent in his imagination.

As Crusoe begins to reevaluate his condition in comparison to his previous life or his first years on the island, he begins to read the Bible each day. An echo of Augustine's conversion emerges when, in a moment of sadness, he opens his Bible and imputes a personal application to the passage he reads:[18] "One Morning being very sad, I open'd the Bible upon these Words, *I will never, never leave thee, nor forsake thee;* immediately it occurr'd, That these Words were to me, Why else should they be directed in such a Manner, just at the Moment when I was mourning over my Condition, as one forsaken of God and Man?" (90). The *sortes Biblicae* was popular as a Puritan reading practice that celebrated the direct connection of the believer with God's word.[19] Yet while Augustine's *sortes* passage told him to turn away from the sins of the flesh—an external command to alter his behavior within the context of a new belief system—Crusoe's passage comforts him with an assurance of divine protection. In both cases, the reader is exhorted to change from a material to a spiritual understanding of his life, and the passages respond to the questions of deepest concern: escape from corporeal sin for Augustine, safety and companionship for Crusoe.

Until this point, Crusoe has not engaged in the kind of self-analysis that the Puritan believer sought in solitude. Although he applied the precepts of scientific observation to his external circumstances, he did not apply a corresponding intensity in self-analysis. Only within the accident scenes does he begin to examine the implications of his experience. These circumstances need not have the obvious impact of a catastrophe or a blessing, for he includes in this category a lighthearted scene in which he awakens to the call of an unseen voice: "But the Accident . . . tho' it be a Trifle, will be very diverting in its Place" (87):

> I was wak'd out of my Sleep by a Voice calling me by my Name several times, *Robin, Robin, Robin Crusoe,* poor *Robin Crusoe,* where are you *Robin Crusoe?* . . . Where are you, where have you been?
>
> I was so dead asleep at first, being fatigu'd with Rowing, or Paddling, as it is call'd, the first Part of the Day, and with walking the latter Part, that I did not wake thoroughly, but dozing between sleeping and waking, thought I dream'd that some Body spoke to me: But as the Voice continu'd

---

18. See Homer O. Brown, "The Displaced Self in the Novels of Daniel Defoe," *ELH* 38 (1971): 562–90.

19. See J. Paul Hunter, *The Reluctant Pilgrim: Defoe's Emblematic Method and Quest for Form in "Robinson Crusoe"* (Baltimore: Johns Hopkins University Press, 1966), 159.

to repeat *Robin Crusoe, Robin Crusoe,* at last I began to wake more perfectly, and was at first dreadfully frighted, and started up in the utmost Consternation: But no sooner were my Eyes open, than I saw my *Poll* sitting on the Top of the Hedge; and immediately knew that it was he that spoke to me; for just in such bemoaning Language I had used to talk to him, and teach him; and he had learn'd it so perfectly, that he would sit upon my Finger, and lay his Bill close to my Face, and cry, *Poor* Robin Crusoe, *Where are you? Where have you been? How come you here?* And such things as I had taught him. (112)

Although Crusoe's interpretation completely secularizes the situation in Augustine's conversion, it does signify an expanded level of personal awareness. The accident allows him to acknowledge his vulnerability and fear—the physical threat that he might not be alone on the island or—more terrifying still—the threat to his reason. Indeed, the accident is almost an irrational or mad moment in which he hears sounds and interprets them as the voice of "some Body." Rather than substituting for a spiritual vision, the parrot functions as a comical automaton and in the process accentuates the secular dislocation from ontological understanding that characterizes Crusoe's experience.[20] Crusoe's fear remains until he can explain how the bird happened to come to him, and restoring his equanimity is a literary enterprise. Through transcribing the narrative—literally composing himself—he determines what has happened and who he is as a result.

Surprising accidents become epicenters of sensation and reflection for both Crusoe and the reader. Breaking in upon consciousness, they require interpretation. In one sense, we might compare Crusoe's shipwreck to Montaigne's fall from his horse. Both accidents involve violent physical upheavals and alter the accidental qualities that define the condition of the body and state of mind. Yet neither accident induces a transformation that the victim perceives as an alteration of essence. The effects are as external as the impact that causes the event. Just as Crusoe replicated

---

20. Locke recounted an anecdote in which a parrot carries on a conversation with Prince Maurice of Nassau (1604–79) as part of his response to Descartes's assertion that speech distinguishes men from automata. "Whether, I say, [talking parrots] would not have passed for a race of *rational Animals,* but yet whether for all that, they would have been allowed to be Men and not *Parrots?* For I presume 'tis not the *Idea* of a thinking or rational Being alone, that makes the *Idea* of a *Man* in most People's sense; but of a Body so and so shaped joined to it; and if that be the *Idea* of a *Man,* the same successive Body not shifted all at once, must as well as the same immaterial Spirit go to the making of the same *Man*" (II.xxvii.8).

English life on the island, when he returns to England he simply reestablishes his life there, regaining his wealth, his early wanderlust, and becoming perceptibly detached from the religious intensity he experienced when he believed himself guided by a providential design.[21]

The extent to which Crusoe wavers in his conviction of divine guidance parallels the uncertainty about ultimate causes reflected in Locke's "I know not what" and his recognition of the limits of human understanding. Crusoe conceives of the possibility that some kind of intuition—whether spiritual in the Scholastic sense of the word or potentially a capacity to interpret accidental signs—supports the conscious reasoning will:

> This renew'd a Contemplation, which often had come to my Thoughts in former Time, when first I began to see the merciful Dispositions of Heaven, in the Dangers we run through in this Life. How wonderfully we are deliver'd, when we know nothing of it. How when we are in (a *Quandary*, as we call it) a Doubt or Hesitation, whether to go this Way, or that Way, a secret Hint shall direct us this Way, when we intended to go that Way; nay, when Sense, our own Inclination, and perhaps Business has call'd to go the other Way, yet a strange Impression upon the Mind, from we know not what Springs, and by we know not what Power, shall over-rule us to go this Way; and it shall afterwards appear, that had we gone that Way which we should have gone, and even to our Imagination ought to have gone, we should have been ruin'd and lost. (137)

In this passage, he writes within a providential context that rests on his newly acquired beliefs, but his recognition of an uncontrolled or even unconscious force positioned against reason gives the latitude for a secular interpretation. Clearly, the "strange Impression" finds its analogue in Locke's association of ideas. The accidental sign that will become a literary topos for the developing novel achieves its early form in *Robinson Crusoe*.

Even as Crusoe remains fundamentally unchanged, his life on the island creates an element of distance from his youthful self that allows him to reinterpret his shipwreck as a lucky and liberating experience. Like the

---

21. See Todd R. Flanders, "Rousseau's Adventure with Robinson Crusoe," *Interpretation*, 24, no. 3 (Spring 1997): 319–37, for a discussion of interpretations of Crusoe's atheism. Flanders considers Crusoe an example of the modern hybrid individual who finds no tension between bourgeois values and religion.

shipwrecked man who assumed the external qualities of kingship in Pascal's *Three Discourses on the Condition of the Great,* he has been acknowledged as the king of his island. In the process of mastering his physical environment through his labor and ingenuity, he has acquired moral principles that enable him to establish a reign of tolerance in which Friday, Friday's father, and the old Spaniard are both free and protected. Although the language he uses to describe his experiences alludes to spiritual understanding, the results of this exercise in forming his person are primarily secular and social: the rebellious young risk taker becomes a mature representative of the middle-class ethic whose self-fulfillment is linked to capitalist striving.

For the reader, the story of this shift juxtaposes the excitement of being at risk with a reassuring affirmation of providential aid. Although Defoe's Puritanism emphasized direct relations to God and encouraged inward analysis, within the narrative, the first person voice provides a purely secular security, for the conventions of adventure literature ensure that a hero speaking on his own behalf has surmounted any hazards that threatened to overcome him. Critical interpretations that read *Robinson Crusoe* purely as a spiritual autobiography or from an entirely material perspective cannot do justice to the ambiguities involved in determining the cause of his good fortune. Defoe rationalizes his narrative with elements drawn from his engagement with experimental science, interpretations of the philosophical tradition, and applications of probability theory. But the impact of the events expresses something absent from earlier narratives: as records of inwardly turned thought processes, they offer, however briefly, evidence of a fictional character newly engaged in the act of self-contemplation.

III. Art and Order

Although the novel is often seen as an indicator of developing interiority, in the eighteenth century, the phrase "know thyself" carried the meaning of recognizing a social identity or classification. The increasing commodification of fashions that signaled membership in a specific social group, a tradition of portraiture that invested the sitter with symbolic attributes, and the popularity of masquerades all indicated the significance of accidental qualities in a fluctuating social climate.[22] As a result of soci-

22. Wahrman, *The Making of the Modern Self,* 184.

etal emphasis on surface characteristics, experiences that defined a "person" in Locke's theory of identity were viewed primarily from an outward rather than an inward point of view.[23]

The novel worked to redefine this perspective by manipulating both aspects of accident. For example, the character of Robinson Crusoe defines himself by attributes of social status. He adventures to become wealthy, replicates the possessions and signs of wealth on his island, and achieves wealth when he returns to civilization. However, Defoe's narrative encourages the reader to identify Crusoe's inner attributes: his initial recklessness, the ingenuity, industry, self-discipline, and changing state of religious belief he displayed after his shipwreck, and his enduring lust for adventure. The character's awareness focuses outward, but Defoe enables the reader to see beneath the surface. In Henry Fielding's *The History of Tom Jones, a Foundling* (1749), however, the goal of instructing the reader becomes explicit and the pedagogical strategy he adopted fosters recognition of identity in terms of enduring or substantive qualities (the kind of ruling passions we met in Montaigne).

The novel was published to great popular acclaim, and its title established its social orientation.[24] As a foundling left "by an odd accident" in Squire Allworthy's bed in Paradise Hall, Tom has been literally cast away. Lacking a name or parentage, he must be defined by society. The enlightened squire determines to "provide in the same Manner for this poor Infant, as if a legitimate Child had had the Fortune to have been found in the same Place" (II.ii.80), but as Tom grows up, his own imprudence casts him adrift once more. Within this complex narrative of risk and reward, accidents function to unsettle and test the hero, for Fielding's educational project was to show his readers the characteristics and decisions that ultimately enabled Tom to earn his place in society.

Manipulation of the spiritual exercise is evident in the novel's struc-

23. *Fantomina* (1724), written by Eliza Haywood, who joined Fielding's Haymarket acting troupe in 1737, exemplifies this tendency. The heroine reanimates the affections of her lover by assuming the costume and manner of a widow, maid, and wealthy courtesan, and he is unable to penetrate any of her disguises.

24. The book was a best seller. An edition of 2,000 bound copies at eighteen shillings sold out before the official publication date (10 February); 1,500 bound copies of the second edition were sold at sixteen shillings; a third edition of 3,000 copies, reset in small pica at twelve shillings, appeared in April and 3,500 more copies were published in September. A revised fourth edition appeared in 1749 but was dated 1750. Copies were "in every Hand, from the beardless Youth, up to the hoary Hairs of Age." Martin Battestin's "Introduction" to *The History of Tom Jones a Foundling*, ed. Fredson Bowers (Middletown: Wesleyan University Press, 1975), xxi. All citations of *Tom Jones* are from this edition.

ture. Although Fielding's academic training would have made him familiar with classical examples, he borrowed religious references to reframe
this topos for his moral purpose. Through biblical analogies like Tom's
expulsion from Paradise, his conflict with Blifil (his Cain or Essau), and
the temptations he encounters in the Sodom and Gomorrah of London
society, Fielding transferred his pedagogical theme from an aspiration
toward union with the divine will to a purely worldly goal: achieving a
legitimate social identity. Although Defoe could propel Crusoe on such
a journey by using the natural catastrophe of the storm under the guise
of a providential act, the events Fielding chose to drive his story were the
results of human agency. Individual characters may exclaim about the
providential nature of some unexpected outcome, but no specific act can
be attributed to direct divine action. Moreover, the narrator claims the
role of a creator and opposes his creative force to the satanic power of
the critic ("This Work may indeed, be considered as a great Creation of
our own; and for a little Reptile of a Critic to presume to find Fault with
any of its Parts, without knowing the Manner in which the Whole is connected, and before he comes to the final Catastrophe, is a most presumptuous Absurdity" (X.i.524–25).

Occasionally the accidents that occur in *Tom Jones* take the form of
purely physical events—like Sophia's fall from her horse—but coincidences like those found in the romance abound in the novel: accidental
or missed encounters, telling losses or discoveries, or misplaced decisions
that result from the inadvertent absence of crucial information. Fielding's
contribution to the evolving manipulation of accident within the narrative lies in the process of unfolding the meaning of these events. Accidents
do not occur as life-transforming points in time, but only reveal their full
implication over a longer narrative time frame. That is, they carry signification that requires attentive interpretation, the assembling of additional
information, and periods of reflection that elaborate the simple memory
function that Locke required to establish personal identity. For example,
Allworthy's misjudgment sends Jenny Jones away to become Mrs. Waters
(because he believes that she has born an illegitimate child) and costs
schoolmaster Partridge his position (because he is the accused father).
These displacements allow Tom to encounter both Jenny and Partridge in
other roles later in the story and eventually lead not only to his mistaken
belief that he has committed incest, but also to the eventual revelation
of his true parentage. The narrator justifies such coincidences as "a nice
Train of little Circumstances" of the kind that may frequently be observed
in life (XVII.iii.916). Indeed, he warns the reader that every element in

the text may be significant even if its importance is not immediately apparent and advises tracing them to earlier events whose implications may have been overlooked (X.i.524–25).

The notion of what a reader would accept as probable was not something Fielding derived from mathematical theories (like those familiar to Defoe); instead he relied on the discussion of probability that appeared in Locke's *Essay Concerning Human Understanding* (IV.xv–xvi).[25] Generally, eighteenth-century critics understood consistency as a matter of observing so-called literary decorums. These principles stated that so long as a fiction was consistent with accepted opinion and place, time, action, and the social status of its characters, it would appear probable or lifelike in accordance with "nature's will." Locke's criterion of using analogies (to experience or to previously established truths) to determine what was probable was not new in itself. The novelty of his argument lay in isolating this principle for use in literary criticism, and his work was cited so often during the eighteenth century that it became nearly a separate theory of probability.[26]

Fielding applied Locke's principle of analyzing external data to determine the likelihood of something that cannot be verified by external signs to the consideration of human behaviors and motives. His *Essay on the Knowledge of the Characters of Men* (from the *Miscellanies* of 1743) would like to claim that everyone possesses a static, morally unambiguous character, although he acknowledges that most people assume disguises. Nevertheless, faces are marked by the passions, so close observation should be able to identify a masquerading mein. Unfortunately, few people have a sufficiently discerning eye. For that reason, he continues, actions pro-

---

25. Kenneth MacLean, *John Locke and English Literature of the Eighteenth Century* (New Haven:Yale University Press, 1936), 2–3, notes that the chief vogue of the *Essay* began about 1725 and lasted until about 1765, with nine single editions appearing in England in addition to four editions of the collected works.

26. Locke defined probability in applications related to matters of fact in terms of the reliability of authorities who could observe and witness the circumstances. However, matters of speculation—things that cannot be sensed because they are immaterial ("Spirits, Angels, Devils, etc.") or are too small or remote to be observed (such as "intelligent Inhabitants in the Planets and other Mansions of the vast Universe"), or forces of nature whose causes we cannot understand (such as the nature of magnetism or the transformation of a candle into light and heat)—required other means of verification. "*Analogy* in these matters," Locke said, "is the only help we have, and 'tis from that alone we draw all our grounds of Probability" (IV.xvi.12). Locke defined the role of analogy in the production of science, but analogy also played a role in the development of narrative hypotheses. See Douglas Lane Patey, *Probability and Literary Form: Philosophic Theory and Literary Practice in the Augustan Age* (Cambridge: Cambridge University Press, 1984), 24–25.

vide the truest standards for judging thoughts, but this method also is open to bias and corruption.[27]

In the *Essay* Fielding hoped only to draw attention to the pervasive danger of being misled by hypocrites. He did not claim to offer the general reader a sure method for penetrating such disguises, but physiognomists had developed rules comparable to those used by physicians. They could identify aspects of character from studying the appearance of the face just as a trained medical observer could identify the nature of a disease by observing accidental qualities in the body. Tobias Smollett, conversant with these rules through his medical training, defined their application as "sagacity."[28] Fielding's pedagogical design in his novels involved training a reader to be sagacious in the sense of being able to identify the truth of a character by interpreting such signs.

A capacity to interpret accidental signs formed part of Tom's education, but it was not sufficient to make him socially mature. In addition to sagacity, he needed to learn prudence. However, Fielding used the term "prudence" in both an ideal and a pejorative sense. In the 1740s the word was evolving from its original meaning as the supreme rational virtue (the sense in which Aquinas had used it) into its near opposite—the worldly wisdom of middle-class morality or even a villainous hypocrisy. Prudence had begun to signify self-discipline, discretion, and foresight in the service of mercenary gain rather than to achieve the goal of self-knowledge and virtuous conduct through spiritual exercise. By deliberately complicating its meaning through his ambiguous use of the term, Fielding pointed up the difficulty of distinguishing the high ideal of wisdom from mere cunning and deceit—of distinguishing substance from accident.

Accident becomes an occasion for the exercise of prudent judgment whenever Fielding's characters are forced to evaluate whether or not a given circumstance is worthy of belief. When Sophia Western initially attempts to interpret the contradictions in Tom's behavior toward her as signs of love or later must determine the probability that he really proposed to Lady Bellaston, she relies on expectations acquired from experience to determine the truth. As a magistrate, Fielding was well positioned to draw on the tradition of determining the probable on the basis of the authority of witnesses, so when Squire Allworthy misinterprets the testimony of Partridge's wife and condemns him because Jenny cannot ap-

27. *Miscellanies by Henry Fielding, Esq.*, vol. 1, ed. Henry Knight Miller (Middletown: Wesleyan University Press, 1972), 163.

28. Tobias Smollett, *The Adventures of Ferdinand Count Fathom*, ed. O. M. Brack, Jr. (Athens: University of Georgia Press, 1988), 51, 252–53.

pear to explain the truth, Fielding instructs the reader in the subtleties of exercising judgment:

> Certain it is, that whatever was the Truth of the Case, there was Evidence more than sufficient to convict him before *Allworthy;* indeed much less would have satisfied a Bench of Justices on an Order of Bastardy; and yet, notwithstanding the Positiveness of Mrs. *Partridge,* who would have taken the Sacrament upon the Matter, there is a Possibility that the Schoolmaster was entirely innocent; For tho' it appeared clear, on comparing the Time when *Jenny* departed from *Little Baddington,* with that of her Delivery, that she had there conceived this Infant, yet it by no means followed, of Necessity, that *Partridge* must have been its Father: For, to omit other Particulars, there was in the same House a Lad near Eighteen, between whom, and *Jenny,* there had subsisted sufficient Intimacy to found a reasonable Suspicion; and yet, so blind is Jealousy, this Circumstance never once entered into the Head of the enraged Wife. (II.vi.101–2)

Even this additional information from the narrator does not describe the full range of possible interpretations. Part of the pedagogical strategy employed in *Tom Jones* is to make the reader doubt all the evidence: even the narrator proves an insufficient or misleading guide.

In addition to judging correctly, Fielding's characters must embody principles of conduct. Although Squire Allworthy misjudges the paternity case—not only on the level of relying on Mrs. Partridge's accusation, but also because he doesn't know that Jenny's conduct was designed to hide the fact that the Squire's sister was Tom's true mother—his conduct toward Tom represents the principle of charity. Tom also acquires prudence by becoming a better judge of the impact his words and actions have on others. As he languishes in prison after a duel, he experiences a rare moment of introspection. Realizing that his mishaps are the result not of chance but of his own imprudence, he exclaims: "Sure . . . Fortune will never have done with me, till she hath driven me to Distraction. But why do I blame Fortune? I am myself the Cause of all my Misery. All the dreadful Mischiefs which have befallen me, are the Consequences only of my own Folly and Vice" (XVII.ii.915–16). Despite the accidents of mistaken identity that led Tom to this despairing self-analysis, he does not undergo a spiritual change. Fielding's creations experience moments of insight, yet they operate largely within the range of types associated with dominant passions. In this respect they act in accord with what the popular imagination still understood to be human motives. Although Fielding was convinced that the passions control behavior, he envisioned them as mixed within the individual, who would be consistent but neither uniformly selfish nor uniformly virtuous. Thus, the characters in *Tom Jones* appear flat and clear rather than tortured or complex. The plot, however, allows the reader to observe those flat surfaces reflecting many different kinds of light as one situation after another puts the characters to the test. Because Fielding believed that some kinds of knowledge—including even self-knowledge—require looking at things from more than one point of view at once, his method was to let the reader see each character from more than one side.

Fielding's concern with corruption of language also depended on the way in which use affects the meaning of words. For Locke, simple ideas entered into the composition of complex ideas through associations with words in the mind of the speaker. Fielding's point was that the composition of ideas in particular minds has nothing to do with the meanings of words. His example cites the word "love." In book 6, the narrator provides a complex notion of authentic loving as rejoicing in the gratification of the beloved, but he does not agree with Locke's assertion that language represents an attempt to transfer ideas from one mind to another.[29] According to the narrator, only experience can attach any meaning to the word, since all the effects of love flow from this experience:

> Examine your Heart, my good Reader, and resolve whether you do believe these Matters with me. If you do, you may now proceed to their Exemplification in the following Pages; if you do not, you have, I assure you, already read more than you have understood; and it would be wiser to pursue your Business, or your Pleasures (such as they are) than to throw away any more of your Time in reading what you can neither taste nor comprehend. To treat of the Effects of Love to you, must be as absurd as to discourse on Colours to a Man born blind; since possibly your Idea of Love may be as absurd as that which we are told such blind Man once entertained of the Colour Scarlet: that Colour seemed to him to be very much like the sound of a Trumpet; and Love probably may, in your Opinion, very greatly resemble a Dish of Soup, or a Sir-loin of Roast-beef. (VI.i.271–72)[30]

29. See Bernard Harrison, *Henry Fielding's "Tom Jones": The Novelist as Moral Philosopher* (London: Sussex University Press, 1975), 61–63.

30. Fielding referred to an example Locke used in the *Essay* (III.iv.11) as part of his exposition of simple ideas. It was widely believed in the eighteenth century that a man born blind would have no conception of colors. A spatial version of this idea became know as the

By rewarding Tom and defeating Blifil at the end of the novel, Fielding proposed a compromise among conventional Christian beliefs, his view of the role chance plays in human affairs, and the idea that meting out justice requires passing judgment on actions according to the motives that inspired them. Thus, an imperfect, blundering yet good-hearted character like Tom could represent the fruit of an educational process. Over the course of the novel, he improved upon his intrinsic qualities by the application of reason and by ethical responses to the accidents of life. Fielding showed the process of creating in Tom a person in possession of a fully fledged social identity as the enlightened master of himself and of Paradise Hall. But the novel also maintains a close connection to the classical understanding of substance. The infant lump of matter found in the squire's bed possessed potentiality in the classical sense and accidents assume the role Aristotle ascribed to substantial form. Together they realize the composite human being Tom Jones.

IV. A Feeling for Accident

Laurence Sterne's *The Life and Opinions of Tristram Shandy*, published from 1759 to 1767, exemplifies the extent to which the novel incorporated current thinking. His capacity to borrow notions from his competitors and parody their effects helped to bring him commercial success. He played against conventions established by Fielding and Samuel Richardson, exploited typographic conventions, and capitalized on serial publication by manipulating the open-ended form of the fictional memoir.[31] But more important for the history of accident, his work also responded to the scientific ferment surrounding the role of the nervous system in the operation of the mind. Shandyism—the witty free association of feelings and ideas characteristic of his fictional family—became a literary byword.

In both context and form, the novel represents the operation of countless contingencies. Like *Tom Jones*, it begins with accidents of birth, but it conspicuously lacks the order that Fielding imposed upon his narrative. In

---

Molyneux problem, after William Molyneux, a member of the Royal Society and friend of Locke. See Martha Brandt Bolton, "The Real Molyneux Question and the Basis of Locke's Answer," in *Locke's Philosophy: Content and Context*, ed. G. A. J. Rogers (Oxford: Clarendon Press, 1994), 75–99.

31. Thomas Keymer, *Sterne, the Moderns, and the Novel* (Oxford: Oxford University Press, 2002), provides an exhaustive analysis of Sterne's relation to contemporary publishing practices as well as his use of popular literature, critical responses, and imitations of Shandyism.

the sense that circumstances abort each of the conditions Walter Shandy believes can secure his son's future (his conception, name, and nose), Tristram resembles Tom in his need to formulate a viable sense of self. However, his efforts to resolve what we recognize as a never-ending identity crisis demonstrate the persistent impact of accidental events.[32] Sterne domesticated such accidents into details of everyday life, such as the buzzing of a fly, a hot chestnut rolling from a tabletop, or an absent-minded turn of phrase, but by creating an environment in which the self resides primarily in accidental qualities, whose mutability makes them particularly vulnerable to chance, he gives accidents an unprecedented power.

If Fielding's work posed the pedagogical problem of learning how to identify social masks (and forestall the kind of self-deception practiced by a character like Blifil, whose consuming self-interest imprisons his understanding), Sterne presented storytelling as a vehicle for self-creation. What Tristram thinks he knows about himself comes to him from stories he has been told about his conception and birth, events that define him as the "Sport of small accidents" (III.viii). Just as the comedy of his father's or Uncle Toby's mechanical responses to these circumstances blurs the boundary between man and automaton, Tristram's incapacity to ignore contingencies or avoid reflecting upon them marks a degree of his humanity.[33] Although narration fails as a strategy for controlling the continual flux of impressions that strike his mind, his very failure testifies to his liberation. The flashbacks, anticipations, deferrals, and digressions that mark his narrative style not only characterize his thought processes; they represent his anima in the classical sense of an animating spirit. Thus, the process of retelling the story of his life becomes more than a communication of moral conditioning in the tradition of the spiritual exercise; it is an essential act of self-preservation.

Sterne was conversant with Locke's *Essay Concerning Human Understanding,* and he used its theories to map the mental processes of the members of the Shandy family. The association of ideas served as a point

32. Among the papers dealing with the question of identity collected in *Laurence Sterne in Modernism and Postmodernism,* ed. David Pierce and Peter de Voogd (Amsterdam: Rodopi, 1996), see esp. 109–21, Stuart Sim, "'All That Exist Are "Islands of Determinism"': Shandean Sentiment and the Dilemma of Postmodern Physics."

33. Herbert Klein, "Identity Reclaimed: The Art of Being Tristram," in Pierce and de Voogd, *Laurence Sterne in Modernism and Postmodernism,* 126, notes that Walter Shandy and Uncle Toby, who lack the means or awareness to escape from their fixed and self-perpetuating identities, seem to fulfill Newton's law that a moving body will move with the same speed and in the same direction indefinitely unless other forces come to exert an influence upon it. Accident, of course, serves as such a force.

of departure for Tristram's autobiography by adding a subjective dimension to the narrative use of accident. In this reunion of the two aspects of accident, events determine qualities. An explicit example of association intensifying the impact of a chance event on thought and behavior occurs when Tristram observes his Uncle Toby, who has caught a fly:

—Go,—says he, one day at dinner, to an over-grown one which had buzz'd about his nose, and tormented him cruelly all dinner-time,—and which, after infinite attempts, he had caught at last, as it flew by him;—I'll not hurt thee, says my uncle *Toby*, rising from his chair, and going a-cross the room, with the fly in his hand,—I'll not hurt a hair of thy head:—Go, says he, lifting up the sash, and opening his hand as he spoke, to let it escape;— go poor Devil, get thee gone, why should I hurt thee?—This world surely is wide enough to hold both thee and me.

I was but ten years old when this happened;—but whether it was, that the action itself was more in unison to my nerves at that age of pity, which instantly set my whole frame into one vibration of most pleasurable sensation;—or how far the manner and expression of it might go towards it;—or in what degree, or by what secret magick,—a tone of voice and harmony of movement, attuned by mercy, might find a passage to my heart, I know not;—this I know, that the lesson of universal good-will then taught and imprinted by my uncle *Toby*, has never since been worn out of my mind: And tho' I would not depreciate what the study of the *Literae humaniores*, at the university, have done for me in that respect, or discredit the other helps of an expensive education bestowed upon me, both at home and abroad since;—yet I often think that I owe one half of my philanthropy to that one accidental impression.[34]

This passage reflects several extensions of Locke's theory known to Sterne. One, proposed by Reverend John Gay, argued that personal pleasure and happiness encourage the pursuit of virtue more than innate ideas or reason.[35] The other, developed by David Hartley and David Hume, emphasized the link between idea and sensation. Hartley believed that the "vibrations" of pleasurable sensations passed from the nerve endings to the

34. Laurence Sterne, *The Life and Opinions of Tristram Shandy, Gentleman*, vols. 1–3 in *The Florida Edition of the Works of Laurence Sterne*, ed. Melvyn New and Joan New (Gainesville: University of Florida Press, 1978–84), 1.2.12. All citations are by volume and chapter number within the Florida edition.

35. Jonathan Lamb, *Sterne's Fiction and the Double Principle* (Cambridge: Cambridge University Press, 1989), 63.

brain. When sensate vibrations subside, they leave behind impressions of themselves, a tendency to fainter vibrations, called "vibratiuncles." These impressions on the brain represent the origin of simple ideas. The brain stores a miniaturized form of these vibrations that echo the original sensation whenever they receive a charge of energy.[36] Hume formulated a more generalized theory. He asserted that all ideas were copies of sensory impressions that were linked by resemblance, proximity, cause and effect, or contrast to form ideas.[37] In the example of Toby and the fly, Tristram experiences Toby's compassion as the imprint of a felt sensation and remembers it as such. Most of the situations in *Tristram Shandy* develop an interplay between physical sensation and ideas that corresponds to Hartley's mechanics of association or Hume's theory that taste and feeling influence thought in a species of gravitational pull.

Removing the process of reasoned reflection from the explanation of how ideas are formed both simplified and complicated Sterne's presentation of accidental events. On the one hand, it reduced the emphasis on providential design. For example, Tristram calls the falling of a hot chestnut into the open fly of Phutatorius's breeches an accident. (An ironic note conjectures the nut fell of its own accord into that particular place as an act of retribution during the week of the publication of a second edition of Phutatorius's "filthy and obscene" treatise on keeping concubines.) On the other hand, the emphasis on feeling extended the interpretive impact of accidents by demonstrating how misguided associations could escalate into life-altering acts. Sterne's presentation of the effect of the chestnut's fall on the life of Parson Yorick illustrates how mental processes could lead from a trivial accident to a momentous outcome. After Phutatorius

36. See Hartley, *Observations on Man*, pt. 1, secs. 1–3. In *De partibus corporis humani sensibilibus et irritabilibus* (1752), Albrecht von Haller, the principal physiologist of the Enlightenment, distinguished between two intrinsic properties of tissue: irritability was the inherent contractibility of the muscle fibers independent of the nerves; sensibility was the inherent responsiveness of tissues imbued with nerves. In contrast to the structural uniformity and interchangeability postulated in the mechanical physiology of the passions, this view implied that each constitution possesses a unique capacity or disposition to register feeling. As a principle of nerve physiology, vibration goes back to Newton's appendix to his *Opticks*, in which he suggested that vibrations in the ether, acting on the retina and brain, produce the sensation of light, just as vibrations in the air, acting on the inner ear, cause the sensation of sound. He extended this idea to motor functions, and it was a short step from there to emotions (shaking with anger, for example). Hartley's *Observations on Man* linked Newton's vibrations to the Locke's association of ideas and thus offered a mental and physical explanation of memory, imagination, habit, and emotion. Joseph R. Roach, *The Player's Passion: Studies in the Science of Acting* (Ann Arbor: University of Michigan Press, 1993), 105, 98–106.

37. David Hume, *An Enquiry Concerning Human Understanding*, ed. Tom L. Beauchamp (Oxford: Clarendon Press, 2000), sec. 3.

plucked the chestnut from his breeches and flung it away with an exclamation, it was picked up by Yorick:

> It is curious to observe the triumph of slight incidents over the mind:—
> What incredible weight they have in forming and governing our opinions,
> both of men and things,—that trifles light as air, shall waft a belief into the
> soul, and plant it so immoveably within it,—that *Euclid's* demonstrations,
> could they be brought to batter it in breach, should not all have power to
> overthrow it.
>
> *Yorick*, I said, picked up the chesnut which *Phutatorius's* wrath had flung
> down—the action was trifling—I am ashamed to account for it—he did
> it, for no reason, but that he thought the chesnut not a jot worse for the
> adventure—and that he held a good chesnut worth stooping for.—But this
> incident, trifling as it was, wrought differently in *Phutatorius's* head: He
> considered this act of *Yorick's*, in getting off his chair, and picking up the
> chesnut, as a plain acknowledgment in him, that the chesnut was originally his,—and in course, that it must have been the owner of the chesnut,
> and no one else, who could have plaid him such a prank with it: What
> greatly confirmed him in this opinion, was this, that the table being parallelogramical and very narrow, it afforded a fair opportunity for *Yorick*,
> who sat directly over-against *Phutatorius*, of slipping the chesnut in—and
> consequently that he did it. (1.4.27)

The other observers consider Yorick's act a witty expression of his well-known dislike of Phutatorius's treatise and appropriate coming from one they associate with Shakespeare's Yorick as a "man of jest."[38] Moreover, long experience with being considered a prankster has conditioned Yorick to wait for time to absolve him rather than refuting such assump-

---

38. The description of Yorick stooping for the chestnut echoes the language Iago uses to describe how he will trap Othello with Desdemona's handkerchief (a "trifle light as air"). Points of resemblance between *Hamlet* and *Tristram Shandy* include a common thread of sexual innuendo, the theme of the meaning of words, the motif of martial honor, and the ruling element of chance. Richard A. Lanham, *Tristram Shandy: The Games of Pleasure* (Berkeley: University of California Press, 1973), 141ff., provides an extended comparison between the play and the novel. Sterne resumed the analysis of the dominance of chance that informed Shakespeare's tragedy, but rather than showing the paralytic effect chance exercises on Hamlet, he showed his characters capitalizing on chance events for their own purposes. While Hamlet disdains "seeming" and can neither play his central role of revenge hero nor reason himself into any other role, Tristram remains secure beneath his many masks in the fixed nature of a comic hero. Both characters are marked by self-imposed delays as well as external interruptions. Although the character of Yorick suggests the most obvious link between the novel and the play, it is Tristram and Hamlet who engage in a comparable quest for self-realization.

tions. Thus, Phutatorius can threaten him under the guise of sharing a joke. To the complex interplay of these reactions to the accident, Sterne adds another layer. The gap in the breeches occasions a hiatus in the narrative, and the recipe for curing the burn alludes to the power of words to disturb or heal: the compress of printed paper used to spread the soothing oil contains no inflammatory passages.

Sterne adapted Locke's theory of accidental association to show the irrational aspects of communication. Locke had justified his idea that the association of ideas produced knowledge by noting great variations in what individuals know: "If our Knowledge were altogether necessary, all Men's Knowledge would not only be alike, but every Man would know all that is knowable: and if it were wholly voluntary, some Men so little regard or value it, that they would have extreme little, or none at all" (*Essay Concerning Human Understanding*, IV.xiii.1). By applying this idea at face value, Sterne suggested that associations confuse communication. He considered them subjective phenomena that isolate one person's understanding from that of another. The accident of the hot chestnut painfully reveals the limitations of the association process.

Both Locke and Sterne experienced the lack of communication as one of life's central problems. Locke responded by rationalizing the connection between ideas and language, but Sterne doubted that fallible human beings could apply Locke's methods or that the results would be appropriate in ordinary life. According to Tristram, three causes of confusion complicate Locke's description of how ideas are imprinted on the blank page of the mind: the dull organs of the perceiver, the slight and transient nature of impressions, and "a memory like unto a sieve, not able to retain what it has received" (1.2.2). In other words, accidental qualities as well as accidental events are implicated in the process. To prove this assertion, he employed a teasing reference to Aristotle's well-established metaphor of wax. If Dolly the chambermaid, he argued, allows the red sealing wax she drops on the letter she has written to Robin to become too hard, it cannot receive the mark of her thimble, if it is beeswax, and therefore soft, it will not hold this impression, or if she is too hasty, the impression will be distorted (1.2.2). By analogy, any type of contingency could rupture the link between an experience and its memory. For similar reasons, Tristram agrees with Locke that words cannot capture the essence of thought. He asserts that "unsteady" uses of words "have perplexed the clearest and most exalted understandings" (1.2.2).

Sterne's conviction that distortions were inherent in language and created barriers to communication was an idea we met in Pascal and one that Fielding also shared. They all believed that the attitudes of both the speaker and the hearer affect the meaning of the words they exchange. Confusion occurs precisely because both participants regard the words they use as common property while the associations they have formed around them differ. As a result, each employs language in a unique way that is further individualized by associations brought to the situation itself. In other words, Sterne assumes that subjective factors are encoded into the language and become explicit in the creative process of communication.[39]

Tristram Shandy served as a test case for these assumptions. The scene in which Tristram's father attempts to explain his theory of the significance of the nose to Uncle Toby demonstrates a failure of understanding not only between the two brothers, but also on the part of the hypothetical figure of Locke himself. If the "great reasoner" had observed Uncle's Toby's close attention, Tristram says, and the meditative way he examined his pipe when he took it from his mouth, he would have concluded that Toby was "syllogizing and measuring with it the truth of each hypothesis of long noses, in order as my father laid them before him" (1.3.40). But he would have been mistaken. A remark by Toby opens a conceptual gulf that enrages Walter Shandy:

> 'Tis a pity, said my father, that truth can only be on one side, brother *Toby*,—considering what ingenuity these learned men have all shewn in their solutions of noses.—Can noses be dissolved? replied my uncle Toby.
>
> —My father thrust back his chair,—rose up,—put on his hat,—took four long strides to the door,—jerked it open,—thrust his head half way out,—shut the door again,—took no notice of the bad hinge,—returned to the table,—pluck'd my mother's thread-paper out of *Slawkenbergius's* book,—went hastily to his bureau,—walk'd slowly back, twisting my mother's thread-paper about his thumb,—unbutton'd his waistcoat,— threw my mother's thread-paper into the fire,—bit her sattin pin-cushion in two, fill'd his mouth with bran,—confounded it;—but mark!—the oath of confusion was levell'd at my uncle *Toby's* brain,—which was e'en confused enough already. . . .
>
> 'Twas all one to my uncle *Toby*,—he smoaked his pipe on, with unvaried composure,—his heart never intended offence to his brother,—and as his head could seldom find out where the sting of it lay,—he always gave my

---

39. Wolfgang Iser , *Lawrence Sterne: "Tristram Shandy,"* trans. David Henry Wilson (Cambridge: Cambridge University Press, 1988), 41.

father the credit of cooling by himself.—He was five minutes and thirty-five seconds about it in the present case. (1.3.41)

Toby's nonsensical response shows how a mistaken association can alter a situation and deflect the narrative in a fresh direction. Walter's emotional and physical reaction typifies the way in which Sterne's characters communicate their emotional experiences through symbolic expressions. Just as Fielding chose public actions and dialogue to delineate his characters, Sterne used spontaneous or accidental expressions of emotions as external signals of individuality. When linguistic communication breaks down, body language becomes the vehicle of communication. As in the scene when Tristram was moved by Toby's care for the captured fly, Toby and Walter's responses are anchored in action rather than reason. Their emotions are transferred to a level of seemingly involuntary motions. Although the characters do not grasp the idiosyncratic nature of their behavior (or the ethical implications of their gestures), Sterne's vivid depiction of body language forces readers to use their own patterns of association to interpret these responses.[40]

Tristram's sense of himself constitutes a clear example of the period's perception that identity was nourished from the outside. We see this explicitly in the formative influence he ascribes to Uncle Toby's sensibility to the fly. However, Adam Smith's *Theory of Moral Sentiments* (1759) hypothesized that the sentiment of sympathy involved a transfer and metamorphosis of self. This notion reflects some of the issues Locke faced when he contemplated whether detaching the hand from the body would create a doubled consciousness. Smith believed a person could come to empathize with another's situation by degrees. Evoking sympathy might involve altering the external circumstances, altering one's own character and person, or crossing the boundary between external sensations and internal reflection or feeling.[41] This mobility of personal identity would permit transference without loss of identity. Reading novels fostered precisely this experience of vicarious identification.

The possibility of doubleness also provided a key to the relation between reader and narrator. Fielding alternately cajoled and berated his reader to adopt the position of an impartial yet sympathetic spectator, an imaginary "inmate of the breast" that passes judgment on our conduct.

---

40. Ibid., 47–48.

41. Raymond Martin and John Barresi, *Naturalization of the Soul: Self and Personal Identity in the Eighteenth Century* (London: Routledge, 2000), 95.

But Sterne's awareness that the mental isolation of the individual made communication a social necessity alerted him to the fact that a tangle of attitudes lay open to the minds of his readers just as to the minds of his fictional characters.[42] His representations of the minute convolutions of association and response in the thoughts of his characters have been considered a psychological innovation in the development of the novel; however, his exploration of mental states represents less a technical innovation than evidence of his firm grasp of contemporary theories about the operations of the mind.

Sterne signaled his intention to explore issues of how people acquire knowledge of the world (or of themselves) in terms of mental communication rather than physical action by replacing the conventional title of "The Life and Adventures" with "The Life and Opinions." Locke had assumed (and Fielding wished to believe) that rational analysis could lead to moral behavior, and the late eighteenth century placed extraordinary faith in the assumption that even the most mindless pattern of causation eventually could be explained as the result of some mechanical cause. However, for Sterne, human affairs consisted of such a tissue of improbabilities that rational conjecture became almost impossible. Within the mental landscape of Shandy Hall, what appears probable and what appears certain form a Lockean continuum. Each character processes experience with results that are distinctive and unique, but their categorical assumptions that their idiosyncratic ways of combining ideas represent reality lead them into confused or even catastrophic interactions.

What Sterne attempted to teach—and we recognize the persistently pedagogic purpose in his work—was not precisely analogous to the act of judgment that formed such an essential part of Fielding's pedagogical goal but an art of communication that acknowledged the dangers of inordinate reliance on the formation of judgments alongside the possibilities inherent in the process of association. One of his strategies was to shift the Aristotelian emphasis on the faculty of discerning categorical *differences* among ideas or things to the faculty of discerning unexpected *correspondences* or correlations. This shift allocated greater importance to wit. Sterne believed Locke should have regarded this quality more highly, for it allowed men to be ridiculous, as they inevitably would be, yet to be

---

42. See Keymer, *Sterne, the Moderns, and the Novel*, 36–48, on the playful yet perturbed awareness of variations in reader interpretations by Richardson and Fielding as well as by Sterne.

perceived as such without sacrificing their fundamental humanity.[43] Tristram argues for the necessity of both judgment and wit as the "hardest to come at" yet "most calamitous to be without" of the ornaments of the mind, but it is judgment, not wit, that has deceived him so often in his life that he always suspects it "right or wrong" (1.3.20 and 1.5.11).

In the last decades of the century, a flurry of critical and popular attention to Sterne's work propelled novelists toward a more subjective examination of character. His principle of internal consistency allowed greater flexibility in delineating human behavior because it was premised on a new perception of the variations in the ways people think and feel. The extent to which qualities of mind were conditioned by mental as well as physical accidents became an accepted literary understanding. Throughout the literary community, the old notion of the individual as a discrete unit of matter sharing a common human form was replaced by a cerebral notion of what constitutes individuality.

43. John Traugott, *Tristram Shandy's World: Sterne's Philosophical Rhetoric* (New York: Russell and Russell, 1954), 31–32. Tristram's authorial preface mocks Locke's attack on wit ("the great Locke, who was seldom outwitted by false sounds—was nevertheless bubbled here"; 1.3.20), making it clear that he expected the philosopher who had refuted so many errors to have examined the needful role of wit more clearly before joining the "great wigs" who condemned it.

CHAPTER SIX

The Textual Self: Opportunity and Emotion in the Creation of the Individual

I. Illumination

Within the culture of the early novel, complex interrelations between reading and writing formed a crucible for understanding the self. For English authors like Richardson, Fielding, or Sterne, the interaction between the narrator and the reader had become a critical issue in the novelist's craft. In their correspondence as well as in their experiments with the narrative voice, they acknowledged the extent to which they believed that temperament, associations, and prior experience urged readers to create texts in their own image, to discover themselves in the words of another. What determined the impact of the reading experience involved not only the book but also the circumstances, point in time, and state of the reader's understanding. In France, where the publishing market was more unstable and authors less inclined to seek commercial alternatives to patronage, the literary work was understood primarily as a medium for intense, interpersonal experience.[1] Jean-Jacques Rousseau's passionate

---

1. France shared in the late eighteenth-century epidemic of reading that occurred across Europe. After 1750 novels, travel books, and works on natural history crowded out the classics in libraries of nobles, and wealthy bourgeois and library catalogs bulged with works by authors now completely forgotten. Salons, public libraries, and reading rooms became social centers, and although prices for membership in book-lending societies were high, the renting of books became commonplace. Reading habits also appeared to change, evolving from concentrated attention on a few accessible texts to a passion for acquiring and reading larger quantities of books. Inexpensive *bibliothèque bleue* volumes presented simplified tales and risqué humor showing man enslaved by passions, driven by astrological forces and mixtures of the four humors and the four elements that polite society had rejected in the seventeenth century. In other words, much of that material lagged far behind the ideas of the Enlightenment. However, astrology and mythical tales were beginning to give way

epistolary novel, *La Nouvelle Héloise* (1761), was continental Europe's best seller.[2]

Rousseau described the novel's popularity among women and among those courtly Parisian readers still possessed of "that exquisite sense which thrills the heart," a virtue that somehow managed to survive amid corrupted moral conditions.[3] His analysis of his readers reflected his social aspirations and exemplified the imaginative reconstruction of reality that appears throughout his work, but readers did identify themselves with his characters, make pilgrimages to Vevey, and attempt to imitate fictional situations represented in the novel. Above all, they identified him with Saint Preux.[4] Indeed, although he protested that his work reflected the intensity of an ecstatic imagination rather than events in his own life, he treasured files of letters from infatuated readers, and his sense of himself as a romantic hero became deeply embedded in his autobiographical projects.[5] In the case of Rousseau, therefore, both readers and author

---

to new attitudes toward death, human nature, social relations, and natural forces. Robert Darnton, *The Great Cat Massacre and Other Episodes in French Cultural History* (New York: Vintage, 1985), chap. 4, summarizes the French publishing environment at that time. See also Raymond Birn, "Malesherbes and the Call for a Free Press," in *Revolution in Print*, ed. Robert Darnton and Daniel Roche (Berkeley: University of California Press, 1989), 50–66. According to Jack R. Censer, *The French Press in the Age of Enlightenment* (London: Routledge, 1994), 139, enough periodicals had more than a three-year run during the period from 1740 to 1788 to require a special category within the censor's office. On the basis of a study of prospectuses for these periodicals, Censer suggests that readers were drawn primarily from the elite class (both commoners and nobles) and approximately 15–20 percent were women.

2. Rousseau was lionized in the Paris salons after his novel was published. Geoffrey Turnovsky, "The Enlightenment Literary Market: Rousseau, Authorship, and the Book Trade," *Eighteenth-Century Studies* 36, no. 3 (2003): 387–410, notes that while the substantial payments Rousseau received enhanced his reputation, the passionate and sincere image he strove to present to the public was more important to him. He insisted on identifying himself, although most books at the time were published anonymously, and refused to accept even seemingly trivial textual changes or corrections from his publisher.

3. Jean-Jacques Rousseau, *The Confessions and Correspondence, Including the Letters to Malesherbes*, vol. 5 of *The Collected Writings of Rousseau*, trans. Christopher Kelly, ed. Christopher Kelly, Roger D. Masters, and Peter G. Stillman, 11 vols. (Hanover: University Press of New England, 1990), XI.456. Unless noted all future citations of Rousseau's work are taken from this edition.

4. See Jean Starobinski, *Jean-Jacques Rousseau: Transparency and Obstruction*, trans. Arthur Goldhammer (Chicago: University of Chicago Press, 1988), especially his discussion of Rousseau's report on the generation of the novel and its appeal, 338–46.

5. Not all of his admirers were women. Robert Darnton, "Readers Respond to Rousseau," in *The Great Cat Massacre*, 217–22, recounts how Jean Ransom, a La Rochelle bookseller, idolized the author.

begin to explore the possibility that a fictive text can serve as an author's alternative self.

Rousseau's status as novelist and as an autobiographer who vividly recorded the impact of his early reading experiences presents us with an exemplary figure of an eighteenth-century individual formed by reading.[6] As a young boy, he read the "novels" that had belonged to his mother, who died at his birth. At first he and his father read aloud together after supper simply to make the practice of reading more amusing, but soon they shared a consuming interest in these narratives. We can only hypothesize about what works they read, but in the *Confessions* he wrote that this "dangerous method" of learning shaped his emotions into a "different stamp":

> I do not know how I learned to read; I remember only my first readings and their effect on me. This is the time from which I date the uninterrupted consciousness of myself. . . . By this dangerous method I acquired in a short time not only an extraordinary facility in reading and understanding, but also an intelligence about the passions that was unique for my age. I had no idea whatsoever about matters whose feelings were all known to me already. I had conceived nothing; I had felt everything. These confused emotions which I experienced one after the other did not at all impair my reason which I did not yet have: but they formed one of a different stamp in me, and gave me bizarre and romantic concepts about human life, from which experience and reflection have never been able to cure me completely. (V.i.7–8)

---

6. For an overview of the semantic history of the word "individual," see Raymond Williams, *Keywords: A Vocabulary of Culture and Society* (New York: Oxford University Press, 1983), 161–65. Edward W. Tayler, "The First Individual," in *Soundings of Things Done: Essays in Early Modern Literature in Honor of S. K. Heninger, Jr.*, ed. Peter E. Medine and Joseph Wittreich (Newark: University of Delaware Press, 1997), 251–59, offers Henry More as a case history of the first individual. Evidently, between 1635–37 More experienced a crisis concerning the individuality of the soul. He refused to regard substance as a union of form and matter or accept the principle that individuals are formally similar but distinct in matter. He posited a Christian-Platonic interpretation, colored by atomism, in which an individual is the center of light and energy, free, active, and vital. According to Tayler, the term *individuum* (indivisible), referring to the member of a species, became naturalized by the end of the sixteenth century but lost out to "individual." The seventeenth century gradually became comfortable with "individual" as referring to a single human being distinct from family or society. Someone trained to think of the self as substance would find it hard to conceive of an "individual."

References to sensation and reflection in this passage are reminiscent of Locke's two fountains of knowledge as well as his theories of the association of ideas and of the power of early impressions on a child's mind. Rousseau recognized that he had been formed by print culture, identifying a mode of self-consciousness that evolved from the act of reading, even as he acknowledged the risk of taking dangerous (and lasting) impressions into his mind. The passage also expresses a fundamental aspect of his retrospective interpretation of this experience, which presents feelings as prior to reason.

Altering any of the events that led to this moment in Rousseau's childhood might have broken the formative chain of circumstances. If his mother had not been a prescient reader, if his father had not chosen her books for his pedagogical purpose, and if he had not confessed himself "more of a child than you are" (V.i.7) after a *nuit blanche* spent reading, Rousseau's mind might not have been stamped at an early age by popular fiction.[7] From his earliest recollections, therefore, this exemplary representative of the Enlightenment reveals accident as a determining force in his development.

Rousseau recorded countless accidents in his autobiographical writings. Some are physical calamities like crushing his finger in a printing press or being temporarily blinded by an exploding ink bottle. Others appear as seemingly unrelated events like the nightly locking of the gates of Geneva that led him to cast off the apprenticeship he hated, abandon his native town, make his way across the Alps to Turin, and at last arrive in Chambery, where he began his affair with his "dear Mamma," Mme de Warens. He appears deflected from his course by one chance occasion after another. What made him unique, he believed, was not random events but essential qualities that determined their impact upon him: his sensibility and the power of his imagination. Both of these characteristics intersected in the life-altering accident he experienced in the summer of 1749.

While walking along the road from Paris to Vincennes, he read in his

---

7. Keymer, "Sterne and the 'New Species of Writing,'" in *Sterne, the Moderns, and the Novel* (Oxford: Oxford University Press, 2002), argues that Sterne read popular fiction omnivorously, as indicated not only by his use of contemporary work, but also by the contents of his personal library. For Sterne the reading of experimental examples of a new genre represented a deliberate choice on the part of a mature author. Even if we take into account the fact that the works Rousseau read were written prior to this efflorescence, he associated their impact with his distinctive originality. The immense popular success of *La Nouvelle Héloise* demonstrates the degree to which his readers empathized with the opposition of feeling to reason (in the characters of Saint Preux and Wolmar) that he described as fundamental to his own development.

newspaper the notice of a competition for the best response to a question posed by the Academy of Dijon.[8] At that moment of chance reading he experienced an epiphany that has come to be known as his "illumination on the road to Vincennes":

> That year 1749 the Summer was excessively hot. From Paris to Vincennes adds up to two leagues. Hardly in a condition to pay for cabs, at two o'clock in the afternoon I went on foot when I was alone, and I went quickly so as to arrive earlier. The trees on the road, always pruned in the fashion of the country, gave almost no shade, and often exhausted from the heat and fatigue, I spread out on the ground when I was not able to go any farther. I took it into my head to take some book along to moderate my pace. One day I took the *Mercury of France* and while walking and glancing over it I fell upon this question proposed by the Academy of Dijon for the prize for the following year: *Has the progress of the sciences and arts tended to corrupt or purify morals?*
>
> At the moment of that reading I saw another universe and I became another man. (V.viii.294)

Rousseau gave us a specific moment in time. He spoke of his restricted finances, the lopped branches of the trees, and the heat of the road. Deftly and economically, he created an empirical setting that highlighted the shock of his chance reading and presented a thoroughly modern tableau. Yet by using reading to slow his pace and block the sensations of the roadway and the heat of the sun from his mind, he created a world of reading that existed alongside the empirical world he sketched. Thus, even before he began to write his fictions, he joined the world of reading with the world of experience.

Ideas rushed into Rousseau's mind when he read the question posed by the academy. He envisioned a universe shining with truths that seemed to him as immutable as the stars. A chance reading—an encounter in a public place with information available to anyone who had access to a popular newspaper—created a unique and intensely private experience.

8. In "The Great Divide: Rousseau on the Route to Vincennes," in *George Washington's False Teeth: An Unconventional Guide to the Eighteenth Century* (New York: W. W. Norton, 2003), 107–18, Robert Darnton portrays Rousseau as an "intellectual tramp" who turned to the companionship of the philosophes after failing in his attempt to enter French society. He interprets Rousseau's attack on the arts and sciences as a reflection of his alienation from the salons. By inaugurating his publishing career, the illumination transformed a pattern of failed projects and repeated humiliations into a resounding public success (which ironically caused him to be swept up as a curiosity into the high society he had decried).

This illumination constituted all of his thought, he wrote later, and the experience became a touchstone, a foundation for his autobiographical attempts. He rewrote his life obsessively around this moment, chronicling both his physical and mental sensations, as if he could never quite grasp what had happened to him on the road to Vincennes.

Rousseau described his experience in the *Confessions* (1766–70), the "Letter to Christophe de Beaumont" (1763), the *Dialogues* (1772–76), and the *Reveries of the Solitary Walker* (1776–78), but most extensively in his "Second Letter to Malesherbes" (1762). "Je tombe sur la question," he wrote in his letter—"I fell across the question"—and then recounted how he enacted this idiomatic expression by falling to the ground:

> If anything has ever resembled a sudden inspiration, it is the motion that was caused in me by that reading; suddenly I felt my mind dazzled by a thousand lights; crowds of lively ideas presented themselves at the same time with a strength and a confusion that threw me into an inexpressible perturbation; I feel my head seized by a dizziness similar to drunkenness. A violent palpitation oppresses me, makes me sick to my stomach; not being able to breathe anymore while walking, I let myself fall under one of the trees of the avenue, and I pass a half-hour there in such an agitation that when I got up again I noticed the whole front of my coat soaked with my tears without having felt that I shed them. ("Second Letter to Malesherbes," V.575)

While his spirit rose, "dazzled by a thousand lights," his body fell, oppressed and panting. The scene invokes a division of spirit and body. It is "real" in the sense that it is grounded in the detail of the moment, but beneath these circumstantial details lie old narratives.

Rousseau's illumination echoes two of the most famous conversion narratives in Western thought: Paul's conversion on the road to Damascus and Augustine's conversion through a chance reading, narrated in his *Confessions*. When the light of God shone down on Paul, blinding him and knocking him down, it directly manifested God's presence. When Augustine overheard a voice that he interpreted as a direction to read and opened Paul's *Epistle to the Romans*, his conversion signified a mediation of God's power through reading the holy words.[9] Rousseau, however,

---

9. Patrick Riley, "The Inversion of Conversion: Rousseau's Rewriting of Augustinian Autobiography," *Studies in Eighteenth-Century Culture* 28 (1999): 229–55, argues that Rousseau's confessional anecdotes ascribe his calamities to chance and deform the natural dispositions of the self.

received his illumination when his glance fell on a newspaper notice. In short, we have traveled from a direct moment of illumination through increasing distance from providential light to a secular act of reading. No longer theological, Rousseau's illumination described his experience within the world. It was not God who entered into his heart in a moment of spiritual vocation, but rather an idea. Nor did his transformation bring him into a community of believers. Instead, it reinforced his differences, his uniqueness in a new community composed of writer and reader.

The experience was at once intellectual and deeply personal. We know he often wandered in the countryside for pleasure, either alone or with a beloved companion like Mme d'Houdetot, but on the day of his illumination, he was on his way to visit his friend and fellow thinker Denis Diderot.[10] Diderot, whose *Philosophical Thoughts* had been condemned by the censor shortly after its publication in 1746, was under arrest in the Château of Vincennes for having written his *Letter on the Blind*, which employed the well-established philosophical problem of the nature of sight as a metaphor for his critique of Enlightenment reason. His confinement was emblematic of state control over the French press, which attempted to censor all works opposed to the monarchy, the church, or morality.[11] Because Rousseau's own efforts to make a name for himself, such as his project for a new musical notation, an opera, and his play *Narcissus*, had failed to materialize, his sympathy for his friend's situation must have been colored by the fact that someone from a similar artisan background had managed to achieve distinction, indeed notoriety, in the literary field.

Reading the question posed for the academy's competition appeared perilous to Rousseau because of the visceral and intense response that accompanied his chance reading, yet he regarded it as a "happy chance" in the sense that it gave him ideas that would win the prize and define his future career: "Suddenly a fortunate chance happened to enlighten me about what I had to do for myself, and to think about my fellows about whom my heart was ceaselessly in contradiction with my mind,

10. For a discussion of Rousseau as the emblematic walker see Celeste Langan, *Romantic Vagrancy: Wordsworth and the Simulation of Freedom* (Cambridge: Cambridge University Press, 1995), chap. 1.

11. Daniel Roche, "Censorship and the Publishing Industry," in *Revolution in Print: The Press in France, 1775–1800*, ed. Robert Darnton and Daniel Roche (Berkeley: University of California Press, 1989), 3–26. According to Roche, 513 of the prisoners placed in the Bastille between 1740 and 1749 (19 percent of the total) were under arrest for breaking the book laws. The percentage rose to 40 percent between 1750 and 1759.

and whom I still felt myself brought to love along with so many reasons to hate them."[12] His exact words were *heureux hasard.* While in English usage the word hazard generally signifies a risk or peril, especially one that will produce bodily harm, the French term *hasard* is less restrictive and denotes chance.[13]

Rousseau's association of self-risk with chance also alluded to the culture of gambling so pervasive in eighteenth-century France.[14] Along with narratives of risk and reward appearing in periodicals and novels that featured happy or unhappy outcomes of accidental events, gambling played a role in informing a shift in the possibilities of self-definition. All types of accidental experience began to acquire significance as elements that could form the course of a life. For the nobility, risking large sums at play became an analogy for risking one's life in battle. Having the courage to risk and winning or losing with equal equanimity demonstrated indifference

12. Jean-Jacques Rousseau, *Letters to Malesherbes,* in *The Collected Writings,* V.575.

13. The etymology of *hasard* emphasizes the secular implications of the word, which probably derives from the Arab plural *az-zahr,* meaning *dice.* Another possible origin derives from a game of dice played by the Crusaders and named after their place of encampment, the castle Hasart. Both definitions show the origin of the term in a game of dice—hence the generic name for gambling, *jeux de hasard.* However, something of the original Latin word for chance (*sors*) also hovers over the word in relation to Rousseau's illumination. *Sors* derived from the Roman word for the tokens used in casting lots for government jobs, so that chance was linked by association to events that determined one's "lot in life." For more on the etymological origins of *hasard,* see Clément Rosset, *Logique du pire: Éléments pour une philosophie tragique* (Paris: Presses universitaires des France, 1971), 9–10.

14. Louis XIV held *appartements du roi* given over to gambling three times a week at Versailles, the queen hosted a nightly game, and courtiers scheduled additional occasions for play. Hosts so frequently acted as bankers for games to entertain their guests that satirists, chroniclers, and moralists complained that compulsive gambling had destroyed other forms of social entertainment. In Paris ten authorized *maisons de jeux* operated games involving some degree of skill (*jeux de commerce*), but essentially they served as fronts for more lucrative chance-driven games (*jeux de hasard*). Gambling also took place at the two great Paris fairs during almost four months of the year, all year long at foreign embassies, and eventually at gambling houses at the Hôtel de Gesvres and later at the Hôtel de Soissons. In addition to these legal venues, the large number of clandestine Parisian gaming rooms, lighted by *tripots,* made one visitor comment that "flaming pots set Paris ablaze," and gambling was by no means restricted to Paris. The "Age des Lumières" was lighted by gambling. In *Enlightenment and the Shadows of Chance: The Novel and the Culture of Gambling in Eighteenth-Century France* (Baltimore: Johns Hopkins University Press, 1993), 30–32, Thomas Kavanagh provides a more detailed history of the gambling craze from 1674 into the reign of Louis XVI. His seminal study positions contingency as a force operating within the conventional characterization of Enlightenment reason and determinism. See also F. N. David, *Games, Gods and Gambling: The Origins and History of Probability and Statistical Ideas from the Earliest Times to the Newtonian Era* (New York: Hafner, 1962); and Gerd Gigerenzer et al., *The Empire of Chance: How Probability Changed Science and Everyday Life* (Cambridge: Cambridge University Press, 1989).

to material gain and thus served as a means of displaying hereditary status. When the marquis de Dangeau, a recently ennobled Huguenot, won several fortunes at court through his skillful play, he was not accused of cheating but of applying his vaunted study of probabilities in the service of venal gain. Dangeau's consistent success not only signaled the end of the aristocratic posture of superiority to money, it affirmed the primacy of mathematical probability and sanctified bourgeois economic expertise. Areas of life that had previously appeared to escape deterministic laws had been tamed by mathematical analysis, enabling those skilled in the science of probability to master events that previously seemed to lie beyond conscious direction. Awareness of the potentially determining role of chance or accident was accompanied by a sense that the self could be defined by the way the individual responded to such events.

Rousseau may have associated *hasard* with Diderot, whom he was on his way to visit at the moment of his illumination. Not only had Diderot drafted an ironic proposal for a compulsory French lottery designed to replace the tax system, he invoked chance and probability to critique notions of providence in the *Philosophical Thoughts*, which had been proscribed by the French censor.[15] In a paragraph that Rousseau later cut from his response to Voltaire's *Poem on the Lisbon Earthquake* (1756), he recalled reading the twenty-first of Diderot's *Philosophical Thoughts*: "I remember that what has struck me most forcibly in my whole life, on the fortuitous arrangement of the universe, is the twenty-first philosophical thought, where is shown by the laws of analysis of chance that when the quantity of the throws is infinite, the difficulty of the event is more than sufficiently compensated by the multiplicity of the throws, and that consequently the mind ought to be more astonished by the hypothetical continuation of chaos than by the real birth of the universe" ("Letter to Voltaire," III.117–18). In the passage that impressed Rousseau so dramatically, Diderot's materialism replaced providence with probability in

15. Ian Hacking discusses the shift from deterministic models of scientific understanding and the invention of probability theory in *The Taming of Chance* (Cambridge: Cambridge University Press, 1990). See also his "Was There a Probabilistic Revolution 1800–1930?" in *The Probabilistic Revolution*, ed. Lorenz Krüger, Lorrain J. Daston, and Michael Heidelberger (Cambridge, MA: MIT Press, 1987). For a discussion of contingency in Diderot's work see Kavanagh, *Enlightenment and the Shadows of Chance*, 162–84; Lester G. Crocker, *Diderot's Chaotic Order: Approach to Synthesis* (Princeton: Princeton University Press, 1974); and Geoffrey Bremner, *Order and Chance: The Pattern of Diderot's Thought* (Cambridge: Cambridge University Press, 1983). A more general consideration of these issues that focuses on the nineteenth-century French novel can be found in David F. Bell, *Circumstances: Chance in the Literary Text* (Lincoln: University of Nebraska Press, 1993).

such a way that chaos was controlled by an underlying structure. Within the contemporary scientific community, the workings of the physical (and even the moral) world had come to be understood as controlled by laws of cause and effect even though the techniques were not yet available to demonstrate this truth in all cases. Although some believed a divine principle directed these forces as their primary cause, others did not. Therefore, Diderot's *Encyclopédie* calls chance a "fiction, a chimera bereft of possibility and existence." The article gave a theological support for this assertion: "For God, knowing all causes and all effects, actual as well as potential, in the clearest detail, nothing can be an effect of chance." [16] The agnostic Diderot refused to subordinate human knowledge to the workings of any theological principle, so this entry suggests that his imprisonment had given him a greater respect for the power of censorship. Overall, however, the *Encyclopédie* reflected his faith in human potential to advance (however chaotically) along the pathways of discovery. [17]

In Rousseau's illumination, *hasard* arrived suddenly—"tout à coup"—and in the *jeux de hasard* a *coup* is a throw of the dice. Thus, by reading and responding to the academy's question, he gambled himself to win the prize and become a published author. The longed-for literary career that had seemed to be out of reach for a watchmaker's son within the stratified structure of French society once again hovered within his grasp; suddenly he understood how he could single himself out through his original perspective and his unique sensitivity. In one sense, he could emulate Dangeau's success at the gaming tables by his play with words.

Although the force of *hasard* literally knocked Rousseau down on the road to Vincennes and Diderot's probabalistic reading of *hazard* may have encouraged him to imagine winning the competition, he refused to believe that the laws of probability could account for all human activity. He explicitly exempted the writing of a great work of art. As he explained in his "Letter to Voltaire" (1756): "Let someone come to tell me that, from a fortuitous throw of letters [Voltaire's] *Henriade* was composed, I would deny it without hesitating; it is more possible for chance to bring it about than for my mind to believe it, and I feel that there is a point where moral impossibilities are for me equivalent to a physical certainty" (III.118). In

16. "Chance [*le hasard*] is nothing. It is a fiction, a chimera bereft of possibility and existence. People attribute to chance effects whose causes they do not understand. But for God, knowing all causes and all effects, actual as well as potential, in the clearest detail, nothing can be an effect of chance" (my translation). Denis Diderot, *Encyclopédie*, vols. 14–17 of *Oeuvres complètes* (Paris: Garnier, 1875–77), 14:84–85.

17. Kavanaugh, *Enlightenment and the Shadows of Chance*, 246ff.

other words, while Rousseau may have accepted the operation of the laws of probability in relation to the physical world, his sense of individualism excluded their operation in the moral realm. He could no more admit that talent was the fruit of chance than Diderot would consider it a God-given gift.

Although Rousseau wrote some articles for the *Encyclopédie*, he rejected its embrace of progress through the arts and sciences in favor of his evolving perception of the primacy of innate or instinctive feelings. Both his secularism and the significance he accorded to chance measure his increasing separation from the idea that lives are determined by divine plan. In fact, later he expressed the wish that his own works might provide the basis for some future *sortes Rousseau:* "I like to flatter myself that some day there will be a statesman who is [also] a citizen [and] that by some lucky chance he will cast his eyes on this book [*Second Discourse*], that my loose ideas will inspire in him more useful ones, that he will devote himself to making men better or happier. . . . My writing has been guided by this fantasy."[18]

If we read Rousseau's description of his illumination literally, he was not enlightened by what he read or by the act of reading but by chance itself. *Hasard* represents a concatenation of accidental circumstances that alters the outcome of an intended act. Again in his letter to d'Alembert on the theater, he evoked its power through the metaphor of gambling: "Chance, countless accidental causes, countless unforeseen circumstances, do what force and reason could not; or, rather, it is precisely because chance directs them that force can do nothing; like the dice which leave the hand, whatever impulsion is given them does not bring up the desired point any more easily" ("Letter to d'Alembert," X.305). Even though the results of casting the dice evade the thrower's control, the result is not chaotic because *hasard* directs. This is the sense in which Rousseau invoked *heureux hasard* in the narrative of his illumination. He summoned luck—the luck of his entry—but he also ascribed a higher power to *hasard* within an allusion to emerging notions of probability theory that investigated how readily certain combinations would occur when dice were thrown. Probabilistic calculations evaded the traditional understanding of chance operating within providential control, so that this latent allusion provides another measure of the secularization of Rousseau's thought. Moreover, by evoking this probabilistic model to explain

---

18. Jean-Jacques Rousseau, "Fragments politiques," in *Oeuvres complètes* (Paris: Gallimard, 1959), 3:474.

his transformation, he accentuated his belief that unexpected circum-stances—those that evade "strength and reason"—control the process of self-definition.

II. Probability and Sensibility

The only piece Rousseau wrote directly under the force of his illumina-tion, the *prosopopoeia* of Fabricius, involved the assumption of a new voice and character.[19] The word *prosopopoeia*—which derives from the Greek for "face (*prósopon*)" and "making (*poieîn*)"—was a rhetorical figure studied in the classical curriculum in which the student adopts the persona of an earlier writer to declaim in his voice. In other words, in this moment he created or was occupied by a literary character. A similar process of developing a narrative persona was at work in contemporary England. For example, when Joseph Addison invented the character of Bickerstaff to be the author of his *Spectator* papers or Daniel Defoe based Robinson Crusoe on the actual shipwreck experience of Alexander Selkirk, the mul-tiplication of the authorial persona introduced the possibility of creating a deepened (multifaceted) textual self for the author.

To inveigh against "vain talents," Rousseau chose the persona of a Roman whose poverty signaled his virtue:[20] "What has become of those thatched roofs and those rustic hearths where moderation and virtue used to dwell? What disastrous splendor has succeeded Roman simplic-ity? What is this strange language? What are these effeminate morals? What is the meaning of these statues, these Paintings, these buildings? . . . Romans, hasten to tear down these Amphitheaters, break these marble statues, burn these paintings, chase out these slaves who subjugate you and whose fatal arts corrupt you. Let other hands win fame by vain tal-ents; the only talent worthy of Rome is that of conquering the world and making virtue reign in it" (*First Discourse*, II.11). Reflecting on the great

19. He included this piece at the end of the first part of his *First Discourse*, published in January 1751.

20. Given Rousseau's financial state at the time (he walked to Vincennes because he could not afford a fiacre), we can understand his attraction to this figure, for in the *Aeneid*, Fabricius is briefly described as "parvo potentem: powerful in poverty" (VI.843). See Virgil, *Aeneid*, trans. H. Rushton Fairclough (Cambridge, MA: Harvard University Press, 1940–46). Fabricius also is present in Dante's *Purgatorio*, where he appears just before the completion of Dante's penance and is greeted as "O buon Fabrizio, / con povertà volesti anzi virtute / che gran riccezza posseder con vizio" ("O good Fabricius, thou chosest for thy possessions virtue with poverty rather than great riches with wickedness"). Dante Alighieri, *The Divine Comedy*, trans. John D. Sinclair (London: Bodley Head, 1958), XX.25–27.

crowd of ideas that visited him at the moment of his illumination had led Rousseau to a conclusion that incorporated a subtle paradox: man is naturally good but is made evil by the social institutions that civilize him. The critique of civilization that he put into the mouth of Fabricius reflected this perception, but Rousseau asserted that the corrupting influence was not confined to Rome or to eighteenth-century France but was part of the universal history of mankind. "What did I have this great man say," he explained, "that I might not have put into the mouth of Louis XII or Henry IV?" (II.11). Yet even as he spoke through Fabricius, a creator or fabricator contemptuous of unworthy talents, he made Fabricius invoke the departed Cineas, the ambassador of Pyrrhus, who had admired the Roman senate for its virtue.

In other words, what appears as a conventional rhetorical exercise worked to create an enhanced textual self, and the classical technique began to signify in a new and unsettling way. Even as Rousseau attached himself to the moral authority of great men by adopting a series of literary personae, he also expressed a fundamental uncertainty about who was truly speaking or writing. "Putting on of a face" led only to another mask, another *prosopopoeia*, so that his authorial self was endlessly dislocated backward in a process of cultural archaeology until he uncovered the archetypal figure of Natural Man.[21]

When Rousseau fell to the ground on his way to Vincennes, he experienced an instinctive manifestation of emotion. Separated from his spirit, his body acted in ways he recognized only after he returned to consciousness. Upon reflection, his palpitations and spontaneous tears testified to the sincerity of his illumination, but he also came to believe they signaled a natural response of the kind that society had forced him to mask. He realized that by imposing a reign of reason, civilization had destroyed such "natural purity."[22] In the golden age of Natural Man, neo-Aristotelian

21. In *Metaromanticism: Aesthetics, Literature, Theory* (Chicago: University of Chicago Press, 2003), 48–49, Paul Hamilton argues that Rousseau needed to establish a base for self-understanding outside the tradition of the arts and sciences he had inherited. The more Rousseau risked exposing his idiosyncrasies, the more he tried to suggest that he was abstracting the discussion from the usual preconceptions.

22. George Armstrong Kelly, "A General Overview," in *The Cambridge Companion to Rousseau*, ed. Patrick Riley (Cambridge: Cambridge University Press, 2001), 14, notes that Rousseau became convinced that philosophers had not imagined man's condition sufficiently. Locke's attack on innate ideas responded to the question of man's essence by citing reports of savages with tails, women with beards, and so on, to show that we know only nominal essences and asked where one might discover Descartes's innate ideas in the mind of a child. Rousseau contended that although a child would not display ideas of God, or of duty,

classifications did not apply. "How," he wrote in his *Second Discourse*, "would they have imagined or understood the words matter, mind, substance, mode, figure, movement, since . . . they found no model of them in Nature?" (III.93). Moreover, the entry of "reason" corrupted Natural Man's protective love of the self (*l'amour de soi-même*) into self-love (*amour propre*), the vanity characteristic of civilized man. Pity's empathy with the sufferings of others became self-reflexive: "Reason engenders amour-propre and reflection fortifies it; reason turns man back upon himself, it separates him from all that bothers and afflicts him. Philosophy isolates him; because of it he says in secret, at the sight of a suffering man: perish if you will, I am safe" (*Second Discourse*, III.37). A contemporary example of this phenomenon would be the fascination with car crashes Americans call rubbernecking. For Rousseau erosion of pity posed an ethical problem in which the narcissism of the reasoning self encouraged distinctions that separated civilized man from his fellows and promoted inequality.[23] As a result, he argued, the "various contingencies" that perfect human reason cause the species to deteriorate and make "a being evil while making him sociable" (III.42).[24] In other words, the accidents that play a role in forming Natural Man also help transform him into civilized man through his capacity to adapt to changes in external circumstances.

Before his illumination, Rousseau's thoughts had turned incessantly upon his relation to his fellow men. When he described his experience in the "Second Letter to Malesherbes," he referred to them as "mes semblables," literally "those like me" (V.575). However, the term *semblable* contains a cultural memory of an Aristotelian and neo-Scholastic notion of categories based upon formal similarity. For Aristotle, as for the Scholastics, an individual differed from his "semblable" only because each man was composed of an individual unit of the same matter. But the notion of being like other men tormented Rousseau. He asserted his uniqueness when he wrote that his illumination had transformed him

---

or of complex reason, he would be free from the stain of corruption. *Émile*, of course, proposes how to protect such a child from the wounding effects of society.

23. According to Eric Auerbach, *Mimesis: The Representation of Reality in Western Literature*, trans. Willard R. Trask (Princeton: Princeton University Press, 1953), 466–67, the great disillusionment that occurred when Rousseau's idyllic concept of nature revealed itself as absolutely opposed to the established historical reality prepared for the rise of the modern conception of reality; for the first time, the eighteenth-century style of historically unproblematic and unmoved presentation of life became valueless.

24. Kelly, "A General Overview," 20–21, discusses the antiteleological implications of Rousseau's understanding of the way chance deflects men into specialized ways of life in which they lose a part of their integrity for the sake of necessity or advantage.

into another man (*autre homme*), a use of *autre* reminiscent of his declaration of difference at the beginning of the *Confessions:* "Myself alone. I feel
my heart and I know men. I am not made like any of the ones I have seen;
I dare to believe that I am not made like any that exist. If I am worth no
more, at least I am different [*au moins je suis autre*]. Whether nature has
done well or ill in breaking the mold in which it cast me, is something
which cannot be judged until I have been read" (V.i.5). Understood in
the neo-Scholastic sense, the mold represents the infinitely reproducible
semblables. Through his narrative of the illumination, Rousseau mytholo-
gized the violence of breaking this mold as the liberation of self through
the experience of *hasard.* Thus, chance events or accidents function as
sites around which narratives of individual difference can collocate.

For Rousseau the pedagogical function of these scenes became a point
at which to distinguish his unique responses from those of the average
man. For example, in the *Confessions* he recounts a beating he received as
a boy from Mlle Lambercier. The unusual nature of his reaction came as
a surprise, for he realized a "precocious sexual instinct" in the increase of
affection he felt for her after the punishment: "Who would believe that
this childhood punishment received at eight years of age from the hand
of a woman of thirty, determined my tastes, my desires, my passions, my
self for the rest of my life, and this, precisely in the opposite sense to the
one that ought to follow naturally? At the same time that my senses were
inflamed, my desires were so well put off the track, that—being limited to
what I had experienced—they did not venture to look for anything else"
(V.i.13–14). When Rousseau was spanked, his body responded with an
erection. He described the intensity of his childish sexuality as "depraved
and insane" and its channeling into masochism as a false turn (literally
a perversion), yet this quality—which could not have been recognized as
determining individuality within a neo-Aristotelian schema (and would
be disowned by the new statistically "normal" man)—acquired significance within his understanding of the self by marking him as unique.

Through a series of circumstances, as Rousseau realized in retrospect,
sensuality had created one of the most vigorous elements in his character.
His imagination allowed him to transfer his feelings for Mlle Lambercier
to other women, and he remained chaste, he said, by recreating the scenario of pleasurable punishment with these imaginary creations. Even in
his maturity, he received "the most delicate pleasure" from falling on his
knees and begging forgiveness from a beloved woman. The act of writing
offered an equivalent to this gratifying act of self-exposure and submission to another's judgment. It resulted in "an undertaking which has no

precedent" (V.i.5), the creation of a textual self engaged in a complex process of amorous pleading, sublimation, and deferred gratification.[25]

III. Jacques the Fatalist

"How had they met? By chance like everybody else."[26] The opening words of Diderot's *Jacques the Fatalist and His Master* (written from the 1760s to the 1780s and published posthumously in 1796) announce its theme of chance. In this plotless narrative, chance encounters are ubiquitous. While Rousseau based his analysis of contemporary morality on the natural goodness of man, Diderot explored the relationship between moral behavior and man's understanding of chance events. Although fatalism assumes that all events are foreordained, the fatalist cannot know what will happen until after the events take place. Thus, in Diderot's view, fatalism offers no better guide for making moral decisions than a belief in chance and indeed, by reducing the role of free will, it eliminates moral responsibility.[27]

Diderot's understanding of the problem of cause and effect reflected the Enlightenment idea that matter acts in ways that will be revealed as

25. Although Rousseau evoked a deliberate comparison to Augustine's *Confessions* in his choice of the title for his work as well as elements of individual events, Augustine could not have conceived of making the self the center of his attempt to write his life. In the sense that he understood events, movements of time, and social, intellectual, and psychological states as things made and known by human beings, capturing them in language was hard work but not impossible. Rousseau, on the other hand, striving to make the chaos of his feelings transparent to his reader, did not so much remember as reexperience the emotions that constituted the past for him. He recreated them in the present as he wrote. And because he immediately forgot whatever he consigned to paper (one of the peculiarities of his memory that he felt deserved mention; VIII.294), the act of transcribing his experiences in order to preserve his ideas, the creation of that textual self, simultaneously represented a loss of self. James Olney, *Memory and Narrative: The Weave of Life-Writing* (Chicago: University of Chicago Press, 1998), 411.

26. Denis Diderot, *Jacques le fatalist*, trans. David Coward (Oxford: Oxford University Press, 1999), 3. All citations are taken from this text.

27. Spinoza, whose works Jacques claims to know by heart, was considered the leading proponent of fatalism. The *Encyclopédie* article "Spinosistes" agreed with contemporary understanding of his theories in declaring that his modern followers believe "matter is all that exists; and that it is enough to explain everything." To change the ruling laws of nature would render everything unpredictable, so that fatalism, which makes people passive instruments of natural forces, restricts freedom even more than determinism, which permits individuals to choose how to behave. (Eighteenth-century critics ignored the fact that Spinoza also had argued that behavior can be modified by the threat of punishment or reward.) See Jean Terrasse, "Aspects de l'espace-temps dans *Jacques le fataliste*," *Eighteenth-Century Fiction* 6, no. 3 (April 1994): 243–57, on fatalism as a sentiment versus the doctrine of determinism.

scientific knowledge increases over time. This sense of probable cause extended to the metaphysics of mind and soul. In *Jacques the Fatalist*, Diderot created a dialogue that opposed Jacques's point of view to that of his Master, but the result was neither conclusive nor didactic.

References to Cartesian dualism as well as to the ideas of Locke and Sterne are scattered throughout the conversation. The work forms a tissue of sly allusions to both fictional and real-life characters. Diderot adapted events from Corporal Trim's injury and subsequent treatment in *Tristram Shandy* to serve as the basis for Jacques's biography. In the following passage, he alludes (by association) to Walter Shandy's theory of noses and has the Master sense an idea. At the same time, he nods to the criticism of the corrupting influence of fairy tales that appears in Rousseau's *Émile* and to Descartes's comparison between living men and automata:[28]

MASTER: Jacques, do you know the fable about Garo?

JACQUES: Yes.

MASTER: What do you make of it?

JACQUES: It's bad.

MASTER: That's easily said.

JACQUES: And easily demonstrated. If instead of acorns, oak trees produced pumpkins, would Garo the Bumpkin have gone for a snooze under one? And if he hadn't gone for a snooze under an oak tree, what difference would it have made to the shape of his nose if the tree had rained pumpkins or acorns? It's the sort of thing you should give children to read.

MASTER: A philosopher with your name won't hear of it.

JACQUES: Two things: first, every one is entitled to his opinion, and second, Jean-Jacques is not the same as Jacques.

MASTER: Well that's Jacques's hard luck.

JACQUES: Nobody can say that until he's read the last word of the last line of the page devoted to him in the great scroll.

MASTER: What are you thinking?

JACQUES: I was thinking that all the time you've been talking to me and I've been answering, you were talking without wanting to and I was answering without wanting to.

MASTER: And?

JACQUES: And? That we were therefore a couple of living, thinking machines.

MASTER: But what do you want at this moment?

28. Sterne sent Diderot the first six volumes of *Tristram Shandy* in 1762. "The Acorn and the Pumpkin" appears in La Fontaine's *Fables*.

JACQUES: By God, it doesn't matter what I want. All wanting does is to activate
   another set of cogs in both our machines.

MASTER: Activate in what way?

JACQUES: I'll be damned if I can conceive that cogs are activated for no reason.
   My Captain used to say: "Postulate a cause and an effect will follow. A trivial cause will produce a trivial effect. A passing cause will produce a passing effect. An occasional cause will produce an occasional effect. A cause
   that is blocked will produce a reduced effect. When the cause stops, the
   effect is nil."

MASTER: But it seems to me that I can sense inside me that I am free, in the
   same way that I am aware that I am thinking. (220–21)

During the course of their arguments, Jacques and his Master uncover
inconsistencies in their doctrines.[29] Since Jacques believes that all events
are written on the great scroll and he cannot escape what has been written there, he acts as he pleases. Thus, he accepts the absurdity of his relation to his fatalistic belief. Yet when his Master accepts the status quo, his
attitude also could be described as fatalistic. Just as the men reverse their
social roles when Jacques asserts his independence and his Master con-
dones the insubordination, by the last page neither is Jacques the complete fatalist nor Master the complete master. This ambiguity—combined
with multiple additional stories interpolated into the interrupted structure of the narrative—defuses the power of the fatalist interpretation of
events.

To the question of how a person's philosophical perspective affects
behavior, Diderot seems to answer that many alternatives are possible.
For example, in the story of Mme de La Pommeraye, the listeners change
their interpretations of the characters as the narrative unfolds. Their sym-
pathies lie alternately with the young whore forced to masquerade as a
paragon of virtue (although she could be seen as a schemer), with Mme
de la Pommeraye as the betrayed lover (although she could be seen as a
monster of vengeance), or with the dupe of her stratagems (who could
be viewed either as the heartless agent of his own misfortune or, when
he discovers the past of the woman he has been led to marry, a noble
embodiment of forgiveness). Not only do Jacques and his Master view
this story differently; they also revise their own judgments—presumably

29. See Peter V. Conroy, Jr., "Jacques's Fatal Freedom," *Eighteenth-Century Fiction* 2, no. 4
(July 1990): 309–26, on references to Claude-Adrien Helvétius, Julien Offray de La Mettrie,
Étienne Bonnot de Condillac, Locke, and Spinoza in Diderot's thought as well as an ex-
tended analysis of this opening passage.

as the reader must continually revise his or her opinion as the dialogue proceeds. Each of the stories within a story serves to accentuate the paradoxical nature of interpretation.

Diderot was indebted to Sterne's treatment of the problems of communication: the fluidity of language, the extent to which habits reflect a rigidity of mind, and the variation in individual interpretations of circumstances. Nevertheless, his approach also was colored by his work on the *Encyclopédie*.[30] His early *Letter on the Blind* had argued that every human reaction must differ in proportion to physical differences among individuals, and throughout *Jacques* he implies a physiological basis for behavior. It includes not only the Master's habit of taking snuff and looking at his watch or Jacques's limp but also the effects of climate and social milieu. For Diderot, mental capacity supplemented such physiological differences. In other words, he understood behavior as a combination of chance elements that formed an individual's basic attributes with the sense perceptions and associations that derived from experience. This complex of chance elements naturally produced individual moral judgments in every human being.

In addition to variations in body, mind, and experience, Diderot understood that language could also mark an individual. In 1767 he wrote to the sculptor Étienne-Maurice Falconet, "There is no great principle of morality or taste which is not introduced as example by means of words and their diverse meanings, and that vocabulary would thus become at the same time a book of morals." The speed of conversation, he added, made it impossible for anyone to correct for discrepancies in language by pausing to assess the meaning of each word or the collection of ideas it contained.[31] Because the factors that create an individual are infinitely variable, it follows that no one can either understand another person precisely or be precisely understood.

Diderot's work on the *Encyclopédie* already had capitalized on the fortuitous juxtaposition of ideas. Its alphabetical organization did not impose any predefined system of knowledge on the contents. Intersections

30. Laurent Milesi, "'Have You Not Forgot to Wind Up the Clock?' Tristram Shandy and Jacques le Fataliste on the (Post?) Modern Psychoanalytic Couch," in *Laurence Sterne in Modernism and Postmodernism*, ed. David Pierce and Peter de Voogd (Amsterdam: Rodopi, 1996), 179–95, discusses the "Chinese box device" used by both Sterne and Diderot. He regards the drama of suspended endings in *Jacques* as Diderot's original contribution and notes the way in which foretelling and reenactment allows events to become an integral part of the life of the auditor or reader, at least for the duration of the experience.

31. John Robert Loy, *Diderot's Determined Fatalist: A Critical Appreciation of "Jacques le fataliste"* (New York: Columbia University Press, 1950), 176–79.

between ideas were fundamentally coincidental and thus analogous to the coincidences that occur among events in *Jacques*. However, the *Encyclopédie* did impose a degree of order on its components, and he viewed its open-ended gathering of information as both fertile and potentially productive.[32] His fundamentally optimistic view of life celebrated the generative potential of its relative disorder. For him, no overarching system like fatalism could contain either the suggestive richness of information in an encyclopedia or the multiplicity of elements in a novel. *Jacques the Fatalist* demonstrated the narrative fertility of messy experience.

Like Fielding and Sterne, Diderot used a narrative voice in *Jacques* to establish a relationship between the putative author and the reader.[33] His narrative interruptions emphasize the randomness of life and further undermine the fatalist perspective. Although Jacques sees the events in his story as parts of an unbroken chain, the reader experiences a chaos that calls that sequence into question. Jacques's perspective establishes a difference between participating in events and being detached from them. Within the terms of his fatalism, this position of mastery belongs to the creator of the great scroll, but it also is natural to the storyteller.

The process of foretelling and revisiting events in the novel goes beyond Montaigne's earlier recognition that diversity of perceptions confused the understanding of Reformation theologians. Diderot's realization that perceptions also shift over time, as the perceiver alters the significance allocated to sensations or experience, expanded this diversity by orders of magnitude. Unending narrative breaks down the concept of clock-time boundaries. In *Jacques* he compounded his characters' multiple perceptions by introducing the belated discovery that his narrator is unreliable, making him not only suspicious of the text he presents but also in possession of other versions he has hidden from the reader. The result blurs the barrier between truth and fiction.[34]

Jacques's invocation of the great scroll suggests that the experience of

32. See Kavanagh, *Enlightenment and the Shadows of Chance*, esp. 244ff.

33. Kathryn Simpson Vidal, "Diderot and Reader-Response Criticism: The Case of *Jacques le Fataliste*," in *Studies in Eighteenth-Century Culture* 15 (1986): 33–45. Vidal compares Diderot's use of narration with Fielding's.

34. See Alice Fredman, *Diderot and Sterne* (New York: Columbia University Press, 1955), 145. Her observation that the destruction of narrative time works to fuse the real and the imaginary or vicarious experience suggests ways in which Diderot's technique contributed to the expanding repertoire of ways to manipulate the author-reader relationship. See also Marie-Hélène Chabut, "Diderot's *Jacques le Fataliste et son Maître*: Ex-Centricity and the 'Novel,'" *Eighteenth-Century Fiction* 2, no. 1 (October 1989): 53–64, on related aspects of the novel's construction and language.

life resembles an act of reading. His analogy is evocative for the genre of
the novel in particular. On the level of the fictional situation of *Jacques
the Fatalist*, both Jacques and his Master crave the heightened or expanded
sensation that Sterne as well as Diderot mocked in their addresses to their
readers. Like Sterne, Diderot risked frustrating this desire with delays or
interruptions in order to force his readers to acknowledge that the world
is full of experiences, all of them competing for attention. Ironically, the
providential control he assumed over both the fictional lives of his characters and over the submissive reader confronted fatalism in another way:
his manipulation of narrative credibility and time mediated against the
possibility that the reader could be certain of any preordained outcome.
At the same time, blurring the distinction between truth and fiction allowed readers to transform their self-created constructs into elements of
a personal reality. Rousseau's autobiographical projects inverted this process as he conflated real and imagined versions of his experiences over
narrative time.

IV. Vulnerability

In the *Dialogues*, written during the final years of his life, Rousseau returned to the rhetorical device of the *prosopopoeia*, dividing his authorial
persona into a character called the Frenchman and one called Rousseau
who met to discuss the writings of an author named Jean-Jacques. "Rousseau" admires the work of "Jean-Jacques," but public opinion has deterred
the Frenchman from even reading it.[35] Not until "Rousseau" actually
meets "Jean-Jacques," and discovers someone radically different from the
man described by his reputation, and the Frenchman reads the texts for
himself, can they begin to reconcile the man with his published work.[36]

35. In French polite society, new writing was commonly read aloud in salons and the
writer appeared as a person of good company, deferring to the taste of the interlocutors. After the relative failure of his reading of his *Confessions* in that context, Rousseau attempted to
find a different way to communicate. In effect, he created prefatory material to the *Dialogues*
that entrusted his self to others, and he was profoundly shocked when Condillac reacted
by treating the text as a conventional book and giving advice for improving and marketing
it. See Peter France, "The Commerce of the Self," in *Representations of the Self*, Comparative
Criticism 12, ed. E. S. Shaffer (Cambridge: Cambridge University Press, 1990), 52–53.

36. Rousseau may have modeled this schizophrenic division of self on Plato's dialogues *Theaetetus, Sophist*, and *Statesman*, which contain not only the character of Socrates
but also others who physically resemble him or bear his name, as well as a stranger who
employs characteristics of the Socratic method. The subject of these dialogues is both the
philosophical issue of the relationship between images and originals and the way in which
texts come to be written.

What is at stake in this exchange is interpretive vulnerability, and the *Dialogues* proposed to teach the reader how to respond as justly as "Rousseau" and the Frenchman learned to do: "And that is also all he himself [Jean-Jacques] desires. The hope that his memory be restored someday to the honor it deserves, and that his books become useful through the esteem owed to their Author is henceforth the only hope that can please him in this world. Add to that the sweetness of seeing two decent and true hearts once again open themselves to his own. Let's temper in this way the horror of that solitude in which he is forced to live in the midst of the human race" (I.iii.245). In the *Confessions* Rousseau presented himself as "un autre" to everyone else, but in the *Dialogues* he has become "un autre" to himself.[37] Here his play at self-abasement for the sake of his physical pleasure took the form of confuting what he now viewed as the judgment of a hostile public. His goal was to intensify the readers' regard when they realized their injustices and truly understood him. However, we also recognize in the conflation of "Jean-Jacques" with "Rousseau" and Jean-Jacques Rousseau, who also appears as "I" and even corrects "Rousseau," the dislocation of selves behind a series of masks that appeared in the *prosopopoeia* as well as in Diderot's novel.

In his last autobiographical work, the *Reveries*, Rousseau avoided addressing the reader at any point. His turn inward represents a key moment in the development of a literary representation of self. Rousseau's strategy for writing the *Reveries* mirrored that used by Sterne for capturing the texture of thought in his novels. In the first promenade, he promised to write down his ideas as they came into his head, without regard for logic or connection, allowing them to travel the space of his imagination and letting the sights he encountered spark, as if by chance, memories and associations with past events.[38] But the culture of gambling also was embedded in his method, for he sketched his notes on the backs of playing cards as he walked, as if inviting *hasard* to enter into the very structure

37. The "History of the Preceding Writing" that Rousseau appended to the *Dialogues* affirms the validity of this comparison of text to spirit, for rather than submitting his manuscript to a publisher, he attempted to hand it over to providence by placing the pages on the altar of Notre Dame. When he found the gate to the altar locked, he experienced a moment of dizziness and "an upheaval of my whole being such that I cannot recall suffering anything like it" (248). Later he gave copies to Condillac and one of his English visitors and even tried to press them on strangers in the street, joining them with a handwritten plea for justice and a return to the affection he once enjoyed from the French public.

38. For a deconstructive reading of this moment, see E. S. Burt, "Mapping City Walks: The Topography of Memory in Rousseau's Second and Seventh Promenades," *Yale French Studies* 74 (1988): 231–47.

of the book. Indeed, this random technique seems designed to counter any formal restraints of plot or genre, a rhetoric of spontaneity intended to ensure the essential purity of his revelations:[39] "Having, then, formed the project of describing the habitual state of my soul in the strangest position in which a mortal could ever find himself, I saw no simpler and surer way to carry out this enterprise than to keep a faithful record of my solitary walks and of the reveries which fill them when I leave my head entirely free and let my ideas follow their bent without resistance or constraint" (*Reveries of the Solitary Walker*, VIII.i.9).

What interested Rousseau most were plants. He took pleasure in the simplicity and objectivity inherent in the rhetoric of botanical writing and in Linnaeus's system of botanical categorization, in which the Aristotelian qualities survived in a classification of plants according to genus, family, and species. At the time, more active collection of demographic data accompanied the popular practice of collecting specimens from nature. Although the results did not yet allow individuals to ask how they compared with universal standards of the "average man" or the "normal man," as they would in the nineteenth century, the word "statistics" had emerged during the seventeenth century, and this new science was beginning to make it possible to compare a person's own actions with data that related to the rest of society.[40] In that sense, statistical demographics laid the foundation for a sociological version of the Linnaean system. Indeed, Rousseau's study of plants—which recognized the essence of each specimen while relating it to others—responded to his enduring concern with his own position in relation to the human species. As we might expect, he was attracted to the rarest of flowers. In the second promenade, for example, he described how he took special pleasure in the *Cerastium aquaticum*, one of three specimens that caught his attention on a walk through the pastoral fields on the way to Charonne. Pressing this rarity into the

39. In his *Second Dialogue*, Rousseau had described how letting his senses receive random impressions of external objects rested his imagination: "He perceives nothing except perhaps some movement at his ear or in front of his eyes, but that is enough for him. Not only do a parade at a fair, a review, an exercise, a procession amuse him, but the crane, the windlass, the sheep, the working of some machine, a boat that passes by, a windmill that turns, a cowherd at work, people bowling or playing with a racquet, the flowing river, the flying bird attract his gaze. He even stops at sights without movement, as long as variety takes its place. Trinkets on display, books of which he reads only the titles lying open on the quay, images on walls at which he gazes with a stupid eye, all these things stop him and amuse him when his tired imagination needs rest" (II, 121).

40. Theodore M. Porter, *Rise of Statistical Thinking, 1820–1900* (Princeton: Princeton University Press, 1986), 25.

book he was carrying was an act of preservation analogous to preserving himself in the pages of his written texts (VIII.ii.10).[41]

Immediately after this moment of "self-preservation," he experienced an accident that recalled his illumination on the road to Vincennes. As he passed in front of the inn known as the Gallant Gardener, a dog and coach careened toward him out of nowhere. The crowd parted for the dog, but Rousseau attempted to jump over him:[42] "I judged that the only means I had to avoid being knocked to the ground was to make a great leap, so well-timed that the dog would pass under me while I was still in the air. This idea, quicker than a flash and which I had the time neither to think through nor carry out, was the last before my accident" (VIII.ii.11). Before he could jump, the dog knocked him down, and he fell headfirst into the path of the carriage. He barely escaped death and regained consciousness hours later in the arms of strangers, unable to remember where he was or what his name was (VIII.ii.12).

Rousseau's description of his accident represents an ambitious and conscious rewriting of the accident Montaigne described in his essay "On Practice."[43] After Montaigne was thrown from his horse when a larger man and mount collided with him, he did not know *where* he was, but loss of memory became for Rousseau the loss of self-knowledge, of *who* he was. As with his earlier illumination, he returned again and again to the ecstasy produced by this moment of separation from his physical body. "I felt a rapturous calm in my whole being," he wrote, "and each time I remember it, I find nothing comparable to it in all the activity of known pleasures" (VIII.ii.12).

Feeling born again, Rousseau had no memory, yet "it seemed to me

41. Bernhard Kuhn, "Natural History and the History of the Self: Botany, Geology, and Autobiography in the Works of Goethe and Rousseau," *Colloquium Helveticum* 25 (1997): 41–62. In his *Dictionnaire*, Rousseau described the hermaphroditic plant as the most complete flower, relating it to his hypothesis that primitive man lacked a rigidly defined sexual role in society. Equating the plant's leaves to the masks of convention, he regarded the flower as emblematic of the authentic self that conceals nothing beneath its surface. He often used "leaf" for "page" in his writing.

42. Like Fielding's fictional characters, who attempt to hide their motives while giving themselves away to the reader through their words or actions, Rousseau did not register the incongruity of being knocked down by a dog or the bizarre aspect of his plan to jump. He could not appreciate the humor of his response because he was never detached from his introspection. The primacy of sensation over reflection in Rousseau's thought shows with particular clarity if we compare the capacity for analytical distance exhibited by Augustine or Montaigne.

43. As Rousseau says in the *Reveries:* "My enterprise is the same as Montaigne's, but my goal is the complete opposite of his: he wrote his *Essays* only for others, and I write my reveries only for myself" (I, 8).

that I filled all the objects I perceived with my frail existence" (VIII.ii.12). This atemporal sense of presence is powerfully reminiscent of the Neoplatonic goal in which the soul, leaving behind the qualities of the body, dissolves into a union with the One. Through the shock of his accident, Rousseau's accidental qualities, the masks of selfhood, disappeared and he had "no distinct notion of my person." Thus, he looked down on his bleeding body as he "would have watched a brook flow," without thinking that the blood had anything to do with him. The alliteration between Rousseau and stream (*ruisseau*) suggests a lingering concept of self, but this notion of substantial selfhood is a sign of his fundamental identification with nature. In other words, an example of the kind of *hasard* that explained the fall from a natural to a civilized state of being had allowed him to glimpse the pure state of existence that he once associated with Natural Man.[44]

Part of the calm Rousseau felt immediately after his fall was linked to his physical shock. Only when his wife saw him did he realize he had been injured. However, the accident temporarily calmed his paranoia as well. The harm he experienced was literal and its direct cause perceptible— as devoid of malice as the accidents that confronted Natural Man. The shock of the event replaced his hypothesis that everyone he met was involved in a nebulous pattern of malign intentions. Although the accident appears surreal to the modern reader, by suddenly and unexpectedly realizing the harm Rousseau anticipated, it brought with it a calming lucidity. Because paranoia cannot coexist with an actual accident, his experience on the road to Charonne allowed him to achieve a self-defining moment of inner stability.

As soon as Rousseau left the sphere of the accident, however, his paranoia returned. He interpreted his visitors, such as the secretary of M. Lenoir, the chief of police, or Mme d'Ormoy, whom he suspected of trying to make use of his authorial persona, as participants in a plot against him. And when he read in the newspaper that a funeral oration was being prepared, the preview of its "outrages and indignities" confirmed

---

44. Jacques Derrida's *Of Grammatology*, trans. Gayatri Chakravorty Spivak (Baltimore: Johns Hopkins University Press, 1998), considers the metaphysics of presence in Rousseau's "Essay on the Origin of Language." For a discussion of the applicability of his reading to the *Reveries*, see Eve Grace, "The Restlessness of 'Being': Rousseau's Protean Sentiment of Existence," *History of European Ideas* 272 (2001): 133–51. Grace attempts to resolve the contradiction between the interpretation of Rousseau's "sentiment of existence" as a passive state that requires minimum development and the alternative that it is contingent on development of the "whole being," including reason and imagination. In her interpretation, reverie represents a reprieve from the activity imposed by self-love and the imagination.

his paranoia (VIII.ii.14). His career as an author had begun in a chance reading of the *Mercury of France*; the *Avignon Courrier* reported his death. Finally, he chanced to learn that a subscription had been opened to print any manuscripts found in his apartment, and he interpreted this as proof that his enemies had "a collection of fabricated writings available just for the purpose of attributing them to me right after my death." He wore himself out making "a thousand commentaries on it all and trying to understand the mysteries they rendered inexplicable for me. The only constant result of so many enigmas was to confirm all of my previous conclusions, to wit, that my personal fate and that of my reputation have been so fastened by the connivance of the whole present generation that no effort on my part could shield me, since it is completely impossible for me to transmit any bequest to other ages without making it pass in this age through the hands of those interested in suppressing it" (VIII.ii.15). Between the illumination on the road to Vincennes, which offered a solution to the tension between Rousseau's individuality and the pressures of social determination, and the accident on the road near Charonne, which allowed a remission of his paranoia, we see him taking pleasure in the experience of accident as a mode of self-realization. But he also expressed an underlying instability indicative of his gradual disillusionment with the promises of deterministic reasoning. As a young man, he had adopted the confident posture implicit in a mastery of the laws of probability and gambled his future on a chance opportunity. Now he shared Diderot's and Voltaire's disillusion with the promises of Enlightenment reason. He began to doubt that human will could master nature and envisioned his life as a stacked game in which he no longer controlled the odds: "Then I began to see myself alone on earth and I understood that in relation to me my contemporaries were nothing more than automatons who acted only on impulse and whose actions I could calculate only from the laws of motion" (VIII.viii.72).

Rousseau's lifelong attempt to explore the connection between reason and feeling ended with the realization that he could deploy a unique blend of these qualities. Other men might act on the basis of instincts and show themselves in possession of elaborate mechanical functions, but they lacked his capacity to respond to life experiences or to articulate those responses. Writing them down could give his readers access to heightened sensibilities. In this context, Rousseau envisioned Descartes's notion that speech distinguishes a man from an automaton in fresh terms. Rather than applying rhetorical or literary techniques to communicate an intellectual system, as Descartes (or Locke) had done, he used them to animate the emotions.

Print culture was deeply implicated in this transformation. On the one hand, it fostered a sociological change in communication, as the pleasure of conversation (or of reading aloud in a group of "semblables") evolved into the pleasure of reading alone. Other changes accompanied this shift: a new relationship between reader and author affected the relation between thought and feeling. Increasingly, reading served as a vehicle for communion between isolated individuals. And because that communication stressed emotional correspondences, it began to blur the separation between philosophy and storytelling. We see this in Rousseau's own career as a political theorist and best-selling novelist. By expressing his wish that "decent and true hearts once again open themselves to his own," he suggested that exchanges of feeling—like his vicarious introduction to passion through the novel or the revelation of his future vocation on the road to Vincennes—might transform and illuminate the reader.

Within the pulse between determinism and contingency emblematic of the decades that precede the French Revolution, Rousseau captures the ungrounded isolation of the individual cognizant of both the promises and the deceptions of the Enlightenment. His autobiographical writings reveal a complex narrative of risk and reward, expectation and confirmation, serendipity and desire that reflect his position on the cusp of a major shift in perception. Born into a society inflamed by gambling, maturing during the secularization of accident that opposed deterministic philosophy, he structured a textual identity around the manipulative response to contingency as a vehicle for self-actualization.

CHAPTER SEVEN

The Accidental Sublime: Returning Substance to Accidental Events

I. Accidental Signs

While Rousseau's autobiographical projects were separated in time from William Wordsworth's *Prelude* by what their contemporaries understood as a cataclysmic upheaval in thought, the two men responded to Enlightenment empiricism with many shared concerns.[1] Like Rousseau, Wordsworth struggled to distinguish his genius as a means of self-explanation or validation to his readers. He addressed the difficulty of reconciling intellectual control with unruly emotions. And although his reticence with respect to his private life created ambiguities comparable to those posed by Rousseau's oblique or devious insights, he attempted to resolve past actions into a mature personal identity. Nevertheless, the different ways in which accident appears in their work signal a shift in approach to the question of interiority. Instead of presenting his sensitive responses to contingency as an arena for self-display—as Rousseau did even while botanizing—Wordsworth demonstrated his capacity to interpret accidental signs found in nature.

The subordination of substance and increased emphasis on accident articulated in Locke's *Essay Concerning Human Understanding* and explored in the fiction of Defoe, Fielding, Sterne, and Diderot as well as in Rousseau make accidental events the source of an abundance of possibilities for interpreting experience. Dissolving the original Aristotelian opposition be-

---

1. Wordsworth had read *The Social Contract* and *Émile*. Probably he knew at least the content of the posthumously published *Confessions*. W. J. T. Mitchell, "Influence, Autobiography and Literary History: Rousseau's *Confessions* and Wordsworth's *The Prelude*," *ELH* 57 (1990): 643–65, discusses both correspondences and differences.

tween essential substance and inessential qualities in this way opened up the possibility of recalibrating the importance of what had been deemed inessential. Wordsworth capitalized on what we might term this protode-constructivist perspective toward accident when he transformed details in nature or mundane objects into signs of philosophical import. In that sense, he transmuted the inessential into the essential. Our awareness of the role substance has played so far in the history of accident allows us to grasp the extent to which he exhumed and reanimated the concept in his poetic work.

When Wordsworth aligned the image-making power of the imagination with aesthetic emotions, his experience transferred his response from the sensory object itself into an intellectual and moral sphere. In his descriptions of memorable moments in his youth, therefore, we recognize both the oscillation from a perception of vulnerability within the natural world to one of power and echoes of the effects of violent accident described by Montaigne and Rousseau.

During 1798, the annus mirabilis of their creative collaboration, Samuel Taylor Coleridge shared with Wordsworth an extensive knowledge of associationism, the technical name for a school of thought David Hartley developed directly from Locke's work.[2] Thus, although Wordsworth was never a student of philosophy, his use of the varied implications of accident drew not only on the general cultural awareness of Locke's work or on the classical education he received as a boy at Hawkshead Grammar School, but also on his intellectual friendships, not only with Coleridge but also with Tom Wedgwood and William Hazlitt.[3]

2. Coleridge knew Hartley through a recently republished edition abridged by Joseph Priestley, *Hartley's Theory of the Human Mind, on the Principle of the Association of Ideas* (London, 1790). Coleridge named his son Hartley after David Hartley, whom he called "the great master of Christian philosophy"; see his letter to Thomas Poole, 24 September 1796, in *Collected Letters of Samuel Taylor Coleridge*, ed. Earle Leslie Griggs, 6 vols. (Oxford: Clarendon Press, 1956–71), 1:236.

3. See Stephen Gill, *William Wordsworth: A Life* (Oxford: Oxford University Press, 1990), chap. 5. For a list of Wordsworth's early reading, consult Duncan Wu, *Wordsworth's Reading, 1770–1799* (Cambridge: Cambridge University Press, 1993). Francis F. Steen, "'The Time of Unrememberable Being': Wordsworth's Autobiography of the Imagination," *Auto/Biography Studies* 13, no. 1 (Spring 1998): 11, notes Wordsworth's perception of the absurdity of Wedgwood's proposal to raise children in laboratory conditions where sensory development would not be overloaded by random and meaningless data as one of the triggers for the poet's project of illustrating the growth of the mind in response to natural objects. Book 5 of *The Prelude, 1798–1799*, ed. Stephen Parrish (Ithaca: Cornell University Press, 1977), expresses the hope that "Sages, who in their prescience would controul / All accidents, and to

The project of writing what Coleridge called "the first genuinely philosophic poem" was intended to respond to the changes in taste that he and Wordsworth ascribed to readers as the result of the rise of sensationalism in the periodical press.[4] In the "Preface" to their *Lyrical Ballads* (1802), Wordsworth argued that the minds of readers were being blunted by the quantity of coincidences or other surprising and violent events disseminated in print.[5] The tedium of workers' occupations, he asserted, produced a craving for extraordinary incident that was gratified in "frantic novels, sickly and stupid German Tragedies, and deluges of idle and extravagant stories in verse." The combined effect had corroded reader sensibilities "to a state of almost savage torpor."[6]

Wordsworth's dismay did not cause him to turn away from accident as subject matter. On the contrary, both accidental events and accidents in the sense of familiar, common, or seemingly inconsequential aspects of experience appear everywhere in his early work. By presenting his material in a way that would induce a "state of excitement" in his readers, he proposed to arouse their passions without relying on vulgar sensationalism and lead them through a process of remembrance and contemplation that would stimulate their association of ideas. In much of his finest early poetry, some accidental object that serves as a sign to the sensitive observer reveals a violent or tragic event buried in history. Margaret's broken bowl in "The Ruined Cottage," the unfinished sheepfold in "Michael," and the garments left on the shore by the drowned man of Esthwaite in *The Prelude* are extant signs that memorialize the "numerous accidents in flood and field . . . tragic facts of rural history." A pattern of a chance encounter or mishap that becomes imprinted on the memory through its association with a powerful emotion recurs in all these examples and forms the structure of the famous "spots of time."

When Wordsworth began his intellectual and poetic collaboration with Coleridge in the summer of 1797, one of the first things he read to him was an early version of his poem "The Ruined Cottage." The following

---

the very road / Which they have fashioned would confine us down / Like engines" will learn that "in the unreasoning progress of the world / A wiser spirit is at work" (1805, V.350–55).

4. See Mary Jacobus, *Tradition and Experiment in Wordsworth's Lyrical Ballads (1798)* (Oxford: Clarendon Press, 1976).

5. Wordsworth's early poetry coincided with a marked upswing in print culture after a century of relative stagnation. See Clifford Siskin, *The Work of Writing: Literature and Social Change in Britain, 1700–1830* (Baltimore: Johns Hopkins University Press, 1998), chap. 6.

6. *The Prose Works of William Wordsworth*, ed. W. J. B. Owen and Jane Worthington Smyser, vol. 1 (Oxford: Clarendon Press, 1974), 126.

year, under Coleridge's influence, he revised it to shift the pastoral tragedy into his new pedagogical project.[7] In the poem, after toiling over "the
slippery ground" of a commons bared to the sun with the "insect host"
buzzing around his face, the narrator encounters the walls of a ruined cottage. "'Twas a spot!" he exclaims, marking this place as a locus of heightened significance.[8] On a bench near the cottage door, he discovers the
Pedlar who will help him decipher the history hidden in this spot. This
chance encounter with a figure representing the archetype of the natural
philosopher will transform the young poet's understanding.[9]

The Pedlar draws the narrator's attention to accidental signs that might
pass unnoticed by an unsympathetic mind, traces of human history hidden in the cottage ruins and the "useless fragment of a wooden bowl"
(line 145).[10] A draft of "The Ruined Cottage" explicitly states their function as signs that can engender empathy:

> And never for each other shall we feel
> As we may feel till we have sympathy
> With nature in her forms inanimate
> With objects such as have no power to hold

7. Wordsworth played a vital role in the late eighteenth-century revival of the pastoral.
For a transhistorical analysis of the genre, see Annabel Patterson, *Pastoral and Ideology: Virgil
to Valéry* (Berkeley: University of California Press, 1987).

8. *"The Ruined Cottage" and "The Pedlar,"* ed. James Butler (Ithaca: Cornell University
Press, 1979), MS. B, line 31. Additional references in this paragraph come from lines 19–23.
Unless noted, future citations are from this manuscript. The poem exists in a number of
drafts, the principal ones being MS. A (March–June of 1797), MS. B (1798), and MS. D, a
copy made by Dorothy Wordsworth during some point between February and November
1799. MS. D offers the most coherent version of the poem. As Butler notes on page 6 of his
edition, the poem represents "the culmination of elements present in Wordsworth's poetry from the beginning. In 'An Evening Walk,' for example, a female beggar—her husband
killed in the American war—wanders along the road with her two babes. . . . The woman in
'Salisbury Plain' was once living happily with her husband and children, as was Margaret in
'The Ruined Cottage.'"

9. As a natural philosopher "in the dead lore of the schools undisciplined" ("The Ruined Cottage"; MS. B, line 75), the Pedlar speaks what Wordsworth described in the 1802
"Preface" to *Lyrical Ballads* as "a more permanent and a far more philosophical language
than that which is frequently substituted for it by Poets" (app. 3, lines 84–86, p. 744). That
is, he speaks in "common English" and not in what Wordsworth viewed as the overblown
rhetoric of earlier poetry. See John Guillory, *Cultural Capital: The Problem of Literary Canon
Formation* (Chicago: University of Chicago Press, 1993), 126ff.

10. Much later, in 1843, Wordsworth explained that the Pedlar "represented" his idea of
what his "own character" might have become if he had been born into a class that deprived
him of a liberal education (quoted by James Butler in his introduction to *"The Ruined Cottage" and "The Pedlar,"* 17).

Articulate language. In all forms of things
There is a mind . . .[11]

Wordsworth's radical assertion that mind is present in "all forms of things" echoes both the classical idea that a defining substance gives form to everything and the Cartesian notion that an animating power of thought underlies the material world. In this early expression of his idea of nature, Wordsworth suggests that some force or quality that links all things enables inarticulate objects to convey their meaning. Here the poet hypothesizes that some substantive quality binds all phenomena and empowers seemingly insensate objects to communicate to man.

What the Pedlar knows of the human history of the inhabitants of the cottage and the attention he has paid to every detail present on the spot enables him to construct the history of Margaret and her family. Once she offered water from her well to refresh all travelers who passed her cottage. Failed harvests and the "plague of war" (line 136) brought hardship to the family, her husband Robert contracted a fever, and anxiety unsettled his mind. The desperation that resulted from his "hour of accident" (line 204) compelled him to enlist secretly in military service.[12] His departure devastated Margaret, and she slid slowly into madness, losing both of her children before she died. The Pedlar, returning every season, traced her decline in the gradual ruin of her cottage and the weeds that overran her garden, and the spot remains for him a sign of Margaret's life and suffering. Her tale was composed of events (like the fever and later disordering of her husband's mind and then her own madness) that appear as accidents both because they unbalance the stable tenor of life and because each action in the chain of events appears to be an arbitrary or incidental occurrence. These insubstantial or transitory experiences have vanished, and only ruins remain to convey this history.

Midway in the Pedlar's account, he admonishes the young man against viewing the accidents that have occurred to others as entertainment—or using their sufferings to buttress his own sense of self-protection. In other words, he counsels resistance to the narcissistic self-regard that Rousseau identified as one of the results of civilizing the instinctive empathy of Natural Man. He warns him not to hold "vain dalliance with the misery / Even

11. "Alfoxden Notebook" (20v–21r), in *"The Ruined Cottage" and "The Pedlar,"* lines 120–23.

12. These details accurately reflect current social conditions. The failed harvest of 1794 and the harsh winter of 1794–95 led to bread riots. T. S. Ashton, *An Economic History of England: The Eighteenth Century* (London: Methuen, 1955), 239.

of the dead" (lines 282–83), but to attend to the humble signs that would be overlooked by a seeker of sensation:

> 'Tis a common tale,
> By moving accidents uncharactered,
> A tale of silent suffering, hardly clothed
> In bodily form, and to the grosser sense
> But ill adapted, scarcely palpable
> To him who does not think.
>
> (lines 290–95)

After inviting the narrator to drink at Margaret's half-choked well, the Pedlar describes his own impressions of the scene. His meditation concludes by focusing on the bowl that symbolizes for him the daily welcome Margaret once gave to travelers, the physical destruction that replicates her broken state of mind, and the pitiful remnant that memorializes her existence. It is useless—except as a sign.

The Pedlar's instruction succeeds, for when the narrator learns to read accidental signs, he forms new patterns of association. In the future he will "no longer read / The forms of things with an unworthy eye" (MS. D, lines 510–11). The work of the imagination that enables him to empathize with Margaret's suffering proceeds in three stages: close attention to inanimate forms in nature, recovery of the meaning of these signs, and formation of more deeply felt associations with them. The sense of calm and happiness the narrator carries away from the ruined cottage is the opposite of indifference or detachment. Moved by what he has learned, he has discovered how to respond to a world fraught with "ruin and . . . change" (MS. D, line 521) by drawing on the stabilizing power of the forces of nature:

> "She sleeps in the calm earth, and peace is here.
> I well remember that those very plumes,
> Those weeds, and the high spear-grass on that wall,
> By mist and silent rain-drops silver'd o'er,
> As once I passed did to my heart convey
> So still an image of tranquillity,
> So calm and still, and looked so beautiful
> Amid the uneasy thoughts which filled my mind,
> That what we feel of sorrow and despair
> From ruin and from change, and all the grief
> The passing shews of being leave behind,

Appeared an idle dream that could not live
Where meditation was."

(MS. D, lines 512–24)

Wordsworth completes his meditative ordering of apparently incidental experiences into accidental signs by linking this new sense of calm
to the beauty of nature. The sight of the misted spear-grass refreshes the
Pedlar-philosopher just as earlier travelers were once refreshed by the water from Margaret's bowl. His aesthetic response extends the implications
of the pastoral mood Wordsworth evoked at the beginning of the poem,
but he transforms the conventional function of the pastoral from a refuge
to an underlying power that restabilizes the uneasy mind.

Rather than using images from nature allegorically to disguise political or personal concerns in the manner of the pastoral, Wordsworth argued that objects in nature communicate through a language of form. We
have already seen that reading signs requires an alteration in perception,
and how the fragment of the wooden bowl acquires its meaning for the
narrator through the medium of words when the Pedlar articulates its
history. The spear-grass shares this level of narrative reference as one of
the weeds that have taken over Margaret's garden, but to the philosophical mind the calm it instills derives from an aesthetic beauty associated
with the act of contemplation.

II. "Such Consciousness I Deem but Accidents"

"The Ruined Cottage" demonstrates how transient or accidental forms can
lead the poetic perception toward a new appreciation of nature. In the so-
called Goslar fragment, a draft passage from *The Prelude* that Wordsworth
wrote during his self-imposed exile in Germany during the winter of
1798–99, he extended this insight to associate an aesthetic response to nature with a metaphysical relationship between substance and accident:[13]

I seemed to learn
That what we see of forms and images

13. Eventually published as the *Two-Part Prelude* in 1974, this poem has a complicated
textual history. Wordsworth began part 1 in Goslar in 1798 and completed part 2 in England
1799. A fair copy was transcribed in Dove Cottage that December. The untitled work was
revised many times, notably in thirteen books in 1805, before being published as the four-
teen-book *Prelude* in 1850. Part 1, the Goslar poetry, provides Wordsworth's most radical engagement with nature, self, and accident. For a full textual history of the poem, see Jonathan
Wordsworth and Stephen Gill, "The *Two-Part Prelude* of 1798–99," *JEGP* 62 (1973): 503–25.

Which float along our minds & what we feel
Of active or recognizable thought
Prospectiveness or intellect or will
Not only is not worthy to be deemed
Our being, to be prized as what we are
But is the very littleness of life.
Such consciousness I deem but accidents,
Relapses from that one interior life
That lives in all things sacred from the touch
Of that false secondary power by which
In weakness we create distinctions, then
Believe that all our puny boundaries are things
Which we perceive and not which we have made
—In which all beings live with god themselves
Are God existing in one mighty whole
As indistinguishable as the cloudless east
At noon is from the cloudless west when all
The hemisphere is one cerulean blue.[14]

In this passage Wordsworth offers a crucial ontological reformulation of accident. Having developed its pedagogical importance, he acknowledged its negative aspect. An overabundance of sensory stimuli can create mental clutter or mess that blocks the interior life by demanding too much imaginative energy. In this guise of "littleness," accidents confuse and conceal the "one interior life that lives in all things" by clouding the understanding with inessentials. In other words, under certain circumstances, he conceives of accidents functioning in relation to the essence of thought as Aristotle claimed that accidental qualities functioned as inessentials in relation to substance. However, his concept is not a purely Aristotelian one. Instead of maintaining that accidents must be understood in opposition to substance, he shifts the frame of reference to the idea of delusory perceptions. Reliance on sensory distinctions—the physical manifestation of accidental qualities—has become an impediment, he argues, to the realization of the substantive unity of nature.

Just as Locke criticized Scholastic semantic complexities, Wordsworth saw that the application of categorical distinctions obscured the fundamental union between beings within the natural world and God

---

14. This version, written in 1799, is from the Dove Cottage MS. 33. The passage opened part 2 in the 1799 version but disappeared in succeeding versions.

that binds disparate natural phenomena into "one mighty whole." When the act of aesthetic contemplation dissolves these conceptual boundaries, the inner life fuses into the sublime vision he equated with an overarching hemisphere of "one cerulean blue."[15] Nature and the inner life have assumed the role of substance.

The "spots of time" is perhaps the most powerful and best-known concept in Wordsworth's poetry, and many efforts have been made to interpret it.[16] However, the interpretation of these nodal points has ignored their patterning of accident. A series of scenes involving accidents scattered through the *Two-Part Prelude* recounted events from his childhood that had remained in his mind.[17] As spots of time, they structure Wordsworth's later interpretations of experience in the way that Locke argued

15. Wordsworth's analogy between the inner life and the heavens has a biological source. Research has discovered that the neurological locus ceruleus (a nuclear structure in the pons, located just above the medulla oblongata and bordering on the fourth ventricle, whose cell bodies manufacture the neurotransmitter norepinephrine, which is visible to the naked eye) functions to inhibit the activity of the neurons that induce the REM state and its phantasmagoric dreams. Coleridge had affinities with medical theories of neurophysiological mechanisms of the body that were forming in the 1780s and 1790s in Germany. There he attended lectures by Johann Friedrich Blumenbach that countered Locke's associationist philosophy and Hartley's vibrationism by applying knowledge that imputed nervous sensibility to racial constitutions and may have encountered anthologies dealing with the subject, like Christian Friedrich Ludwig's *Scriptores neurologici minores selecti* (1791–95). George S. Rousseau, *Nervous Acts: Essays on Literature, Culture and Sensibility* (London: Palgrave, 2004), 39.

16. Jonathan Bishop's article "Wordsworth and the 'Spots of Time,'" *ELH* 26 (March 1959): 45–65, remains one of the best readings of the spots as a whole, and it underscores their centrality to both Wordsworth and English romanticism generally. Geoffrey Hartman in *Wordsworth's Poetry, 1787–1814* (New Haven: Yale University Press, 1964) as well as *The Unremarkable Wordsworth* (Minneapolis: University of Minnesota Press, 1987) combines New Critical close reading with the insights of Continental theory, while the articles that make up "Wordsworth and the Production of Poetry," ed. Andrzej Warminski and Cynthia Chase, special issue, *Diacritics* 17, no. 4 (Winter 1987), propose deconstructive readings of many of the spots. David Ellis provides psychoanalytic readings of the "scene of visionary dreariness" and the "Christmas-time spot" in *Wordsworth, Freud and the Spots of Time* (Cambridge: Cambridge University Press, 1985). See also Richard Lansdown, "Transitional Objects: The Spots of Time in the Prelude of 1799," *Critical Review* 42 (2002): 14–34. Yet if the spots have proved hospitable to language-based criticism as well as psychoanalytic theory, the revival of historically minded theories and criticism has shied away from the childhood spots. Thus, Alan Liu looks at the Simplon Pass spot in *Wordsworth: The Sense of History* (Stanford: Stanford University Press, 1989) and concentrates on books 9–13 of the *Prelude*. Renewed interest in textual and formalist criticism has returned to these seminal spots; see Susan Wolfson's chapter on the "Drowned Man" spot in *Formal Charges: The Shaping of Poetry in British Romanticism* (Stanford: Stanford University Press, 1997).

17. Wordsworth, *The Prelude, 1798–1799*, 280–83. All further citations of the *Two-Part Prelude* are from this edition, by book and line number unless otherwise noted.

that accidental associations imprinted on the mind formed the basis for formulating new ideas. In a passage that appears only in the 1799 version of the poem, Wordsworth described how he distilled random stimuli into lasting images:

> I might advert
> To numerous accidents in flood or field,
> Quarry or moor, or 'mid the winter snows,
> Distresses and disasters, tragic facts
> Of rural history that impressed my mind
> With images, to which in following years
> Far other feelings were attached, with forms
> That yet exist with independent life,
> And, like their archetypes, know no decay.
>
> (lines 279–87)

This passage reconciles the substance-accident dichotomy: what remained accidental was the transitory observations and the fluctuating feelings that became attached to memories; what he recognized as substantive was the preservation of such accidents of experience in the form of eternal images. By association, other feelings became attached to the original forms, drawing his mind toward subjects of importance and creating lasting impressions.[18] The capacity to retain monumental experiences allowed him to glimpse the essence of nature and provided a touchstone for his developing poetic imagination. Childhood accidents afforded material for his later work and also shielded his imagination against the trivia of daily life; they both nourished and ordered his thought:

> There are in our existence spots of time
> Which with distinct pre-eminence retain
> A fructifying virtue, whence, depressed
> By trivial occupations and the round
> Of ordinary intercourse, our minds
> (Especially the imaginative power)
> Are nourished, and invisibly repaired.

18. Wordsworth borrowed his allusion to "numerous accidents in flood and field" from Othello's wooing of Desdemona with a narration of his military career: "Wherein I spake of most disastrous chances, / Of moving accidents by flood and field." *Othello*, 1.3.134–35. This example of the power of narrated accidents in itself exemplifies the process of association.

> Such moments chiefly seem to have their date
> In our first childhood.
>
> (lines 288–96)

To become a "spot of time," an experience must transcend the material world of flux and decay and achieve a "distinct pre-eminence." Thus, it carries both spatial and temporal resonance. Wordsworth's primary use of the word "spot" signifies a place, such as the ruined cottage. This interest in place was in keeping with the eighteenth-century tradition of loco-descriptive poetry. However, he transformed it into a form of self-definition. The imprint made by a sympathetic response to a place or object served as a catalyst that conditioned the way he received and incorporated future experiences and in the process made him a unique individual.

Spots began as specific moments (spots *in* time), and an experience that existed at some point in time could be revisited in a historical sense as an element of remembered past. But the powerful impression made by a spot *of* time was reanimated when it was recalled and became the site of new emotions and insights that were not available at the moment of the initial encounter. Thus, "far other feelings" could become attached to a spot *of* time during the course of the individual's maturation.

In this way, Wordsworth suggested that within the context of mutable experiences, certain details from the external world possessed an enduring substance. While a spot remains unaltered when it recurs, the implications it projects are analogous to shifting accidental qualities. Independent of the mutable existence of the person who conjures them, these qualities are capable of evoking a variety of emotions and poetic expressions. We might compare Wordsworth's concept of the lasting impression made by experiences in nature to Aristotle's example of a plant undergoing substantial change over time yet remaining recognizably the same: while associations attached to the spot of time may grow, blossom, or decay, the original memory endures unchanged.

Wordsworth's description of imaginative recall altered the function of narration and memory in self-understanding. His process of creating over time a set of what might be called semantic memories retains its basic plausibility in contemporary neurological understanding. Thinking that is not devoted to processing perceptions or to motor control can produce a form of cognitive simulation that functions in certain restricted circumstances, such as dream states. Wordsworth's capacity to sustain such simulations without any sensory stimulus appears to be a novel aspect of his memory. As Wordsworth recognized, the creation and recording of autobiographical visions that possess vivid perceptual as well as emotionally satisfying properties alter the parameters for determining biographical reality.[19] He abandoned claims like those made by Rousseau that he reexperienced past emotions in the process of writing about them or that his stories recorded a literal truth about his being. Implicitly, he also abandoned the Cartesian identification of thought processes with proof of the existence and significance of the self. Instead, he dismissed the recollection of experiential details as the "littleness of life" in favor of the "one interior life" whose value rested on a transcendent (and substantively featureless) embrace of the natural world.

The so-called stolen boat episode, which Wordsworth wrote in Goslar in 1798, joins the spot-as-site-of-emotion with the spot-as-sign-of-guilt (in the sense of the spots that stain Gertrude's soul in *Hamlet* or those that Lady Macbeth cannot wash from her hands). Although links with violence intensified the imprint the spots made on Wordsworth's mind, personal guilt is latent or indirect. The narrative depends on a seemingly impromptu decision to steal a shepherd's boat, and this theft provides an undercurrent of "trouble" that intensifies the boy's response to the natural scene. By including this detail, Wordsworth presented two features that would characterize the "spots of time." First, the experience was embedded within a narrative construction. Second, it required a conjunction between a specific moment and an individual who engaged it. The individual's sensibility and capacity to remember and contemplate were as crucial as the surrounding circumstances. Although the event retains an accidental aspect because it occurs without intention, it represents an intersection between an event and the infinitely variable qualities of mind and experience that the individual brings to it. Since the boy who stole the boat on that moonlit night was Wordsworth, the place and the moment effected an illumination.

When the boy leaves the shore and rows onto the lake, the stars are mirrored in the dark surface and the strokes of his oars leave circles (the perfect Euclidean form) on the water that "melted all into one track / Of

19. Evidence for memory transformation appears in *The Prelude* in parallels between the story of Vaudrecoeur and Julia and Wordsworth's affair with Annette Vallon, but his use of material from Dorothy's journals presents other examples. See, for example, Anne K. Mellor, "Writing the Self / Self Writing: William Wordsworth's *Prelude* / Dorothy Wordsworth's Journals," in *Romanticism and Gender*, ed. Anne K. Mellor (New York: Routledge, 1993), 144–69; and Kurt Heinzelman, "The Cult of Domesticity: Dorothy and William Wordsworth at Grasmere," in *Romanticism and Feminism*, ed Anne K. Mellor (Bloomington: University of Indiana Press, 1988), 52–78.

sparkling light" (lines 394–95). He finds himself suspended within an elemental scene suffused with the terms of natural philosophy and where material objects have become invisible. But his communion with nature breaks suddenly when a huge cliff appears to rise up, blocking his view of the stars, and seems to stride after him (line 412). After this terrifying moment, he experiences an inner darkness which draws his imagination from the natural world with all its familiar qualities of color and shape to conceive of a mighty abstraction that did not "live / Like living men" (lines 426–27)—a monstrous apparition:

> and after I had seen
> That spectacle, for many days my brain
> Worked with a dim and undetermined sense
> Of unknown modes of being: In my thoughts
> There was a darkness, call it solitude
> Or blank desertion; no familiar shapes
> Of hourly objects, images of trees,
> Of sea or sky, no colours of green fields:
> But huge and mighty forms, that do not live
> Like living men, moved slowly though my mind
> By day, and were the trouble of my dreams.
>   (lines 119–29)

Wordsworth associated the inner world with permanence, but in the boating scene, the dark form that acquires such disruptive agency in the boy's imagination embodies a new way of incorporating the marvelous within a commonplace context. Traditionally, the appearance of some marvel inspires wonder and thus leads to new knowledge. Here the appearance of the dark form causes the boy to meditate on the "grandeur in the beatings of the heart" (line 141). Shocked from his sense of oneness with the beauty of the natural world, his imagination opens to a dim perception of other spiritual energies lying beneath the surface.[20] By cap-

---

20. The term "nature" bears a charged meaning among critics too intricate to develop here. Briefly, phenomenological critics from M. H. Abrams to Geoffrey Hartman emphasize the dialectical encounter between self and nature as a process of self-discovery. My reading of the role of accident has most in common with this perspective. In that sense, we simply acknowledge that two other points of view are current in the literature: New Historicists, such as Jerome McGann, Marjorie Levinson, and Alan Liu, argue that Wordsworth's invocation of nature displaces his political anxiety into a solitary and self-affirming relationship that evades political reality, while ecologically minded critics, such as Jona-

turing the temporal break in consciousness caused by an unexpected or accidental event, the boating scene expresses another aspect of experience: a moment of awareness sweeps the self into an altered state of being. A word to name the type of substantive accident capable of producing such spiritual elevation was available in the eighteenth century: it was known as the sublime.

III. Kant's Aesthetic

Wordsworth was familiar with the understanding of the sublime found in Edmund Burke's *A Philosophical Enquiry into the Original of Our Ideas of the Sublime and the Beautiful* (1757) as was Emmanuel Kant. While there is no evidence that Wordsworth was directly (or even indirectly) influenced by Kant's work, both men expressed a conviction of a profound relation between nature and morality. For them, that relation enriched Burke's materialist understanding of the experience of intense emotional response to the power of nature. And in some ways, Kant's analysis of the sublime in his *Critique of the Power of Judgment* (1790)—separated by less than a decade from the *Two-Part Prelude*—provides a more evocative comparison with Wordsworth's position.

Kant's aesthetic of the sublime retained Locke's assertion that sensations provide the basis for formulating clear ideas, but his embrace of metaphysics separated his doctrine from either Enlightenment empiricism or rationalism. Kant believed that limiting the study of the understanding to the processing of sensory experience placed a naive restriction on human reason and that Rousseau's attempt to discover man's hidden nature by observing human emotions and actions reduced the unity of moral law to ethical norms. To him, whether the question of being was understood as a fixed state that could be used as the basis for knowing other things or as a reality that the mind could access and assimilate, it posed a basic question about the limits of reason. He conceived of the sublime as an experience that could transcend those limits.

The *Critique of the Power of Judgment* contains ideas Kant had been formulating in his lectures as early as the mid-1770s. He conceived of this work as a practical complement to his theoretical metaphysics that would set out the principles of both taste and morality. When he reasoned that taste required nothing more than empirical knowledge, which could be

---

than Bate and James McKusich, interpret the interest in nature as an expression of prescient environmentalism.

learned by comparing personal responses with those of others, he discarded the project. Apparently, he resumed it again when he recognized that judgment had the power to mediate between the concepts of nature and freedom.

Kant applied his aesthetic to man-made objects as well as to natural ones, for he held that appreciation resides in the perception of beauty without regard to the concepts the subject holds about the object or the fact that it is natural rather than artificial. In its pure form, therefore, aesthetic judgment rests on a perception either that the form of an object (in the sense of its boundaries) evokes pleasure or that it possesses a quality capable of arousing a feeling of immensity or boundlessness. The judgment of sublimity involves this second type of experience. A third type of aesthetic judgment, based on whether the beholder experiences the accidental qualities of the object as agreeable, held no interest for him. Such perceptions varied with the perceiver and thus had no claim to universal validity. In each case, however, he understood the pleasure derived from beauty as the result of a harmonious interaction between the play of the imagination (which arranges sensory data to produce form) and of the understanding (which monitors and constrains this play within the limits of what can be conceived).[21]

Burke's essay had defined the sublime according to the emotion of astonishment or terror an object could produce in the beholder. By focusing on the object, he limited the creativity of the imagination to a Lockean function of representing remembered sensory impressions to the mind and recombining them into new patterns. Kant dramatically revised this position. Although he recognized the role of sensory perception, his aesthetic shifted its focus to the perceiver, in keeping with his metaphysical critique of the concept of the self (ego) as well as his critique of the concept of the object:[22] "Hitherto it has been assumed that all our knowledge must conform to objects. But all attempts to extend our knowledge of objects by establishing something in regard to them *a priori*, by means

21. Malcolm Budd, "Delight in the Natural World: Kant on the Aesthetic Appreciation of Nature," pt. 1, "Natural Beauty," *British Journal of Aesthetics* 38, no. 1 (January 1998): 14–15, notes a fourth type of aesthetic judgment in nature—one based on the qualitative perfection of an object independent of either the perceiver's response or any reference to pleasure but due to the ways in which natural functions are realized, as when, for example, a gazelle leaps. Kant did not include it in his system, although it fits his criteria. My discussion depends heavily on Budd's interpretation of Kant's aesthetic of the sublime in nature.

22. Ernst Cassirer, *Kant's Life and Thought*, trans. James Haden (New Haven: Yale University Press, 1981), 194–95.

of concepts, have, on this assumption, ended in failure. We must therefore make trial whether we may not have more success in the tasks of
metaphysics, if we suppose that objects must conform to our knowledge.
This would agree better with what is desired, namely, that it should be
possible to have knowledge of objects *a priori*, determining something
in regard to them prior to their being given."[23] Kant's perception that the
knowledge of objects and self-knowledge were inescapably linked undermined the Cartesian assumption that knowledge of our inner states can
be derived without any knowledge of the external world and that it is
necessary to infer the latter from the former. By arguing that both self-
knowledge and the knowledge of objects were intrinsically judgmental,
he also undermined the Lockean project of discovering the foundations
of all knowledge through sensation and reflection.[24]

According to Kant, sensations cannot provide the basis for a univer-
sally valid truth because they are wholly contingent, varying from moment to moment as well as from subject to subject and dependent on
the individual's circumstances. Decades earlier, Diderot had postulated
a comparable subjective understanding of perception, but Kant added
the argument that the equally variable and subjective desire for pleasure
might serve as a basis for a universal moral law. Since he recognized that
universality would require a bond between theoretical and practical reasoning, he sought a principle that would enable individuals to submit
desire to a moral law that knew no exceptions yet could be recognized as
their own creation. Because artistic intuition was experienced both as a
feeling of self and as a feeling of union with the world and life, it met this
criterion. It allowed the self to be detached without being destroyed. This
degree of aesthetic objectification, he believed, found its expression in
the sublime.[25]

When Kant classified aesthetic judgments, he determined that only
the judgment of the agreeable—the one that he had dismissed as irrel-
evant for his purposes—aroused the desire for more objects of the same
kind. Pure judgment of taste did not generate that interest. Beauty in
nature cost the pursuer some effort. It would not be sought merely for
enjoyment, but for the sake of admiration or love of the beautiful. As a

23. Immanuel Kant, *Critique of Pure Reason*, trans. Norman Kemp Smith (London: Macmillan, 1929), preface to the second edition, xvi. All future references are to this edition.

24. Paul Guyer, "Transcendental Deduction of the Categories," in *The Cambridge Companion to Kant*, ed. Paul Guyer (Cambridge: Cambridge University Press, 1992), 155.

25. Cassirer, *Kant's Life and Thought*, 318–19, 330–31.

result, he could ascribe at least the potential for moral worth to a taste for natural beauty. This connection was of crucial importance because it allowed aesthetic judgment to change theory to the practice that he hoped to achieve: delight in the natural world could lead to moral feeling. This sequence from judgment to the understanding of moral law was analogous to the perception that Wordsworth's natural philosopher in "The Ruined Cottage" gained by contemplating the accidental sign embodied in Margaret's broken bowl.[26]

Kant distinguished between the restful sensations produced by the contemplation of the beautiful and the mental agitation aroused by the sublime. To induce the experience of sublimity, he argued, the object must make the beholder conscious of being a powerful rational agent. The first step in this heightened consciousness would be an emotional oscillation between attraction to the object and repulsion from it. For example, a realization of the immensity of nature impresses upon the beholder the inadequacy of human power, and at the same time engenders a compensatory sense of man's moral superiority over nature. While the senses may be overwhelmed by the seemingly limitless extent of the heavens because the scale exceeds the imagination's capacity to determine a unit of measurement, infinity can be envisioned as a whole only in thought.[27] Awareness that mental power is superior to the senses constitutes what is known as the mathematical aspect of Kant's sublime. The second, so-called dynamic aspect involves the beholder's awareness of being physically vulnerable to nature's might. This perception is accompanied by an awareness that physical goods (including self-preservation) are of no moral consequence. Kant assumed that this double perception engenders a feel-

26. Malcolm Budd, "Delight in the Natural World: Kant on the Aesthetic Appreciation of Nature," pt. 2, "Natural Beauty and Morality," *British Journal of Aesthetics* 38, no. 2 (April 1998): 123–24, explains that Kant understood the judgment about taste to derive from pleasure in an object's form, while moral judgment derives pleasure from the form of the principle. He did not expect the ordinary person, whose ideas of beauty and moral good were "confused" or "indistinct," to have any articulated awareness of this analogy.

27. Malcolm Budd, "Delight in the Natural World: Kant on the Aesthetic Appreciation of Nature," pt. 3, "The Sublime in Nature," *British Journal of Aesthetics* 38, no. 3 (July 1998): 235–40, sees multiple problems in Kant's treatment of the infinite as well as in the ambiguous role of imagination. He argues that Kant considered all estimations of size fundamentally aesthetic. The difficulty of grasping infinity appeared in Pascal's wager to support his belief in God, while in the secularizing climate of the Enlightenment, Kant used it to support his theory of aesthetic intuition. Both Pascal and Kant associate awareness of infinity with fear, but the Kantian system reasserts the power of reason on a human scale.

ing of supremacy that counteracts the normal state of self-centeredness. Thus, pleasure succeeds the initial shock:

> Two things fill the mind with ever new and increasing wonder and awe, the oftener and the more steadily we reflect on them: the starry heavens above me and the moral law within me. I do not merely conjecture them and seek them as though obscured in darkness or in the transcendent region beyond my horizon: I see them before me, and I associate them directly with the consciousness of my own existence. The heavens begin at the place I occupy in the external world of sense, and broaden the connection in which I stand into an unbounded magnitude of worlds beyond worlds and systems of systems and into the limitless times of their periodic motion, their beginning and their duration.[28]

Both the negative or painful aspects of an experience of sublimity and its positive effects derive from the same root.[29] In this doubleness we recognize analogies to the experience that Montaigne described when he was knocked from his horse and Rousseau described when he collided with the coach. Overwhelmed first by a natural event and suffering pain from the encounter, each recorded a secondary experience of pleasure or spiritual elevation. In the boating scene, Wordsworth described a less violent physical experience, but it engendered a comparable sense of emotional turmoil. However, after meditating on what had happened, he also recognized an elevated sense of the power of nature. All three examples of accident, in other words, denominated an experience Kant would name sublime.

Although Wordsworth's initial debt to Burke has been amply demonstrated in his association of fear and love with the sublime, he began to concentrate less on sensations than on an aspiration toward the infinite, an inward search for what lay under appearances.[30] In a fragmentary essay

28. Immanuel Kant, *Critique of Practical Reason*, trans. Lewis White Beck (New York: Macmillan, 1993), 169.

29. Thomas Huhn, "The Kantian Sublime and the Nostalgia for Violence," *Journal of Aesthetics and Art Criticism* 53, no. 3 (Summer 1995): 72, makes a similar point about the complementary relation of imagined external distance between the self and nature and imagined internal distance between the self and the fear of nature. In the sublime, he says, our realization of power over the supposed power of nature allows us to pay homage to the fear we have overcome.

30. See W. J. B. Owen, "Wordsworth's Aesthetics of Landscape," *Wordsworth Circle* 7, no. 2 (Spring 1976): 70–82, and "The Sublime and the Beautiful in 'The Prelude,'" *Wordsworth Circle* 2 (1973): 67–86. See also Eve Walsh Stoddard, "Flashes of the Invisible World: Read-

of 1811, entitled "The Sublime and the Beautiful," he attributed the power of the sublime to two aspects of the experience, a doubleness that can be compared to Kant's analysis. On the one hand, Wordsworth believed that in an encounter with the sublime, the imagination failed to grasp what it strove to attain yet felt the force of its striving: "Power awakens the sublime either when it rouses us to a sympathetic energy & calls upon the mind to grasp at something towards which it can make approaches but which it is incapable of attaining—yet so that it participates in the force which is acting upon it." On the other hand, he recognized the importance of surmounting the trauma inherent in the experience. For him, the second aspect of the sublime allowed the mind to feel superior to its fears: "Or, 2ndly, by producing a humiliation or prostration of the mind before some external agency which it presumes not to make an effort to participate, but is absorbed in the contemplation of the might in the external power, &, as far as it has any consciousness of itself, its grandeur subsists in the naked fact of being conscious of external Power at once awful & immeasurable."[31] The resemblance between these two statements and Kant's mathematical and dynamic classifications of the sublime is evident.

Wordsworth was aware of the potential danger of allowing an absolute power over the mind. In that sense, his concern with the moral aspects of the sublime also appears closer to Kant than to Burke. He shared Kant's interest in freeing the imagination to allow transcendent insight. Nevertheless, his poetic purpose embraced the entire scale of aesthetic experience: the beholder whose telescopic vision stretches to infinity can focus with equal intensity of feeling on the microscopic detail of a blade of grass silvered with dew.

IV. Spots of Time

Each of the "spots of time" involves the interpretation of an accidental sign. The challenge of interpreting such signs in terms of the arbitrari-

---

ing *The Prelude* in the Context of the Kantian Sublime," *Wordsworth Circle* 16, no. 1 (Winter 1985): 33. Her etymological breakdown of the term to accentuate the sense of under (sub-lime) is reminiscent of Locke's understanding of substance. She also emphasizes that the degree to which Wordsworth replaced Burke's understanding of the sublime, in which man's knowledge and actions are determined by the sense, as a passive experience with a position closer to the Kantian aesthetic, which offered man freedom for self-determined moral actions.

31. William Wordsworth, "The Sublime and the Beautiful," in *Prose Works of William Wordsworth*, II, 354.

ness of rhetorical language has tended to obscure Wordsworth's own use of a lingering metaphysics of substance and accident in these scenes of accidental illumination. For example, in the 1805 *Prelude,* Wordsworth introduced the spot of the "Drowned Man" by describing the boy "roving up and down alone, / Seeking I knew not what" (V.431–32). As we already have recognized in the context of other transforming or illuminating experiences of accident, his questing mood fulfills a precondition for the surfacing of an accidental encounter that will carry substantive significance.[32] Moreover, the entire image carries echoes of Locke's hunter after truth who (in this case) instinctively pursues the substance he derided as "I know not what."

When the boy crosses a field that extends into the Esthwaite and comes upon a heap of garments lying "on the opposite shore" (1805, I.264–69), he already knows how to read an arbitrary sign. Despite the twilight, he sees the abandoned garments clearly. Encountered "by chance" within a natural scene, they present themselves to the prescient eight-year-old as a site of interpretation. Transfixed, he does not call out for the owner of the garments, or run for help, but waits and watches:

> Half an hour I watched
> And no one owned them: meanwhile the calm lake
> Grew dark with all the shadows on its breast,
> And now and then a leaping fish disturbed
> The breathless stillness. The succeeding day
> There came a company, and in their boat
> Sounded with iron hooks and with long poles.
> At length the dead man, 'mid that beauteous scene
> Of trees, and hills, and water, bolt upright
> Rose with his ghastly face.
>
> (1799, I.270–80)

The breathless stillness of the scene and the anthropomorphic imagery of the peninsula "shaped like ears" suggest a brooding presence that echoes the uncertain mood of the boating scene and intensifies the moment of interpretation that is to come. It creates a reciprocity between the

32. This spot is a privileged site for deconstructive approaches to both Wordsworth and romanticism generally. See especially Paul de Man, "Autobiography as De-Facement," in *The Rhetoric of Romanticism* (New York: Columbia University Press, 1984), 67–81; and Cynthia Chase, *Decomposing Figures: Rhetorical Readings in the Romantic Tradition* (Baltimore: Johns Hopkins University Press, 1986).

drowned man and the boy who does not act but drinks in the scene and broods upon it.

To initiate a lasting impression, an accidental sign need not possesses features that would create a comparable effect on any beholder. The sight of the pile of clothing acquires its power from the boy's state of mind and perceptions. For Wordsworth, poetic election provided a "disposition to be affected more than other men by absent things as if they were present; an ability of conjuring up in himself passions, which are indeed far from being the same as those produced by real events, yet (especially in those parts of the general sympathy which are pleasing and delightful) do more nearly resemble the passions produced by real events, than anything which, from the motions of their own minds merely, other men are accustomed to feel in themselves."[33] Watching beside the Esthwaite in expectation of some undefined illumination, the boy achieved a talismanic memory that the poet would develop into a personal mythology.

As in the boating scene, Wordsworth employed various aspects of distance to allow the external stimulus to penetrate his imagination. Physically removed from the abandoned garments by the body of water, the boy is separated in time from the death that occurred at some unspecified previous moment. When the "ghastly face" of the drowned man surfaces " 'mid that beauteous scene / Of trees, and hills, and water," aesthetic distance contains the terror of the event. The role of aesthetic distance becomes even more pronounced in the 1805 *Prelude*, when Wordsworth adds:

> And yet no vulgar fear,
> Young as I was, a child not nine years old,
> Possessed me, for my inner eye had seen
> Such sights before among the shining streams
> Of fairyland, the forests of romance—
> Thence came a spirit hallowing what I saw
> With decoration and ideal grace,
> A dignity, a smoothness, like the words
> Of Grecian art and purest poesy.
>
> (V.473–81)

The muted sense of shock that pervades both descriptions conveys a slippage between real experiences and literary ones. Associations of awe or terror deepened the impression made by the event and meditation trans-

33. Wordsworth, "Preface" to *Lyrical Ballads*, app. 3, lines 302–8, p. 751.

muted these negative associations into elevated feelings of calm and inspiration. Through the passage of time, the spot that once signified physical corruption becomes linked to memories drawn from books and art.
Wordsworth said that his aesthetic experiences buffered him from "vulgar fear." Indeed, in the fifth book of the 1805 *Prelude,* he used garments
as a metonymy for books (V.23), and here the "hallowing spirit" derived
from romance and fairy tales turns the "ghastly" (implicitly rotting)
face of the drowned man into the form of a Grecian statue: a form of
knowledge.

Wordsworth believed that "hallowing" spirits that intended him for
his poetic vocation guided him to formative experiences.[34] His use of
literary associations also supports his claim of poetic election, and he
drew on biblical associations for the same reason. Placing the garments
on the "opposite shore" alludes to a traditional Christian image of the
afterworld. The leaping fish that breaks the water's stillness is an iconographic symbol of Christ. And the garments themselves echo the discovery of "linen clothes laid by themselves" that predicted the return of
Christ's living body.[35] If Christ's abandoned clothes marked his triumph
over mutable time and ascent to immortality, the abandoned garments of
the drowned man assert a different kind of immortality: through this vision the poet's imagination was empowered to create an archetypal "spot
of time" that transcended the mutable world.

Both the concluding "spots of time" in part 1 of the *Two-Part Prelude*
follow the scenario of guilt and murder we have already encountered. The
"tragic facts of rural history" recognize the darker sides of feeling. While
Wordsworth appears linked to such emotions by his capacity for imaginative interpretation, he distances himself from violence by using the
pattern of the chance or accidental encounter to dissolve direct responsibility for past events.

One key element in his general pattern for constructing an accident
scene is the narrator's separation from a guide or companion. In the so-
called Double spot, the frightened boy, separated by "some mischance"
from his servant, finds himself alone at a place where "in former times / A
man, the murderer of his wife, was hung / In irons" (1799, I.309–10). Like

34. For example, in the boating scene he notes, "one evening led by them [spirits] / I
went alone into a shepherd's boat" (lines 81–82). When Wordsworth revised this passage
for the 1805 *Prelude,* he named Nature as his guide: "But I believe / That Nature, oftentimes,
when she would frame / A favored being, from his earliest dawn / Of infancy doth open out
the clouds" (1805, I.363–66).

35. See Luke 24:12 and John 20:5, 7.

the encounter with the heap of garments, this experience on the moor invokes a scene of reading:

> Mouldered was the gibbet mast,
> The bones were gone, the iron and the wood,
> Only a long green ridge of turf remained
> Whose shape was like a grave.
>
> (1799, I.310–13)

As Wordsworth recounted in the 1805 version, what he actually saw on this spot was a mouldering gibbet post driven into the ground.[36] Removing the physical relic, as he did in this passage, transforms the long green ridge into an arbitrary sign invested with a grim history. Association, which led him to imagine the ridge as a grave containing a hidden body, turned the spot as place into a spot of time. Rather than falling prey to uncontrollable accidental associations (the process Locke feared could lure the mind into madness), he showed in various versions of the remembered event his full control over the experiential material: he could move imaginatively closer to or further from complicity between himself and the past. Since no overt connection mediates between the gibbet spot and the scene of "visionary dreariness" (a caesura is the sole separation between them), this transition appears as a dramatic example of the process of association:

> I left the spot,
> And, reascending the bare slope, I saw
> A naked pool that lay beneath the hills,
> The beacon on the summit, and more near
> A girl who bore a pitcher on her head
> And seemed with difficult steps to force her way
> Against the blowing wind.
>
> (1805, I.313–19)

This passage does not draw an explicit association between the girl and the grave; it describes a process of attention that consists of seemingly

36. The gibbet spot appears to conflate two historical events, a murder by Thomas Lancaster that took place in 1672 and one by Thomas Nicholson in 1767. Although the 1805 *Prelude* suggests that letters identifying the murderer were carved on the turf at the base of the post, the *History of Penrith* (1858) identifies them as TPM (Thomas Parker Murdered), so it is possible that Wordsworth never saw the letters himself.

random observations. The girl's appearance to the boy after he leaves the grave seems to be an accident, for if he had climbed the hill earlier or later, he might not have seen her. Unworldly or even uncanny, she appears on the borders of consciousness, on the edges of the probable world. As a heroic figure making her way against the strong wind, she embodies the uncertainty of accidental events.[37] In effect, to fulfill his stated goal of arousing emotions, Wordsworth withheld the type of direct pedagogical assertion represented in the Pedlar's explanation of the fragment of Margaret's bowl. Instead, by forcing the reader to pay concentrated attention to ambiguous details, he elicited active contemplation of the relation between aspects of the experience that could parallel his own associations with them.

Wordsworth characterized this experience as an "ordinary sight" although he claimed it defied his powers of description:

It was in truth
An ordinary sight but I should need
Colours and words that are unknown to man
To paint the visionary dreariness
Which, while I looked all round for my lost guide,
Did, at that time, invest the naked pool,
The beacon on the lonely eminence,
The woman and her garments vexed and tossed
By the strong wind.

(1799, I.319–27)

Here "visionary dreariness" takes on the aspect of the sublime, although Wordsworth's experience does not agree with all aspects of Kant's classification system. What constitutes sublimity in this vision does not reside in qualities inherent in the objects the boy perceives, for they are "ordinary" sights, but in the perception of the viewer. As noted, those perceptions had been conditioned by transient and accidental circumstances: if the boy had not encountered the gibbet spot before he saw the girl with the pitcher, he would not have had such a powerful experience. The sequence

37. Bishop, "Wordsworth and the 'Spots of Time,'" esp. 56–57, recognizes the way in which Wordsworth used descriptive detachment to control the emotional response to this vision without denying its impact: "Can we read the extraordinary concentration upon the separate images of pool, beacon, and girl as a displacement of feeling from the evidences of crime and punishment to accidental concomitants of an experience too overwhelming to be faced directly?"

or preconditions that engender the juxtaposition presented for interpretation determine its impact. In that sense, the experience is most like the aesthetic judgment Kant identified not with the universal pure judgment of the sublime but with the mutable judgment of the agreeable. We might say, therefore, that insofar as solitude, morbidity, and temporal sequence appear as necessary yet unpredictable or unstable conditions that create a "spot of time" and the effect of the experience elevates the mind, Wordsworth's variation on the Kantian sublime was predicated on accidental qualities.[38]

A powerful expression of this kind of accidental sublime occurs when the scene of "visionary dreariness" shifts immediately to the "Christmastime" spot.[39] Once again the boy's solitary experience occupies a powerful place in the poet's imagination. "Feverish, and tired, and restless" (1799, I.332), the agitated or overexcited boy climbs up to a crag from which he can see two roads, either of which might be the route taken by the coach sent to fetch him home for his Christmas holidays. Unlike the other spots that he entered "by chance" and interpreted in retrospect, the image of the divergent roads directs this experience toward the future and dramatizes a play with chance. The descriptive elements of the scene mirror his state of mind:

> 'Twas a day
> Stormy, and rough, and wild, and on the grass
> I sate, half-sheltered by a naked wall;
> Upon my right hand was a single sheep,
> A whistling hawthorn on my left, and there,
> Those two companions at my side, I watched

38. André Breton described similar preconditions for the surrealist illumination he named "objective chance." See his description of the aleatory walk that preceded his meeting with his muse in *Nadja*, trans. Richard Howard (New York: Grove Press, 1960), 63–64.

39. Wordsworth's first long poem, "The Vale of Esthwaite," completed when he was seventeen, presented an earlier version of this moment and underlined the significance of the term "spot." "No spot but claims the tender tear / By joy or grief to memory dear," he wrote, and went on to describe the scene on a "steepy rock" with a "sharp Hawthorn" and "poor flocks all pinch'd with cold" (in *Early Poems and Fragments, 1785–97*, ed. Carol Landon and Jared Curtis [Ithaca: Cornell University Press, 1997], 446, lines 272–76). The feverish state in the 1799 *Prelude* is presented more as melancholy and sadness, for the boy has "swimming eyes," suggesting that he was aware of the perilous state of his father's health and knew what was to come. This sensibility is interestingly (and characteristically) sublimated into the boy's awareness of the natural scene in his later retelling of this pathetic tale. For further discussion of the two versions, see Duncan Wu, "Tautology and Imaginative Vision in Wordsworth," *Charles Lamb Bulletin*, n.s., 96 (October 1996), 174–84.

With eyes intensely straining as the mist
Gave intermitting prospects of the wood
And plain beneath.

(1799, I.341–49)

In this description, Wordsworth gave the wall, the hawthorn, and the sheep, which could have passed unnoticed as random elements within the landscape, an emphasis like his deliberate focus of attention on the pond, beacon, and girl in the scene of visionary dreariness. From his position on the summit, the boy is tempted to believe that he possesses an all-seeing eye and can control chance. Wordsworth did not describe the arrival of the horses, the road by which they finally came, or what reception awaited him at his widowed father's home. Instead, the next lines reveal that his father died within ten days and he and his brothers followed the body to its grave.

Shocked from being a son to being an orphan, he associated the summit where he played with chance with his father's death. If he had not wished so feverishly to determine the horses' route, perhaps the outcome might have been different and his father would not have died. He displaced his guilt into a memory of the prior event so that the spot came to represent a complex interplay of intention and accident around death. The sequence of events altered his position in the world from that of a presumptuous son who "looked in such anxiety of hope, / With trite reflections of morality" (1799, I.357–58) to that of an orphan who "bowed low / To God, who thus corrected my desires" (1799, I.359–60). However, the boy's religious insight does not complete the process of contemplation. Repeated meditations on this transforming moment restored to him a sense of the substantive significance of his original pleasure in the natural scene:

And all the business of the elements,
The single sheep, and the one blasted tree,
And the bleak music of that old stone wall,
The noise of wood and water, and the mist
Which on the line of each of those two roads
Advanced in such indisputable shapes,
All these were spectacles and sounds to which
I often would repair, and thence would drink
As at a fountain, and I do not doubt
That in this later time when storm and rain

Beat on my roof at midnight, or by day
When I am in the woods, unknown to me
The workings of my spirit thence are brought.

(1805, I.361–74)

In essence, with the passage of time he discarded his feelings of "trite morality" to achieve the restorative wholeness he described in fragment written in Goslar, "In which all beings live with god themselves / Are God, existing in one mighty whole" (Dove Cottage MS. 33, lines 16–17).

While the spot passed essentially unchanged from the *Two-Part Prelude* of 1799 to the *Prelude* of 1805, Wordsworth gave it a fresh introduction:

The days gone by
Come back upon me from the dawn almost
Of life; the hiding-places of my power
Seem open, I approach, and then they close;
I see by glimpses now, when age comes on
May scarcely see at all; and I would give
While yet we may, as far as words can give,
A substance and a life to what I feel:
I would enshrine the spirit of the past
For future restoration.

(1805, XI.333–42)

Initially, he had tried to see past the mist, but now he fixed on its flickering nature as a figure for his fragile and partial understanding and his desire to secure a final interpretation. As a boy, he assumed he could penetrate the mists to achieve his hopes and desires. The early mist appeared diaphanous and shifting, but when he returned to his memory, it assumed "indisputable shapes" that closed around past experiences as he attempted to retrieve them. When age came on, he feared he might become unable to access these sources of his poetic power. He needed the spots of time more than ever, because they represented defining elements of his poetic election. If he could not preserve their memory, he would lose this vital sense of self.

Part 1 of the *Prelude* established a psychology of perception in fundamental agreement with Locke's theory of association that was framed within Wordsworth's poetic purpose. Things in nature, he averred, communicate through a language of form which can be recognized by a person who approaches them in a mood of heightened receptivity. Emotional associations attach to these encounters either from the past or through associations formed by unplanned or chance events that surround the experience. Given sufficient native or learned sensitivity, an individual can read additional meaning into these events. When all the conditions are fulfilled in the individual as well as in the experience, even a humble occasion can become a "spot of time" and future contemplation will develop its significance.

Wordsworth recognized that the operation of such a sequence of perceptions is conditioned by the degree of awareness possessed by the individual—the scope of the beholder's perceptive possibilities. For him, the intensity of this process gave evidence of his vocation, but the double significance of accident (as a quality opposed to the timeless or eternal and as an event beyond reasoned control) also provided a conceptual basis for his poetical project. By elevating perception beyond the trivial, trite, or ill-considered response, the transformation of the accidental through contemplation both stimulated and protected his imagination. In these early works, moments of sublime awareness produced a liberating calm. They allowed him to envision the substantive unity of the natural world.

CHAPTER EIGHT

Altered States: The Macroscopic Impact of Accidental Qualities

I. Under the Microscope

The shifts of consciousness that marked the final decades of the eighteenth century have served as important markers of modernity. However, despite perceptible changes in how people wrote or thought about themselves, the conflict between whether identity resided in qualities that were acquired through experience or qualities that were innate or inherent did not disappear in the nineteenth century. Indeed, it became a focus of expanded debate. Charles Darwin's demonstration that the principle of natural selection could produce evolutionary change crystallized the excitement (or unease) regarding empirical and scientific discoveries and unsettled existing notions of man's place in the universe. But mutations in the concept of identity such as those traced over the past four chapters—enormous alterations wrought over a long period of time from what appeared to be anomalous or insignificant accidents—could be viewed as analogous to his concept of species drift.

"Personality," in the sense of "that quality or assemblage of qualities which makes a person what he is, as distinct from other persons" appeared in 1795.[1] This new definition (which removed the disparaging connotation the term had carried during the middle of the century) indicates broad acceptance of a shift from self-definition in terms of qualities held in common with others to the perception of individual uniqueness

---

1. Dror Wahrman, *The Making of the Modern Self: Identity and Culture in Eighteenth-Century England* (New Haven: Yale University Press, 2004), 276. Tension between the uniqueness of each individual and identifying categories would become an inescapable aspect of modern notions of identity (and continues in today's identity politics). Categories of religion and nation did not shift along with categories like gender, race, and class. See esp. 279–81.

that Rousseau and Wordsworth prized in themselves. The early eighteenth century had been sufficiently secure in its classification of people according to qualities such as class, gender, or nation to be able to accommodate or even take pleasure in deviations from the group, but changing commercial and technological circumstances as well as sociological shifts undermined that security. Old categories began to be perceived as uncomfortably rigid or increasingly penetrable. We experience this phenomenon retrospectively when we attempt to apply period demarcations, such as Enlightenment or romanticism, or sort individual authors into these categories. In effect, resistance to generic as well as historical labels begins to appear as a modern phenomenon.[2]

The multiplicity and diversity of nineteenth-century texts require me to offer a more explicit justification of the examples chosen for this chapter. Its center is Darwin, who appears as the author of a seminal change in the perceived function of accident that signals the cumulative effect of many individual accidents within a contingent environment. Jane Austen and George Eliot, authors chosen from a vastly expanded field of literary candidates, reflect important changes in both authorship and readership. Austen sought popular success in the dominant form of fiction produced in the first quarter of the century, and *Persuasion* is the novel in which she most clearly communicates the fissures appearing in a rigidly conservative social structure.[3] Eliot occupies a parallel position as the dominant novelist of the later century, a multilingual polymath familiar with the most innovative science and philosophy of her day, and the double plot of *Daniel Deronda* postulates identity in newly psychological and nationalistic terms that directly evoke the issue of innate qualities. Moreover, because both women cultivated a pedagogical relation with their readers, their work revisits the relationship of self-formation to reading established by Fielding and Sterne.

The novels that dominated the 1810s, when Austen was creating her body of work, were written about and for women in a market that resem-

2. Clifford Siskin, *The Work of Writing: Literature and Social Change in Britain, 1700–1830* (Baltimore: Johns Hopkins University Press, 1998), pt. 1, on the emergence of disciplinarity.

3. Paul Hamilton, *Metaromanticism: Aesthetics, Literature, Theory* (Chicago: University of Chicago Press, 2003), 160, offers the example from *Persuasion* of Anne's verdict that she had been rightly persuaded to do the wrong thing by Lady Russell, a substitute for the right person (her late mother). By repeatedly isolating her heroines from parental control (as a paradigm of conservative authority), Austen has her characters compensate for an absent authority or one in abeyance, conserving the principle of ancien régime or monarchy despite having to be loyal to stand-ins who seem inferior or mistaken.

bled the mass-marketing environment of romance novels today. A relatively small number of publishers controlled it, directing their product to specific groups of readers through association with the name of the publishing house. The power of the typical individual author was negligible, and both the structure and content of the books were determined largely by marketing considerations. All these factors influenced Austen's work. Her books appeared anonymously, and marriage plots like those she used were virtually the only type of fiction publishable by women. Her books were titled in ways that would have been easily recognizable to patrons (for example, *Sense and Sensibility* and *Pride and Prejudice* announce a conventional theme of the heroine's education), and they were designed to offer a "quick read" with a satisfying climax at the conclusion of each volume to patrons of circulating libraries that required brief lending periods to ensure their profits.[4] Nevertheless, one of the ways in which Austen pressed the boundaries of what had become highly formulaic writing appears in her use of accident.

Austen compared her method to miniature painting: "the little bit (two Inches wide) of Ivory on which I work with so fine a Brush, as produces little effect after much labour."[5] This famous comparison could be understood as a self-deprecating association with an artistic medium familiar to women of the day or an allusion to the genteel workmanship suited to a woman's hands. But it also reflected her awareness of the explosive eighteenth-century development of new kinds of scientific apparatus (like telescopes or microscopes). For example, by enlarging a specimen under the lens, the microscope intensified normal vision to reveal a world of detail once hidden from sight. This new technology inspired pictorial artists to translate its visual precision into both the techniques used to represent objects in their paintings and a more circumscribed focus of attention. In effect, therefore, Austen was announcing that her work placed society under a microscope and claiming validity for her interpretations as an ardent observer of her world.

A century after Locke theorized that repeated associations could create mental habits, both authors and readers had come to accept the notion that any accidental event could induce a change or transformation

4. See Barbara M. Benedict, "Sensibility by the Numbers: Austen's Work as Regency Popular Fiction," in *Janeites: Austen's Disciples and Devotees*, ed. Deirdre Lynch (Princeton: Princeton University Press, 2000), 63–86; and more generally Darryl Jones, *Critical Issues: Jane Austen* (Houndmills: Palgrave, 2004), 8–13.

5. Jane Austen, *Selected Letters, 1796–1817*, ed. R. W. Chapman (Oxford: Oxford University Press, 1985), 189.

of character. Accidents no longer needed to crash onto the page like the great wave that hurled Robinson Crusoe onto his island. Sterne's depiction of states of mind could make sparing a fly buzzing around the dinner table at Shandy Hall just as significant. Austen recognized that domestic routines offered a myriad of events (unexpected encounters, overheard remarks, impulsive statements, or missteps in timing) that could bring into focus the delicate operations of the mind and heart.

As a transitional novelist, Austen gave her characters traits we have met in eighteenth-century examples: they were presented in balanced pairs (pride and prejudice, sense and sensibility), constant or stable temperaments were seen as ideal, and social values were essentially conservative. Yet the pattern of self-recognition in Austen's novels shifted the problem of moral action to an interior register of a new dimension. Her characters are not simply "mixed," as Fielding drew his; they are prey to sensations or feelings they can neither explain nor understand (although they constantly attempt to do both). Internal conflicts give the characters an aspect of being rounded and mutable rather than bounded within the tradition of the humors or dominant passions. They also condition the character's ability to interpret accidental events.[6]

Austen's characters, especially her heroines, are skilled in reading the signs provided by speech, manner, or conduct. In *Persuasion* (1818), Anne Elliot exhibits a wry grasp of her sister's character as she endeavors to understand the motives of a cousin who has suddenly reestablished his connection with the family after a long period passed without any contact:

> She could offer one solution; it was, perhaps, for Elizabeth's sake. There might really have been a liking formerly, though convenience and accident had drawn him a different way, and now that he could afford to please himself, he might mean to pay his addresses to her. Elizabeth was certainly very handsome, with well-bred, elegant manners, and her character might never have been penetrated by Mr. Elliot, knowing her but in public, and when very young himself. How her temper and understanding might bear the investigation of his present keener time of life was another con-

---

6. David Medalie, "'Only the Event Decides': Contingency in *Persuasion*," *Essays in Criticism* 49, no. 2 (April 1999): 153, argues that Anne both accepts and rejects the power of contingency in human affairs when she justifies in retrospect her submission to Lady Russell's advice. In effect, she says that contingency determines the viability of moral positions, yet injunctions from established authority cannot be disregarded for the sake of contingent circumstances. Nevertheless, the novel disparages Sir Walter's fixation on superficial guarantees of identity (such as his reflection in the mirror or in Burke's *Peerage*).

cern, and rather a fearful one. Most earnestly did she wish that he might not be too nice, or too observant, if Elizabeth were his object.[7]

Anne mistrusts her cousin William Elliot because his words or behavior are not spontaneous. She feels she "could so much more depend upon the sincerity of those who sometimes looked or said a careless or a hasty thing, than of those whose presence of mind never varied, whose tongue never slipped" (II.v.153). She reads for accidents. Although her skill in deciphering the man beneath the manner shields her when her cousin insinuates that his affections rest on her, her insight is of no use in making the critical leap into defining her own future. In a social context filled with flattery, deceit, and hidden motives, the prudence Fielding recommended to his readers is not sufficient to ensure Anne's happiness.

A series of coincidences unmask William's past when Anne visits Mrs. Smith, but what she learns from her former schoolmate also clarifies her understanding of enduring values. Her friend lives cheerfully in reduced circumstances and ill health, yet, as Anne recognizes, she has not allowed change to control her life. Accidents of fate, illness, a husband's death, and the loss of fortune and family have effected only surface alterations in her appearance and her lifestyle; they have not substantially altered who she is. An essential quality in her nature—which Anne identifies as an "elasticity of mind" that carries her out of herself—allows her to transcend her misfortunes.

Surrounded by a society in which making judgments trivializes experience and stunts the inner life, Anne's struggle for interpretive clarity produces a cumulative effect of distress.[8] She withdraws to protect herself from family demands and an abundance of stimuli. Austen discarded the role of overt guide to lead the reader solely through indirection, but her "fine Brush" made clear that Anne's self-effacing role in society offered an imperfect shelter from the psychic accidents that resulted when Captain Wentworth reentered her life. On his first evening as part of the company, she takes her accustomed place at the piano, watching the other women flirt with him while she accompanies the dancing:

> Her fingers were mechanically at work, proceeding for half an hour together, equally without error, and without consciousness. *Once* she felt

7. Jane Austen, *Persuasion*, ed. John Davie (Oxford: Oxford University Press, 1971), II.iii.133. All future citations refer to this edition.

8. Adela Pinch, *Strange Fits of Passion* (Stanford: Stanford University Press, 1996), 148–49.

that he was looking at herself—observing her altered features, perhaps, trying to trace in them the ruins of the face which had once charmed him; and *once* she knew that he must have spoken of her;—she was hardly aware of it, till she heard the answer; but then she was sure of his having asked his partner whether Miss Elliot never danced? The answer was, "Oh! no, never; she has quite given up dancing. She had rather play. She is never tired of playing." Once, too, he spoke to her. She had left the instrument on the dancing being over, and he had sat down to try to make out an air which he wished to give the Miss Musgroves an idea of. Unintentionally she returned to that part of the room; he saw her, and, instantly rising, said, with studied politeness, "I beg your pardon, madam, this is your seat." (I.viii.71–72)

On one level, Anne is performing like one of the eighteenth-century automatons. In a striking division of body from spirit, she assumed the "ruin" of her face while her consciousness turned outward to "read" the scene.[9] The motions of her hands are as mechanical as the movements of the eye across a page of text. However, ambiguities in the evidence on which she bases her interpretation allow the reader to outpace Anne's understanding of herself (pained by Wentworth's remark that she has altered beyond his knowledge and "unintentionally" drawn to him) or of Wentworth (actively inquiring about Anne from another partner).

Although Austen's contemporaries admired the empirical care with which she recorded life around her, such passages in *Persuasion* reflect aspects of mental operation in an innovative style that shows her appreciation for both unconscious and half-conscious functions of mental life. In this respect, her sophistication was in advance of the biological

9. The study of physiognomy had lost its significance from the late seventeenth century, declining into a form of fortune-telling. But Johann Kaspar Lavater's *Essays on Physiognomy* appeared in one or more editions per year between 1792 and 1810. He proposed (using the image of a bird flying free within the confines of its cage) that the body was bound within certain parameters and the range of the mind also was determined. Therefore, the inner core of selfhood and the impermeable boundaries of identity were not essentially inscribed in the physical body; rather, the inner substance made a feature that was in itself accidental, and thus of infinite variety, indicative of a person's true character. (Blake noted in his copy of Lavater: "Substance gives tincture to the accident, and makes it physiognomic.") Another solution proposed that physiognomic knowledge was itself part of the innate essence of human identity. For example, Charles Bell, in *Essays on the Anatomy of Expression in Painting* (1806), assumed that ability to read faces was inborn. The period's vogue for wax figures and silhouette artists responded to the premium on embodied, unique, and unmediated physiognomy. See Wahrman, *The Making of the Modern Self,* 295–99.

science of her era.[10] Her interest in the interaction of mind and body has become the focus of increased critical interest as part of our own growing awareness of brain function. Thus, we now recognize periods when internal sensations create confusion in Anne's mind as part of a continuum of what we might call cognitive self-possession. When her emotions are most affected, she acts automatically, but at moments of physical crisis, such as Louisa Musgrove's fall, she responds with empathy and control.

Wentworth's courtship of Louisa is particularly poignant for Anne because it recalls her feelings for him almost a decade earlier. When social obligations place her in his vicinity throughout the narrative, she overhears many comments that she interprets in isolation. On a walk near Uppercross Farm, for example, she happens to seat herself under the cover of a hedgerow while Louisa and Wentworth search for nuts and thus overhears Wentworth tell Louisa that a good impression may not be durable but people who are happy are of a firm mind: "'—Here is a nut,' said he, catching one down from an upper bough. 'To exemplify,—a beautiful glossy nut, which, blessed with original strength, has outlived all the storms of autumn. Not a puncture, not a weak spot any where.— This nut,' he continued, with playful solemnity,—'while so many of its brethren have fallen and been trodden under foot, is still in possession of all the happiness that a hazel-nut can be supposed capable of'" (I.x.86). The reader experiences this scene with Anne and must interpret the example. Wentworth does not mention Anne, but implicit in her interpretation is the memory of the storm in their relationship in which she did not hold firm. Characteristically, she gives the least flattering interpretation to his words, devaluing the extent to which her continued love expresses precisely the constancy he describes and ignoring the unyielding conservatism and gendered stereotypes implicit in his analogy. If Louisa interprets his reference as praise for her own willfulness, the structure of the novel highlights how Anne's character differs from that of the energetic and flirtatious Louisa.

An accident that occurs at the midpoint of the novel forces Anne to alter her passive behavior for the first time in Wentworth's presence. The physicality and dramatic intensity of Louisa's fall at Lyme Regis make this moment unprecedented in Austen's fiction although she traces the way

10. Alan Richardson, "Of Heartache and Head Injury: Reading Minds in Persuasion," *Poetics Today* 23, no. 1 (Spring 2002): 141–60, discusses the shift from environmental to biological approaches to psychological behavior during the period.

in which it resonates for each of the participants with her habitual microscopic care. As the characters stroll along the upper part of the stone quay, they decide to descend a narrow set of stairs to the lower level:

> All were contented to pass quietly and carefully down the steep flight, excepting Louisa; she must be jumped down them by Captain Wentworth. In all their walks, he had had to jump her from the stiles; the sensation was delightful to her. The hardness of the pavement for her feet, made him less willing upon the present occasion; he did it, however; she was safely down, and instantly, to shew her enjoyment, ran up the steps to be jumped down again. He advised her against it, thought the jar too great; but no, he reasoned and talked in vain; she smiled and said, "I am determined I will:" he put out his hands; she was too precipitate by half a second, she fell on the pavement on the Lower Cobb, and was taken up lifeless! (I.xii.106)

In this "half a second," Austen intervened to transform Louisa's pleasurable jump into an unanticipated punishment for her willfulness. Louisa intended Wentworth to catch her—as a symbol of catching her in marriage—but instead she fell and hit her head on the hard stone.[11] This accident alters the direction of the plot. On the one hand, it applies a moral judgment: Louisa's head suffers as a result of her headstrong determination. The fall influenced "her health, her nerves, her courage, her character to the end of her life, as thoroughly as it appeared to have influenced her fate" (II.vi.158).[12] On the other hand, because the reader is never privy

---

11. Concussions served as frequent examples of neuropathology at the time. In August 1815, a few months before Austen began writing *Persuasion*, the *Edinburgh Review* published a long article on the implications of localized brain injury that exemplified the tension between the two contemporary notions of mind-body relations: a dualistic interpretation that conformed to orthodox notions of the soul and identification of discrete brain functions in a materialist interpretation. See Richardson, "Of Heartache and Head Injury," 145–48.

12. At this time Charles Bell, Erasmus Darwin, and William Lawrence in Britain as well as Franz Joseph Gall and Pierre-Jean-Georges Cabanis on the Continent were exploring the notion of a biological basis for the mind, its embodiment in the brain, and the innate and internally active nature of some basic faculties. Darwin espoused the idea of two different nervous systems. His *Temple of Nature* (published posthumously in 1803—on the heels of the *Lyrical Ballads*) incorporated neuroanatomical views from his "Mechanism of the Human Body" (1798), which reasoned upward from flowers and small animals to human beings, whose ideas were formed through a series of "nervous links" in the body, each consisting of successive trains of motions conducted through the extremity of the nerve tip. He claimed that the sensation that nerves permitted had been the great evolutionary step. New sensations evoked new passions and degrees of self-reflection, which gave rise to emotions that defined human beings as creatures of sensibility. George S. Rousseau, *Nervous Acts: Essays on Literature, Culture and Sensibility* (London: Palgrave, 2004), 42–43. Such neurosci-

to Louisa's mental processes, the account is less personal than social. The accident removes her from the rivalry for Wentworth's affections because Captain Benwick attends her during her convalescence and (demonstrably inconstant) she falls in love with him. But the full implication of the event rests on the observers. Austen showed the reader how the accident affected Anne and Wentworth; although they were physically untouched by the experience, it altered their lives as deeply as it altered Louisa's. The shock of the accident reverberates within their consciousness, and their interpretation of the event becomes the new subject of the reader's attention. Anne remembers an earlier remark of Wentworth's: "Anne wondered whether it ever occurred to him now, to question the justness of his own previous opinion as to the universal felicity and advantage of firmness of character; and whether it might not strike him, that, like all other qualities of the mind, it should have its proportions and limits. She thought it could scarcely escape him to feel, that a persuadable temper might sometimes be as much in favour of happiness as a very resolute character" (I.xii.113). Her imagery links the physical striking of Louisa's head against the stone, which produces such changes of fortune, with an idea striking the mind and effecting a change in understanding. Indeed, Louisa's accident and the period of reflection that follows it allow Wentworth to "distinguish between the steadiness of principle and the obstinacy of self-will, between the darings of heedlessness and the resolution of a collected mind" (II.xi.228). He contrasts Louisa's behavior with Anne's and recognizes, as he explains to her at the end of the novel, that he has been "constant unconsciously, nay unintentionally" (II.xi.227). The shock of Louisa's accident allowed the realization of the value of control and order to break through into his consciousness.

Anne recognizes and quickly responds to the accidental experience, for hers is a "collected mind." In one sense, she is the collector of quotations and impressions that have had a formative influence on her, but she also is a collector in the additional sense of being a composer or a person who recollects. Her capacity for reflection operates like a Wordsworthian spot

---

entific theories reinforced the emphasis on the ideas of an innately active mind and the maturation of individual uniqueness that were common to literary romanticism but radically different from the externalized understanding of the self during the earlier eighteenth century. Wahrman, *The Making of the Modern Self*, 293. Margaret Anne Doody, "Self, Love, and Memory," *Eighteenth-Century Fiction* 14, no. 1 (October 2001): 67–94, also notes the interest in the nerves as intermediaries between the outer and inner world that paved the way toward making the material into the spiritual. *Pride and Prejudice* serves as her example from Austen's work.

of time: her love for Wentworth made an enduring mark on her being. It is not simply Louisa's behavior that makes Wentworth realize his true desire; it is also Anne's substance, her essential and unchanging nature.

The crucial accident in the penultimate chapter of *Persuasion* offers a more typical example of the reduction in scale that characterizes moments of illumination in Austen's novels. It is an event that will soon come to be called serendipitous.[13] Wentworth overhears Anne defending the constancy of women in a discussion with Captain Harville. She tells him that women's feelings are more tender and long-lived than those of men, and her voice falters with the intensity of her feeling. Wentworth's shock of emotion causes him to drop his pen. Startled, Anne wonders if he heard her words. A complex interpretation travels between the two characters in a moment of shock; through the mechanism of accident, Austen achieves the transparency of one mind to another. Wentworth's knowledge of Anne's feeling arrives from outside rather than through any assemblage of prior experience. It confronts him as a moment of epiphany and pain ("you pierce my soul"; II.xi.223).

If the traditional experience of accident involved overtly expressed physical as well as mental anguish, in this passage the impact of the event involves a moment of psychic transport. The determining force of the accident bears no relation to its delicate cause, and its effects can be concealed from the observers. Significantly, instead of transforming Wentworth's character, it reveals his unchanged love for Anne.

Wentworth's feelings caused him to drop his pen, but Anne's argument stimulates him to pick it up again to prove himself: "I offer myself to you again with a heart even more your own, than when you almost broke it eight years and a half ago. Dare not say that man forgets sooner than woman, that his love has an earlier death. I have loved none but you. Unjust I may have been, weak and resentful I have been, but never inconstant" (II.xi.223). After the interpretive uncertainties of Anne and Wentworth's relationship during the course of the novel, the plot comes to rest on the old idea of immutable substance. He has drawn up a romantic contract, an explicit avowal of feelings whose importance within his sense of himself he fully understands. The receipt of this letter is "an overpowering happiness" to Anne.

Austen's novels enacted a species of social anthropology that surveyed

---

13. According to Robert K. Merton and Elinor Barber, *The Travels and Adventures of Serendipity* (Princeton: Princeton University Press, 2003), chap. 1, the term "serendipity" was coined by Horace Walpole in 1754 but lay dormant until the 1830s.

the rules and contingencies involved in the English marriage market, where her heroines' chief tactical advantage was their sharp observation of the moral and marital implications presented to them in the accidents of daily life. A constant and focused reader of experience could avoid marital mishaps, as Anne resists William Elliot, and secure a mate whose stability and constancy matches her own. In *Pride and Prejudice*, Charlotte Lucas says, "Happiness in marriage is entirely a matter of chance."[14] The word "happiness" derives from "hap," and its etymology suggests an emotional state in which good luck acquires an element of permanence. In Austen's novels, however, the unhappy characters demonstrate that securing happiness is never a matter of chance. Charlotte believes any man will change so much during the course of a marriage that his present personality is inconsequential when deciding whether to accept or refuse him. Taking her chances, she accepts Mr. Collins and condemns herself to a loveless marriage with a foolish man. Unlike Anne, Charlotte cannot discern the unchanging aspects of character. Like Louisa Musgrove, she is an unwise reader of both her circumstances and of human nature.

A conservative interpretation of Austen might emphasize both her efforts to safeguard aristocratic principles and conventional use of accident to delineate or represent the effect of ruptures in accepted behavior or serve as a providential or deterministic cause of reform for the better. Louisa's fall might be seen in those terms.[15] Nevertheless, if we read *Persuasion* for its treatment of accidental qualities rather than exclusively for its accidental events, we recognize that the novelty of her work lies in her shift from external accidents to subjective ones. In that respect, the intellectual atmosphere of *Persuasion* appears to extend the representation of identity that we began to trace in Locke's *Essay Concerning Human*

14. Jane Austen, *Pride and Prejudice*, ed. James Kinsley (Oxford: Oxford University Press, 1980), I.vi.19.

15. Lorrie Clark, "Transfiguring the Romantic Sublime in *Persuasion*," in *Jane Austen's Business: Her World and Her Profession*, ed. Juliet McMaster and Bruce Stovel (New York: St. Martin's Press, 1996), 30–41, argues that the novel asserts a context of risk (the destructive financial forces set in motion by Sir Walter that precipitate the loss of the estate or the play with physical risk that the Admiral engages in with his overturning carriage or that Mary Musgrove flirts with in her hypochondria). Risk resolves into the pleasure of a feeling of freedom analogous to the sublime. However, she sees in Anne a philosophical balance that refuses to abandon reason for ecstatic emotion yet does not deny the force of nature. See also Paul A. Cantor, "The Class Act: *Persuasion* and the Lingering Death of the Aristocracy," *Philosophy and Literature* 28 (1999): 135–36; and Terry Eagleton, *The English Novel: An Introduction* (London: Blackwell, 2005), chap. 5. Eagleton agrees with Cantor, taking Austen to be an exemplary conservative intent on reforming the aristocracy in light of the threat posed by the social instability of Regency England.

Understanding. Indeed, Anne and Wentworth's love for one another takes the form of an enduring accidental association, an imprinting of experience that will not be extinguished, in Anne's words, "when existence or when hope is gone" (II.xi,222). But this is possible not solely as the result of the developmental process described in the novel; it also asserts the presence of an innate disposition for constancy and depth of feeling. The shock Anne and Wentworth experience in the penultimate chapter arises less from any exchange of new thoughts than from the impact of what they hear on hearts already prepared by the memories of their earlier love. Austen's last romance testifies to the way in which the idea of love can operate unconsciously (for Wentworth) and triumph over social persuasion (for Anne) to surface after eight years through an intensified reading of accidental signs and shocking moments of inner recognition.

II. A Dynamic Mechanism

We have seen how closely Austen's work relates to eighteenth-century traditions, but her late novels in particular reveal her attempt to impose control on an increasingly complex and mutable climate of experience. In 1821, Richard Whateley reviewed Austen's posthumously published novels, *Northanger Abbey* and *Persuasion*.[16] "Her fables," he wrote, "do not consist (like those of some of the writers who have attempted this kind of common-life novel writing) of a string of unconnected events which have little or no bearing on one main plot, and are introduced evidently for the sole purpose of bringing in characters and conversations; but all have that compactness of plan and unity of action which is generally produced by a sacrifice of probability: yet they have little or nothing that is not probable."[17] Minute observation, coupled with attention to the repeatability of social situations, extended her resources for establishing what

---

16. *Northanger Abbey* had been written in 1797–98, although perhaps reworked sometime between 1803 and 1816. *Persuasion* was written in 1816.

17. Richard Whateley, "Review of *Northanger Abbey* and *Persuasion*," in *Persuasion*, ed. Patricia Meyer Spacks (New York: W. W. Norton, 1995), 196–205, esp. 197. Walter Scott's review recognized that earlier novels had described characters in terms of genus rather than individuation. One of his own goals was an active search for characters who were original and individual and projected outward from their inner nature. Deirdre S. Lynch, *The Economy of Character: Novels, Market Culture, and the Business of Inner Meaning* (Chicago: University or Chicago Press, 1998), 125 and *passim*, dates this shift in consciousness from about 1779 to the late 1780s.

could be regarded as probable behavior or circumstances and in the process gave her portraits of contemporary society a documentary freshness.

As a body of work, Austen's novels resemble experimental situations. For example, on one level, each one explores what qualities enable a heroine to overcome the disabilities created by her family environment. Thus, in *Persuasion* and *Emma* the heroines have lost their mothers. In *Sense and Sensibility* and *Pride and Prejudice*, the daughters have been indulged by their mothers and the fathers are absent or detached. In *Mansfield Park*, Fanny obediently leaves the large impoverished family that resulted from her mother's misalliance to live with her uncle, while in *Northanger Abbey*, the self-ruling Catherine Moreland leaves her large family to travel under the dubious care of a neighbor.[18] If such accidents of birth (including all the qualities of mind, body, or circumstance that concerned Sterne) establish the basis for social survival, interpretation of the accidents that occur in the course of daily existence provides an adaptive tool that ensures those fittest for the struggle will succeed. In that sense, Austen's heroines behave in a proto-Darwinian manner.

An avalanche of data that began to appear in periodicals from approximately 1820 to 1840 extended the collection of overlooked information assembled by literary observers like Austen. Sponsored by scientific academies formed in London, Paris, and Berlin, these figures offered far more detailed information than earlier English or French mortality statistics, and from the 1830s they began to be used to define human behavior. For example, murders and suicides were classified according to multiple possible motives, and it appears that people may not have ascribed these motives to actions until they were apprised of such classifications. In the sense that counting created new modes of self-conception, it had the effect of making up people.[19]

The astronomer Adolphe Quetelet took the radical step of applying mathematical laws of error (which had been used to calculate the proportionate number of times a coin might fall heads in a number of tosses or to identify celestial positions) to biological and social phenomena. He transformed the statistical mean into a real quantity, and almost immediately all kinds of human attributes, both physical and moral, were

18. See Juliet McMaster, "Class," and Edward Copeland, "Money," in *Cambridge Companion to Jane Austen*, ed. Copeland and McMaster (Cambridge: Cambridge University Press, 1997), 115–30, 131–48.

19. Ian Hacking, *Historical Ontology* (Cambridge, MA: Harvard University Press, 2002) 113.

investigated and plotted on distribution curves.[20] The concept of an "average man" postulated qualities against which people could measure their own lives. Differences became deviations from these norms. Thus, within the field of empirical analysis, statistical intelligence led to an increasingly precise awareness of anomalous or accidental data. Concomitantly, the creation of an "average" or "normal" self had the effect of reducing the individual to a single statistic within a sequence of random events, and the awareness that many people shared the same experiences stimulated fresh attempts to particularize the individual within a crowd of rivals for status or success. Faith in the regularity of numbers formed the basis of increasingly sophisticated statistical laws that gradually eroded the eighteenth-century's deterministic understanding of the world and created a powerful new awareness of arbitrary, random, or meaningless events. In principle, this documentary apparatus offered the possibility of control over minute aspects of behavior in the name of ensuring the welfare of the population. A web of control increasingly allowed the state to specify individuality: the paranoid scenario that Rousseau envisioned was becoming a technological reality.

One of the most influential applications of the evolving statistical theory of probability was Charles Darwin's *On the Origin of Species* (1859). The possibility of locating deviations in quantitative data patterns provided a tool he could apply to the biological phenomena that formed the focus of his interest. However, his work represents the culmination of extended interest in evolutionary change stimulated by *Vestiges of the Natural History of Creation*, which was published anonymously in 1844 but written by a nonscientist, Robert Chambers, the copublisher of *Chamber's Edinburgh Journal*.

By 1844, with a circulation of ninety thousand, Chambers's journal occupied an established position within the proliferating journalistic milieu of the period. His familiarity with the needs and expectations of readers enabled him to write a scientific book that created unprecedented attention. Although the work was criticized by prominent men of science as well as theologians, it exercised a profound influence on the general public. In fact, copies of *Vestiges* continued to sell long after Darwin published his *Origin*. Darwin was aware that his own theory would be approached in relation to the earlier book, so he deliberately wrote in ways that would distinguish his style from that of journalists or novelists and paid careful

---

20. See Lambert Adolphe Quetelet, *A Treatise on Man and the Development of His Faculties* (Edinburgh: W. and R. Chambers, 1842), esp. his introduction and book 4.

attention to marketing it through a reputable publisher as well as reminding his readers that his highly respected, multivolume study of barnacles provided genuinely scientific evidence for his discoveries.[21]

Darwin had begun to consider questions surrounding the creation of species during his voyage around the world (1831–36) as the ship's naturalist on the HMS *Beagle*. In the Galapagos, he noted the way in which finches differed from island to island and theorized that these differences signaled the mutability of species, an idea broached but never realized in the work of his grandfather Erasmus Darwin as well as other scientists:[22] "Although much remains obscure, and will long remain obscure, I can entertain no doubt, after the most deliberate study and dispassionate judgment of which I am capable, that the view which most naturalists entertain, and which I formerly entertained—namely, that each species has been independently created—is erroneous. I am fully convinced that species are not immutable."[23] His work required a long gestation period, and he hesitated to publish his controversial material until he learned that the naturalist Alfred Russel Wallace had arrived at similar conclusions based on observations in the Malay Archipelago. Two obstacles had impeded Darwin's reinterpretation of the natural world. One was reliance on the notion of immutable substance that had formed the basis of natural philosophy from Aristotle through Linnaeus. The other was the explanation of the creation of man and animals revealed in Genesis. Darwin's careful accumulation of fact and the power of his observations enabled him to depose both the biblical account and the substantial immutability of species.

On the Origin of Species begins with a consideration of the variation among species that occurs in man's breeding of domestic animals. Observing that breeders tried to possess and breed from the best individual animals, he realized that they intended only to better their own stock,

21. This discussion of *Vestiges* depends on James A. Secord's study of the book's cultural context and influence, *Victorian Sensation: The Extraordinary Publication, Reception and Secret Authorship of "Vestiges of the Natural History of Creation"* (Chicago, University of Chicago Press, 2000). Secord (512–16) makes the point that while Darwin's work gave fresh impetus to debates about the meaning of science, he owed his central position as the heroic author of one of the few interdisciplinary texts published at the time and his entry into the literary canon to the division of learning into academic disciplines. Rebecca Stott's *Darwin and the Barnacle* (New York: Norton, 2003) recounts the role research on barnacles played in Darwin's career.

22. See Edward Manier, *The Young Darwin and His Cultural Circle* (Doredrecht: D. Reidel, 1978), 14–20.

23. Charles Darwin, *On the Origin of Species by Means of Natural Selection*, ed. Joseph Carroll (Peterborough: Broadview, 2003), introduction, 98. All future citations are of this edition.

not to alter the breed. Over the centuries, he added, "this very same process, only carried on more methodically, did greatly modify, even during their own lifetimes, the forms and qualities of their cattle" (I.116). That is, breeders did not intend to change the species, but merely to effect some desired improvement in each successive animal, and the cumulative effect of individual choices brought about the broader changes. Darwin defined the process that caused species change in domestic animals over time as "unconscious selection" (I.119). In other words, he acknowledged accident as a driving force.

In developing his theory, he postulated three conditions that favor species change. First, an increase in the number of specimens being bred permits more variations among them and thus a broader range of choices. Second, an increase in time allows more variations to occur. Third, an increase in the value placed upon the species encourages greater attention paid to variations and selection based on those differences. For example, he noted: "I have seen it gravely remarked, that it was most fortunate that the strawberry began to vary just when gardeners began to attend closely to this plant. No doubt the strawberry had always varied since it was cultivated, but the slight varieties had been neglected. As soon, however, as gardeners picked out individual plants with slightly larger, earlier, or better fruit, and raised seedlings from them, and again picked out the best seedlings and bred from them, then, there appeared (aided by some crossing with distinct species) those many admirable varieties of the strawberry which have been raised during the last thirty or forty years" (I.120). In this microhistory of strawberry cultivation, Darwin displayed his characteristically admirable command of fact and recognized the way in which natural things were acquiring value and significance in nineteenth-century society.[24] I argued that Austen's meticulous observation reflected a microscopic view of her social environment, and here we see Darwin applying a similar close examination to the behavior of plants and animals and of the farm economy. Austen recommended that young women be cultivated and enhanced just as the woodland strawberry is

24. Probably the strawberries that became fashionable in London markets about 1831 were gathered in the wild, but Thomas Andrew Knight, president of the Royal Horticultural Society from from 1811 until 1838, made the first large-scale attempt to crossbreed strawberry varieties in 1817. His example and support encouraged market gardeners, notably Michael Keens of Isleworth and Myatt of Deptford, to develop varieties with improved flavor, color, size, and productivity. Thomas Laxton, an experimenter who worked for Darwin mainly on peas, conducted an extensive strawberry-breeding program during the 1860s, introducing his first results in 1872.

being nurtured and controlled and with the same goal of increasing perceived value.[25] As we observed in *Persuasion,* rather than suggesting her heroines would become fitter by enhancing superficial characteristics, she demonstrated that the qualities that ultimately allowed Anne to succeed were her combination of emotional integrity and her Darwinian capacity to adjust to changing circumstances.

This similarity in conceptual understanding results from the established literary perception that human behavior must be consistent in the face of narrative upheaval. Fielding's classical aesthetic had required a character to behave in accordance with what would appear plausible, and this principle was maintained within Rousseau's frank exposure of his feelings, Wordsworth's intense investment in childhood memories, and Austen's altered perception of both character and context. Today, when psychologists interested in memory or scientists interested in the function of the senses acknowledge the degree to which literary work anticipated current understanding, they are recognizing the empirical function inherent in fictional portrayals of experience. Like Darwin, authors perceived accidents in ways that did not conform to existing ideological systems and took the risk of publishing their findings.

No more than Austen did Darwin focus on major events like earthquakes or on life-transforming circumstances like infectious disease. His attention permeated the smallest details of things in nature, giving new value to the occurrence of accident: "We see these beautiful co-adaptations most plainly in the woodpecker and missletoe; and only a little less plainly in the humblest parasite which clings to the hairs of a quadruped or feathers of a bird; in the structure of the beetle which dives through the water; in the plumed seed which is wafted by the gentlest breeze; in short, we see beautiful adaptations everywhere and in every part of the organic world" (III.132).

Darwin perceived beauty in the adaptive strategies that made a particular organism victorious in the struggle to survive. His respect for parasites or predators did not derive from an abstract aesthetic appreciation of form but rather from the function they fulfilled within the system of interdependent relationships operating in the natural world. In his perception,

---

25. Amy M. King, *Bloom: The Botanical Vernacular in the English Novel* (Oxford: Oxford University Press, 2003), traces the relation between the rhetorical study of Linnaean botany in England and the courtship novels of the late eighteenth and nineteenth centuries. Her analysis of *Persuasion* (124–31) describes Anne as the botanical equivalent of a flower that blooms twice in a season. Adaptive resilience to a climate chilled by family neglect and early disappointment enables her to survive and flourish.

all things could be considered accidental parasites, in the sense that each depended on other species for survival and each element vied for continued existence. Transformations over long periods of time and the complexity of the relations between individuals and circumstances impressed him with an immensity of scale analogous to Kant's mathematical sublime.

Yet Darwin's understanding of natural selection did not imply moral judgments or give primacy to the beautiful or sublime in nature. It simply recognized practical achievement. He understood that within a world of finite resources, a geometric increase in any population would result in struggles among individuals or species. His aesthetic celebrated survival in a Malthusian world:

> Nothing is easier than to admit in words the truth of the universal struggle for life, or more difficult—at least I have found it so—than constantly to bear this conclusion in mind. Yet unless it be thoroughly engrained in the mind, I am convinced that the whole economy of nature, with every fact on distribution, rarity, abundance, extinction, and variation, will be dimly seen or quite misunderstood. We behold the face of nature bright with gladness, we often see superabundance of food; we do not see, or we forget, that the birds which are idly singing round us mostly live on insects or seeds, and are thus constantly destroying life; or we forget how largely these songsters, or their eggs, or their nestlings, are destroyed by birds and beasts of prey. (III.133)

The mechanism needed to drive the process of natural selection involved not only qualities manifested by the individual but also environmental contingencies, for Darwin presented nature as a dynamic economy in which all living things struggle for existence.

We recognize in the terms Darwin used to describe this economy the reappearance of the Aristotelian accidental quality and accidental event in a new and active guise. His holistic understanding of the interplay between qualities in the organism and qualities operating at a specific time and place, such as abundance, distribution, variation, and rarity, saw all these factors signifying in relation to one another. He recognized in this interplay the violent struggles that underlie a more romantic perception of the natural world.[26] In this amoral system what is bad is what hinders

26. Gillian Beer calls Darwin a "romantic materialist." *Darwin's Plots: Evolutionary Narrative in Darwin, George Eliot, and Nineteenth-Century Fiction* (London: Routledge and Kegan Paul, 1983), 48.

survival and what is good is what improves the odds of survival: "Can we doubt (remembering that many more individuals are born than can possibly survive) that individuals having any advantage, however slight, over others, would have the best chance of surviving and of procreating their kind? On the other hand, we may feel sure that any variation in the least degree injurious would be rigidly destroyed. This preservation of favourable variations and the rejection of injurious variations, I call Natural Selection." (IV.144). As determinism confronted the challenges posed by statistical probability, the notion of causation was pressured to accommodate greater complexity. Thus, the intersection of multiple causes might be required to explain what appeared to be a chance result. In this passage, Darwin explained that any variation from such an integrated system of causes would alter the chance of survival. Moreover, in his theory, events appear within the arena of a struggle that rendered them significant if they produce advantageous or disadvantageous results over time. When they appear with increasing frequency, they acquire a statistical significance. In other words, if an accident occurs once, it may or may not have lasting significance. On the other hand, if the accidental factor is reproduced a number of times, it acquires new power: it can generate or destroy an individual or a species.

Darwin's theory of species change did not recognize individuality as modeled around the idea of eccentricity or deep self in the way Rousseau or Wordsworth understood it in their autobiographical writings. However, even as he blurred the individual into a statistic, his thought remained individualistic because he recognized that variation takes place within the individual, and that an individual quality or act could begin the process of pulling a new species apart from the old. Crucial changes cannot be perceived at the time. At any given moment, an event appears accidental because the ordering principles are of such complexity that they are not readily apparent. When Darwin studied finches in the Galapagos, he was not seeking visual understanding of their substantial finchness but hoped that the accidental variations that occurred on each island could provide tangible evidence for the "slow progress" of change. His treelike diagram (fig. 4) shows a jumble of inadvertent and unintentional changes transformed into an orderly design.[27]

27. In fact, the evidence of fossilized trees, which Sir Charles Lyell documented at sixty-eight different levels in a site in Nova Scotia, provided literal support for Darwin's treelike construction of accidental change in "long-past geological ages." Lyell published the three volumes of his *Principles of Geology* from 1830 to 1833. His study of fossilized shell deposits

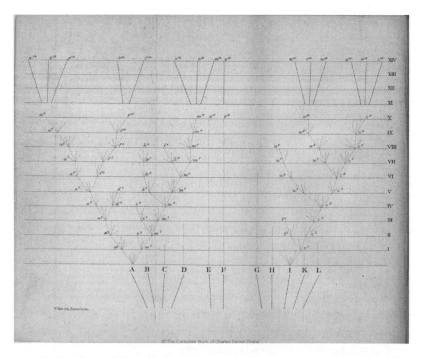

4. Charles Darwin, "Diagram of Common Descent," from *The Origin of Species* (1859).
From The Complete Work of Charles Darwin Online, University of Cambridge
(http://darwin-online.org.uk).

Darwin understood that the actions and reactions of plants and mammals, butterflies and worms, barnacles and bees might be contingently beneficial as well as predatory or harmful. In the final paragraph of the *Origin*—made famous by its concluding reference to evolution—he meditated on the visible and invisible actions that animated an earthen bank. He presented this complex, interdependent tangle of biological life as a creative force. His model was nonprovidential. It replaced the myth of the single creative sequence with a theory of continuing creation and maintenance.[28] Although the result was the first comprehensive yet fully secular interpretation of accident, Darwin could not escape the theological or moral implications of his work. As he wrote to the American botanist Asa

in Italy enabled him to develop his theory of uniformitarianism, which argued that gradual changes over time explain the earth's history. In the eighteenth century, representations of the classical diagram showing the knowledge of fixed substances that was commonly known as "Porphyry's tree" were revived in the literal image of a tree.

28. For an extended discussion of these ideas see Adam Phillips, *Darwin's Worms* (London: Faber and Faber, 1999).

Gray: "With respect to the theological view of the question. This is always painful to me. I am bewildered. I had no intention to write atheistically. But I own that I cannot see as plainly as others do, and as I should wish to do, evidence of design and beneficence on all sides of us. There seems to me too much misery in the world. . . . I am inclined to look at everything as resulting from designed laws, with the details, whether good or bad, left to the working out of what we may call chance. . . . (May 22, 1860)."[29]

Darwin's sense of the creative power of mess (and the growing influence of statistics that suffused many other fields of endeavor during the second half of the nineteenth century) was reflected in the emergence of a new vocabulary used to describe accidental variations. "Abnormal" and "deviation" derived directly from the practice of statistics (although "deviant" did not come into use until the early twentieth century). By the end of the century, "random" also acquired a specifically statistical meaning as something that involved equal chances for each hypothetical member of a population, and it carried the added significance of rendering the product of such a process completely unpredictable in its details. "Messy" had appeared early in the century to describe a state or situation of confusion or muddle, and by midcentury the word acquired the additional connotation of a dirty state or place.[30] However, such negative associations of "mess" were balanced by awareness that the messes might do more than change or disrupt the existing order: Darwin had shown how necessary and constructive they could be.

By turning randomness into a creative force, Darwin gave chance events a place in the natural order, but he could not explain what caused the accidents that drove his process of natural selection. At the same time, statistical laws that identified sociological norms were forced to recognize deviations whose causes were unclear. By the mid-nineteenth century, scientific analysis suggested that events might appear regular without being subservient to laws of nature.[31] As determinism faded away under these pressures, unexpected or arbitrary occurrences continued to demand ex-

29. Reprinted in Carrol's edition of the *Origin*, 492.

30. David Trotter, *Cooking with Mud: The Idea of Mess in Nineteenth-Century Art and Fiction* (Oxford: Oxford University Press, 2000), esp. chap. 3, "Mess and Modernity," 79–114.

31. Gregor Mendel's seminal work on genetics was published in 1866 but not appreciated until independent researchers rediscovered it in 1906. According to Jacques Monod, *Chance and Necessity: An Essay on the Natural Philosophy of Modern Biology*, trans. Austryn Wainhouse (New York: Knopf, 1971), 24, the full implications of Darwin's own theory, which implicitly depends on the chemical mechanisms that enable reproductive invariance, did not become apparent until the 1950s.

planations. And now verifiable evidence became the standard of proof. The fresh and unsettling awareness of the power of contingency spread broadly into society, bringing with it a heightened or expanded level of conceptual uncertainty.

III. Wished-For Accidents

Darwin functioned as a great codifier of the concepts of historical change that had acquired the name "gradualism" in the 1830s. The notion that evolution proceeded in slow and steady stages, which became one of the most popular markers for Darwinian thought, did not contradict gradualist belief. Because the *Origin* was revised six times (in increasingly conservative formulations), his own writings fostered uncertainty about how accident operated within his theory. Meanwhile, early realist novelists, such as Anthony Trollope—who abhorred surprises—had embraced gradualism. They strove to banish coincidences from their narrative structures and illuminating or transforming accidents from the delineation of character. However, Darwin needed chance variations to advance his argument, and realism also required chance to advance the narrative. In both cases the difficulty of explaining the energy or agency that motivated change left room for various deterministic interpretations. As a result, interpretation of accident became a marker for the understanding of historical change.

The two plots of George Eliot's final novel, *Daniel Deronda* (1876), Deronda's quest for his identity and Gwendolen's quest to become a better person, are joined precisely in terms of the force that accident directs on their development. Famously difficult to reconcile artistically, this double structure illustrates Eliot's attempt to integrate a sophisticated awareness of current scientific knowledge with what she understood as the pedagogical reason for writing.[32] In a letter she wrote to Joseph Payne a few days before the publication of the novel, she explained her goal: "But my writing is simply a set of experiments in life—an endeavour to see what our thought and emotion may be capable of—what stores of

---

32. Suzanne Graver, *George Eliot and Community: A Study in Social Theory and Fictional Form* (Berkeley: University of California Press, 1984), 11, notes that Eliot aspired to create a serious engagement with the text on the part of the reader. Her goal was to "so [present] our human life as to help my readers in getting a clearer conception and a more active admiration of those vital elements which bind men together and give a higher worthiness to their existence; and also to help them in gradually dissociating these elements from the more transient forms on which an outworn teaching tends to make them dependent" (George Eliot, *The George Eliot Letters*, ed. Gordon S. Haight [New Haven: Yale University Press, 1955], 4:472). Readers' letters and contemporary reviews suggest she often evoked this response.

motive, actual or hinted as possible, give promise of a better after which we may strive—what gains from past revelations and discipline we must strive to keep hold of as something more sure than shifting theory."[33] Eliot, who had defended *Vestiges* in an essay published in *Westminster*, read Darwin's *Origin* as soon as it was published and regarded it as an epochal work. In an unpublished essay she applied the idea of natural selection to the development of art: "Fortunate irregularities are discoveries in art; they are stages of its development, and go on living according to a natural selection."[34] In her application of Darwin's theories, she became aware of experiences that break the ordered pattern of existence. This realization occurred involuntarily—accidentally as it were—and exploiting it created a developmental stage in her own evolution.

Eliot's intellectual association with her companion, the philosopher, scientist, and editor George Henry Lewes, was remarkably strong, for they shared their reading and studied each other's work.[35] His evolving social and scientific theory was closely related to the changes in her understanding of the social and psychological implications of organicist thought, a belief in the interrelation of all things. He attempted to integrate metaphysical speculations on sensation and associationism (including the work of Locke and Hartley, among others) with the physiological psychology that had become influential in the early and mid-nineteenth century. According to Lewes, eighteenth-century theories of individualism were founded on a false premise: that individuals could not be understood apart from the society in which they lived. Moreover, he believed that social determinism extended to emotions, perceptions, and thoughts. Therefore, accumulations of knowledge, belief, prejudice, and tendencies conditioned not only institutions, but also the way in which generations felt and thought. In his view, the individual was not merely constrained by external coercive forces but internalized them in an adaptive development. Eliot was profoundly affected by these theories in both her social analysis and her psychological conceptions, and her novels attempted to balance her belief in individual difference with the social implications of Lewes's philosophy.[36]

33. Letter from Eliot to Payne, 26 January 1876, in Eliot, *Letters*, 6:216.

34. George Eliot, autograph manuscript notebook no. 7, Beinecke Rare Book and Manuscript Library, Yale University.

35. Eliot revised and completed the last two volumes of Lewes's *Problems of Life and Mind* for posthumous publication in 1878.

36. Sally Shuttleworth, *George Eliot and Nineteenth-Century Science: The Make-Believe of a Beginning* (Cambridge: Cambridge University Press, 1984), 19. Secord, *Victorian*

Random events permeate *Daniel Deronda*. It opens in medias res, at a gambling casino, a scene that records how the idea for the book came to Eliot, who was struck by the sight of Byron's young grandniece playing at a table filled with haggard gamesters. In her beauty and vitality, Gwendolen Harleth stands out from this obsessive crowd, but when she reads an implicit reproach into Deronda's gaze, she deliberately begins to play with greater recklessness. Ironically, she imagines assuming the guise of a modern goddess of fortune just as her luck deserts her: "She had begun to believe in her luck, others had begun to believe in it: she had visions of being followed by a *cortège* who would worship her as a goddess of luck and watch her play as a directing augury. Such things had been known of male gamblers; why should not a woman have a like supremacy?"[37] Gwendolen considers herself superior to those around her and glories in her recklessness. In effect, she has inherited the characteristics that made Austen's Mary Crawford so compelling both to the inhabitants of Mansfield Park and to later critics. Like Mary Crawford, who lacked the talent to read experience accurately despite her wit and charm, Gwendolen is morally insecure and cannot save herself from a lethal combination of bad behavior and bad luck. The chance that fixes Deronda's attention is a life-transforming accident for her, but the sight of Gwendolen also unsettles Deronda. He experiences a desire to look at her again but questions the nature of her appeal: "Was she beautiful or not beautiful? and what was the secret of form or expression which gave the dynamic quality to her glance? Was the good or the evil genius dominant in those beams? Probably the evil; else why was the effect that of unrest rather than of undisturbed charm? Why was the wish to look again felt as coercion, and not as a longing in which the whole being consents?" (I.i.3).[38] Gwendolen's

---

Sensation, 488–89, argues that Eliot owed her realist approach to the novel primarily to George Combe's *Constitution*, Herbert Spencer's *Westminster* essays, and *Vestiges*. Nancy L. Paxton, *George Eliot and Herbert Spencer: Feminism, Evolutionism, and the Reconstruction of Gender* (Princeton: Princeton University Press, 1991), accentuates sexual development in *Daniel Deronda* as evidence of Eliot's reaction to role of gender issues in Spencer's promulgation of evolutionary theory, but she also notes that his sociology became the focus of the treatment of race and nationality in book 1. See also A. S. Byatt's introduction to *George Eliot: Selected Essays, Poems and Other Writings*, ed. A. S. Byatt and Nicholas Warren (London: Penguin, 1990), xxxi–xxxii, on Eliot's "Notes on Form in Art" (1868) in relation to the interplay between scientific and metaphorical language in her last two novels.

37. George Eliot, *Daniel Deronda*, ed. Graham Handley (Oxford: Clarendon Press, 1984), I.i.6. All future citations are of this edition.

38. "Dynamic" was a scientific word at the time (invoking a force producing motion as well as the motion of bodies acting mutually on one another). According to the OED, the psychological dimension Eliot gave the term was original.

awareness of her attraction carries a biological power that demonstrates Eliot's attention to the aspect of sexual selection in Darwin's work. In *Daniel Deronda* a poorly chosen marriage cannot result merely in a mismatch in terms of money or social status (as it might have done for one of Austen's characters): it affects the development of the species. Although Deronda is unaware of his Jewish heredity, instinctively he is protected from responding sexually to Gwendolen, and despite the moral terms Eliot chooses to express Deronda's thoughts, he is not passing judgment or attempting to position her within conventional Christian morality.

As an observer in quest of his own identity and direction in life, Deronda suggests an English example of Baudelaire's flaneur, a wanderer who rests his gaze solely by chance. The way in which he singles Gwendolen out from the crowd of gamblers emphasizes the aleatory nature of his glance. And testing Gwendolen's capacity to survive becomes a part of Eliot's experiment, just as Deronda's ability to resist her tests his own fate. Moreover, the disturbing structure Eliot gave the novel, which seems to present two independent narrative strands bound only by coincidences, generates a comparable impression that she has relinquished authorial control to chance.

Both the narcotized expressions on the gamblers' faces and the hypnotic exchange between Deronda and Gwendolen partake of the interest in mesmerism during the mid-nineteenth century. Eliot was fully familiar with the neurological advances that led to greater curiosity about levels of consciousness. The body of the mesmerized individual obeys commands like an automaton; the conscious self is not in control. "Unconscious" as a term to describe involuntary behavior had come into use in the early 1700s, and by the middle of the nineteenth century large numbers of periodical articles testified to popular interest in the subject. Lewes read Eduard von Hartmann's enormously popular *Philosophy of the Unconscious* in 1869 and again in 1872, but his own theory of organic interaction argued against Hartmann's idea of a guiding intelligence. For Lewes, consciousness was "not an agent, but a symptom."[39] He conceived of the mind as a palimpsest. In his version of Locke's associationism, the mind was composed of sensations derived equally from consciousness and the unconscious. He made no distinction between the two levels, considering their relation to one another a gradation. By defining mind as the activities of the whole organism in correspondence with a

---

39. George H. Lewes, *Problems of Life and Mind,* 2nd ser., *The Physical Basis of Mind* (London: Trübner, 1879), 363.

psychic and social medium, Lewes not only undercut the Cartesian division between mind and body and Descartes's identification of the self with conscious thought, but also anticipated aspects of later nineteenth- and twentieth-century theories of the unconscious.[40]

Gwendolen's remaining gamble after she faces the news that her family has been "totally ruined" is marriage. At this point of crisis, she accepts Grandcourt, even though she knows that he has cast off the mother of his three illegitimate children, and much of the novel describes their pathological relationship.[41] Grandcourt, possessed of a will so powerful it seems uncontrolled, exerts a sadistic power over his wife, yet his response to Deronda's growing influence over her leads to his destruction. To escape the possibility of some reckless act on Gwendolen's part, he takes her to the Continent. But the three accidentally meet again in Genoa, where Grandcourt drowns in a boating accident before Gwendolen's eyes, his face appearing like the death's head she had foreseen earlier in the narrative. Hysterically, she tells Deronda that she is a murderess and compares her "evil longings" for Grandcourt's death to a "writing of fire": "I don't know how it was—he was turning the sail—there was a gust—he was struck—I know nothing—I only know that I saw my wish outside of me" (VII.lvi.648). This sentence, the most powerful expression of the unconscious in the novel, brings repressed understanding to the surface. The mysterious gust suggests a murderous wish fulfillment, and the shocking physical accident that follows alienates her from her rational self, effectively creating a divided consciousness. Gwendolen tells Deronda that she had contemplated killing Grandcourt, but she lost the key to the drawer where she had hidden a dagger. Her suppression of self-understanding ("I know nothing") first subverts her wish in the loss of the key, then allows chance to become the agent of her desire. Her response to the accidental event presents the true moral test, and her

40. The opening scene of *Daniel Deronda* makes a game of chance the object of hypnotic fascination for the gamblers, who appear as puppets of chance. However, Gwendolen's hysterical behavior later in the novel also exhibits moments of fear and repressed desire that surface as uncontrollable displays of emotion. For example, when she recovers from her terror at unexpectedly seeing a painted death's head joined to a fleeing figure, she "wonder[s] at herself in these occasional experiences, which seemed like a brief remembered madness, an unexplained exception from her normal life" (I.vi.56). Eliot's solution to the problem of how to render such conflicts and contradictions of the psyche was to interweave terminology borrowed from the romantic-Gothic literary tradition with her interpretation of Lewes's psychological theory.

41. See Marlene Tromp, *The Private Rod: Marital Violence, Sensation, and the Law in Victorian Britain* (Charlottesville: University Press of Virginia, 2000), 199–239.

paralysis as Grandcourt struggles to save himself constitutes a moment of negative self-definition in which Eliot inverts the issue of moral striving. Gwendolyn has not committed murder, yet she knows herself to be capable of it. Grandcourt's "accident" has become an association opposed to the comfort offered in Wordsworth's spots of time while retaining equal transformative power. We can compare the radical alteration of her life to the effect of the head injury which completely changed Louisa Musgrove after her fall: the physical cracking open of Louisa's head has metamorphosed into the subjective splitting of consciousness.[42]

In a final halting interview, both characters recognize the spiritual dimension of their relationship. "I said . . . it should be better . . . better with me," Gwendolen tells Deronda, "for having known you." And he replies, "Now we can perhaps never see each other again. But our minds may get nearer" (VIII.lxix.750). Deronda's response illustrates Eliot's version of the transparency of minds. She has not constructed a novel about a man in love with two women at the same time or of a willful woman desperate for a romantic alliance, but a relationship both internalized and therapeutic. Deronda has become Gwendolen's close observer, a screen on which she projects her desires; and by becoming "better" in a moral and psychological sense, she becomes a survivor. Freud, who later embraced sympathetic resonance as integral to psychoanalysis, was amazed by *Daniel Deronda*.[43]

The second strand of the novel involves Deronda's own sense of self in a visionary narrative that entwines Eliot's psychological experiment with a sociological one. She translated the topos of a foundling—an accident—who earns his position in society into a story of cultural identity. At the moment of Deronda's defining accident, his rescue of Mirah, which prefigures his destiny as a savior of the Jews, he is literally adrift, rowing aimlessly on the Thames, a man who cannot be classified in terms of family ties and refuses to be classified by status or profession.[44] He has

---

42. Deronda hardly knows how to reply to Gwendolen's confession, but his capacity for listening allows him to offer her solace without judging her. Victorian scientific and technological innovations (which included the telephone and phonograph, which appeared in the late 1870s) shifted the focus of the senses from the intense visual emphasis celebrated by Wordsworth to an emphasis on the capacity to listen. Eliot not only accentuated the defining role of music in this novel; she also translated the new science of acoustics, and the theory of sympathetic vibrations formulated by Hermann von Helmholtz, into a metaphor for mutual understanding and emotional connections. John M. Picker, *Victorian Soundscapes* (New York: Oxford University Press, 2003), 84–88.

43. Ibid., 107.

44. According to Terry Eagleton, *The English Novel*, 184, a romantic brand of politics makes *Daniel Deronda*, the only novel Eliot set in her own time, a utopian work which counters

abandoned himself to chance events. Reversing the emotions with which Gwendolen watched Grandcourt sink into the water, he perceives the appearance of the delicate girl as a vision of something vital that lies "outside" himself. For Eliot, Deronda's aimless quest constitutes a qualified endorsement of the fertility of a random substitute for rational problem solving. Mirah immediately recognizes Deronda's rescue as "God's command," but he only gradually comes to understand the far-reaching consequences of his chance meeting with a Jewess and his subsequent discovery of his own Jewish blood.[45] The way in which he postpones learning his identity further diminishes the role of sequential cause and effect. His drifting behavior presents an analogue to free association, opposed to the tradition of the well-plotted novel in which time reveals accidental events as plausible and significant. Deronda represents the flaneur's way to be modern.[46]

Eliot's explanation for this behavior rested on her rejection of the notion that identity can be strictly defined or quantified as well as on her critique of characters (like Grandcourt) who judge issues according to predefined categories. The scene in which Deronda meets Mirah's brother Mordecai on Blackfriars Bridge illustrates her shift from a transformation of the subject's inner sense of self that has no connection to the external cause of the accident to a recognition of self directly in accord with the

---

the "chilling" lack of vision that exemplified English society with the goal-oriented concepts of Judaism and Zionism. If English society lacked an emotional and spiritual authority comparable to Jewish national feeling, the fact that the Jewish characters in the novel are also English brings out the exclusionary formation of English national consciousness. The early 1870s ended a period in which Jews were struggling against their exclusion from public life and had begun to remove their political and civil disadvantages at the institutional level. See David Feldman, *Englishmen and Jews: Social Relations and Political Culture, 1840–1914* (New Haven: Yale University Press, 1994).

45. Eliot became sufficiently proficient in her study of Hebrew with Talmudist Emanuel O. Deutsch of the British Museum's oriental department to translate Spinoza's *Ethics*. For one analysis of the extent to which *Daniel Deronda* represents Victorian Christian Zionism see Edward W. Said, *The Question of Palestine* (New York: Vintage Books, 1992), chap. 2, esp. 60–66.

46. Deronda's wandering adverts to the myth of the Wandering Jew. Even before he learns of his heritage, he ascribes his restlessness to an inherited yearning and his mother recognizes in him a latent obstinacy of race. Mordecai envisions a future in which inherited racial memory absorbs the idea of difference: "The heritage of Israel is beating in the pulse of millions; it lives in their veins as a power without understanding, like the morning exultation of herds; it is the inborn half of memory, moving as in a dream among writings on the wall, which it sees dimly but cannot divide into speech" (457). Pauline Nestor, *Critical Issues: George Eliot* (Houndmills: Palgrave, 2002), 154–55, also notes the primacy of nature over nurture in the biological vocabulary of the novel with the suggestion that genes confer a fundamental identity.

causative agent. The encounter is plausible on a literal level. Mordecai often comes to this spot at sunset (for he has had a vision of meeting his prefigured second self on the river). Deronda happens to travel there by wherry rather than taking a cab, intending to seek out the remarkable man he had met before at a nearby bookshop. Nevertheless, as he rows down the river with the setting sun at his back, these accidental circumstances transform the scene into precisely what Mordecai had foreseen: the sunset representing his own physical decline has brought him his alter ego, his new life. However, by tacitly assuming the identity of Mordecai's friend, Deronda becomes what Mordecai claims him to be. In this accidental context, the self has been defined not from inner experience but from without. His fortune has found him.

Giving Deronda a Jewish identity allowed Eliot to develop his role as an outsider—vulnerable to social prejudices yet detached from participating in them—in order to apply a reforming purpose to her analysis of British society. In the process, she identified blood and race as new markers of self-definition. Deronda's fate has been determined by bloodlines that give an unalterable certainty to the question of self.[47] Although Eliot chose a scientific rationale over a providential one, she still controlled the messy and changing world of the second half of the century within a recognizably deterministic viewpoint. Deronda is not unique in the sense that he represents and belongs to a people. His substance is Jewish. When he reveals this fact to Hans Meyrick, however, it elicits from his friend and rival a caustic meditation on substance. Referring to Mordecai, Meyrick writes: "I leave it to him to settle our basis, never yet having seen a basis which is not a world-supporting elephant, more or less powerful and expensive to keep. My means will not allow me to keep a private elephant. I go into mystery instead, as cheaper and more lasting—a sort

47. David Kaufmann, a Jewish scholar and Eliot's contemporary, recognized that a sharp idea of nationality had reappeared in *Daniel Deronda*: "It must be noted that the Jews themselves have begun to recognise a nationality in Judaism—and a nationality which cannot be laid aside like a garment." Quoted in Hao Li, *Memory and History in George Eliot* (New York: St. Martin's Press, 2000), 153. However, the idea of identity as clothing takes on various implications in the novel. The fusion of national traits makes Deronda's English reserve and self-possession appear as a veneer over his romantic sensibility, and Graver, *George Eliot and Community*, 241–43, points out instances of ironic reference that undercut the elevated mode of his transformed identity. For example, when he returns to share the news of his heritage, Eliot notes with irony that he is wearing the summer clothing of his contemporaries—as other heroes must have done (639). In that sense, the references to garments and identity hark back to the earlier eighteenth-century notion of a shiftable, externally defined self. Eliot's treatment of Mordecai and the tentative introduction of the visionary theme also point to notions of spiritual versus corporeal identity.

of gas which is likely to be continually supplied by the decomposition of the elephants" (VII.lii.598). Meyrick mocks Mordecai's ontological certainty of the primacy of all things Jewish by invoking Locke's figure of the Indian philosopher who saw the world supported by a great elephant. Here the anecdote Locke used to question the basis of all things as postulated in late Scholastic thought returns to satirize the possibility that race, blood, or marks of physiognomy can better define a man's essence. All such theories, Meyrick suggests, prove costly and are only partially successful. A visionary in his own right, the painter proposes another solution, the mysterious, self-renewing gas that emanates from decaying ideas of substance. His ironic suggestion recognizes an irresolvable and self-perpetuating quest that moves both backward and forward in time. The epigraph that begins the novel alludes to the same idea with reference to another seventeenth-century source, Bernard Fontenelle's *Entretiens sur la Pluralité des Mondes* (1686). "Men can do nothing without the make-believe of a beginning," says Fontenelle, who argues that both Science and its less accurate grandmother, Poetry, look backward as well as forward (I.i.3). A scientific experiment cannot begin without a hypothesis to test; Eliot's novel could not take shape until some conjunction of "fortunate irrelevancies" directed the author's imagination. *Daniel Deronda*, an "experiment in life," simultaneously looked backward to the perennial desire for a stable sense of self and forward to an idea of cultural identity. At the end of the novel, Deronda sails into the increasing instability and uncertainty of modern life.

CHAPTER NINE

The Form of Accident:
The Boundaries of Perception

I. Visual Forms

During the final decades of the nineteenth century characteristics of unease and struggle permeated all fields of endeavor. The accumulation of empirical data had not achieved the Enlightenment ideal of an orderly or secure body of knowledge. Like the gas Meyerick envisioned being expelled by decomposing theories of substance in Eliot's *Daniel Deronda*, explanations of events in nature or the vagaries of human behavior appeared to be drifting into an intangible and increasingly indefinite future. At the same time, new technologies were developing that would radically shift modes of perceiving events within daily life and science remained a source of understanding and creative stimulus.

As a new information technology, photography had proved its capacity to expand the boundaries of what was visible through X-ray and microscopic photographs or the chronophotographic experiments of Eadweard Muybridge and Étienne-Jules Marey. Photographs could record fleeting or contingent experiences, preserve images of people and places, and even (through double exposures and other techniques) manufacture images that projected an illusion of reality. Photographs appeared on visiting cards, in publications and were gathered into albums or displayed in shops and exhibition halls. This accumulation of visual data made distant scenes more widely accessible while the ease with which ordinary people could obtain photographs of loved-ones created a reservoir of images resonant with emotion. Writers and visual artists were fascinated by both the recording and the memorializing aspects of the new technology, so that Émile Zola and August Strindberg as well as painters like Pierre

Bonnard or Edvard Munch left extensive photographic records of intimate aspects of their lives.[1]

One of the most self-consciously aware of the amateur artist-photographers was Edgar Degas. As someone who knew Claude Monet and Auguste Renoir, Pierre Bonnard and Pablo Picasso, Marcel Proust and Paul Valéry, he participated in the ideational transformations under way during the 1890s as well as in an evolving relationship between words and images. This chronological position allows his photographs to serve as visual markers of a significant transitional moment in the history of accident. As in earlier periods in which conventional contexts provide glimpses of dynamic conceptual change, his work appears Janus faced, embracing both past and future. Just as Raphael captured the Scholastic synthesis on the brink of a shift to post-Reformation turmoil, Degas sought to define forms and motion—to abstract and preserve their essence—on the cusp of a radical shift in the representation of the inner as well as the external world. Despite obvious differences in visual style and subject matter between the Stanza and one of Degas's portrait photographs—the architectural public space of the Vatican walls giving way to domestic interiors suffused in murky lamplight and the intellectual clarity of Raphael's iconographic program being replaced by Degas's fascination with the subtle range of physiognomic expression—both artists preserve traces of cultural memory.

"The snapshot is photography and nothing more," Degas wrote to the Danish painter Lorentz Frölich in 1872. His early extant notebooks include two such snapshots and a sketch reproducing the composition of one of André-Adolphe-Eugène Disdéri's photographs of two women, but sometime between 1878 and 1881, he discovered the work of Muybridge and Marey, and by the spring of 1884 he was actively taking pictures.[2] His interest coincided with the alteration in the position of the photograph within the tradition of the visual arts that occurred during the same time. The assumption that a striking photographic image resulted from

1. For a discussion of the general impact of photography on visual perception see Dorothy Kosinski, "Vision and Visionaries: The Camera in the Context of Symbolist Aesthetics," in *The Artist and Camera: Degas to Picasso*, ed. Dorothy Kosinski (New Haven: Yale University Press, 1999), 12–23.

2. See Theodore Reff, *The Notebooks of Edgar Degas*, 2 vols. (Oxford: Clarendon Press, 1976). Both Julie Manet and Daniel Halévy recount Degas's photographic enthusiasm. See accounts quoted in Malcolm Daniel, *Edgar Degas, Photographer* (New York, 1998), 35 and 36. Elizabeth C. Childs, "Habits of the Eye: Degas, Photography, and Modes of Vision," in Kosinski, *The Artist and Camera*, 77, dates Degas's photographic activity to 1894–96.

accident rather than the photographer's skill, sensitivity, or knowledge of the visual arts was being actively disputed in the work of photographers in America as well as on the Continent. A photographic style emerged that came to be known as pictorialism. Rather than depending on technological characteristics of the medium, pictorialism was conceptualized around the work of the impressionists as well as an earlier naturalism that shared the ideological aim of symbolist poets to express "eternal meanings."[3]

In the 1880s, a number of Degas's colleagues experienced a loss of faith in their own abilities. Paul Cézanne longed for the skills of the Italian masters. Renoir questioned his capacity to draw and wondered whether he had been traveling down a blind alley with impressionism.[4] Degas made radical experiments to recapture the Renaissance techniques of underglaze painting and adapt them to his work with pastels. He also experimented with various recipes to fix the colors in cumulative layers. Working on the smooth surfaces of tracing paper (rather than the "toothed" papers in conventional use) allowed him to manipulate the surrounding space, combine figures, and gradually enlarge them to achieve the monumentality characteristic of his late work. By creating multiple copies of the same image, he could also explore intense and unpredictable color harmonies, finally selecting one version of the subject to bring to completion. Paul Valéry regarded the separation of form from color resulting from these procedures as evidence that Degas belonged to the "family of abstract artists."[5]

In a portrait of Auguste Renoir and Stéphane Mallarmé that Degas took in 1895, he is partly visible within a blaze of light reflected in the large mirror that forms the background of the photograph (fig. 5). The portrayal of the three men conjoined in this way is emblematic of the interplay between contemporary theoretical positions with regard to the making of images and the technical capacities of the photographic medium—the impressionist Renoir looks directly into the camera, the symbolist poet withdraws into himself, and Degas as the master of the new technology mediates between them. Motifs of the mirror and the dimly lit interior are characteristic of many of Degas's photographic portrait

3. Anne Hammond, "Naturalistic Vision and Symbolist Image: The Pictorial Impulse," in *The New History of Photography*, ed. Michel Frizot (Cologne: Könemann, 1998), 293.

4. Richard Kendall, *Degas: Beyond Impressionism* (London: National Gallery, 1996), 65.

5. Ibid., 77–104. Kendall refers to Degas's experimental approach as "quasi-Darwinian."

5. Edgar Degas, *Pierre Auguste Renoir and Stéphane Mallarmé* (1895). Gelatin-silver print, 15 3/8 × 11 3/16 in. Gift of Paul F. Walter (00207.89). The Museum of Modern Art, New York, New York, USA. (Digital image © The Museum of Modern Art / Licensed by Scala / Art Resource, New York.)

studies. The halo of light that blots out his face would not have disturbed him, for he pushed the technical limits of this new medium in his attempt to realize the quality of artificial light and the play of shadow. Moreover, acceptance of unintended results was characteristic of his concurrent experimental manipulation of pastels in his drawings of bathers and dancers.

In another photograph of the same date, a group portrait taken at the home of Ludovic Halévy (fig. 6), a double exposure superimposes two vertical figures on four figures arranged in a horizontal format. Although the double exposure was unintentional, Degas accepted the result, having several prints made of the image. Because of his fascination with lighting effects he left portions of the composition in deep shadow, making the figures seem partly substantial and partly transparent against the dark background.[6] Just as he capitalized on unexpected results in his work with pastels to convey a tension between a momentary gesture and an iconic human form stripped of inessentials, he acknowledged the evocative nature of this technical accident. Thus, while the photographic process allowed a chance effect, the eye of the artist determined both the enabling contexts and the value of the end result.

"If Degas had died at fifty," Renoir wrote, "he would have been remembered as an excellent painter, no more: it is after his fiftieth year that his work broadened out and that he really became Degas."[7] In that sense, he claims that his fellow painter's essence rests on his experimental pushing of visual limits. If photography stimulated Degas, his painting exploited ways of seeing that photographers would not consciously pursue for decades: showing movement by being in movement, framing a view, creating breakdowns of scenes and low-angle shots, filling the picture, emptying it, inventing off-center, oblique compositions, employing dissolves, close-ups, cropping—a legacy of enduring qualities.[8] Nothing emphasizes Degas's right to serve as an emblem of a turn-of-the-century revitalization of visual form more than his invention of so many of the visual techniques that eventually would be applied to cinema.

Although Degas expressed little sympathy with symbolist literary work, his photograph of Mallarmé is recognized as one of the most expressive portraits of the poet, and the two men shared a fascination with

6. Daniel, *Edgar Degas, Photographer,* 32–34.

7. Quoted in Kendall, *Degas,* 10.

8. Elvire Perego, "Intimate Moments and Secret Gardens: The Artist as Amateur Photographer," in Frizot, *New History of Photography,* 345.

6. Edgar Degas, *Mathilde and Jeanne Niaudet, Daniel Halévy, Henriette Taschereau, Ludovic Halévy, Elie Halévy* (1895). Glass negative with silver gelatino-bromure. Photograph: Hervé Lewandowski. Musée d'Orsay, Paris, France. (Photograph © Réunion des Musées Nationaux / Art Resource, New York.)

technical experimentation. We can obtain indications of their commonality from Valéry, who was a close friend of both men. He recounts how Degas complained to the poet of the difficulty of completing his own sonnets even though he had no lack of ideas. Mallarmé replied, "But, Degas, you can't make a poem with ideas. . . . *You make it with words.*" When Valéry recorded this exchange, he recognized that both men prized the form that underlay the distinction between words and images: "Degas saying that drawing was *a way of seeing form,* Mallarmé teaching that *poetry is made with words,* were summing up, each for his own craft, a truth."[9]

Mallarmé responded with surprising sympathy to the introduction of free verse in 1886, but it presented him with a crisis of method comparable to that experienced by Degas and other members of the

9. See Theodore Reff, *Degas: The Artist's Mind* (New York: Harper and Row, 1976), 191. According to Reff, Degas knew many of the symbolist writers in the 1870s, while Mallarmé was involved in Berthe Morisot's circle of impressionists and had written about Degas's art as early as 1876.

impressionist circle.[10] "Un Coup de dés" represents his response to this challenge, a poem whose great originality consists in the visual form given to the words. One of the difficulties posed by the poem lies in the lack of an authoritative version of the text.[11] However, without a doubt Mallarmé invested extraordinary care in its typographic form. Like Degas, who was fascinated by the process of printing photographs, Mallarmé learned about book production and typography. Choosing the Didier font—noted for its elegant use of space within and between characters and its harmony between the Roman and italic alphabets—he employed many different sizes of type, contravened typographic rules in his pictorial placement of words on the page, and rendered the form of the four-page signature an important aspect of the interplay between sense and space.[12]

When Valéry saw the draft of the poem, it was laid out on squared paper, a fact that reminds us how intensely mathematical thinking was implicated in Mallarmé's respect for Descartes's vision of mathematics as a language. In an interesting corollary observation, Valéry noted that "art, for [Degas], was simply a series of problems in a more subtle kind of mathematics than the real one."[13] In that sense, the process Degas used to shift the placement of figures in space by cropping and reprinting his photographs, adding paper to the margins of his drawings, or applying the principle of the "close-up" to intensify his study of the human form has parallels to the processes Mallarmé used in creating the poem in space. One frequently noted example is the way in which the distribution of words projects a tentative visualization of the subject matter—such as the flotsam resulting from the wrecked ship or the floating plume—but

10. Clive Scott, *Vers Libre: The Emergence of Free Verse in France, 1886–1914* (Oxford: Oxford University Press, 1990), 70–71.

11. The edition proposed by Ambroise Vollard was abandoned after the poet's death. Proofs corrected in Mallarmé's hand (the Lahure proofs) provided the basis for the edition by Mitsou Ronat and Tibor Papp (Paris: Groupe d'Atelier, 1980), which preserves the page size, typography, and other elements of the Vollard project.

12. Aspects of Mallarmé's typographic design are discussed in detail by Roger Pearson, *Unfolding Mallarmé: The Development of a Poetic Art* (Oxford: Clarendon Press, 1996); Robert Greer Cohn, *Mallarmé's "Un coup de dés": An Exegesis* (New York: AMS Press, 1980 (which offers a version of the physical text); Virginia A. La Charité, *The Dynamics of Space: Mallarmé's "Un coup de dés jamais n'abolira le hasard"* (Lexington, KY: French Forum, 1987); and René Lindkens, *Dans l'espace de l'image* (Paris: Aux Amateurs de Livres, 1986), which provides a schematic representation to support his analysis. Their conclusions are not entirely compatible, but Pearson outlines the main features of the debate.

13. Reff, *Degas: The Artist's Mind*, 274.

the relation of recto to verso, as in the chiasmus that centers the poem across pages six and seven, or the struggle between lines of Roman and lines of italic type around the bold LE HASARD on page 10 are evidence of a spatial geometry of remarkable sensitivity.[14] The result is a visual icon whose form exposes the latent semantic content.

Recognizing the connotative fluidity of language as a defect that would inhibit the realization of his goal of a "pure" poetry, Mallarmé asserts that in a linguistic sense every thought involves chance. Linguistic rules cannot be abolished by a throw of the dice (in the sense that dice games are bound by rules as well as laws of probability). Although the poet annuls normal syntax, abolishes punctuation, and calls on space to aid his words, the struggle with contingent language ends by acknowledging an inescapable ambiguity: "Toute Pensée émet un Coup de Dés."

Ambiguity exists on the level of the event portrayed in the poem. The shipwreck is evoked through the presentation of the ocean from which the captain's arm thrusts upward, ready to throw the dice. However, the dice are never thrown. Mallarmé presents only the eternal hesitation that expresses the stakes of "making an event out of the thought of the event."[15] From the standpoint of interpreting the situation, the reader must bet on the cast of the dice, that is, on the words thrown across the blank page. The parallel with Pascal's wager is evident although secularized to a plane of artistic truth. Just as the essence of the poem would be sacrificed by scraping the words (which we might align with accidental qualities) from the page that is necessary to the whole, the essence of the event would be equally lost if the dice were thrown or the gesture never realized. On the one hand, the essential undecidability of the event would vanish in the presence of the sum of the numbers on the faces of

14. The Mallarmé literature, including the works cited above, is characterized in large part by page-by-page, line-by-line demonstrations of this point.

15. Alain Badiou, *Being and Event*, trans. Oliver Feltham (London: Continuum, 2003), 192–96. Meditation 19 consists of an extended discussion of "Un Coup de dés." In it Badiou reads the numerical implications of casting the dice in terms of his own theory of the essence of the event as a result (something countable and enclosed with the limits of possibly having begun and possibly having ended) that emerges from its disappearance into the multiple (the situation as the sum of its constituent elements). In that sense, if the dice were cast, the essence of the event would escape into chance and no longer be capable of representing the absolute notion of "there is." He argues, with reference to his own theory that a human being actualizes him- or herself as a subject by keeping faith with recognition of the status of the event within a situation, that if undecidability constitutes a rational attribute of the event, and the salvatory guarantee of its nonbeing, the vigilance of becoming consists as much in the anxiety of hesitation (the feather) as through the courage of the outside place (the star, "up high perhaps"), 197–98.

the dice. On the other hand, nothing would take place. In other words, Mallarmé simultaneously privileges the accidental or contingent as a poetic necessity and denies it an interpretive fulfillment.

Experiments with photographic images show that viewers confronted with interpretive ambiguity respond by making deductions of a narrative cast even when nothing present in the image represents an act. Interpretations of the feather as a plume on a hat, a pen, a spray of ocean foam, to take only one example from "Un Coup de dés," suggest that Mallarmé's iconic verbal images are capable of producing similar narratological responses. Although an explanation for this phenomenon remains elusive, such investigations work to reorder the noetic relationships between words and images, disturbing the primacy of language as an originary mode of making sense and allocating a comparable power to insinuate conceptual understanding to the visual image. For both images and language, sensation becomes a skin over more intricate mental processes.[16] An intuition of this kind may have lain behind Degas's sarcastic aphorism: "Literature explains art without understanding it, art understands literature without explaining it."[17]

The interpretive process that generates an abstract concept in response to concrete images (struggle, for example, construed from the splay of words across page 10 of "Un Coup de dés") appears to proceed from a general impression to specific details rather than the reverse.[18] In terms of the relation between accidental qualities and substance, this notion becomes extremely suggestive when applied to the artistic process. Paring away the markings of individuality, as Degas did in his late renderings of bathers or dancers, or defusing the connotative aspects of language, as Mallarmé did by making the blank page as relevant as his text, allowed both to move away from literal representation while proclaiming the inexplicable. Mallarmé's assertion that his work would be comprehensible to a reader who read between the lines signals his awareness of possibilities for decoding text that escaped semantic limitations. An ability to read form generates a shifting relationship between word and image that characterizes not only the twentieth-century proliferation of photographic images but also the new medium of film.

16. See Lindkens, *Dans l'espace de l'image*, 40–42. He based his experimental work (asking subjects to verbalize their response to photographic images) on a hypothesis derived in part from the work of Jean Piaget.

17. Reported by G. Rouault, *Souvenirs intimes* (Paris, 1927), 98.

18. Lindkens, *Dans l'espace de l'image*, 44–65, posits this argument in detail, accentuating its application to photography and cinema in particular.

II. The Pearl

In their final work, both Degas and Mallarmé express a search for essence within a context based on contingency—Mallarmé in terms of his subject matter as well as his poetic innovation, Degas in terms of his experimental technical processes and his exploration of human emotion in his portrait photography. In these portraits emotions are concentrated in faces and hands that emerge from deep shadows and are accentuated by sequential cropping and enlargement as though Degas wished to approach his subjects so closely that he could capture every nuance of their thought. His stated goal was not to reproduce a likeness but to discover a pattern of human emotions that would replace the painter Charles Le Brun's 1698 catalog of facial expressions.[19] This project combined a fascination with the representation of states of mind and an awareness that among his contemporaries they comprised emotions of far greater complexity than Le Brun's simple modes of "anger," "joy," or "melancholy."

Degas's project remained unrealized, but the impulse to obtain a more penetrating and universal understanding of states of mind also lay behind the utopian project Sigmund Freud conceived in the spring of 1895. He proposed to "investigate what form the theory of mental functioning assumes if one introduces the quantitative point of view, a sort of economics of nerve forces, and second, to extract from psychopathology a gain for normal psychology." After months of intense effort, he discarded this project for a scientific psychology, but seminal ideas regarding the operation of the mind appeared in a draft for this project, couched in the mechanistic and technical vocabulary of his medical training. His *Outline of Psychoanalysis*, left unfinished when he died in 1939, echoed this early program in almost every detail and reaffirmed his desire to establish psychoanalysis among the natural sciences.[20]

In order to construct a psychosomatic interpretation of accidental events, Freud gathered examples from his reading, from friends, and from the patients he saw as part of his therapeutic practice in Vienna. He defined three conditions that a psychic accident must fulfill. It must not exceed certain dimensions fixed by judgment to lie "within the limits of the normal." It must be a momentary disturbance of a function that the subject is capable of performing correctly. Finally, the patient must

---

19. Reff, *The Notebooks of Edgar Degas*, 1:26–27.

20. Peter Gay, *Freud: A Life for Our Time* (New York: Doubleday, 1988), 79. Gay quotes from Freud's letter to Wilhelm Fliess of 25 May 1895.

immediately recognize the performed function as wrong. Lacking any perceptible motivation, a psychic accident will tempt the individual to explain it as "inattentiveness," or put it down to "chance." In this way, Freud turned the former assertion of a chance event as something the individual cannot control into a symptom of repression. Although Freud's theory allowed for chance events, all psychic accidents were understood to be signs of the unconscious: "I do not believe that an event in whose occurrence my mental life plays no part can teach me any hidden thing about the future shape of reality; but I believe that an unintentional manifestation of my own mental activity *does* on the other hand disclose something hidden, though again it is something that belongs only to my mental life. I believe in external (real) chance, it is true, but not in internal (psychical) accidental events."[21] To illustrate the difference between chance events and psychic accidents, Freud described how he used to visit a ninety-year-old patient so frequently that all the cabdrivers at the rank in front of his house knew the patient's address. However, one day, a cabdriver happened to stop in front of a house with the same number but located in a parallel street. While this event might have been a psychic mistake on the part of the cab driver or interpreted by a superstitious person as an omen of the woman's probable death, for Freud it was merely "an accident without any further meaning." On the other hand, he wrote, if he had walked to the wrong house through absentmindedness, he would have considered his mistake a psychic accident "that had an unconscious aim and required interpretation" (327–28).

Freud interrupted his work on *The Psychopathology of Everyday Life* to write the case history of Ida Bauer, whom he described as Dora in *An Analysis of a Case of Hysteria.*[22] Written in 1901 but not published until 1905, the study recorded his incomplete analysis of "a hysterical girl

---

21. Sigmund Freud, *The Psychopathology of Everyday Life*, vol. 6 of *The Standard Edition of the Complete Psychological Works*, 24 vols., ed. James Strachey (London: Hogarth Press, 1953–74), 328. All further references are to this edition.

22. *The Psychopathology* includes a reference to the unconscious overdetermination of the apparently arbitrary choice of the pseudonym Dora for his patient. "With a view to preparing the case history of one of my women patients for publication I considered what first name I should give her in my account. There appeared to be a very wide choice; some names, it is true, were ruled out from the start—the real name in the first place, then the names of members of my own family, to which I should object, and perhaps some other women's names with an especially peculiar sound. But otherwise there was no need for me to be at a loss for a name. It might have been expected—and I myself expected—that a whole host of women's names would be at my disposal. Instead, one name and only one occurred to me—the name 'Dora'" (308).

of nineteen" who displayed the commonest of somatic and medical symptoms—notably a nervous cough, attacks of aphonia, or muteness—as well as suicidal tendencies.

For late nineteenth-century physicians, hysteria retained elements of earlier gendered theories of nervous sensibility. The majority of hysteric patients were women, diagnosed as suffering from abnormalities in their sexual function, but the disease produced a baffling array of symptoms. By the last decades of the century, four thousand madwomen were incarcerated as incurables in the Salpêtrière Hospital in Paris, where Freud spent several months studying with Jean-Marie Charcot, the leading French neurologist of the 1890s. Charcot used photographic observations as a means to identify what he considered the "lies," or false symptoms, produced by the hysterical body. Freud saw these photographs as providing new evidence that the hysteric unconsciously acted out what she could not accomplish. Although the experience at Salpêtrière made Freud uneasy, and he disowned his initial notion of the unconscious as a camera storing images that could be printed later, the experience led him to identify the hysteric's illness with memory. Nothing in mental life gets lost, he conjectured. It continues to work and protest and disturb the mind.

In the course of Dora's analysis, Freud sought to work out the implications of her accidental acts and interpret her dreams. The *Analysis*, therefore, accompanied his work on *The Psychopathology* and allows us to consider the implications of accident within the analytic process. In it, he presented the analyst as a detective who must take events that appear to be accidental and reveal their unconscious motivation. During one session, for example, Dora played continually with her reticule, opening and closing it and inserting a finger into the opening. He identified her reticule as a representation of her genitals and diagnosed her gestures with it as masturbation. Freud's analysis of the significance of her gestures led him to categorize all such seemingly involuntary acts as symptoms: "I give the name of symptomatic acts to those acts which people perform, as we say, automatically, unconsciously, without attending to them, or as if in a moment of distraction. They are actions to which people would like to deny any significance, and which, if questioned about them, they would explain as being indifferent and accidental."[23] A hysterical subject would describe such events as accidents to conceal something she unconsciously wished to remain hidden, just as a murderer might hope to have

---

23. Sigmund Freud, *Dora: An Analysis of a Case of Hysteria* (New York: Macmillan, 1963), 68. All further references are to this edition.

his crime appear to be an accident. Freud argued that a hysteric represses some physical or psychic trauma that created intense anxiety in a person predisposed to feel its effect. Like an inversion of the Wordsworthian spot of time, this trauma incubates in the memory and infects experience with hidden associations.

In this interpretation, a trauma lay at the core of the identity the patient had established. A wound inflicted on the body or mind breached the psychic defense system. To shield itself from the negative effects of this latent presence, the self must be repeatedly refashioned by the memory.[24] In this process of self-revision, the hysteric becomes susceptible to new wounds that are in some way reminiscent of the imperfectly suppressed or only partially resolved initial trauma.

Although Freud failed to identify Dora's "Ur-trauma," he was able to detect the somatic representations of a complex web of remembered psychic wounds revolving around her love of her father, Herr K. (her father's friend), and Herr K.'s wife. Her somatizations emerged in scenarios involving bed-wetting, masturbation, sexual aggression, and victimization that she was compelled to repress in turn. The accidental symptoms that brought Dora for therapy, such as her catarrh, concerned parts of her body that signified for her as erotogenic zones. Freud compared these symptoms to the grain of sand around which an oyster creates a pearl: "In the lowest stratum we must assume the presence of a real and organically determined irritation of the throat—which acted like the grain of sand around which an oyster forms its pearl. This irritation was susceptible to fixation, because it concerned a part of the body which in Dora had to a high degree retained its significance as an erotogenic zone. And the irritation was consequently well fitted to give expression to excited states of the libido" (74). When Dora rejected Freud's claims that she was "in love" with her father, Herr K., and his wife, he asserted that she had repressed her desire, that no meant yes, and that just as there are no mental accidents, "there is no such thing as an unconscious 'No.'" His later interpretation of Dora's dream, in which a fire threatens her mother's jewel case, led to a vertiginous interpretation that linked childhood accidents of bed-wetting, Dora's sexual awareness, and her belief that her father had infected her mother, and thence herself, with syphilis. According to Freud, the multivalent symptom, like the pearl composed of nacreous layers, contains several meanings at the same time or can express several

---

24. Elisabeth Bronfen, *The Knotted Subject: Hysteria and Its Discontents* (Princeton: Princeton University Press, 1998), 34–35.

meanings in succession (46). The self that the subject describes during analysis is haunted by stories of past experiences that are no more under control than the symptoms that symbolize them. When the parasitic memories are contained or absent from consciousness, the patient is in a normal psychological state. Thus, intermittent loss of control over the boundary between the conscious and the unconscious states—a blurring of those boundaries during the hysteric attack—is what distinguishes the hysteric subject.[25]

In *The Psychopathology* Freud argued that paranoid behavior also reflects aspects of the unconscious of normal and neurotic people. In one sense, the paranoiac perceives the unconscious more clearly than someone of normal intellectual capacity, but this knowledge is rendered worthless, because he projects what is unconsciously present in his own mind onto the mental life of other people. Everything he observes in others appears full of significance to him; everything can be interpreted. Freud gave the example of a paranoiac who "concluded that there was a general understanding in his environment, because when his train was moving out of the station the people had made a particular movement with one hand."[26]

Freud's own paranoia surfaced during Dora's analysis. His psychoanalytic goal could not be satisfied by simply listening to her story of her relationships (as Daniel Deronda attended to Gwendolen's confession) or even by interpreting the symptomatic signs. In the guise of a cure to be effected by transforming her understanding, he proposed a forcible, even manipulative, imposition of his Oedipal theory. He sought to solve her problem as a detective solves his case, achieving a conclusive ending or closure for the story of her psychic woundings.

Dora resisted Freud's interpretations. After one of his sexual interpretations, she exclaimed, "I knew you would say that!" but he countered by glossing her comment as a "common way of putting aside a piece of knowledge that emerges from the repressed" (61). What formed from their encounter was a mutual crisis of self-definition. Far from allowing Freud to draw a clear boundary between his knowledge and her own

25. In Jacques Lacan's *Four Fundamental Concepts of Psycho-analysis,* trans. Alan Sheridan, ed. Jacques-Alain Miller (New York: W. W. Norton, 1981), 24–25, he underlines the accidentality of the unconscious, whose elaborate functions produce surprising (possibly transitory) solutions that recapture a harmony with the real, yet disappear as soon as they are discovered. Thus, the unconscious presents essential form as a vacillating discontinuity.

26. Rousseau's paranoia led him to believe even children conspired against him, and the social plot he described in his *Reveries* constitutes an interpretive model analogous to the one Freud analyzed in detail.

presumably deviant symptoms, she drew him into an exchange. Dora's analysis revealed to Freud critical complexities of the subject-analyst relationship that could not be adequately represented through a metaphor of prying open an oyster "with his collection of picklocks" to reveal a pearl.[27] The intersection between two selves, he realized, altered the nature of the process and the outcome in unanticipated ways.[28] He came to believe that Dora had projected her frustrations and trauma onto him and interpreted her rejection of therapy as a reenactment of her rejection of Herr K.'s advances. He wondered whether if he had changed himself to accommodate her, he might have been able to complete her case history. In other words, the resistance of this intelligent hysteric infected him with a sense that any interpretive resolution—any narrative of the self—must necessarily be incomplete, contradictory, and fallible. The *Analysis* laid the groundwork for his theory of transference and eventually of countertransference.

In historical accounts of physical accidents, such as Montaigne's fall from his horse, we saw not only the fear of bodily injury instilled by these traumatic events but also a temporary detachment of spirit from body and the way in which such experiences became sites of self-definition through interpretation. Freud recognized that he possessed the skills of an exceptional reader of both originary accidents and the symptomatic accidents thrown up as psychic defenses. What he now began to envision was the possibility that the unconscious self fears that if it can be completely read, it will be destroyed. Cutting the knot of psychic responses would undo the existing self, a change it resists with all its power. In that sense, the normative or healthy state that Freud hoped to instill involved a species of self-destruction: not only would it dissolve the pearl; it would also unravel the messy knot that constitutes the self. In the conflict between analyst and subject, therefore, the subject's resistance expressed a struggle for life on the part of the wounded unconscious but also its fundamental need to remain unknowable.

The word Freud used to explain the unconscious, *Unbewusste*, literally means "that which cannot be known." As a rhetorical gesture, this formulation echoes Locke's "I know not what." In that sense, Freud's idea of

---

27. *The Complete Letters of Sigmund Freud to Wilhelm Fliess*, trans. Jeffrey Moussaieff Masson (Cambridge, MA: Harvard University, Belknap Press, 1985), 427.

28. See, for example, Bronfen's reading of the case of Emma Ekstein, in which she notes the many parallels between the patient's near death after a bungled operation on her nose to remove the supposed physical cause of her hysterical symptoms and Freud's own physical and psychic condition at the time (*The Knotted Subject*, 243–57).

the unconscious resurrects the old notion of substance as the immutable, atemporal quality that can be known only through its accidents. Within the Freudian system these qualities translate into symptoms—words or gestures that inhere in the unconscious. These accidental signs become the sole means of gaining knowledge about what is hidden from the conscious mind. Locke had postulated that proper interpretation could "cure" dangerous or debilitating associations; two centuries later Freud constructed an elaborate adaptation of this earlier model.

III. Precision and Soul

Robert Musil's *Man without Qualities* (1930–33) displays a deep understanding of scientific practice as well as of contemporary psychological and philosophical currents of thought. Although the novel incorporates the double aspects of accidental qualities and accidental events into the hero's quest for identity, Musil did not believe old ideologies offered any protection from the dehumanizing impact of new technology or that they could accommodate dramatic sociopolitical changes. While he considered the natural sciences ahead of less precise disciplines, he recognized that the scientific method excluded subjective factors that he valued as part of experiential reality, and he admired the emotional flexibility and loss of moral prohibitions in the arts of his time. By transferring the lack of bias assumed by a laboratory technician to the examination of morality, he aspired to produce a character able to transcend the "qualities" that impeded realization of the "one knowledge" that had been the goal of rationalist Enlightenment.[29] This ideal remained unrealized at his death, and the final volumes of his work are incomplete.

To demonstrate the far-reaching impact of science and technology on all aspects of contemporary experience, Musil opened his novel with an automobile accident. He described the qualities attached to the event. The

---

29. Musil coined the word "ratoid" to identify fields of knowledge characterized by dependably regular and unambiguous facts. He believed that the notion that only reason could produce knowledge was merely a historical convention, although he also described the resistance to reason expressed by the Catholic Church as evidence of senility and a misperception of the value of the irrational aspects within its own traditions: "Only once did the church demonstrate, in Scholasticism, that it could construct an intellectual system of this sort—the kind that makes man the goal of metaphysics—whatever else this system may be." He argued that the system collapsed simply because it was built on Aristotle, whose "teachings had developed dry rot after two thousand years of service." Robert Musil, "Political Confessions," in *Precision and Soul: Essays and Addresses*, ed. and trans. Burton Pike and David S. Luft (Chicago: University of Chicago Press, 1990), 23, 25.

time is 1913—a fine August day, according to all the available weather statistics and astronomical calculations—the place, the busy streets of prewar Vienna. Urban noise creates a texture of sound whose rhythms are unique to this city. Pedestrians form cloudlike clusters, trickling, oscillating, splintering off, and then dissipating like molecules in a chemical compound. "Like all big cities," he wrote, "it was made up of irregularity, change, forward spurts, failures to keep step, collisions of objects and interests, punctuated by unfathomable silences; made up of pathways and untrodden ways, of one great rhythmic beat as well as the chronic discord and mutual displacement of all its contending rhythms."[30]

Automobiles shoot from narrow streets into bright squares. An upper-class couple of uncertain identity (possibly characters who appear later in the novel) is walking through the streets when one of the rushing vehicles hits an unknown pedestrian. A crowd swarms to the spot:

> Like bees clustering around the entrance to their hive people had instantly surrounded a small spot on the pavement, which they left open in their midst. In it stood the truck driver, gray as packing paper, clumsily waving his arms as he tried to explain the accident. The glances of the newcomers turned to him, then warily dropped to the bottom of the hole where a man who lay there as if dead had been bedded against the curb. It was by his own carelessness that he had come to grief, as everyone agreed. People took turns kneeling beside him, vaguely wanting to help; unbuttoning his jacket, then closing it again; trying to prop him up, then laying him down again. They were really only marking time while waiting for the ambulance to bring someone who would know what to do and have the right to do it. (I.4–5)

In the first two chapters, Musil used his narrative perspective to capture the conflict between subjectivity and objectivity. Scientific data abstracted and distanced to the equivalent of an aerial view of the scene conflicts with an impressionistic presentation of what equally abstracted

30. Robert Musil, *The Man without Qualities*, trans. Sophie Wilkins, 2 vols. (New York: Alfred A. Knopf, 1995), 1:3. All further citations are taken from this edition. J. P. Stern, *The Dear Purchase: A Theme in German Modernism* (Cambridge: Cambridge University Press, 1995), 139–40, notes that Musil's knowledge of Wittgenstein's perception of nonspecific knowledge underlies this passage: "But is a blurred concept a concept at all? Is an indistinct photograph a picture at all? Is it indeed always an advantage to replace an indistinct picture by a sharp one? Isn't the indistinct one often just what we need?" Ludwig Wittgenstein, *Philosophical Investigations*, trans. G. E. M. Anscombe (New York: Macmillan, 1958), 198.

264 / Chapter Nine

narrative figures experience on the street level. Nevertheless, his narration also plays with the subjective perspective familiar from the earlier novel. In one passage the unknown man uses his knowledge of American accident statistics (one hundred ninety thousand killed and four hundred fifty thousand injured) to reassure his companion. Adding an ironic commentary allows Musil to capture the woman's inability to assimilate the data she has received as well as the ambiguities inherent in her emotional response: "'Do you think he's dead?' his companion asked, still on the unjustified assumption that she had experienced something unusual" (I.5). These divergent perspectives work to deny meaning to the situation by excluding one another. Thus, Musil approaches the problem of representing reality by juxtaposing ways of recording experience so that the result becomes inconclusive.

Not only did Musil accentuate the chaotic ambiance of modern culture; he also identified how social constructs developed to deal with contingency, like an ambulance service, reduced crowd responses to a hivelike conformity. Judgments have become uniform and dispassionate, actions uncertain and contradictory. The violence of the accident contrasts with its lack of emotional impact as he articulates how reasoning defuses engagement with experience and shows the crowd awaiting the ambulance as an agent that will "know what to do and have the right to do it."

On a symbolic level, this crowd represents Vienna awaiting the rise of Fascism. Musil understood the nation as an "enormous, heterogeneous mass, on which nothing can quite make an impression, which cannot quite express itself, whose composition changes every day as much as the stimuli that act upon it."[31] The continued dominance of nationalism and racism after the war led him to reject the idea that human beings are inherently rational or inherently good, and he became convinced that situations and events shaped both individuals and groups of individuals. A shared language was all he recognized in a nation. Neither individuals nor nations expressed any inborn disposition that time would reveal to be their essence. In his view, therefore, postwar national and individual identities were formless, lacking firm feelings, ideas, or resolutions. Such "identities" are made, unmade, or reinforced by psychic and material needs, he argued, and cannot be analyzed in terms of substance.[32]

31. Musil, "The 'Nation' as Ideal and Reality," in *Precision and Soul*, 111.
32. Stefan Jonsson, *Subject without Nation: Robert Musil and the History of Modern Identity* (Durham: Duke University Press, 2000), 16–17. Musil noted (in a somewhat uncanny association in terms of my narrative) that man is equally capable of writing *The Critique of Pure Reason* or becoming a cannibal (*Precision and Soul*, 101–33, 150–92).

Like the accident scene that symbolizes modern culture, the house of Ulrich, the "man without qualities," symbolizes the modern self. Musil, who read widely in philosophy, traced the influence of three centuries in the architectural details of this structure.[33] The description of the house refers to his sense that the Cartesian and rationalist interpretation of the self had undergone a historical transformation and he dryly alluded to the lodge established by Locke's hunter after experience, the Rousseauean love nest, and misinterpretations introduced by the nineteenth century that blurred the whole tradition into an understanding as confused as a bungled photograph:

> Had the distinguished couple [who witnessed the auto accident] followed [the street's] course a little longer, they would have come upon a sight that would certainly have pleased them: an old garden, still retaining some of its eighteenth- or even seventeenth-century character, with wrought-iron railings through which one could glimpse, in passing, through the trees on a well-clipped lawn, a sort of little château with short wings, a hunting lodge or rococo love nest of times past. More specifically, it was basically seventeenth-century, while the park and the upper story showed an eighteenth-century influence and the façade had been restored and somewhat spoiled in the nineteenth century, so that the whole had something blurred about it, like a double-exposed photograph. (I.6)[34]

Looking through the windows of Ulrich's house reveals the book-lined study of a scholar, and in one sense, Musil's dense and literate novel

33. In 1908 Musil wrote his doctoral dissertation on the philosopher Ernst Mach, who replaced the idea of causality (in which the self depends on the necessary link between a substance and its effects or manifestations) with the idea that the self constitutes a force field in which nonpersonal elements crystallize and then dissolve again in a series of responses to the environment.

34. The opening accident remains unresolved and plays no direct part in the developing plot of the novel. In another transposition of point of view, Ulrich views the crowd from the window of his house, but when he enters the street, he is set upon by hooligans and engages in a fight that leads narratologically to his meeting with his future lover, Bonadea. Together, however, the scenes express the central notion that historical events and individual consciousness are both products of circumstance. An event becomes negligible or exceptional, depending on whether the narrator employs scientific detachment or the omniscience of the nineteenth-century novel. Irony undercuts every situation. "But today," says Ulrich, "responsibility's center of gravity is not in people but in circumstances. Have we not noticed that experiences have made themselves independent of people? They have gone on the stage, into books, into the reports of research institutes and explorers, into ideological or religious communities, which foster certain kinds of experience at the expense of others as if they are conducting a kind of social experiment" (1:158).

sums up seventeenth-, eighteenth-, and nineteenth-century thought. If the ways in which Degas and Mallarmé embraced technology allow us to recognize allusions to the enduring problem of discerning substance amid the chaos of sensations, *The Man without Qualities* refers more self-consciously to the tradition of Aristotle's categories. However, Musil does so within the context of contemporary chemical and molecular discoveries:

> All moral events take place in a field of energy whose constellation charges them with meaning. They contain good and evil the way an atom contains the possibilities of certain chemical combinations. They are what they will become, so to speak; and just as the word "hard" denotes four entirely different essences, depending on whether it is connected with love, brutality, zeal, or discipline, the significance of all moral events seemed to [Ulrich] to be the function of other events on which they depended. In this way an open-ended system of relationships arises, in which independent meanings, such as are ascribed to actions and qualities by way of a rough first approximation in ordinary life, no longer exist at all. What is seemingly solid in this system becomes a porous pretext for many possible meanings; the event occurring becomes a symbol of something that perhaps may not be happening but makes itself felt through the symbol; and man as the quintessence of his possibilities, potential man, the unwritten poem of his existence, confronts man as recorded fact, as reality, as character. (I.270)

This passage encapsulates various strands of thought that Musil addressed as plot and character in the larger scale of the novel. His familiarity with Aristotelian terminology is evident, and his understanding of the relationship between essential and inessential echoes Aristotle's earlier formulation. In Musil's understanding, however, qualities that once appeared solid have become inessentials. Everyone in the novel is defined by contemporary versions of Aristotle's nine qualities (professional, national, state, class, geographical, sexual, consciousness, unconsciousness, private) plus a tenth quality that occupies a status that resembles that of substance while inverting its unchanging nature.[35] This "tenth" quality cancels out or supersedes the identity society ascribes to any individual. For Musil, what might be denominated the soul was more properly un-

---

35. These terms are David Luft's (*Robert Musil and the Crisis of European Culture, 1880–1942* (Los Angeles: University of California Press, 1980), 223. However, the analysis of the "tenth" quality comes from Jonsson, *Subject without Nation*, 264.

derstood as a fantasy of spaces yet unfilled, the unlimited human potential to become something else. The tenth quality allows a person every possibility except one: taking seriously what happens to the other nine qualities or what they do.[36]

Using his command of both statistics and psychology, Musil made Ulrich observe that each person possesses roughly the same qualities and capacities.[37] These qualities are shared so vastly that no attribute can be considered self-defining. Anyone who identifies his or her uniqueness as the result of possessing them misunderstands the contingent nature of selfhood.[38] Within different contexts, Ulrich says, "a murder can appear to us as a crime or a heroic act, and making love as a feather that has

36. One example of more recent philosophical exploration of this problem occurs in Saul A. Kripke, *Naming and Necessity* (Cambridge, MA: Harvard University Press, 1972), 73–77. He opposes a statement that would assert that if X exists, then the notion that X has most of the properties of X is a necessary truth. We may pick a man out by an accidental property, he notes, but we use the name to designate him in all possible worlds. The property we use need not be regarded in any way as necessary or essential. For example, Aristotle's most important property rests on his philosophical work, but he might have lacked these properties altogether. He could have had a completely different career. Thus, important properties are not automatically essential unless importance is used as a synonym for essence. Slavoj Žižek, *The Sublime Object of Ideology* (London: Verso, 1989), 87–129, develops examples taken from Kripke into an extended (and politicized) discussion of identity.

37. Philip Payne, *Robert Musil's "The Man without Qualities": A Critical Study* (Cambridge: Cambridge University Press, 1988), 117, notes that Ulrich's capacity for transferential analysis appears in the thought experiment in chap. 7 involving the serial murderer Moosbrugger, who represents one extreme of Ulrich's range of psychic possibilities. Payne links this analysis to Musil's knowledge of Husserl's *Phenomenological Psychology*, which gives priority of subjective awareness to the examination of the operation of consciousness and the perception of objects. The only way to directly experience how others feel, Husserl argued, is by an imaginative act that draws analogies to the feelings the perceiver has experienced in his or her own body. Musil worked with the psychologist Carl Stumpf just as Husserl had worked with him earlier in his career, so this kind of thinking appeared valid to him. He also read Ernst Kretschmer's *Medical Psychology*, which argued that human awareness is formed of two interwoven strands: in the objective strand, man sees himself from without as a creature of flesh and blood and prone to influences of nature and environment he observes in other men, but the subjective strand also involves consciousness of inner experiences, the feeling of being the center of a universe that moves when he moves. These states carry on a continuous dialogue with each other in the normal individual. Mental health stems from self-criticism by the mind of its interpretation of reality. See Payne, *Robert Musil's "The Man without Qualities,"* 133. In other words, Musil possessed a theoretical foundation for depicting the divided self that Eliot struggled to express in *Daniel Deronda*, one that mediates between the tradition of the modernist novel and postmodern interpretations.

38. For Musil, Daniel Deronda's identification with his Jewish blood would be no more valid or laudable than defining himself as an English citizen or as Mirah's husband (although he might be better satisfied with Deronda's feeling of brotherhood and his openness to risk).

fallen from the wing of an angel or that of a goose" (I. 270). Normal categories of identity are simply temporary classifications applied within a narrative to allow a person to be recognized as the same over time. They conceal the essential formlessness that constitutes the underlying reality of a biological entity. When such categories are buttressed by ideologies, they become fixed identities that block the development of any additional possibilities.

Ulrich's quest for *das rechte Leben* forms the central action of the novel. His interior monologues and passionate attempts to formulate his changing perceptions of reality occur throughout the work as moments that fracture an existing viewpoint and awaken new meanings. Thus, while Musil's "man without qualities" shares with Daniel Deronda something of the flaneur's respect for the creative potential in accident, he expanded the interiority of the psychic accident that we met in Eliot's treatment of Gwendolen Harleth into a structural principle that dominated his novel: "The drive of [Ulrich's] own nature to keep developing prevents him from believing that anything is final and complete, yet everything he encounters behaves as though it were final and complete. He suspects that the given order of things is not as solid as it pretends to be; no thing, no self, no form, no principle, is safe, everything is undergoing an invisible but ceaseless transformation, the unsettled holds more of the future than the settled, and the present is nothing but a hypothesis that has not yet been surmounted" (I.269).

As Ulrich explains in a later passage, the inner man is "nothing but an unstable, shifting mist." Experience, he adds, encrusts and traps the soul the way a piece of flypaper catches a fly, first by a "tiny hair," then hampering movement, and gradually enveloping it until a thick coating covers the original shape (I.137). No longer recognizable as the youth he was, man seeks to regain his freedom if only in a gesture. He may express it outwardly as an accidental sign, such as a new mustache, or inwardly as a new idea. In other words, Musil drew an analogy between ideas and mental accidents; he understood both as mutable, paradoxical, and to some extent self-defining.

We have recognized how narratives require characters to make both valid and mistaken interpretations of accidental events, but Musil claimed that life consists of making interpretations. Because the mutability of life unfixes people, they become susceptible to a single-minded man with qualities. He identified Arnheim, the wealthy capitalist who stands as one of Ulrich's conceptual opponents, as such a person. In other words, on a metaphorical level he asserted that modern life derives a semblance of form from capitalism. At the same time, he saw the kind of certainty symbolized by a flag, a celebration, or an idolized leader as the dominant and dangerous condition of contemporary society. His interpretation of history emphasized pervasive randomness as characteristic of the past and the future as well as the present:

> Examined close up, our history looks rather vague and messy, like a morass only partially made safe for pedestrian traffic, though oddly enough in the end there does seem to be a path across it, that very "path of history" of which nobody knows the starting point. This business of serving as "the stuff of history" infuriated Ulrich. The luminous, swaying [streetcar] in which he was riding seemed to be a machine in which several hundred kilos of people were being rattled around, by way of being processed into "the future." A hundred years earlier they had sat in a mail coach with the same look on their faces, and a hundred years hence, whatever was going on, they would be sitting as new people in exactly the same way in their updated transport machines. (I.390–91)[39]

Rational skepticism provides Ulrich with the means to interpret experience and challenge received opinions, yet he comprehends the necessity of an intuitive approach to the problem of how to live. In *The Man without Qualities* circumstances operate at a sociohistorical level just as they do in terms of the character development of an individual. In effect, Musil suggests that "history" has evolved from the intersection of unrelated circumstances and that our perception of historical circumstances conditions our knowledge of it. People are pawns of chance encounters.

---

39. The "essayism" Ulrich espouses not only fractures the surface of the narrative; it also disrupts any movement toward closure. Thus, the structure of the novel is equally essayistic, which coincides with the absence of a single privileged perspective as well as Musil's refusal to delineate any overarching force moving the narrative along a predetermined path. (The lack of closure for the unfinished novel has been extensively discussed, most recently by Stefan Jonsson in *Subject without Nation*.) Although the density of historical and social observation might appear to be a diversion from the spiritual autobiography tradition of the nineteenth-century novel, Musil would not accept the idea that World War I represented a predetermined rather than an accidental event: "Time was making a fresh start then (it does so all the time)" (I.15). In fact, anachronisms frequently blur the datable events mentioned in the text. Just as modernists replaced traditional storytelling with inconsequential series of private nonevents and disappointed expectations, Musil inferred that absence of causality was a necessary condition for telling historical truth; therefore, inconsequential narrative represented the only way in which his contemporaries could write history. Stern, *The Dear Purchase*, 158, notes the resemblance between Musil's representation of time and that in *Tristram Shandy*.

The characters that Musil favors, like Ulrich, a rational scientist who suspects everything he knows, understand this truth and strive against it.[40]
Moved by arbitrary circumstances, at every moment Ulrich longs for a different way of living and behaving. He summarizes this tension through a
version of Darwin's evolutionary tree:

> These two trees were the shape his life had taken, like a two-pronged fork.
> He could not say when it had entered into the sign of the tree with the
> hard, tangled branchwork, but it had happened early on, for even his im-
> mature Napoleonic plans had shown him to be a man who looked on life
> as a problem he had set himself, something it was his vocation to work
> out. This urge to attack life and master it had always been clearly discern-
> ible in him, whether it had manifested itself as a rejection of the existing
> order or as various forms of striving for a new one, as logical or moral
> needs or even merely as an urge to keep the body in fighting trim. And ev-
> erything that, as time went on, he had called essayism, the sense of possi-
> bility, and imaginative in contrast with pedantic precision; his suggestions
> that history was something one had to invent, that one should live the his-
> tory of ideas instead of the history of the world, that one should get a grip
> on whatever cannot quite be realized in practice and should perhaps end
> up trying to live as if one were a character in a book, a figure with all the
> inessential elements left out, so that what was left would consolidate itself
> as some magical entity—all these different versions of his thinking, all in
> their extreme formulations against reality, had just one thing in common:
> an unmistakable, ruthless passion to influence reality. Harder to recognize
> because more shadowy and dreamlike were the ramifications of the other
> tree that formed an image for his life, rooted perhaps in some primal mem-
> ory of a childlike relationship to the world, all trustfulness and yielding,
> which had lived on as a haunting sense of having once beheld the whole
> vast earth in what normally only fills the flowerpot in which the herbs of
> morality send up their stunted sprouts. No doubt that regrettably absurd
> affair of the major's wife was his only attempt to reach a full development
> on this gentle shadow side of his life; it was also the beginning of a recoil

40. The irony of the novel rests on accurate predictions of the future by characters who
do not seem capable of such insight as well as on the pathological characters (like Moosbrugger or Clarissa) as representative of individuals who have escaped the boundaries of rational thought. As a result the reader is forced to realize that none of the characters (including Ulrich) possess credible modes of thought. See Michael André Bernstein's analysis in
Five Portraits: Modernity and the Imagination in Twentieth-Century German Writing (Evanston:
Northwestern University Press, 2000).

that had never stopped. Since then, the leaves and twigs always drifting on the surface were the only sign that the tree still existed, though it had disappeared from view. This dormant half of his personality perhaps revealed itself most clearly in his instinctive assumption that the active and busy side of him was only standing in for the real self, an assumption that cast a shadow on his active self. (I.646–47)[41]

The first tree suggests the complexity of intellectual striving. Here Ulrich appears to equate the history of ideas with an ideal process of conceptual development. Nevertheless, he recognizes the human desire to control the arbitrary and expunge the accidental. The second tree postulates that the essence of humanity cannot reside in the intellect (although ultimately Musil said that intellect must play a role in harmonizing the disparate aspects of existence). By remembering his youthful passion for the major's wife, Ulrich acknowledges the role of feeling as a substantive component of the self and expresses a profound sense of loss. A Wordsworthian image of childhood trailing clouds of immortality hovers over this passage, making even the ferocious energy implied in Darwin's natural selection elegiac. For Ulrich, half of the tree of life exists like a relic struggling for survival within a polluted environment.

In terms of the history of accident, therefore, we recognize that its omnipresence in Musil's vision radically revised its interpretive potential. In an environment in which everything is accidental, no accidental event can exert a transforming power. Moreover, as the accidental qualities that make up social identity are stripped away, layer by layer, the absence of

41. In a text withdrawn by Musil in the proof stage entitled "Ulrich and the Two Worlds of Feeling," Ulrich arranges a list of names given to feelings in two sets. Both have instinctual origins. Musil's term *Triebe* invoked nineteenth-century materialism. (However, in *Four Fundamental Concepts of Psycho-analysis*, Lacan stressed that "instinct" mistranslates Freud's *Triebe*, which he believed more properly signifies "urgency.") Ulrich's first set is made up of definite, determinate, and specific feelings aroused by outside events that demand a response; the second of indefinite, indeterminate, general feelings more like moods. The less that was known about what caused these feelings, the stronger their effect. Once established, the task is to connect these groups. Ulrich theorizes that transformation rather than development leads from the indeterminate, intentionless moods to purposeful feelings. Thus, mental life is condemned to transitoriness and frailty, while moods and mental dispositions are relatively stable and unchanging. In an age which claims to place the highest value on inwardness, he observed, outward feelings and action are at a premium. The chapter ends with Ulrich reading a passage from Swedenborg about the way angels are said to experience what we call space and time. Stern, *The Dear Purchase*, 178–80, conjectures that the reason Musil broke off this version was his realization (along with that of the character) of the devastating nonresult of Ulrich's year of self-examination and the formal limitations of the literary form.

substance appears as a frightening emptiness.[42] To the extent that the potentially liberating freedom to choose roles offered by modern society results in a psyche that is scattered and floating free of will or reason, the self defined as pure possibility has become devoid of content.[43] Musil struggled to surmount this problem through a transcendent fusion of being represented in Ulrich's relation to his sister Agathe. Nevertheless, *The Man without Qualities* expresses the exhaustion of the form of the novel as a site for philosophical introspection, not simply because the work remained unfinished but because its structure represents the impossibility of employing narrative to embody the central formlessness of modern experience.

42. The notion that the novel presages postmodernist theories of lack or nothingness represents the theme of Jonsson's study of Musil, *Subject without Nation*. He chose Julia Kristeva, Paul Ricoeur, and Giorgio Agamben as his postmodernist points of comparison, recognizing that his selection did not imply any direct influence.

43 Anthony J. Cascardi, *The Subject of Modernity* (Cambridge: Cambridge University Press, 1992), 36–39.

CHAPTER TEN

Envisioning Accident: Searching for Substance in an Accidental World

I. Objective Chance

Throughout the earlier history of accident thinkers asserted numerous mutations in the understanding of substance: Montaigne proposed the idea of the ruling passion, Descartes thinking substance, Locke "I know not what," Wordsworth the power of nature, Eliot cultural identity, and Freud the unconscious. Although the immense influence of Freudian theories carried "germs" of ontological thinking into the twentieth century, as Musil demonstrates in *The Man without Qualities,* in the wake of World War I, the possibility of achieving a secure understanding of existence was giving way to a perception of vulnerability and doubt. This change affected the perception of accidental qualities and realigned their relation to substance.

At the same time, media technologies gave renewed importance to catastrophic accidents. Repetitions expanded the scale of dangerous events, while photographs could capture the sensory impact of ephemeral sights and sounds and films could replicate their shocking suddenness. By bringing train wrecks, airplane crashes, and collapsing bridges or buildings vividly before the mind, the new media altered the function of reflection.[1] Opportunities to bring associations acquired over the passage of time to bear on the act of interpreting events diminished with the flood of dramatic encounters. The pervasive immediacy of vicarious

---

1. Douwe Draaisma, *Metaphors of Memory: A History of Ideas about the Mind,* trans. Paul Vincent (Cambridge: Cambridge University Press, 2000), chaps. 4 and 5, discusses the phonograph and photograph as memory technologies whose importance is comparable to writing.

accidental experiences also encouraged emotions rooted in the terror of the sublime to predominate over rational analysis.

The previous chapter ended with accidental events acquiring symbolic value, as in the opening of Musil's novel, when he used the image of a hive of people clustering around the site of a car accident to stand for contemporary conformism. In this chapter we confront another pattern of twentieth-century image making in which the psychological implications surrounding accidents trigger responses that are primarily subjective rather than intellectualized. In the case of the surrealists, the scale of an event did not delimit its impact and the accident experience was extensively theorized. However, mediated experiences, including those created through digital technologies, increasingly privileged skills in processing and manipulating visual forms and expanded the central role of vision as a means of acquiring information. Just as the explosion of eighteenth-century print culture produced familiarity with shocks and catastrophes that tended to dull the emotional impact of individual events, a surfeit of mediated encounters led to an increasingly obsessive focus on intense accident experiences. Under the pressure of a barrage of visual sensations, virtual accidents were diminished to the level of casual entertainments, while global catastrophes reached a scale that scarcely could be comprehended in rational terms. These shifts in perception stimulated reformulations of enduring issues of substance and accident in predominantly visual form.

The surrealists aspired to remake the world by jolting the public from what they perceived to be their state of reactionary self-satisfaction. Shock served as a key tactic in this attempt. The strategies they employed in their imagistic writing and visual arts involved the use of accidental events as a means to destabilize perceptions as well as the use of deformations of visual experience, which made otherwise normal qualities suddenly "accidental" in an Aristotelian sense by appearing in unexpected contexts.

In the first surrealist manifesto (1924), André Breton, the "pope" of the movement, proclaimed freedom from the control of reason as well as aesthetic or moral constraints. The manifesto recognized the impact of Freud's theory of the unconscious. Although the surrealists had only a partial and second-hand knowledge of Freud's ideas, Breton's medical training had provided him with some experience in psychoanalytic practice, and he believed Freud had not fully grasped the philosophical importance of his own work as a mode of liberating the imagination.[2]

---

2. In "Le Cinquantenaire de l'hysterie," *La Révolution surrealiste* 11 (15 March 1928): 20–22, Breton and the poet and novelist Louis Aragon declared the hysterical symptom to

For Breton, a systematic analysis of events in a person's life could neither reveal deep-seated motivations nor help to define a course of action, but because he envisioned the artist's role as that of a therapist for the times, he did not abandon a sense of intellectual control over the raw materials of accidental associations. He also rejected Freud's suggestion that psychic reality must be understood as separate from material reality. Instead, Breton revalued the importance of the subconscious as the more significant part of reality:

> The imagination is perhaps on the point of reasserting itself, of reclaiming its rights. If the depths of our mind contain within it strange forces capable of augmenting those on the surface, or of waging a victorious battle against them, there is every reason to seize them—first to seize them, then, if need be, to submit them to the control of our reason. The analysts themselves have everything to gain by it. But it is worth noting that no means has been designated a priori for carrying out this undertaking, that until further notice it can be construed to be the province of poets as well as scholars, and that its success is not dependent upon the more or less capricious paths that will be followed.[3]

To Breton, metaphor and other literary modes of association seemed inadequate as a means to achieve the sensation of illumination he and his collaborators desired, so they experimented with various ways to detach imagination from rational processes. Initially, they adopted the strategies of the ready-made employed by Dada artists who used them to affront and stimulate the exhausted sensibilities of viewers. Surrealist visual artists took objects out of context and juxtaposed them in incongruous ways that made them seem unfamiliar. Their goal was to endow objects "with a persuasive strength rigorously proportional to the violence of the initial shock they produced."[4] Surrealist automatic writing attempted to estab-

---

be the "greatest poetic discovery of the later nineteenth century." Freud's early writings had been translated into French in 1921.

3. André Breton, *Manifesto of Surrealism* (1924), reprinted in *Manifestoes of Surrealism*, trans. Richard Seaver and Helen R. Lane (Ann Arbor: University of Michigan Press, 1969), 10.

4. André Breton, *Mad Love*, trans. Mary Ann Caws (Lincoln: University of Nebraska Press, 1987), 88. All future citations refer to this edition. Karl Heinz Bohrer, *Suddenness: On the Moment of Aesthetic Appearance*, trans. Ruth Crowley (New York: Columbia University Press, 1994), 78, argues that Breton was more interested in a sort of epistemological wit that originates when an observer or reader is put into a situation in which the unique character of what is seen shakes the dominant perceptual norms and values.

lish a direct relation between thought and language. Through the swift motion of the pen, the use of suggestive stimulant phrases, and even hypnotic or trance states, their automatism tried to duplicate the workings of the unconscious during dreams. Breton referred to automatic writings as "spoken thoughts." His term did not imply a degradation of thought into language but a method of giving intangible thought a form. Corporeal and almost mechanical, automatic writing opened the mind to contingency.[5]

By allowing the unconscious to manifest itself spontaneously when inhibiting constraints were suppressed, surrealist practices provided a way to access Freud's *Unbewusste*. They also deliberately tried to reproduce what we recognize as the effect of a violent accident. Breton became fascinated by chance, whether expressed in the collage of objects randomly juxtaposed on a painted canvas or in actual encounters with objects or people. As he described them, such juxtapositions took on the "character of things revealed," causing moments of "sublime illumination" that were experienced as dislocations in which the individual felt simultaneously like and unlike himself. In other words, they had the impact produced by physical accidents as articulated in Rousseau's illumination.

Aleatory walking was a surrealist activity parallel with automatic writing, and again we can recognize elements of a play with chance comparable to the walks during which Rousseau scribbled on cards the thoughts that he would reformulate later into his *Reveries*. For Breton, chance encounters that occurred on his nondirected walks through Paris formed an experience based on a state of expectancy. He was a flaneur awaiting a disruption of the surface of life, the appearance of the type of sublime accident that Wordsworth had denominated a "spot of time."

Breton's surrealist theory made the nature of such experiences more precise. They consisted of a sequence of related events that began with some signal designed to catch the attention and could be realized only when a negative precondition, which he described as a sense of torpor, was replaced by an abrupt mobilization of all the faculties. *Nadja* (1928), Breton's narrative of a love affair that might equally well be considered a model of life surrendered to contingent impulses, an account of psychotic transference, or an antinovel, demonstrates this surrealist experience. His description of his first meeting with Nadja illustrates the desired outcome of an aleatory walk. This passage details the aspects of

5. See Jacqueline Chénieux-Gendron, *Surrealism*, trans. Vivian Folkenflik (New York: Columbia University Press, 1990), 54ff.

time and place that precondition the event and indicate its emotional charge:

> Last October fourth, toward the end of one of those idle, gloomy after-noons I know so well how to spend, I happened to be in the Rue Lafayette: after stopping a few minutes at the stall outside the *Humanité* bookstore and buying Trotsky's latest work, I continued aimlessly in the direction of the Opéra . . . there were more people in the street now. I unconsciously watched their faces, their clothes, their way of walking. No, it was not yet these who would be ready to create the Revolution . . . suddenly, perhaps still ten feet away, I saw a young poorly dressed woman walking toward me, she had noticed me too, or perhaps had been watching me for several moments. She carried her head high, unlike everyone else on the sidewalk. And she looked so delicate she scarcely seemed to touch the ground as she walked . . . I had never seen such eyes. Without a moment's hesitation, I spoke to this unknown woman.[6]

Here the first moment of the surrealist sequence is composed of random observations of other people on a crowded street. The references to Trotsky and the bookstore named Humanité allude to the political context attached not only to surrealism but to other avant-garde artis-tic movements such as Dada and Futurism, and as he moves toward the Opera, a symbol of cultural decadence and outworn art forms, the street becomes crowded with people whom he recognizes as unprepared for the revolution he and his associates find so necessary. The poorly dressed young woman, however, is a *semblable*, encountered in what came to be known as an "objective chance."

In *Mad Love* (1937), Breton described chance as objective because for him it represented an intersection between some natural necessity and a desire or fear that projected itself onto an object.[7] In the experience of the

---

6. André Breton, *Nadja*, trans. Richard Howard (New York: Grove Press, 1960), 63–64. All future references are to this edition.

7. Breton, *Mad Love*, sec. 2, 19–25. Breton's inspiration was a survey that asked the ques-tions "What do you consider the essential encounter of your life? To what extent did this encounter seem to you, and does it seem to you now, to be fortuitous or foreordained?" He printed the results of the survey in the art journal *Minotaure*, which he directed in 1932. Remarking that the mind's "hesitations" have been responsible for the "sluggish evolution" of the concept of chance, he traced it from Aristotle's definition ("an accidental cause of exceptional or accessory effects taking on the appearance of finality"), to Cournot's ("an event brought about by the combination or the encounter of phenomena which belong to independent series in the order of causality"), to Poincaré's ("event rigorously determined,

278 / Chapter Ten

objective chance, seemingly unrelated phenomena, noticed without affect, nevertheless signal the act of interpretation:

> But the distinction between what is plausible and what is not is no less telling for me than for others. I am no less subject than they to the need to observe how life outside me develops apart from my own individuality; if I accept to reflect at each moment as only I can upon the spectacle playing itself out beyond me, it is nevertheless odd, strangely so, to see how this spectacle suddenly appears to be set up for me alone. . . . It is in fact impossible for this mind not to experience in [this conjunction of events or signs] both a remarkable happiness and disturbance, a mixture of *panic-provoking* terror and joy. It is as if suddenly, the deepest night of human existence were to be penetrated, natural and logical necessity coinciding, all things being rendered totally transparent, linked by a chain of glass without one link missing. (39–40)

Breton's evocation of this experience recalls Kant's description of the sublime in both the initially panic-stricken and ultimately triumphant realization of relationships that stretch in unbroken sequence to infinity. In *Nadja*, Breton created the prototype of such an experience. There he introduced into the text a photograph of the facade of the Humanité bookstore, where a notice Sign Here (*On signe ici*) provides a subconscious call to action. Such insignificant details mark one extreme of the objective chance experience. They are the *faits-glissances*, tenuous occurrences of negligible impact, which nevertheless provide a context for the *faits-précipices*, the indelible and overwhelming events themselves. The appearance of Nadja, a figure utterly unlike those around her, provided the revolutionary impetus that gave meaning to these trivial observations.

Links between the *faits-glissances* and the *faits-précipices* are not part of any chain of causes—both his observations and his associations happened by chance—but they acquire significance through psychic mechanisms of condensation and displacement. Nadja tells him that her name comes from the first two syllables of the Russian word for hope (*nadezhda*). She is the beginning of hope. Meeting her promises the emotional engagement Breton desired, but it does not fulfill it; Nadja falls in love

---

but such that an extremely small difference in its causes would have produced a considerable difference in the facts"), and finally to the "modern materialist" attempt to reconcile Engels with Freud ("chance is the form of manifestation of the exterior necessity that traces its path in the human unconscious").

with him but he does not love her. Therefore, her name gives an explicit interpretation to the entire sequence of events as a beginning (but only a beginning) of the wished-for love. As we saw in Wordsworth's claim of poetic election, illuminations of this kind happen only to people whose attention focuses on deciphering the links between forms and words. Breton called this a "lyric behavior" that required a condition of openness, eagerness, a childlike spirit, or emotional turbulence or nostalgia to enable someone to have such an experience.[8]

Breton's explanation of the life-transforming power of such accidental events involved nineteenth-century ideas of the interdependence between identity and society alongside Freud's theory of the unconscious. He saw the self being invented in accord with psychic and material pressures. *Nadja* presents an evocative stage in this exploration, for, on the one hand, it attempts to record chance directly while, on the other hand, it contains that experience within an authorial framework. The text emulates a case study by presenting the data that attracted Breton's attention and his responses as characteristics of a unique or even idiosyncratic individual. In that regard, *Nadja* not only allows the reader to witness his experience, it presents the way in which he experienced it. The central section, which recounts his affair with Nadja, contains an extended diatribe against the methods of the asylum where she was later imprisoned in which Breton rejects the psychoanalytic attempt to control chance and deprive it of its potential as a creative tool. However, he places this section between an introduction and a forward-moving conclusion. The introduction sketches a portrait of himself as the experimental subject—providing a sociological and cultural context and delineating, in effect, his qualities—and the conclusion returns to the question of the subject's identity.

If we remember Aristotle's distinction between accidental qualities that are separable from substance (those that may alter without negating it) and those that are inseparable from it (those whose absence would transform the substance) and Locke's interpretation of personal identity evoked over time, we can see how Breton was haunted by a notion that he might have no substantive essence. He wondered whether the self varied as a function of time. Or perhaps it was a mutable quality that changed with the perceptions of others or could be transferred from one individual to another.[9]

8. Chénieux-Gendron, *Surrealism*, 86.
9. Breton inserted photographs and sketches throughout *Nadja*. On the one hand, they served to add conviction to the text. On the other hand, they extended the content by reformulating the problem of identity. A studio portrait of Breton appears at first to answer the question, Who am I? yet this "normal" image possesses no guarantee of being the "true"

Nadja opens with this question: "Who am I? If this once I were to rely on a proverb, then perhaps everything would amount to knowing whom I 'haunt.' I must admit that this last word is misleading, tending to establish between certain beings and myself relations that are stranger, more inescapable, more disturbing than I intended. Such a word means much more than it says, makes me, still alive, play a ghostly part, evidently referring to what I must have ceased to be in order to be who I am" (11).

Breton's insecurity allowed chance to play a critical role in the process of self-definition. For this reason, he understood a defining experience, like his affair with Nadja, as a collaboration between his inner being and chance. In fact, their relationship was defined both literally and figuratively in terms of cataclysmic accident. Apart from birth and death, the most significant chance phenomenon for him was the *coup de foudre* like the feeling he experienced at their meeting. He considered such an experience more marvelous because its intense emotional impact resulted from two arbitrary trajectories that stretched the law of probability.[10] But *Nadja* climaxes in a narrowly averted physical accident that fuses violence with love, sex, and death: "I was driving a car along the road from Versailles to Paris, the woman sitting beside me (who was Nadja, but who might have been anyone else, after all, or even *someone else*) pressed her foot down on mine on the accelerator, tried to cover my eyes with her hands in the oblivion of an interminable kiss, desiring to extinguish us, doubtless forever, save to each other, so that we should collide at full speed with the splendid trees along the road. . . . In imagination, at least, I often find myself, eyes blindfolded, back at the wheel of that wild car" (152–53). Nadja's potentially fatal kiss communicated not only her own incipient madness but also reanimated chance in its threatening guise.[11] Blinded at the steering wheel, Breton had internalized Blind Fortune with her wheel. Although his affair with Nadja remained one-sided (and the concluding section of the book apostrophizes a fully beloved woman), her capricious spontaneity and defiance of conventions remained memorable

---

self. In fact, the text is full of references to confusions of identity (for example, being mistaken for a dead friend, Breton's discovery that all the figures in Watteau's "Embarcation for Cythera" repeat the same couple, or the story of an obscure horror film in which "thousands of replicas of a Chinaman" invade New York City).

10. Anna Balakian, *André Breton: Magus of Surrealism* (New York: Oxford University Press, 1971), 120.

11. Nadja's delusions, panic, and lapses of attention are symptoms of breakdown, and her drawings present the stylistic features of schizophrenia. See Roger Cardinal on Breton's failure to acknowledge these symptoms. *Breton, "Nadja"* (London: Grant and Cutler, 1986), 47–48.

for him. Whether he pulled back from the danger inherent in the surrealist model from an instinct for self-preservation, his reason, or his incomplete love of Nadja remains unclear. Nevertheless, the idea that ultimate beauty must be linked to some spasm or act of destruction appears in the final words of the text: "Beauty will be CONVULSIVE or will not be at all." Breton concluded with the example of a train that ceaselessly roars out of the Gare de Lyon, never leaving or able to leave. "It consists of jolts and shocks, many of which do not have much importance, but which we know are destined to produce one *Shock*, which does. Which has all the importance I do not want to arrogate to myself" (160).

Surrealists regarded the creative process as analogous to the law of objective chance that created serendipitous meetings or other real-life accidents. Both in life and in art, the results not only allowed desire to be expressed without conscious intervention but also could be interpreted to presage predestined outcomes. Breton had no illusions about surrealism's ability to help him resolve the problem of his destiny or its lasting impact on modern life. Yet in the concluding words of the first manifesto he recognized the illusory aspect of sensory perceptions of color or matter. He defended the power of the arbitrary to identify them as such, strip away these accidental qualities with the laserlike power of the imagination, and thus hope to access a more profound understanding of existence: "Surrealism is the 'invisible ray' which will one day enable us to win out over our opponents. 'You are no longer trembling, carcass.' This summer the roses are blue; the wood is of glass. The earth, draped in its verdant cloak, makes as little impression upon me as a ghost. It is living and ceasing to live that are imaginary solutions. Existence is elsewhere" (*First Manifesto*, 47).

II. Invulnerable Bodies

The new technology of cinema was especially congenial to the surrealists. Man Ray, Luis Buñuel, Salvatore Dali, and René Clair were among the early practitioners who achieved notable work in this medium, but all the surrealists were regular patrons of silent films. They applied their aleatory method to filmgoing, watching segments at random and focusing on isolated images. Breton described both the way in which he attended the cinema and the effect of his method: "I never began by consulting the amusement pages to find out what film might chance to be the best, nor did I find out the time the film was to begin. I agreed wholeheartedly with Jacques Vaché in appreciating nothing so much as dropping into the cinema when whatever was playing was playing, at any point in the show, and leaving at the first hint of boredom . . . to rush off to another cinema where we behaved in the same way. . . . I have never known anything more *magnetizing:* it goes without saying that more often than not we left our seats without even knowing the title of the film which was of no importance to us anyway." [12]

Not only were the surrealists struck by the juxtaposition of images with words in the use of intertitles and the way in which montage could realize dreamlike free associations and reverse natural laws of space and time, but the improvisations and slapstick routines of silent comedians were also immediately recognizable as expressions of surrealist anarchy. They were more excited by the formal experimentation in the films of Buster Keaton than by what they judged were the more sentimental, narratological films of Charlie Chaplin.

Keaton's mechanical genius encouraged him to exploit both the physical properties of objects within his films and the potential of cinematic illusions, while his acrobatic training in vaudeville allowed him to perform for the camera with thrilling invulnerability. The surrealists particularly appreciated a famous section of *Sherlock, Jr.* (1923) in which Keaton falls asleep while working as a projectionist at a movie theater and his doppelgänger leaves his body to enter the movie projected on the screen. This film-within-a-film sequence realized the surrealist goal of seeing the object in a dramatically fresh way and actualized what psychologists denominated transference.

A startling special effect sequence in the film enabled Keaton to evoke the seemingly illogical associations produced by the unconscious. At the moment the projectionist dreams he enters the world of the film, a graphic-match montage creates accident after accident as the environment around him metamorphoses. A walled garden turns into a busy street, where he is almost run down by a car, and then into a cliff overlooking a gorge. The gorge turns into a jungle inhabited by lions, which turns into a desert, where a passing train nearly runs him down and the mound of sand he uses as a seat turns into a rock in the ocean. A huge wave washes over him, but when he tries to dive into the water, he lands headfirst in a snow bank. Leaning against a tree, he falls back into the original garden.

---

12. Breton, "As in a Wood," trans. Paul Hammond, in *The Shadow and Its Shadow: Surrealist Writing on the Cinema,* ed. Paul Hammond (Edinburgh: Polygon, 1991), 81. Of course, the vast majority of moviegoers neither could engage in aleatory filmgoing nor wished to do so.

The comedy springs from the repeated misfire of his instinctive attempts to stabilize the threat of a disorderly environment.

We might compare Jacques Lacan's analysis of the role the symptom plays in transference to the effect of this sequence. What is repressed from the past, he argued, derives its interpretive meaning from a signifying context. In Keaton's gag sequence this would be equivalent to the underlying danger the character experiences in each new situation. For Lacan, any experiential rupture retroactively restructures the subject's historical narrative, making it readable in another way. The psychoanalytic subject can only change within the field of this "hallucinatory mise-en-scène of the fact."[13] Thus, the projectionist responds to each threat posed by his environment by changing his position, not by changing his escape strategy. Lacan also theorized that an imaginary self can exist only if the subject misrecognizes its own conditions. In an analogous way, throughout the gag sequence, the projectionist misrecognizes the cinematic illusion—taking it for real—but each adjustment in his perception also dissolves into a fresh misconception. As in psychoanalysis, under these circumstances knowledge becomes an "impossible-real" and the subject must place the self at risk in order to obtain it.

Two related factors are in play here. On the one hand, the *jouissance* (Lacan's principle of pleasure carried to the point of pain), which he identified as the "substance" behind illusionary misrecognitions, must be repaid with the loss of enjoyment. Thus, both the viewer's transferential enjoyment and the projectionist's relief at being saved from threats or discomforts oscillate between pleasure and pain. On the other hand, Lacan argued that the condition of this enjoyment is a kind of ignorance: to experience the thrills involved in the match sequence, the projectionist must suspend his knowledge of the dream state and the viewer his or her knowledge of the editing technology that supports the illusion.

During this riff on cinematic alchemy, Keaton remains both mute and expressionless within his persona of the "great stone face." Both qualities represent a refusal of identity, simultaneously representing a subjective nothingness while demonstrating that nothingness is not the same as nothing.[14] In the next sequence he demonstrates the medium's capacity to

13. All quoted terminology in this passage derives from Slavoj Žižek, *The Sublime Object of Ideology* (London: Verso, 1989), 56 and 67.

14. Stefan Jonsson, *Subject without Nation: Robert Musil and the History of Modern Identity* (Durham: Duke University Press, 2000), 176–77, sketches the traditional characteristics of

restructure identity when, after passing the test of his adaptive abilities, the doppelgänger takes on the persona of a famous detective called in to solve the case of the missing pearls. In this role he once again survives through his mastery of the accidental situation. Impervious to damage, he inadvertently foils attempts to decapitate or poison him, avoids being blown up by a billiard ball loaded with explosives through his skillful play, and rescues the heroine in a spectacular chase in which he careens unharmed through city traffic and countryside on the handlebars of a riderless cycle. This long gag sequence contains a dazzling exhibition of Keaton's skills as a performer and as a director. Sections like the long single take in which the meeting of two trucks allows him to pass over a gap in a railway bridge that then collapses gently to deposit him on level ground in time to barely miss the dynamiting of a log barring his way combine astonishing physical prowess with a visual imagination that compels amazement.[15]

Slapstick comedy often is seen just as the surrealists viewed it—as a subversion of the social constraints that work to prevent violent actions, a dismemberment of social mores in which the invulnerability of the star renders the resulting chaos amusing. The viewer comprehends the threat by analogy to real-life situations he or she has experienced, yet the cinematic suspension of norms achieves the pleasure of vicarious control. By allowing the audience to experience simulated accidents, rendering them "safe," adding acrobatics to exaggerate the impact, yet at the same time removing the viewer from real risk, the film detaches pleasure from any

---

the Pierrot figure, whose historical function, he says, is analogous to that of a trace element in the natural sciences. It normally appears in cultural periods marked by ideological disorientation and in situations where collective identities of class, gender, and ethnicity are being restructured. Modernism represented a triumphant era for the Pierrot figure in the works of Pablo Picasso, Henri Rousseau, Paul Klee, Paul Cézanne, the Ballets Russes, Charles Baudelaire, Paul Verlaine, Guillaume Apollinaire, Wallace Stevens, Federico Fellini, Ingmar Bergman, Jean-Luc Godard, and others. Jonsson does not mention Keaton, but clearly he belongs within this tradition.

15. Keaton came to film after more than twenty years as a vaudeville performer. The typical vaudeville program consisted of a series of acts eight to twenty minutes long that had no narrative interconnection. Early films presented similarly self-contained moments; the gag sequences that halted the development of any story line were composed of an ingenious array of repetitions and variations played on a chosen motif and structured to build toward closure in a shock finish. Repetitions were necessary to intensify the comic effect. As Lisa Trahir notes in her work on Keaton ("The Ghost in the Machine: The Comedy of Technology in the Cinema of Buster Keaton," *South Atlantic Quarterly* 101, no. 3 [Summer 2002]: 573–90, and "Short-Circuiting the Dialectic: Narrative and Slapstick in the Cinema of Buster Keaton," *Narrative* 10, no. 3 [October 2002]: 307–25), he was able to integrate this vertical dimension of the gag sequence with the horizontality of the narrative structure.

actual pain. As a superhero, Keaton both endures danger and triumphs over it on behalf of the audience.[16] Thus, cinema technology pushed physical invulnerability to accident beyond previous human limits.

In the final frames of *Sherlock, Jr.*, the transference implicit in the opening sequence becomes the subject for comic irony when the projectionist (awakened from his dream) studies the star of the inner film in order to apply his method of courtship in the "real" world of the outer film. At this moment, as so often in the silent film, the actions performed by Keaton's character tend to be unorthodox or obsessive. They are not what a normal person could or would do under the circumstances, yet any signs that might have revealed the internal self to a psychoanalyst have been subsumed within the exquisite control he exercised over his body and his face. His miraculous competence hid Keaton's effort so effectively that the principal impression his films convey is of the character's extraordinary good luck. In other words, the psychological underpinnings inherent in cinematic techniques carry no psychoanalytic reference.

Rather than serving as a means of exploring unconscious behavior or expanding self-knowledge, what cinematic transference accomplished was a species of cultural transference, epitomized in the celebrity culture that emerged alongside the explosive development of the American film industry. The star system that powered the rise of the great Hollywood studios fostered a focus on the performer as an object rather than on the individuality of the characters. Despite the faintly subversive final frames of *Sherlock, Jr.* (in which Keaton regards with bafflement—and possibly dismay—the on-screen kiss that dissolves into a shot of an on-screen family), the projectionist's experience is recognizably linked to the passive experience of the filmgoer: stars formed objects of hope and desire.

Whatever notion of identity filmgoers possess can be reembodied in a screen illusion. In this transference, the possibilities of being are unlimited. At the same time, mechanical reproduction controls the qualities of things and individuals. Film portrays forms that "do not live like living men." The power of the technology lay in its capacity to represent illusions of reality, replicate dream states, and invoke the shock and surprise of the unknown. As American films gradually moved away from gag sequences toward a formula that combined specifically cinematic devices with narrative patterns drawn from the novel and the theater, the

16. Another example of substitution occurs in the use of canned laughter or other audience responses in television shows. Mechanical reproduction replaces the viewer's actual response.

star consistently triumphed over both accidental and intentional events that eventually resolved the action in accord with expected sentimental values.

Because the star was sacrosanct and events led to secure outcomes, the intervening action could exploit violence of all kinds. Although plot and character were capable of endless manipulation, audience expectations remained constant, and any aesthetic distance fostered by the gag sequence that typified silent comedy faded into emotional involvement. Defused of significance and diminished in interpretive content, accident became simply a formal element, a locus of visual rather than conceptual interest. Viewer identification with the immutable persona of a star moving from one film to another rather than with the characters portrayed in the cinematic situations joined the affectless rendering of physical accidents to trivialize and further diminish the pedagogical role that accident had played during the formative development of the novel.

III. Future Alienation

A film might be viewed as a thought technology—analogous to innovative scientific technologies like nanotechnology or magnetic resonance imaging or to the computer's power to search, synthesize, and disseminate information. In that guise it might serve as a laboratory for conducting experiments in how the mind works or a site where experiences frozen in time could be dismembered into abstracted forms of understanding. On the other hand, filmgoing (or later watching television) could be viewed as a branch of techno-determinism, turning the members of the audience into automatons whose inner void becomes filled with preprogrammed, externally imposed experiences. In this guise, film would offer to assuage the wounded or uncertain self by allowing the viewer to participate in vicarious experiences of physical desirability or physical power. Romantic or adventure films exploit this second aspect of film, while science-fiction films presume to fill the first.

Like suspense and horror movies, science-fiction films exploit the principle of pleasure in pain. Just as accident evolved into an affectless experience within silent film comedy, in these films life-threatening violence operates within strictly defined controls. This formula enables the audience to thrill to vicarious dangers as readily as it had laughed at silent comedy violence. But because shock loses its power over time, filmmakers continually were forced to heighten their effects. The formulas on which suspense, horror, and science-fiction genres were based were self-consuming. Pressure to innovate intensified the visual sophistication of the film medium, but to ensure commercial survival, cinematic accidents increasingly attempted to effect violent entry into the minds of the viewers.

Ridley Scott's *Alien* (1979), the first film in a quartet depicting the encounters between humans and a species that requires their bodies as reproductive hosts, draws on established conventions of both horror and science-fiction genres. The horror film had trained viewers to recognize the camera's inexorable progress through the compartments of the space ship during the opening minutes of the film as a prelude to a shocking experience. The camera's eye-level angle could readily be equated with the perspective of a person traveling through the cabin. Its pace forced attention to every trace of human occupancy or quiver of motion caused by a mechanical operation, a movement of air, or a flutter of coded signals appearing on a computer screen. No detail carries directly perceptible meaning (although an old-fashioned perpetual motion toy of a bird dipping its beak in water adds a surreal note). The only legible words operate like Breton's *faits-glissances.* "Emergency" suddenly begins to blink on a helmet and the name of the ship appears on an incoming computer message: *Nostromo,* or "our man." By association, therefore, the undercurrent of heartbeats and breathing on the sound track accentuates a sense of foreboding that vies with the torpor induced by the long panning shot. In this opening sequence, Scott compels the viewer to become a flaneur—ready for illumination. As a door slides open to admit the camera into the room where the crew members are encased in a circle of transparent pods for their hypersleep, the lights go on, fulfilling this expectation in the most literal way.

The setting establishes the parameters of the *Nostromo's* high-tech world by deliberately contrasting the antiseptic minimalism of the pods against shadowed corridors lined with circuitry of baroque yet vaguely organic complexity that appear subject to breakage or dysfunction (and thus to human accidents). In *The Question Concerning Technology,* Heidegger described how technology comes to appear ordinary, ceasing to arouse awe, and in the process destroys the human capacity to feel wonder. Even early technologies, he wrote, flattened life by comparison to the animation implicit in the pre-Socratic notion of being: "For what presences by means of *physis* [being] has the bursting open belonging to bringing-forth, e.g., the bursting of a blossom into bloom in itself. In contrast, what is brought forth by the artisan or the artist, the silver chalice, has a bringing forth belonging to bringing forth not in itself, but in another, in the craftsman or artist."[17] In the modern age, this effect has become so extreme that beauty assumes the form of the monstrous, as the dominance of technology voids human nature. Thus, Heidegger's interpretation of Kant's sublime transformed his ecstatic perception of the starry night into a threatening confrontation with an abyss. The stylistic self-consciousness of *Alien*—in which the transparent lids of the pods swing open like blossoming petals or the alien egg unfurls before Kane, the enraptured crew member who discovers it—gives cinematic technology that kind of monstrous, quasi-natural beauty.

Technology enables the crew to overcome the limitations of the body, giving them properties (such as the capacity for hypersleep) that transcend time and space, but it also has made them dependent on technology for survival. Now the human beings who developed technology as an instrument are predicated on that technology; they have become accidental to it. Although the frame of the film involves the motif of dreaming (in which the central section constitutes a nightmarish experience), in the opening scene the crew is reborn to consciousness from the womblike equipment of the mothering ship. The name given to the ship's computer, Mother, underscores the ambiguities of nurture in the film as well as the theme of dependence on technology.

What appear to be a series of accidents—an unexpected diversion in the ship's path, the discovery that the wrecked space ship the crew has been sent to investigate contains mysterious leathery eggs, the alien bursting from one of the eggs to attach itself to the face of Kane, the subsequent contamination of the *Nostromo* by the alien—do not lead to the empowering self-discoveries of Kant's sublime. Instead, they reveal a terrifying world where man is no longer the dominant species. The alien's appearance is always sudden and unexpected, and when it appears it ruptures and redirects the course of the narrative, leaving the characters vulnerable. Reduced to their primary instinct of self-preservation, they become the prey of the alien whose aggressive will to survive and parasitic efficiency exert a literally creative force, for its goal is to incubate its embryo in a human host.[18] Equating all the crew members by defining

17. Martin Heidegger, *The Question Concerning Technology and Other Essays*, trans. and ed. William Lovitt (New York: Harper and Row, 1977), 10–11.
18. Ash, the film's emblem of scientific detachment (revealed later as an android programmed to obey the company's command to bring back a specimen alien), identifies the creature as a perfect adaptive organism, and he admires its essential purity. H. R. Giger, the Swiss surrealist who designed the alien and its environment, visualized the creature as a fusion of machine and organism, phallic components and female function. The android also

them as eligible hosts, the alien echoes the company's recognition that the alien has the potential to give new life to its aging technological arsenal while the workers are expendable. Individual members of the human species, identifiable by their blood (in contrast to the white fluid that flows through the android's operating system or the alien's molecular acid), possess no relevant uniqueness for either the company or the alien. They have been reduced to objects of use—resource materials—by the mechanisms that control the plot.[19]

In *Alien*, the "Mother" ship provides its newly "birthed" human crew with food and information to enable them to serve the interests of the company, but their skills are being rendered obsolete. When the android Ash praises the single-minded purity of the alien's aggression, he is admiring his own integrity of purpose. Since human qualities can be programmed into androids, all that distinguishes a human being is the vulnerability of the body (and its capacity to fulfill the alien's reproductive potential) and the primal drive for self-protection. Recognition of bodily penetrability—its cannibalization by a biotechnology—constitutes the shock of *Alien*. Gone are concerns about unruly associations invading the mind or the notion that reflection can achieve spiritual improvement or analysis return an ailing subject to mental health; the alien incubates in Kane's chest, not his brain, and powers its explosive emergence with a phallic thrust.[20]

Physical and sexual terrors in *Alien* reflect a modernist emphasis on the material body, but also carry metaphorical resonance. Self-defining

---

combines the mastery over the body benignly implied in Keaton's automatic gestures with a murderous power. In *Aliens* and *Alien³*, a second-generation android was programmed to protect the company's investment in humans, but in *Alien Resurrection* this feature was discarded as impractical, and the company scientists cloned a hybrid from a fusion of the DNA of Ripley, the heroine of the series, with alien material.

19. Ironically, what accidental qualities the characters possess were assigned by marketing considerations that surrounded the making of the film. Interviews included in the supplementary materials on casting and reactions to the film that accompany the DVD of the director's cut (2003) note that two characters, Ripley and Lambert, her crewmate, became women in order to expand the audience appeal. *Alien* was the fourth-highest-grossing film of 1979, but, according to associate producer Ivor Powell, the fact that the alien that is "birthed" from Kane's chest repulsed thirty- to forty-year-old women was recognized (post facto) as a box office liability.

20. Jean Baudrillard, *The Vital Illusion*, ed. Julia Witwer (New York: Columbia University Press, 2000), 22–25, argues that automatons, chimeras, and clones will supersede the human race and, as genetic simulations of life, will jeopardize both the individual and the species' capital. Contemporary culture clones people by synchronizing ideas and emotions so that innate differences are annulled. For him, this mental cloning (fostered by media technology) anticipates biological cloning.

qualities have become inessential once again, leaving physical matter as the source of being, and the film frames human freedom with an infinite space where (as the movie's ad slogan taunted) "no one can hear you scream." In this internal and external void, the company's unseen presence assumes a quasi-divine control. Like the alien, it reduces the human beings to the parasitical relationship it requires to fulfill its needs, and the crew becomes the victim of two intersecting wills. In contrast to Darwin's eulogy of the parasite as a beautiful example of coadaptation, the double determinism expressed in *Alien* neither pretends to creative symbiosis nor aspires to redemptive change.

Film exercises more complete control over what is seen or heard than any other medium, giving film companies a power over the audience analogous to the company's control over the experiences available to the crew of the *Nostromo*. When I considered the relationship between the early novel and its audience, I noted how much authors who depended on the publishing economy needed to please and attract the reading public. Commercial considerations place well-known constraints on whether or not a film will be made as well as on its final form, but as filmgoers become more inert or passive consumers of the cinematic product, they more readily internalize the thoughts and values presented to them. In effect, by allowing a filmmaker to instill a uniform unconscious, they permit themselves to be colonized by parasites of the imagination.[21] Just as the content of *Alien* signals a cycling back to earlier notions of determinism that disregarded the defining potential of accident, it manipulates the audience on the level of instinctual drives.

Alien could realize the intellectual illumination promised by its opening sequence only if the vicarious physical suffering imposed by the struggle with the alien resulted in a meditative assimilation of its implied sociological critique. However, the film does not compel a deterministic interpretation. Its accidents are not atomistic single events but constitute a Darwinian assemblage of indirect causes. For a viewer prepared to interpret the film in sociological terms, the result might be analogous to Rousseau's vision of the corrupting power of civilization after his

---

21. Technology's power to repeat enactments of events has created a way of life in which we watch simulated action for longer periods than any other acts. In 1980, when Pauline Kael lamented the jaded condition of moviegoers who wanted "images that move along in an undemanding way, so they can sit and react at the simplest motor level" in her essay "Why Are Movies so Bad? or, the Numbers," she observed that the audience thought *Alien* was terrific "because at least they'd feel something: they'd been brutalized." *Taking It All In* (New York: Holt, Rinehart, and Winston, 1984), 19.

accident on the road to Vincennes. Or a visual artist with a gift for "lyrical behavior" might process the shock as creatively as Breton absorbed his objective chance experiences. For most members of the audience, however, the illusory trauma serves to insulate them from genuine anxieties and inure them to violence. Safe within a cinematic cocoon, viewers experience purging the alien from the ship as an analogue for real power. But to achieve this satisfaction they must submit to the values and solutions made available through film technology. Like the human hosts that the alien confines in its sticky cocoons during the gestation period, the film audience is contaminated through the pleasure it takes in the virtual realization of its own fears and the anodyne of a sentimental resolution.

IV. Viral Thought

Hindsight allows us to recognize the specter of the alien impregnating its human host as a prefiguration of the invasion of the human genome by the AIDS virus, which surfaced as a fatal infection in 1982, three years after the film was released. Both the alien and the virus had remained latent for unknown periods of time until optimal conditions released their destructive potential and revealed their parasitic nature. In both examples, technological advances provided the opportunity for the fatal mutation and the body became the site of the aggression. Human qualities, operating directly within the constitution of the body or via environmental opportunities created by human agency, permitted the transformation from potential or self-limiting threat to virulent assault. In that sense, AIDS morphed the catastrophic man-made accident that takes place at a specific time and place (such as the nuclear accident at Chernobyl) into a global accident that incorporates other accidents in a chain reaction. Thus, paradoxically, the knowledge which the Enlightenment projected would resolve human problems becomes a calamitous power.[22]

Once the nature of the AIDS epidemic entered the popular imagination, it became possible to envision viral operations working by analogy in other contexts. The accidental or contingent nature of the infection appeared not only in the technological vocabulary of the digital revolution but in the metaphors of art and literature, for well-known early AIDS

---

22. This is Paul Virilio's argument in much of his critique of technology. See especially, "The Museum of Accidents," from *Unknown Quantity*, trans. Chris Turner (London: Thames and Hudson, 2003). He notes that since the 1990s, damage resulting from man-made accidents has superseded damage from natural catastrophes.

victims were members of the artistic community. Filmmaker Derek Jarman created *Blue* (1993) as he was dying from AIDS. The film chronicles the war the virus was waging on his body.[23]

As an example of avant-garde high art, Jarman's antirepresentational film differs from *Alien* almost in every conceivable way, yet both works involve concern with the body and a self-conscious play with form. Jarman's earlier films, such as *Sebastiane* (1976), *Angelic Conversation* (1985), *Caravaggio* (1986), *Edward II* (1991), and *Wittgenstein* (1992), reinterpreted historical figures, so it is not surprising that the initial experience portrayed in *Blue* takes the form of an accidental conversion scene. After the opening invocation apostrophizing a boy and the color blue in language that conflates physical and spiritual ecstasy, he describes almost being run over by a bicyclist "flying in from the dark [who] nearly parted my hair." The accident plunged him into a "blue funk," that drove him to the hospital where the retinal tumors symptomatic of AIDS were first discovered: "The doctor in St Bartholomew's Hospital thought he could detect lesions in my retina—the pupils dilated with belladonna—the torch shone into them with a terrible blinding light."[24] His imagery alludes to the blue color of the poisonous flower of the belladonna (reminding us that Jarman was a master gardener). The blinding light of the doctor's torch produced "blue flashes in my eyes" (recalling the neurological origin of the phenomenon of the blue vision Jarman experienced when he lost his sight). And the loss of his sight constitutes a physical inversion of Saul's spiritual illumination. The atheist Jarman has experienced a seroconversion that turns his vision inward, restoring contingency to a position of thematic relevance.[25]

23. The most comprehensive discussions of Jarman's film career can be found in William Pencak, *The Films of Derek Jarman* (Jefferson, NC: McFarland and Company, 2002); and Steven Dillon, *Derek Jarman and the Lyric Film: The Mirror and the Sea* (Austin: University of Texas Press, 2004. See also Tony Peake's biography, *Derek Jarman* (London: Little, Brown, 1999).

24. Derek Jarman, *Chroma: A Book of Colour—June '93* (London: Century, 1994), 107. This journal incorporates the full text of *Blue*. All citations from the sound track refer to this text.

25. Jarman subverted religious references at other points in the work. For example, his mention of "activists invading the Sunday Mass" alluded to a "die-in" in which members of the AIDS Coalition to Unleash Power (ACT-UP) interrupted a mass being celebrated at Saint Patrick's Cathedral in New York City. He also inverted the Eucharistic ritual by making a film whose screening gathered people together to participate in the experience of the virus consuming his body. Although he accepted the potential blasphemy of using himself as a subject in this context, by eliminating physical evidence of his bodily illness or representing his past in literal images he removed the element of spectacle that had characterized his other films, in which he projected his homosexuality to the public by reinterpreting

The film consists of an unchanging screen of blue that replicates the blue of a television screen or video monitor, accompanied by music and voice-over.[26] In Jarman's condition, visual images existed only in his memory, and the blind filmmaker invoked those that were precious to him through his narration. His narrative is composed of accidental associations related to the color blue: delphiniums, lapis lazuli, dead lovers remembered beside a cobalt sea. He plays with linguistic overtones like "I'm blue" or "singing the blues." He offers a feast of references drawn from his intensely visual background. Obviously, loss of sight presented a heightened trauma for the filmmaker, but in the narration he prays to be released from the image, aligning himself with "astronauts of the void" who leave behind the "comfortable" images that "imprison us" (115). He adds, quoting Blake, "If the doors of perception were cleansed then everything would be seen as it is" (113).

Blue evolved from a performance piece entitled "Symphonic Monotone." The happening involved Jarman and Tilda Swinton, dressed in blue, reciting poetry while slides from Jarman's films and passages from an essay on the color blue were projected on a blue screen. Such collages of assembled visual and language materials reoccur in Jarman's journals as well as in what he called the "cut-up" film *War Requiem* (1989).[27]

------

a history that had excluded same-sex desire. *Blue* quickly became an icon in the cultural signification of AIDS and in the politics surrounding gay identity. Parallels between sociopolitical developments, such as the war in Bosnia, that Jarman was discussing immediately before his accident, and the implications of viral transference are readily identifiable in the film. Working at a time when ideas of intention and cause surrounding the transmission of AIDS had reached hysterical proportions, Jarman clearly regarded becoming infected as an accidental event, an act of "blind Fate," as he said in the narration. His position as a gay filmmaker, his early public acknowledgment of his infection, the understanding of self in terms of inherited characteristics that has accompanied identity politics, and his cinematic method mediate against a restrictive interpretation.

26. In Jarman's published journals and scripts, he repeatedly expressed his antipathy to narrative and narrative cinema. What distinguishes his aversion from the reduction of narration characteristic of avant-garde film is the degree to which he contrasted narrative with poetry. As Ludwig Wittgenstein, the subject of the film Jarman made immediately before *Blue* and an important influence on Jarman's association between language and color, wrote in *Zettel*, ed. G. E. M. Anscombe and G. H. von Wright, trans. G. E. M. Anscombe (Berkeley: University of California Press, 1967), no. 160, "Do not forget that a poem, although it is composed in the language of information, is not used in the language game of giving information." Dillon, *Derek Jarman and the Lyric Film*, devotes chap. 1 to a clarification of what poetry signified to the film artists most influential for Jarman's work.

27. Dillon, *Derek Jarman and the Lyric Film*, 40–43, gives an extended reading of "From Gypsy Mar 1 66," one of the poems Jarman published in *A Finger in the Fishes Mouth* (1972), that presents the restless narrator of the volume as a type of flaneur, assembling dreamlike associations between words and postcard images.

His working method deliberately opened the opportunities inherent in accidents. In this regard, he emulated Jean Cocteau, one of the principal exponents of the French antirealist tradition of filmmaking that extended from Georges Mélies to the work Jean-Luc Godard. "As I left St. Mary's," Jarman reported, "I smiled at Jean Cocteau. He gave me a sweet smile back" (123). This surreal accidental encounter pays homage to a fellow visual artist's analogous capacity to subvert past mythologies (as in Cocteau's Orpheus trilogy) as well as his respect for accident as a creative tool. "A great film is an accident," Cocteau wrote in one of his essays, "a banana skin under the feet of dogma."[28]

Jarman's task was to make the inner experience of viral infection visible, to place a banana skin under the received understanding of medical science and of narrative cinema. At a literal level he recounted the progress of his symptoms and the attempted treatments. At a metaphoric level, he drew parallels between political wars and the war the virus was waging on his body. But his seroconversion had altered his understanding of self: events operating randomly across a lifetime of experience have coalesced to define his present and his future. In an echo of Musil's earlier understanding of the arbitrary nature of existence, Jarman implies that the presence or absence of any conceptual or remembered material in experience is fortuitous. The film's abstract form is equally unbounded. Without changing its tone, intensity, or shape the blue screen that initially signified life's promise reveals how it has been poisoned and turns to black at the end of the film. Form turns the disease against itself, using the destruction of Jarman's retina to remake his cinematic vision.

Although Jarman exercised some control over the viewing experience of the audience, his blank blue screen offered extraordinary latitude for the viewer's imagination. In direct opposition to the assumption made by Hollywood films that audience excitement requires a visually charged experience, abundant and complex in its hectic images, he presented a single radically minimal visual sign. He reduced the visual experience of the film to a liminal color essence. Blue mediates between white and black, visual reality and the void. In *Blue*, nothing is visible except the color, but within the screen of the imaginary, Jarman plays out his life. He can move from past to present; he can manipulate time in his memory; he can move from a finite time and space toward an unknown.

28. Quoted in Andre Bernard and Claude Gauteur, eds., *Art of Cinema*, trans. Robin Buss (New York: Marion Boyars, 1992), 51.

The shade of blue Jarman chose to use in his film is close to IKB (International Klein Blue), the color of the paint with which Yves Klein covered the antirepresentational canvases he began to produce in 1957 in order to explore his ideas about color and the void. His monochrome panels invited viewers to bring their own associations to what they saw. In *Camera Lucida*, Roland Barthes's meditation on the association among photographic images, memory, and death, he asserted that a photographic image involves a transformation of its subject into an object imitating the subject to become "that rather terrible thing which is there in every photograph: the return of the dead."[29] Associations between memory and death permeate *Blue*, but by eliminating concrete visual references and providing only aural stimuli, Jarman temporarily transferred to the viewer the experience of blindness that prepared him to receive his insight into death and disease. Cleansed of visual images, the mind's eye opens to his inner reality. His sound track guides his audience, but the blue screen accepts whatever the individual viewer transfers onto it. Thus, on one level, the film offers an experience parallel to Jarman's own, dependent on arbitrary connections that he controls by an effort of self-will. On another level, the result is necessarily accidental, conditioned by the viewer's capacity to draw on his or her own prior experience and the degree to which something of Jarman can colonize his or her imagination. The film's form, in other words, models the afterlife of the process of transference while the interpretation of the experience becomes limitless and accidental for the viewer.

Jarman's work on *Wittgenstein* seems to have informed his long-standing fascination with color, optics, language, and the implications of pure form. In *Remarks on Colour*, Wittgenstein explored the ways people describe their experiences with color perception as a lens through which to understand the interplay between substance and accident. He deconstructed (dismembered) features of perception from one another, breaking ideas about color into separate moments in which accidental qualities could be detached from what circumscribes them. Often he chose examples from the perception of color the viewer invests in a black and white photograph, but twice he took up the question of the cinematic screen. What he proposed was a virtual reality in which the transparency of cinema achieves some aspects of the experience Barthes recognized in the photograph:

29. Roland Barthes, *Camera Lucida*, trans. Richard Howard (New York: Hill and Wang, 1981), sec. 4, p. 9.

In the cinema it is often possible to see the events as though they were occurring behind the screen, as if the screen were transparent like a pane of
glass. At the same time, however, the colour would be removed from these
events and only white, grey and black would come through. But we are
still not tempted to call it a transparent, *white* pane of glass.

How, then, would we see things through a pane of green glass? *One*
difference would, of course, be that the green glass would diminish the
difference between light and dark, while the other one shouldn't have any
effect upon this difference. Then a "grey transparent" pane would somewhat diminish it.[30]

If we substitute "blue" for "green," we recognize Jarman's conceptual accomplishment. The blue screen diminishes the difference between life
and death. The accidents of memory, detached from the real-world contexts that bound them, acquire a separate freedom. In other words, by
dismembering color from shape and shape from body, he performs an act
of imaginative violence, an act whose energy of thought gives the pure
form its substance in nonactuality. In *Phenomenology of Spirit*, Hegel associated the freedom obtained in this way with death: "But that an accident
as such, detached from what circumscribes it, what is bound and is actual
only in its context with others, should attain an existence of its own and
a separate freedom—this is the tremendous power of the negative; it is
the energy of thought, of the pure 'I.' Death, if that is what we want to
call this non-actuality, is of all things the most dreadful, and to hold fast
what is dead requires the greatest strength."[31] Remembering his dead in
the face of his own death, Jarman exhibits this kind of strength, creating
in *Blue* a fin de siècle example of the accidental sublime. He had encountered the first stage of Kant's description of the experience in the trauma
of his own mortality, and the creation of the film provided evidence of
his intellectual triumph over nature.

"Problems are solved, not by giving new information, but by arranging
what we have always known."[32] In the language of the techno-ontology
that we have been tracing Jarman responded to the question of "being"

30. Ludwig Wittgenstein, *Remarks on Colour*, trans. Linda L. McAlister and Margaret
Schättle, ed G. E. M. Anscombe (Berkeley: University of California Press, 1977), no. 184.

31. Slavoj Žižek, *The Ticklish Subject: The Absent Centre of Political Ontology* (London:
Verso, 1999), 30–31, quotes this passage in the context of the "decomposing" or "dismembering" power of the imagination in his reading of Hegel's *Phenomenology*.

32. Ludwig Wittgenstein, *Philosophical Investigations*, trans. G. E. M. Anscombe (New
York: Macmillan, 1958), no. 109.

with an aesthetic meditation on sight and sound. By replacing three-dimensional space with an unmarked two-dimensional one that telescopes outer and inner experience, the blue screen marks a passage from a finite time and space to a boundless unknown where accident—released from its corporeal reality—becomes substantial form.

Pattern Recognition

In drawing a distinction between substance and accident, Aristotle set in motion a system of thought whose conceptual fertility remains astonishing. For over two thousand years, thinkers have puzzled over how to grasp the rules by which it operates, tinkered with its mechanical breakdowns, assigned it new functions, or contrived to replace parts that seemed outmoded without sacrificing the orderliness of the whole. The difficulty of constraining unruly events to preconceived categories of experience vied with an enduring desire to impose order on contingency. Even as new patterns formed and events came to dominate the discourse surrounding accident, Aristotle's axiomatic distinction between substance and accidental qualities persisted to complicate perceptions of break or rupture. In short, continuities latent within discontinuities appear throughout the history of accident.

The twentieth century capitalized on its new technologies to uncover ordering principles within seemingly random natural phenomena occurring on a global scale. Vast accumulations of computer-generated data were used to support the geological theory of plate tectonics, for example, or the algorithms of chaos theory. At the same time, knowledge about the biological operations of the brain is revolutionizing notions of consciousness. In each case, early encounters with new technologies produced unease about their impact on wider audiences, predictions of moral or cultural decline, and fresh tensions regarding individual identity.

As Virilio reminds us, technology hides its potential for damage within the promise of scientific progress—the automobile preparing for car crashes or nuclear power preparing for atomic and hydrogen bombs—but the power to detonate what he regards as the impending cataclysm resides in "thought technology"—film, television, and digital media. By projecting and repeating all kinds of accidents at will, the media instill fear (as people find themselves helpless and incoherent before disasters), and by adding simulated accidents to real ones, they pander to the public's visual delight in violence, making horror banal and terror heroic. The inherent ability of silent film comedy to reverse physical laws worked to remove meaning from accidental events, while the manipulation of time in mediated experience altered the process of reflecting on them. Television and digital simulation further the sense that all acts are equally accidental.

What Virilio sees as characteristic of the twenty-first century appeared in more occluded terms in this history as early as the eighteenth century. Locke's refusal to acknowledge the implications of a marauding "gang" of associations gave us the first glimpse of a fissure in Enlightenment optimism. Wordsworth's taming of the terrible aspect of the accidental sublime into a therapeutic philosophy of nature served as a prelude to nineteenth-century attempts to disarm the threats of the mad or magical with an affirmation of scientific and technological progress. In the absence of a conceptual grounding from either theology or philosophy, the terrible aspect of the sublime gained force within twentieth century techno-scientific events, such as the deployment of the atomic bomb or the collapse of the World Trade Center towers. The media have capitalized on such events to satisfy the popular fascination with uncontrolled disaster. In fashion, the result has been an aesthetic of mutilation, in politics the emergence of suicide bombers.

We have observed repeatedly how an accidental event can alter or realign the qualities that make up the self. However, when such an event has a broad impact, affecting numbers of individuals, the qualities of the cultural time period alter reflexively. This does not necessarily depend on the loss or gain of some particular element within the event. The action of one individual may not have an immediate or perceptible effect. Nor will some alteration in circumstances necessarily exert a determining impact. Rather, changes appear to reflect a rebalancing of multiple factors. Under such circumstances, the enduring symbiosis within Aristotle's double definition of accident made it possible to implement Foucault's strategy of combining a genealogical structure with an archaeological method: the genealogical axis of event to qualities recorded changes in self-perception, while the archaeological axis of substance and accident responded to metaphysical shifts.

Interpretation of the event was a critical factor in this history. Changing the perception of an accidental event is a way of changing the self in relation to existence. In that sense, our work reinforces Badiou's insight that the responding self becomes the key element in change if and when the response fulfills certain conditions of perception and ensuing action. For example, during the eighteenth century, accidental qualities ceased to be generally understood as inhering in an enduring substance and were thought to shift in response to circumstances. Although the evidence is not precise in date, it is generalized enough to appear persuasive, so we might be tempted to conclude that beginning around the 1750s, a dramatic event or willed act of self-transformation had the power to make a person "modern." However, such an assertion would oversimplify my findings. Accident appears in this history less as a shaping force than as a tool used in exploration, an experimental instrument operated by the self becoming "subjectivized."

Let us reformulate the language of the problem to reflect Badiou's theory. If we replace the idea of ascribing agency to an event ("accidents make people modern") with the idea that modernity resides in an *attitude* toward accident (in the double signification of the term), we might see a figure like Plotinus as modern because he conceived of the spiritual exercise as a way to purge the body of its inessential accidents or Aquinas as modern because his moral teachings posed a new way of looking at the problem of being. In this formulation, the defining factor appears to be a perception of self in relation to others that accompanies an experience of unplanned changes in circumstances. The sense in which accident makes people modern, I would argue, lies in its capacity to mark this process of perception by registering a conceptual position within an existing system of thought.

Whether an attitude should be considered conservative or modern rests on the terms used for comparison. We can point to shifts in the value assigned to aspects of accident that demarcate a series of important attitudinal domains: The reign of substance as the enduring quality with respect to accident lasted into the eighteenth century. During the late eighteenth and early nineteenth centuries, a shift occurred from seeking qualitative resemblances to the exploration of differences. Toward the end of the nineteenth century, a second shift replaced the retrospective sense of self with anticipatory self-structuring and gave primacy to inwardly determined self-definition. A third shift, one that began in the twentieth century and is accelerating rapidly, sacrificed the claim of a substantive self. According to critics like Foucault or Virilio, this movement threatens to extinguish the self completely. In the conclusion to *The Order of Things*, Foucault writes: "As the archaeology of our thought easily shows, man is an invention of recent date. And one perhaps nearing its end. If some event were to cause [those arrangements that created the modern understanding of man] to crumble, as the ground of Classical thought did, at the end of the eighteenth century, then one can certainly wager that man would be erased, like a face drawn in sand at the edge of the sea." For his part, Virilio adds at the conclusion of *Negative Horizon*, "*It is hard to imagine a society that would deny the body just as we had progressively denied the soul. This, however, is where we are heading.*"[1]

The history of accident demonstrates that things that are conventional and things that may be regarded as modern coexist in the understanding. In some cases, an individual may adopt an attitude well before his or her peers. For example, Pascal's conception of personal identity appeared far in advance of Locke's more influential and systematic theory. In other cases, an idea that passed unnoticed when it was formulated suddenly emerges with renewed relevance. For example, contemporary philosophers and psychologists interested in fission have returned to passages in Locke's *Essay Concerning Human Understanding*, in which he meditated on the possibility that a finger detached from the body might retain some aspect of consciousness: "Upon separation of this little Finger, should this consciousness go along with the little Finger, and leave the rest of the Body, 'tis evident the little Finger would be the *Person*, the *same Person*; and *self* then would have nothing to do with the rest of the Body" (II.xxvii.17). Would the finger, he wondered, be aware of its former relation to the body? Would consciousness be bifurcated under these circumstances? Locke's graphic image of dismemberment addressed the possible fragmentation of the self (and the goal of reintegration).[2] In other words, three centuries ago, he posed one of the central questions of postmodernity.

Fission permits us to contemplate what may happen if an idea is cut from a system of thought at one point or another—either deliberately or

1. Michel Foucault, *The Order of Things: An Archaeology of the Human Sciences* (New York: Vintage, 1994), 187; Paul Virilio, *Negative Horizon*, trans. Michael Degener (London: Continuum, 2005), 200. The italics are Virilio's.

2. William Hazlitt's innovative theory of personal identity in his *Essay on the Principles of Human Action* (1805) revisioned Locke's notions in ways that also acquired significance for contemporary psychological notions of fission only in the twentieth century. See Raymond Martin and John Barresi, *Naturalization of the Soul: Self and Personal Identity in the Eighteenth Century* (London: Routledge, 2000), 144–46.

through misunderstanding. Will it persist to animate new concepts? Will it sustain a relation to the original context that may not be obvious to the innovator but become clear in retrospect? On behalf of a corpus of thought, we might respond to Locke's questions in the affirmative, postulating that historical ruptures within Aristotle's categorical system have indeed multiplied consciousness, served as modes of reproduction, and through yearning for an earlier wholeness kept methods of understanding alive. Although we are scarcely conscious of the presence of Aristotle's categorical system in everyday life, this study has tracked the presence of the idea of substance—glimpsed like rare sightings of some endangered conceptual species.

Scientists working on memory and other brain functions have begun to acknowledge literary intuitions as previsions of mental processes whose validity has been confirmed by recent research. I have noted in passing how philosophers such as Descartes or scientists such as Darwin employed literary language to communicate ideas that originated in mathematical or statistical proofs. In an essay written in 1868, "Notes on Form in Art," George Eliot suggested that a language of form links the narratives of literature with those of science. For her, form consists of the recognition of differences. Scientific observation finds its complement in the weblike and universalizing juxtapositions of metaphor. Thus, the creation of a character inescapably binds a "multiplex" of differences together—the fingernail, the muscles which produce a shout, and the capacity to see a red spot against the snow representing disparate facets of a human being—so that the resulting whole constitutes the highest form.[3] When qualities perceived as recognizable and stable shift under the pressure of events, the pattern that emerges also represents more than the sum of its parts. The history I have traced shows substance functioning metaphorically within the language of accident: it allows the sum of paired static images, such as body and soul or form and matter, to create a third concept that supersedes them.

The relevance of accident within such a metaphorical version of pattern recognition becomes clearer if we return to the accidental event that opened this book: Giacometti's automobile accident on the place des Pyramides. We know from his own words that the sculptor's lifelong goal was to capture reality as he saw it. Yet his efforts to strip his subject to its essential form led to the near disappearance of the physical body. In that

---

3. *George Eliot: Selected Essays, Poems and Other Writings*, ed. A. S. Byatt and Nicholas Warren (London: Penguin, 1990), 233.

respect, his work resembles Samuel Beckett's attempts to distill narrative experience into words, a project he repeatedly described as impossible to realize. Giacometti's sculptures consist of radically emaciated figures. His early works shrank in size until he was able to carry his total oeuvre from Switzerland to Paris in a matchbox. Later pieces reduced the figure to a detached head or even to a gaze he hoped would embody the whole force of life.[4] Repeated failures to achieve his goal never diminished the intensity of his search: "Why this compulsion to record what one sees? When one loses oneself in the task of recording . . . it's a matter of the same need whether one is a scientist or an artist. Both art and science mean: wanting to understand. Success or failure is unimportant. It's the modern form of adventure for men who are left on their own."[5] Giacometti expressed his obsession with understanding in language that echoes the opening sentence of Aristotle's *Metaphysics* ("All men by nature desire to know"). Although he described his failure in the terms of postmodern anxiety and his forms expressed the threat of dissolution characteristic of the postmodern self, a quest for substance defined his art.

The automobile accident, which left Giacometti using a cane and crutches, like one of Beckett's heroes, evoked a joyous reaction in him precisely because it allowed him a momentary glimpse of an unobtainable whole: sensual reality fused with suspension in time.[6] It confirmed the existence of substance stripped of its experiential inessentials. For us, his experience serves as a reminder that the significance of accident extends beyond the violent events that dominate the modern imagination. Its long history offers a path through the labyrinth of our messy and uncertain world.

4. Matti Megged, *Dialogue in the Void: Beckett and Giacometti* (NY: Lumen Books, 1985), esp. 37–42.

5. Quoted in Reinhold Hohl, *Alberto Giacometti: Sculpture, Painting, Drawing* (London: Thames and Hudson, 1972), 283.

6. This interpretation of Giacometti's accident derives from Jean-Paul Sartre, *The Words*, trans. Bernard Frechtman (New York: Random House, 1981), 232–33. "'So,' he thought to himself, 'I wasn't meant to be a sculptor, nor even to live. I wasn't meant for anything.' What thrilled him was the menacing order of causes that was suddenly unmasked and the act of staring with the petrifying gaze of a cataclysm at the lights of the city, at human beings, at his own body lying flat in the mud." Giacometti quarreled with Sartre over inaccuracies in his account of the accident (and James Lord's biography of the sculptor does not refer to Sartre's version). Thus, this text exemplifies both the fascination with interpreting accidental events and the subjective nature of the individual response.

BIBLIOGRAPHY

PRIMARY TEXTS

Books

Aquinas, Thomas. *In Perihermeneias.* In *The Philosophy of Thomas Aquinas,* trans. and ed. Christopher Martin. London: Routledge, 1988.

Aquinas, Thomas. *Summa contra gentiles.* Trans. Charles J. O'Neill. Garden City, NY: Doubleday, 1957.

Aquinas, Thomas. *Summa theologiae.* Ed. Thomas Gilby, O.P. 60 vols. London: Blackfriars; New York: McGraw-Hill, 1964–80.

Aristotle. *The Complete Works of Aristotle.* Ed. Jonathan Barnes. Princeton: Princeton University Press, 1995.

Aristotle. *Nicomachean Ethics.* Ed. Terence Irwin. 2nd ed. Indianapolis: Hackett, 1999.

Augustine. *Confessions.* Trans. Henry Chadwick. Oxford: Oxford University Press, 1992.

Austen, Jane. *Persuasion.* Ed. John Davie. Oxford: Oxford University Press, 1971.

Austen, Jane. *Pride and Prejudice.* Ed. James Kinsley. Oxford: Oxford University Press, 1980.

Austen, Jane. *Selected Letters, 1796–1817.* Ed. R. W. Chapman. Oxford: Oxford University Press, 1985.

Bacon, Francis. *The New Organon.* Ed. Lisa Jardine and Michael Silverthorne. Cambridge: Cambridge University Press, 2000.

Boethius. *The Consolation of Philosophy.* Trans. V. E. Watts. New York: Penguin, 1969. Rev. ed., 1999.

Breton, André. "As in a Wood." In *The Shadow and Its Shadow: Surrealist Writing on the Cinema,* trans. Paul Hammond, ed. Paul Hammond. Edinburgh: Polygon, 1991.

Breton, André. *Mad Love.* Trans. Mary Ann Caws. Lincoln: University of Nebraska Press, 1987.

Breton, André. *Manifesto of Surrealism.* In *Manifestoes of Surrealism,* trans. Richard Seaver and Helen R. Lane. Ann Arbor: University of Michigan Press, 1969.

Breton, André. *Nadja.* Trans. Richard Howard. New York: Grove Press, 1960.

Calvin, John. *Institutes of the Christian Religion.* Ed. John T. McNeill, trans. Ford Lewis Battles. Vol. 1. London: S. C. M. P., 1961.

Coleridge, Samuel Taylor. *Collected Letters.* Ed. Earle Leslie Griggs. 6 vols. Oxford: Clarendon Press, 1956–71.

Dante Alighieri. *The Inferno.* Trans. Allen Mandelbaum. Berkeley: University of California Press, 1980.

Dante Alighieri. *The Divine Comedy.* Trans. Charles S.Singleton. Princeton: Princeton University Press, 1971–75.

Dante Alighieri. *The Divine Comedy.* Trans. John D. Sinclair. London: Bodley Head, 1958.

Darwin, Charles. *On the Origin of Species by Means of Natural Selection.* Ed. Joseph Carroll. Peterborough: Broadview, 2003.

Defoe, Daniel. *An Essay on Projects.* In *Social Reform,* vol. 8 of *Political and Economic Writings of Daniel Defoe,* ed. W. R. Owens and P. N. Furbank, 27–142. London: Pickering and Chatto, 2000.

Defoe, Daniel. *The Life and Strange Surprising Adventures of Robinson Crusoe.* Ed. Michael Shinagel. New York: Norton, 1975.

Descartes, René. *The Philosophical Writings of Descartes.* Trans. John Cottingham. Cambridge: Cambridge University Press, 1985.

Diderot, Denis. *Encyclopédie.* Vol. 14. Paris: Garnier, 1876.

Diderot, Denis. *Jacques le fataliste.* Trans. David Coward. Oxford: Oxford University Press, 1999.

Eliot, George. *Daniel Deronda.* Ed. Graham Handley. Oxford: Clarendon Press, 1984.

Eliot, George. *George Eliot: Selected Essays, Poems and Other Writings.* Ed. A. S. Byatt and Nicholas Warren. London: Penguin, 1990.

Eliot, George. *The George Eliot Letters.* Ed. Gordon S. Haight. New Haven: Yale University Press, 1955.

Fielding, Henry. *The History of Tom Jones a Foundling.* Ed. Fredson Bowers. Middletown: Wesleyan University Press, 1975.

Fielding, Henry. *Joseph Andrews.* Ed. Martin C. Battestin. Middletown: Wesleyan University Press, 1967.

Fielding, Henry. *Miscellanies by Henry Fielding, Esq.* Ed. Henry Knight Miller. Vol. 1. Middletown: Wesleyan University Press, 1972.

Fontenelle, Bernard. *Entretiens sur la pluralité des mondes.* Ed. Robert Shackleton. Oxford: Clarendon Press, 1955.

Freud, Sigmund. *The Complete Letters of Sigmund Freud to Wilhelm Fliess.* Trans. Jeffrey Moussaieff Masson. Cambridge, MA: Harvard University Press, Belknap Press, 1985.

Freud, Sigmund. *Dora: An Analysis of a Case of Hysteria.* New York: Macmillan, 1963.

Freud, Sigmund. *The Psychopathology of Everyday Life.* Vol. 6 of *The Standard Edition of the Complete Psychological Works,* 24 vols., ed. James Strachey. London: Hogarth Press, 1953–74.

Hartley, David. *Observations on Man, His Frame, His Duty and His Expectations.* London, 1749. Facsimile, Delmar, NY: Scholars' Facsimiles and Reprints, 1976.

Hegel, Georg Wilhelm Friedrich. *Phenomenology of Spirit.* Trans. A. V. Miller. Oxford: Oxford University Press, 1977.

Hume, David. *An Enquiry Concerning Human Understanding.* Ed. Tom L. Beauchamp. Oxford: Clarendon Press, 2000.

Jarman, Derek. *Chroma: A Book of Colour—June '93.* London: Century, 1994.

Kant, Immanuel. *Critique of Practical Reason.* Trans. Lewis White Beck. New York: Macmillan, 1993.

Kant, Immanuel. *Critique of Pure Reason.* Trans. Norman Kemp Smith. London: Macmillan, 1929.

Locke, John. *An Essay Concerning Human Understanding.* Ed. Peter H. Nidditch. Oxford: Clarendon Press, 1979.

Locke, John. *Two Treatises of Government.* Ed. Peter Laslett. Cambridge: Cambridge University Press, 1960.

Luther, Martin. "Letter to the Christians at Strassbourg." Trans. and ed. Conrad Bergendoff. In *Luther's Works*, 40:68. Philadelphia: Muhlenberg, 1958.

Luther, Martin. *A Prelude to the Babylonian Captivity of the Church.* Trans. A. T. W. Steinhäuser. Rev. Frederick C. Ahrens and Abdel Ross Wentz. In *Luther's Works*, 36:31. Philadelphia: Muhlenberg, 1959.

Mirandola, Pico della. *Of Being and Unity.* Trans. Victor M. Hamm. Milwaukee: Marquette University Press, 1943.

Montaigne, Michel de. *The Complete Essays of Montaigne.* Trans. and ed. Donald Frame. Stanford: Stanford University Press, 1957.

Musil, Robert. *The Man without Qualities.* Trans. Sophie Wilkins. 2 vols. New York: Alfred A. Knopf, 1995.

Musil, Robert. *Precision and Soul: Essays and Addresses.* Ed. and trans. Burton Pike and David S. Luft. Chicago: University of Chicago Press, 1990.

Newton, Isaac. *The Principia: Mathematical Principles of Natural Philosophy.* Trans. I. Bernard Cohen and Anne Whitman. Berkeley: University of California Press, 1999.

Pascal, Blaise. *Pensées.* Trans. A. J. Krailsheimer. New York: Penguin, 1966; rev. ed., 1995.

Pascal, Blaise. *Pascal Selections.* Trans. and ed. Richard H. Popkin. New York: Scribner/Macmillan, 1989.

Plotinus. *The Enneads.* Trans. Stephen MacKenna. Ed. B. S. Page. 2nd ed. London: Faber and Faber, 1957.

Porphyry. "On the Life of Plotinus and the Arrangement of his Work." In *The Enneads*, by Plotinus, trans. Stephen MacKenna. New York: Pantheon, 1957.

Quetelet, Lambert Adolphe. *A Treatise on Man and the Development of His Faculties.* Edinburgh: W. and R. Chambers, 1842.

Rousseau, Jean-Jacques. "Art du jouir et autres fragments." In *Oeuvres complètes*, 1:1173–77. Paris: Gallimard, 1959.

Jean-Jacques Rousseau. "Fragments politiques." In *Oeuvres complètes*, 3:474. Paris: Gallimard, 1959.

Rousseau, Jean-Jacques. *The Collected Writings of Rousseau.* Trans. Christopher Kelly, ed. Christopher Kelly, Roger D. Masters, and Peter G. Stillman. 11 vols. Hanover: University Press of New England, 1990–.

Shakespeare, William. *Hamlet.* Ed. Harold Jenkins. London: Routledge, 1990.

Sidney, Sir Philip. *Defence of Poetry.* Ed. J. A. van Dorsten. Oxford: Oxford University Press, 1966.

Smollett, Tobias. *The Adventures of Ferdinand Count Fathom.* Ed. O. M. Brack, Jr. Athens: University of Georgia Press, 1988.

Sophocles. *King Oedipus.* Trans. William Butler Yeats. In *Greek Plays in Modern Translation*, ed. Dudley Fitts. New York: Dial, 1949.

Sterne, Laurence. *The Life and Opinions of Tristram Shandy, Gentleman.* Vols. 1–3 of *The Florida Edition of the Works of Laurence Sterne*, ed. Melvyn New and Joan New. Gainesville: University of Florida Press, 1978–84.

Vasari, Giorgio. *Lives of the Most Eminent Painters Sculptors and Architects.* Trans. Gaston du C. de Vere. New York: Knopf, 1996.

Wittgenstein, Ludwig. *Philosophical Investigations.* Trans. G. E. M. Anscombe. New York: Macmillan, 1958.

Wittgenstein, Ludwig. *Remarks on Colour.* Trans. Linda L. McAlister and Margaret Schättle, ed. G. E. M. Anscombe. Berkeley: University of California Press, 1977.

Wittgenstein, Ludwig. *Zettel.* Trans. G. E. M. Anscombe, ed. G. E. M. Anscombe and G. H. von Wright. Berkeley: University of California Press, 1967.

Wordsworth, William. *Lyrical Ballads and Other Poems, 1797–1800.* Ed. James Butler and Karen Green. Ithaca: Cornell University Press, 1992.

Wordsworth, William. *The Prelude, 1798–1799.* Ed. Stephen Parrish. Ithaca: Cornell University Press, 1977.

Wordsworth, William. *The Prose Works of William Wordsworth.* Ed. W. J. B. Owen and Jane Worthington Smyser. Oxford: Clarendon Press, 1974.

Wordsworth, William. *"The Ruined Cottage" and "The Pedlar."* Ed. James Butler. Ithaca: Cornell University Press, 1979.

Zwingli, Huldrych. *On the Lord's Supper: Zwingli and Bullinger.* Trans. Rev. G. W. Bromiley. Philadelphia: Westminster, 1953.

Zwingli, Huldrych. *Writings.* Ed. E. J. Furcha and H. Wayne Pipkin. Allison Park, PA: Pickwick Publications, 1984.

Films

Alien. Dir. Ridley Scott. 20th Century Fox, 1979.

Alien Resurrection. Dir. David Fincher. 20th Century Fox, 1992.

Aliens. Dir. James Cameron. 20th Century Fox, 1986.

Alien³. Dir. Jean-Pierre Jeunet. 20th Century Fox, 1997.

Angelic Conversation. Dir. Derek Jarman. British Film Institute, 1985.

Blue. Dir. Derek Jarman. Zeitgeist Films, 1993.

Caravaggio. Dir. Derek Jarman. British Film Institute, 1986.

Edward II. Dir. Derek Jarman. British Film Institute, 1991.

Sebastiane. Dir. Derek Jarman. Barcino Films, 1976.

Sherlock, Jr. Dir. Buster Keaton. MGM, 1923.

War Requiem. Dir. Derek Jarman. Anglo International, 1989.

Wittgenstein. Dir. Derek Jarman. British Film Institute, 1992.

SECONDARY WORKS CITED

Aarsleff, Hans. *From Locke to Saussure: Essays on the Study of Language and Intellectual History.* Minneapolis: University of Minnesota Press, 1982.

Abecassis, Jack I. "'Des cannibals' et la logique de la représentation de l'altérité." In *Montaigne et le Nouveau Monde: Actes du Colloque de Paris 18–20 Mai 1992,* ed. Claude Blum, Marie-Luce Demonet, and André Tournon, 195–205. Saint-Pierre-du-Mont: Éditions InterUniversitaires, 1994.

Ackrill, J. L. *Aristotle the Philosopher.* Oxford: Oxford University Press, 1981.

Armour, Leslie. *"Infini Rien": Pascal's Wager and the Human Paradox.* Journal of the History of Philosophy Monograph Series. Carbondale: Southern Illinois University Press, 1993.

Ashcraft, Richard. "John Locke's Library: Portrait of an Intellectual." In *A Locke Miscellany,* ed. Jean S. Yolton. Bristol: Thoemmes, 1990.

Ashton, T. S. *An Economic History of England: The Eighteenth Century*. London: Methuen, 1955.

Auerbach, Eric. *Mimesis: The Representation of Reality in Western Literature*. Trans. Willard R. Trask. Princeton: Princeton University Press, 1953.

Ayers, Michael. "Substance and Mode." In *Locke: Epistemology and Ontology*, vol. 2. London: Routledge, 1991.

Badiou, Alain. *Being and Event*. Trans. Oliver Feltham. London: Continuum, 2003.

Badiou, Alain. *Infinite Thought: Truth and the Return to Philosophy*. Trans. and ed. Oliver Feltham and Justin Clemens. London: Continuum, [2003].

Balakian, Anna. *André Breton: Magus of Surrealism*. New York: Oxford University Press, 1971.

Barnes, Jonathan. *Aristotle*. Oxford: Oxford University Press, 2000.

Barthes, Roland. *Camera Lucida*. Trans. Richard Howard. New York: Hill and Wang, 1981.

Baudrillard, Jean. *The Vital Illusion*. Ed. Julia Witwer. New York: Columbia University Press, 2000.

Beer, Gillian. *Darwin's Plots: Evolutionary Narrative in Darwin, George Eliot, and Nineteenth-Century Fiction*. London: Routledge and Kegan Paul, 1983.

Bell, David F. *Circumstances: Chance in the Literary Text*. Lincoln: University of Nebraska Press, 1993.

Benedict, Barbara M. "Sensibility by the Numbers: Austen's Work as Regency Popular Fiction." In *Janeites: Austen's Disciples and Devotees*, ed. Deidre Lynch, 63–86. Princeton: Princeton University Press, 2000.

Bernard, André, and Claude Gauteur, eds. *Art of Cinema*. Trans. Robin Buss. New York: Marion Boyars, 1992.

Bernstein, Michael André. *Five Portraits: Modernity and the Imagination in Twentieth-Century German Writing*. Evanston: Northwestern University Press, 2000.

Birn, Raymond. "Malesherbes and the Call for a Free Press." In *Revolution in Print*, ed. Robert Darnton and Daniel Roche, 50–66. Berkeley: University of California Press, 1989.

Bishop, Jonathan. "Wordsworth and the 'Spots of Time.'" *ELH* 26 (March 1959): 45–65.

Bobik, Joseph. *Aquinas on Matter and Form and the Elements*. Notre Dame: University of Notre Dame Press, 1998.

Bohrer, Karl Heinz. *Suddenness: On the Moment of Aesthetic Appearance*. Trans. Ruth Crowley. New York: Columbia University Press, 1994.

Bolton, Martha Brandt. "The Real Molyneux Question and the Basis of Locke's Answer." In *Locke's Philosophy: Content and Context*, ed. G. A. J. Rogers, 75–99. Oxford: Clarendon Press, 1994.

Bonitz, Hermann. *Index Aristotelicus*. 2nd ed. Graz: Akademische Druck, 1955.

Bossy, John. "The Mass as a Social Institution, 1200–1700." *Past and Present* 100 (1983): 29–61.

Bowlin, John. *Contingency and Fortune in Aquinas's Ethics*. Cambridge: Cambridge University Press, 1999.

Boyle, Leonard E. *The Setting of the "Summa theologiae" of Saint Thomas*. Toronto: Pontifical Institute of Mediaeval Studies, 1982.

Bremner, Geoffrey. *Order and Chance: The Pattern of Diderot's Thought*. Cambridge: Cambridge University Press, 1983.

Bronfen, Elisabeth. *The Knotted Subject: Hysteria and Its Discontents*. Princeton: Princeton University Press, 1998.

Brown, Homer O. "The Displaced Self in the Novels of Daniel Defoe." *ELH* 38 (1971): 562–90.

Budd, Malcolm. "Delight in the Natural World: Kant on the Aesthetic Appreciation of Nature." Pt. 1, "Natural Beauty"; pt. 2, "Natural Beauty and Morality"; pt. 3, "The Sublime in Nature." *British Journal of Aesthetics* 38, no. 1 (January 1998): 1–18; 38, no. 2 (April 1998):117–26; 38, no. 3 (July 1998): 233–52.

Burnyeat, Myles. *A Map of Metaphysics Zeta*. Pittsburgh: Mathesis Publications, 2001.

Burt, E. S. "Mapping City Walks: The Topography of Memory in Rousseau's Second and Seventh Promenades." *Yale French Studies* 74 (1988): 231–47.

Bynum, Caroline Walker. *Metamorphosis and Identity*. New York: Zone Books, 2001.

Bynum, Caroline Walker. *The Resurrection of the Body*. New York: Columbia University Press, 1995.

Cameron, Euan. *The European Reformation*. Oxford: Clarendon Press, 1991.

Cantor, Paul A. "The Class Act: *Persuasion* and the Lingering Death of the Aristocracy." *Philosophy and Literature* 28 (1999): 127–37.

Cardinal, Roger. Breton, *"Nadja."* London: Grant and Cutler, 1986.

Carriero, John P. "The Second Meditation and the Essence of the Mind." In *Essays on Descartes' "Meditations,"* ed. Amélie Oksenberg Rorty, 199–221. Berkeley: University of California Press, 1986.

Carruthers, Mary J. *The Book of Memory: A Study of Memory in Medieval Culture*. Cambridge: Cambridge University Press, 1990.

Caruth, Cathy. *Empirical Truths and Critical Fictions: Locke, Wordsworth, Kant, Freud*. Baltimore: Johns Hopkins University Press, 1991.

Cascardi, Anthony J. *The Subject of Modernity*. Cambridge: Cambridge University Press, 1992.

Cassirer, Ernst. *Kant's Life and Thought*. Trans. James Haden. New Haven: Yale University Press, 1981.

Cefalu, Paul. *Moral Identity in Early Modern English Literature*. Cambridge: Cambridge University Press, 2004.

Censer, Jack R. *The French Press in the Age of Enlightenment*. London: Routledge, 1994.

Chabut, Marie-Hélène. "Diderot's *Jacques le Fataliste et son Maître:* Ex-Centricity and the 'Novel.'" *Eighteenth-Century Fiction* 2, no. 1 (October 1989): 53–64.

Chase, Cynthia. *Decomposing Figures: Rhetorical Readings in the Romantic Tradition*. Baltimore: Johns Hopkins University Press, 1986.

Chénieux-Gendron, Jacqueline. *Surrealism*. Trans. Vivian Folkenflik. New York: Columbia University Press, 1990.

Childs, Elizabeth C. "Habits of the Eye: Degas, Photography, and Modes of Vision." In *The Artist and Camera: Degas to Picasso*, ed. Dorothy Kosinski, 70–87. New Haven: Yale University Press, 1999.

Clark, Lorrie. "Transfiguring the Romantic Sublime in *Persuasion*." In *Jane Austen's Business: Her World and Her Profession*, ed. Juliet McMaster and Bruce Stovel, 30–41. New York: St. Martin's Press, 1996.

Code, Alan. "Aristotle: Essence and Accident." In *Philosophical Grounds of Rationality*, ed. R. Grandy and R. Warner, 411–13. Oxford: Clarendon Press, 1986.

Cohn, Robert Greer. *Mallarmé's "Un coup de dés": An Exegesis*. New York: AMS Press, 1980.

Coleman, Janet. *Ancient and Medieval Memories: Studies in the Reconstruction of the Past.* Cambridge: Cambridge University Press, 1992.

Conroy, Peter V., Jr. "Jacques's Fatal Freedom." *Eighteenth-Century Fiction* 2, no. 4 (July 1990): 309–26.

Copeland, Edward. "Money." In *Cambridge Companion to Jane Austen,* ed. Edward Copeland and Juliet McMaster, 131–48. Cambridge: Cambridge University Press, 1997.

Courcelle, Pierre. *Recherches sur les "Confessions" de saint Augustin.* Paris: De Boccard, 1950.

Crocker, Lester G. *Diderot's Chaotic Order: Approach to Synthesis.* Princeton: Princeton University Press, 1974.

Curtius, E. R. *European Literature and the Latin Middle Ages.* Trans. Willard Trask. New York: Bollingen, 1953.

Daniel, Malcolm. *Edgar Degas, Photographer.* New York: Metropolitan Museum of Art, 1998.

Darnton, Robert. *George Washington's False Teeth: An Unconventional Guide to the Eighteenth Century.* New York: W. W. Norton, 2003.

Darnton, Robert. *The Great Cat Massacre and Other Episodes in French Cultural History.* New York: Vintage, 1985.

Darnton, Robert, and Daniel Roche, eds. *Revolution in Print.* Berkeley: University of California Press, 1989.

Daston, Lorraine. *Classical Probability in the Enlightenment.* Princeton: Princeton University Press, 1988.

David, F. N. *Games, Gods and Gambling: The Origins and History of Probability and Statistical Ideas from the Earliest Times to the Newtonian Era.* New York: Hafner, 1962.

Davidson, Arnold I. "Ethics as Ascetics: Foucault, the History of Ethics, and Ancient Thought." In *Foucault and the Writing of History,* ed. Jan Ellen Goldstein, 63–80. Oxford: Basil Blackwell, 1994.

Dear, Peter. *Discipline and Experience: The Mathematical Way in the Scientific Revolution.* Chicago: University of Chicago Press, 1995.

Dear, Peter. "A Mechanical Microcosm: Bodily Passions, Good Manners, and Cartesian Mechanism." In *Science Incarnate: Historical Embodiments of Natural Knowledge,* ed. Christopher Lawrence and Steven Shapin, 51–82. Chicago: University of Chicago Press, 1998.

Debus, Allen G. *Man and Nature in the Renaissance.* Cambridge: Cambridge University Press, 1978.

de Man, Paul. "Autobiography as De-Facement." In *The Rhetoric of Romanticism,* 67–81. New York: Columbia University Press, 1984.

de Man, Paul. "The Epistemology of Metaphor." *Critical Inquiry* (Autumn 1978): 13–30. Reprinted in *On Metaphor,* ed. Sheldon Sacks. Chicago: Chicago University Press, 1979.

Derrida, Jacques. *Of Grammatology.* Trans. Gayatri Chakravorty Spivak. Baltimore: Johns Hopkins University Press, 1998.

Des Chene, Dennis. *Physiologia: Natural Philosophy in Late Aristotelian and Cartesian Thought.* Ithaca: Cornell University Press, 1996.

Des Chene, Dennis. *Spirits and Clocks: Machine and Organism in Descartes.* Ithaca: Cornell University Press, 2001.

Dillon, Steven. *Derek Jarman and the Lyric Film: The Mirror and the Sea.* Austin: University of Texas Press, 2004.

Dobbs, Betty Jo Teeter. *The Janus Faces of Genius: The Role of Alchemy in Newton's Thought.* Cambridge: Cambridge University Press, 1991.

Dod, Bernard. "Aristoteles Latinus." In *The Cambridge History of Later Medieval Philosophy: From the Rediscovery of Aristotle to the Disintegration of Scholasticism,* ed. Norman Kretzmann, Anthony Kenny, and Jan Pinborg, 45–79. Cambridge: Cambridge University Press, 1982.

Doody, Margaret Anne. "Self, Love, and Memory." *Eighteenth-Century Fiction* 14, no.1 (October 2001): 67–94, 295–99.

Downie, J. A. "The Making of the English Novel." *Eighteenth-Century Fiction* 9, no. 3 (1997): 249–66.

Draaisma, Douwe. *Metaphors of Memory: A History of Ideas about the Mind.* Trans. Paul Vincent. Cambridge: Cambridge University Press, 2000.

Durham, Frank, and Robert D. Purrington, eds. *Some Truer Method: Reflections on the Heritage of Newton.* New York: Columbia University Press, 1990.

Durling, Robert. "Deceit and Digestion in the Belly of Hell." In *Allegory and Representation: Selected Papers from the English Institute, 1979–80,* ed. Stephen Greenblatt, 61–93. Baltimore: Johns Hopkins University Press, 1981.

Eagleton, Terry. *The English Novel: An Introduction.* London: Blackwell, 2005.

Eden, Kathy. *Poetic and Legal Fiction in the Aristotelian Tradition.* Princeton: Princeton University Press, 1986.

Elden, Stuart. "Reading Genealogy as Historical Ontology." In *Foucault and Heidegger: Critical Encounters,* ed. Alan Milchman and Alan Rosenberg, 187–205. Minneapolis: University of Minnesota Press, 2003.

Elders, Leo J. *The Metaphysics of Being of St. Thomas Aquinas in a Historical Perspective.* Leiden: E. J. Brill, 1993.

Ellis, David. *Wordsworth, Freud and the Spots of Time.* Cambridge: Cambridge University Press, 1985.

Feldman, David. *Englishmen and Jews: Social Relations and Political Culture, 1840–1914.* New Haven: Yale University Press, 1994.

Flanders, Todd R. "Rousseau's Adventure with Robinson Crusoe." *Interpretation* 24, no. 3 (Spring 1997): 319–37.

Foster, Kenelm. *The Two Dantes and Other Studies.* Berkeley: University of California Press, 1977.

Foucault, Michel. "Nietzsche, Genealogy, History." Trans. Donald F. Brouchard and Sherry Simon. In *Aesthetics, Method, and Epistemology,* ed. James D. Faubion, trans. Robert Hurley et al., 369–91. New York: New Press, 1998.

Foucault. Michel. "On the Genealogy of Ethics: An Overview of Work in Progress." In *Ethics: Subjectivity and Truth,* ed. Paul Rabinow, trans. Robert Hurley et al., 253–80. New York: New Press, 1997.

Foucault, Michel. *The Order of Things: An Archaeology of the Human Sciences.* New York: Vintage, 1994.

Foucault, Michel. "What Is Enlightenment?" In *Ethics: Subjectivity and Truth,* ed. Paul Rabinow, trans. Robert Hurley et al., 303–19. New York: New Press, 1997.

France, Peter. "The Commerce of the Self." In *Representations of the Self,* Comparative Criticism 12, ed. E. S. Shaffer, 39–56. Cambridge: Cambridge University Press, 1990.

Franklin, James. *The Science of Conjecture: Evidence and Probability before Pascal.* Baltimore: Johns Hopkins University Press, 2001.

Freccero, John. "Bestial Sign and Bread of Angels: Inferno 32–34." *Yale Italian Studies* 1, no. 1 (Winter 1979): 152–66.

Freccero, John. "Introduction to *Inferno*." In *Cambridge Companion to Dante*, ed. Rachel Jacoff, 181–87. Cambridge: Cambridge University Press, 1993.

Frede, Dorothea. "Necessity, Chance, and 'What Happens for the Most Part' in Aristotle's *Poetics*." In *Essays on Aristotle's "Poetics,"* ed. Amélie Oksenberg Rorty, 197–219. Princeton: Princeton University Press, 1992.

Frede, Michael. *Essays in Ancient Philosophy*. Minneapolis: University of Minnesota Press, 1987.

Frede, Michael, and David Charles. *Aristotle's Metaphysics Lambda: Symposium Aristotelicum*. Oxford: Oxford University Press, 2000.

Fredman, Alice. *Diderot and Sterne*. New York: Columbia University Press, 1955.

Freedberg, Sydney. *Painting of the High Renaissance in Rome and Florence*. Cambridge, MA: Harvard University Press, 1961.

Funkenstein, Amos. *Theology and the Scientific Imagination: From the Middle Ages to the Seventeenth Century*. Princeton: Princeton University Press, 1986.

Gallagher, Catherine, and Stephen Greenblatt. *Practicing New Historicism*. Chicago: University of Chicago Press, 1997.

Gay, Peter. *Freud: A Life for Our Time*. New York: Doubleday, 1988.

Gigerenzer, Gerd, Lorraine Daston, et al. *The Empire of Chance: How Probability Changed Science and Everyday Life*. Cambridge: Cambridge University Press, 1989.

Gill, Stephen. *William Wordsworth: A Life*. Oxford: Oxford University Press, 1990.

Grace, Eve. "The Restlessness of 'Being': Rousseau's Protean Sentiment of Existence." *History of European Ideas* 272 (2001): 133–51.

Graver, Suzanne. *George Eliot and Community: A Study in Social Theory and Fictional Form*. Berkeley: University of California Press, 1984.

Greenblatt, Stephen. *Hamlet in Purgatory*. Princeton: Princeton University Press, 2001.

Greenblatt, Stephen. *Renaissance Self-Fashioning*. Chicago: University of Chicago Press, 1980.

Guillory, John. *Cultural Capital: The Problem of Literary Canon Formation*. Chicago: University of Chicago Press, 1993.

Guillory, John. "'To Please the Wiser Sort': Violence and Philosophy in Hamlet." In *Historicism, Psychoanalysis, and Early Modern Culture*, ed. Carla Mazzio and Trevor Douglas, 82–109. New York: Routledge, 2000.

Guyer, Paul. "Transcendental Deduction of the Categories." In *The Cambridge Companion to Kant*, ed. Paul Guyer, 123–60. Cambridge: Cambridge University Press, 1992.

Hacking, Ian. *Emergence of Probability: A Philosophical Study of Early Ideas about Probability, Induction and Statistical Inference*. Cambridge: Cambridge University Press, 1984.

Hacking, Ian. *Historical Ontology*. Cambridge, MA: Harvard University Press, 2002.

Hacking, Ian. "The Logic of Pascal's Wager." In *Gambling on God: Essays on Pascal's Wager*, ed. Jeff Jordan, 21–29. Lanham, MD: Rowman and Littlefield, 1994.

Hacking, Ian. "Was There a Probabilistic Revolution 1800–1930?" In *The Probabilistic Revolution*, ed. Lorenz Krüger, Lorraine Daston, and Michael Heidelberger, 1:45–55. Cambridge, MA: MIT Press, 1987.

Hacking, Ian. *The Taming of Chance*. Cambridge: Cambridge University Press, 1990.

Hadot, Pierre. *Philosophy as a Way of Life: Spiritual Exercises from Socrates to Foucault*. Trans. Michael Chase, ed. Arnold I. Davidson. Oxford: Basil Blackwell, 1995.

Hadot, Pierre. *What Is Ancient Philosophy?* Trans. Michael Chase. Cambridge, MA: Harvard University Press, 2002.

Halliwell, Stephen. *Aristotle's "Poetics."* Chicago: University of Chicago Press, 1998.

Hamilton, Paul. *Metaromanticism: Aesthetics, Literature, Theory.* Chicago: University of Chicago Press, 2003.

Hammond, Anne. "Naturalistic Vision and Symbolist Image: The Pictorial Impulse." In *The New History of Photography,* ed. Michel Frizot, 293–309. Cologne: Könemann, 1998.

Hankinson, R. James. *Cause and Explanation in Ancient Greek Thought.* Oxford: Clarendon Press, 1998.

Harris, Ian. "The Politics of Christianity." In *Locke's Philosophy,* ed. G. A. J. Rogers, 197–215. Oxford: Clarendon Press, 1994.

Harrison, Bernard. *Henry Fielding's "Tom Jones": The Novelist as Moral Philosopher.* London: Sussex University, 1975.

Hartman, Geoffrey. *The Unremarkable Wordsworth.* Minneapolis: University of Minnesota Press, 1987.

Hartman, Geoffrey. *Wordsworth's Poetry, 1787–1814.* New Haven: Yale University Press, 1964.

Haskins, Charles Homer. *The Renaissance of the Twelfth Century.* Cambridge, MA: Harvard University Press, 1927.

Hatfield, Gary. "Senses and the Fleshless Eye: The Meditations as Cognitive Exercises." In *Essays on Descartes' "Meditations,"* ed. Amélie Oksenberg Rorty, 45–79. Berkeley: University of California Press, 1986.

Heidegger, Martin. *The Question Concerning Technology and Other Essays.* Trans. and ed. William Lovitt. New York: Harper and Row, 1977.

Heinaman, Robert. "Aristotle on Accidents." *Journal of the History of Philosophy* 23, no. 3 (July 1985): 311–24.

Heinzelman, Kurt. "The Cult of Domesticity: Dorothy and William Wordsworth at Grasmere." In *Romanticism and Feminism,* ed. Anne K. Mellor, 52–78. Bloomington: University of Indiana Press, 1988.

Heninger, S. K., Jr. *Touches of Sweet Harmony: Pythagorean Cosmology and Renaissance Poetics.* San Marino, CA: Huntington Library, 1974.

Hentzel, Gary. "'An Itch of Gaming': The South Sea Bubble and the Novels of Daniel Defoe." *Eighteenth-Century Life* 17, no. 1 (February 1993): 32–45.

Herzman, Ronald B. "Cannibalism and Communion in Inferno XXXIII." *Dante Studies* 98 (1980): 53–78.

Hill, James, and J. R. Milton. "The Epitome (*Abrégé*) of Locke's Essay." In *The Philosophy of John Locke: New Perspectives,* ed. Peter Anstey, 3–25. London: Routledge, 2003.

Hoffmann, George. "Anatomy of the Mass: Montaigne's 'Cannibals.'" *PMLA* 117, no. 2 (March 2002): 207–21.

Hohl, Reinhold. *Alberto Giacometti: Sculpture, Painting, Drawing.* London: Thames and Hudson, 1972.

Hollander, Robert. *Allegory in Dante's Commedia.* Princeton: Princeton University Press, 1969.

Huhn, Thomas. "The Kantian Sublime and the Nostalgia for Violence." *Journal of Aesthetics and Art Criticism* 53, no. 3 (Summer 1995): 269–75.

Hunter, J. Paul. *Before Novels: The Cultural Contexts of Eighteenth-Century English Fiction.* New York: W. W. Norton, 1990.

Hunter, J. Paul. *The Reluctant Pilgrim: Defoe's Emblematic Method and Quest for Form in "Robinson Crusoe."* Baltimore: Johns Hopkins University Press, 1966.

Husain, Martha. *Ontology and the Art of Tragedy: An Approach to Aristotle's Poetics.* Albany: State University of New York Press, 2002.

Iorio, Dominick A. *The Aristotelianisms of Renaissance Italy.* Lewiston: Edwin Mellen Press, 1991.

Iser, Wolfgang. *Laurence Sterne: "Tristram Shandy."* Trans. David Henry Wilson. Cambridge: Cambridge University Press, 1988.

Jacobus, Mary. *Tradition and Experiment in Wordsworth's Lyrical Ballads (1798).* Oxford: Clarendon Press, 1976.

Jacoff, Rachel. "The Body in the *Commedia.*" In *Sparks and Seeds: Medieval Literature and Its Afterlife: Essays in Honor of John Freccero,* Binghamton Medieval and Early Modern Studies 2, ed. Dana E. Stewart and Alison Cornish, 119–37. Turnhout: Brepols, 2000.

Jacoff, Rachel. "The Hermeneutics of Hunger." In *Speaking Images: Essays in Honor of V. A. Kolve,* ed. Robert F. Yeager and Charlotte C. Morse, 95–110. Asheville, NC: Pegasus Press, 2000.

James, Susan. *Passion and Action: The Emotions in Seventeenth-Century Philosophy.* Oxford: Clarendon Press, 1997.

Jankins, John I. *Knowledge and Faith in Thomas Aquinas.* Cambridge: Cambridge University Press, 1997.

Jardine, Nicholas. "Epistemology of the Sciences." In *The Cambridge History of Renaissance Philosophy,* ed. Quentin Skinner and Eckhard Kessler, 685–711. Cambridge: Cambridge University Press, 1988.

Jones, Darryl. *Critical Issues: Jane Austen.* Houndmills: Palgrave, 2004.

Jones, Matthew L. *The Good Life in the Scientific Revolution: Descartes, Pascal, Leibniz, and the Cultivation of Virtue.* Chicago: University of Chicago Press, 2006.

Jonsson, Stefan. *Subject without Nation: Robert Musil and the History of Modern Identity.* Durham: Duke University Press, 2000.

Joost-Gaugier, Christiane. *Raphael's Stanza della Segnatura: Meaning and Invention.* Cambridge: Cambridge University Press, 2002.

Jordan, Mark D. *Ordering Wisdom: The Hierarchy of Philosophical Discourses in Aquinas.* Notre Dame: University of Notre Dame Press, 1986.

Kael, Pauline. *Taking It All In.* New York: Holt, Rinehart, and Winston, 1984.

Kantorowicz, Ernst H. *The King's Two Bodies.* Princeton: Princeton University Press, 1957.

Kavanagh, Thomas. *Enlightenment and the Shadows of Chance: The Novel and the Culture of Gambling in Eighteenth-Century France.* Baltimore: Johns Hopkins University Press, 1993.

Kelly, George Armstrong. "A General Overview." In *The Cambridge Companion to Rousseau,* ed. Patrick Riley, 8–56. Cambridge: Cambridge University Press, 2001.

Kendall, Richard. *Degas: Beyond Impressionism.* London: National Gallery, 1996.

Kenney, John Peter. *Mystical Monotheism: A Study in Ancient Platonic Theology.* Providence: Brown University Press; Hanover: University Press of New England, 1991.

Kenny, Anthony. *Aquinas on Being.* Oxford: Clarendon Press, 2002.

Kenny, Anthony. *Essays on the Aristotelian Tradition.* Oxford: Clarendon Press, 2001.

Kernan, Alvin. *Samuel Johnson and the Impact of Print.* Princeton: Princeton University Press, 1987.

Keymer, Thomas. *Sterne, the Moderns, and the Novel*. Oxford: Oxford University Press, 2002.

Kilgour, Maggie. *From Communion to Cannibalism*. Princeton: Princeton University Press, 1990.

King, Amy M. *Bloom: The Botanical Vernacular in the English Novel*. Oxford: Oxford University Press, 2003.

King, Peter. "Aquinas on the Passions." In *Aquinas's Moral Theory: Essays in Honor of Norman Kretzmann*, ed. Scott MacDonald and Eleonore Stump, 101–32. Ithaca: Cornell University Press, 1999.

Klein, Herbert. "Identity Reclaimed: The Art of Being Tristram." In *Laurence Sterne in Modernism and Postmodernism*, ed. David Pierce and Peter de Voogd, 123–32. Amsterdam: Rodopi, 1996.

Klibansky, Raymond. "Plato's *Parmenides* in the Middle Ages and the Renaissance." *Mediaeval and Renaissance Studies* 1 (1941–43): 281–330.

Kosinski, Dorothy. "Vision and Visionaries: The Camera in the Context of Symbolist Aesthetics." In *Artist and Camera: Degas to Picasso*, ed. Dorothy Kosinski, 12–23. New Haven: Yale University Press, 1999.

Kripke, Saul A. *Naming and Necessity*. Cambridge, MA: Harvard University Press, 1972.

Kuhn, Bernhard. "Natural History and the History of the Self: Botany, Geology, and Autobiography in the Works of Goethe and Rousseau." *Colloquium Helveticum* 25 (1997): 41–62.

Lacan, Jacques. *Four Fundamental Concepts of Psycho-analysis*. Trans. Alan Sheridan. Ed. Jacques-Alain Miller. New York: W. W. Norton, 1981.

La Charité, Virginia A. *The Dynamics of Space: Mallarmé's "Un coup de dés jamais n'abolira le hasard."* Lexington, KY: French Forum, 1987.

Lamb, Jonathan. *Sterne's Fiction and the Double Principle*. Cambridge: Cambridge University Press, 1989.

Langan, Celeste. *Romantic Vagrancy: Wordsworth and the Simulation of Freedom*. Cambridge: Cambridge University Press, 1995.

Lanham, Richard A. *Tristram Shandy: The Games of Pleasure*. Berkeley: University of California Press, 1973.

Lansdown, Richard. "Transitional Objects: The Spots of Time in the Prelude of 1799." *Critical Review* 42 (2002): 14–34.

Law, Jules David. *The Rhetoric of Empiricism: Language and Perception from Locke to I. A. Richards*. Ithaca: Cornell University Press, 1993.

Lear, Jonathan. *Aristotle: The Desire to Understand*. New York: Cambridge University Press, 1998.

Lestringant, Frank. *Le Cannibale: Grandeur et décadence*. Paris: Perrin, 1994.

Lewes, George H. *Problems of Life and Mind*. 2nd ser., *The Physical Basis of Mind*. London: Trübner, 1879.

Lezra, Jacques. *Unspeakable Subjects: The Genealogy of the Event in Early Modern Europe*. Stanford: Stanford University Press, 1997.

Li, Hao. *Memory and History in George Eliot*. New York: St. Martin's Press, 2000.

Lindkens, René. *Dans l'espace de l'image*. Paris: Aux Amateurs de Livres, 1986.

Liu, Alan. *Wordsworth: The Sense of History*. Stanford: Stanford University Press, 1989.

Lloyd, A. C. "The Later Neoplatonists." In *The Cambridge History of Later Greek and Early Medieval Philosophy*, ed. A. H. Armstrong, 272–325. Cambridge: Cambridge University Press, 1967.

Lohr, C. H. "The Medieval Interpretation of Aristotle." In *The Cambridge History of Later*

Medieval Philosophy: From the Rediscovery of Aristotle to the Disintegration of Scholasticism, ed. Norman Kretzmann, Anthony Kenny, and Jan Pinborg, 80–98. Cambridge: Cambridge University Press, 1982.

Loy, John Robert. *Diderot's Determined Fatalist: A Critical Appreciation of "Jacques le fataliste."* New York: King's Crown Press, 1950.

Luft, David. *Robert Musil and the Crisis of European Culture, 1880–1942.* Los Angeles: University of California Press, 1980.

Lynch, Deirdre S. *The Economy of Character: Novels, Market Culture, and the Business of Inner Meaning.* Chicago: University of Chicago Press, 1998.

Mackie, John Leslie. *Problems from Locke.* Oxford: Clarendon Press, 1976.

MacLean, Kenneth. *John Locke and English Literature of the Eighteenth Century.* New Haven: Yale University Press, 1936.

Manier, Edward. *The Young Darwin and His Cultural Circle.* Doredrecht: D. Reidel, 1978.

Mann, Wolfgang-Ranier. *The Discovery of Things: Aristotle's Categories and Their Context.* Princeton: Princeton University Press, 2000.

Marin, Louis. *Portrait of the King.* Trans. Martha M. Houle. Minneapolis: University of Minnesota Press, 1988.

Martin, Christopher, ed. *The Philosophy of Thomas Aquinas.* London: Routledge, 1988.

Martin, Raymond, and John Barresi. *Naturalization of the Soul: Self and Personal Identity in the Eighteenth Century.* London: Routledge, 2000.

Matthews, Gareth B. "Accidental Unities." In *Language and Logos: Studies in Ancient Greek Philosophy Presented to G. E. L. Owen,* ed. Malcolm Schofield and Martha Craven Nussbaum, 223–40. Cambridge: Cambridge University Press, 1982.

Maus, Katharine Eisaman. *Inwardness and the Theater in the English Renaissance.* Chicago: University of Chicago Press, 1995.

Mazzotta, Guiseppe. *Dante, Poet of the Desert.* Princeton: Princeton University Press, 1979.

McInerny, R. *Boethius and Aquinas.* Washington: Catholic University of America Press, 1990.

McMaster, Juliet. "Class." In *Cambridge Companion to Jane Austen,* ed. Edward Copeland and Juliet McMaster, 115–30. Cambridge: Cambridge University Press, 1997.

Medalie, David. "'Only the Event Decides': Contingency in *Persuasion.*" *Essays in Criticism* 49, no. 2 (April 1999): 152–69.

Megged, Matti. *Dialogue in the Void: Beckett and Giacometti.* New York: Lumen Books, 1985.

Mellor, Anne K. *Romanticism and Gender.* New York: Routledge, 1993.

Melzer, Sara E. *Discourses of the Fall: A Study of Pascal's "Pensées."* Berkeley: University of California Press, 1986.

Merton, Robert K., and Elinor Barber. *The Travels and Adventures of Serendipity.* Princeton: Princeton University Press, 2003.

Milesi, Laurent. "Have You Not Forgot to Wind Up the Clock? Tristram Shandy and Jacques le Fataliste on the Post? Modern Psycholanalytic Couch." In *Laurence Sterne in Modernism and Postmodernism,* ed. David Pierce and Peter de Voogd, 179–95. Amsterdam: Rodopi, 1996.

Milton, J. R. "Locke at Oxford." In *Locke's Philosophy: Content and Context,* ed. G. A. J. Rogers, 29–47. Oxford: Clarendon Press, 1994.

Mitchell, W. J. T. "Influence, Autobiography and Literary History: Rousseau's *Confessions* and Wordsworth's *The Prelude.*" *ELH* 57 (1990): 643–65.

Monod, Jacques. *Chance and Necessity: An Essay on the Natural Philosophy of Modern Biology.* Trans. Austryn Wainhouse. New York: Knopf, 1971.

Nakam, Geraldé. *Les Essais de Montaigne, miroir et procès de leur temps.* Paris: Honore Champion, 2001.

Nestor, Pauline. *Critical Issues: George Eliot.* Houndmills: Palgrave, 2002.

Newman, William R., and Lawrence M. Principe. *Alchemy Tried in the Fire: Starkey, Boyle, and the Fate of Helmontian Chymistry.* Chicago: University of Chicago Press, 2002.

Nuovo, Victor. "Locke's Christology as a Key to Understanding His Philosophy." In *The Philosophy of John Locke: New Perspectives,* ed. Peter R. Anstey, 129–53. London: Routledge, 2003.

Olney, James. *Memory and Narrative: The Weave of Life-Writing.* Chicago: University of Chicago Press, 1998.

Owen, W. J. B. "The Sublime and the Beautiful in 'The Prelude.'" *Wordsworth Circle* 2 (1973): 67–86.

Owen, W. J. B. "Wordsworth's Aesthetics of Landscape." *Wordsworth Circle* 7, no. 2 (Spring 1976): 70–82.

Panofsky, Erwin. *Gothic Architecture and Scholasticism.* New York: Meridian, 1957.

Pasnau, Robert. "Form, Substance, and Mechanism." *Philosophical Review* 113, no. 1 (2004): 31–88.

Pasnau, Robert. *Thomas Aquinas on Human Nature: A Philosophical Study of "Summa theologiae" Ia.75–89.* Cambridge: Cambridge University Press, 2002.

Patey, Douglas Lane. *Probability and Literary Form: Philosophic Theory and Literary Practice in the Augustan Age.* Cambridge: Cambridge University Press, 1984.

Patterson, Annabel. *Pastoral and Ideology: Virgil to Valéry.* Berkeley: University of California Press, 1987.

Paxton, Nancy L. *George Eliot and Herbert Spencer: Feminism, Evolutionism, and the Reconstruction of Gender.* Princeton: Princeton University Press, 1991.

Payne, Philip. *Robert Musil's "The Man without Qualities": A Critical Study.* Cambridge: Cambridge University Press, 1988.

Peake, Tony. *Derek Jarman.* London: Little, Brown, 1999.

Pearson, Roger. *Unfolding Mallarmé: The Development of a Poetic Art.* Oxford: Clarendon Press, 1996.

Pelikan, Jaroslav. *The Christian Tradition: A History of the Development of Doctrine.* Vol. 4. Chicago: University of Chicago Press, 1984.

Pencak, William. *The Films of Derek Jarman.* Jefferson, NC: McFarland and Company, 2002.

Perego, Elvire. "Intimate Moments and Secret Gardens: The Artist as Amateur Photographer." In *The New History of Photography,* ed. Michel Frizot, 335–45. Cologne: Könemann, 1998.

Phillips, Adam. *Darwin's Worms.* London: Faber and Faber, 1999.

Picker, John M. *Victorian Soundscapes.* New York: Oxford University Press, 2003.

Pierce, David, and Peter de Voogd, eds. *Laurence Sterne in Modernism and Postmodernism,* Amsterdam: Rodopi, 1996.

Pinch, Adela. *Strange Fits of Passion.* Stanford: Stanford University Press, 1996.

Poovey, Mary. *History of the Modern Fact.* Chicago: University of Chicago Press, 1998.

Popkin, Richard H. *The History of Skepticism from Savonarola to Bayle.* Rev. ed. Oxford: Oxford University Press, 2003.

Porter, Theodore M. *Rise of Statistical Thinking, 1820–1900.* Princeton: Princeton University Press, 1986.

Potter, G. R. *Zwingli*. Cambridge: Cambridge University Press, 1976.

Prosser, Eleanor. *Hamlet and Revenge*. Stanford: Stanford University Press, 1967.

Quint, David. *Montaigne and the Quality of Mercy: Ethical and Political Themes in the Essais*. Princeton: Princeton University Press, 1998.

Reff, Theodore. *Degas: The Artist's Mind*. New York: Harper and Row, 1976.

Reff, Theodore. *The Notebooks of Edgar Degas*. 2 vols. Oxford: Clarendon Press, 1976.

Richardson, Alan. "Of Heartache and Head Injury: Reading Minds in Persuasion." *Poetics Today* 23, no. 1 (Spring 2002): 141–60.

Richetti, John J. *Philosophical Writing: Locke, Berkeley, Hume*. Cambridge, MA: Harvard University Press, 1983.

Riley, Patrick. "The Inversion of Conversion: Rousseau's Rewriting of Augustinian Autobiography." *Studies in Eighteenth-Century Culture* 28 (1999): 229–55.

Roach, Joseph R. *The Player's Passion: Studies in the Science of Acting*. Ann Arbor: University of Michigan Press, 1993.

Roche, Daniel. "Censorship and the Publishing Industry." In *Revolution in Print: The Press in France 1775–1800*, ed. Robert Darnton and Daniel Roche, 3–26. Berkeley: University of California Press, 1989.

Rogers, G. A. J. *Locke's Enlightenment: Aspects of the Origin, Nature and Impact of His Philosophy*. Hildesheim: Georg Olms Verlag, 1998.

Rosset, Clément. *Logique du pire: Éléments pour une philosophie tragique*. Paris: Presses universitaires des France, 1971.

Rouault, G. *Souvenirs intimes*. Paris, 1927.

Rousseau, George S. *Nervous Acts: Essays on Literature, Culture and Sensibility*. London: Palgrave, 2004.

Rozemond, Maureen. *Descartes's Dualism*. Cambridge, MA: Harvard University Press, 1998.

Rubin, Miri. *Corpus Christi: The Eucharist in Late Medieval Culture*. New York: Cambridge University Press, 1991.

Ryan, Christopher. "The Theology of Dante." In *Cambridge Companion to Dante*, ed. Rachel Jacoff, 136–52. Cambridge: Cambridge University Press, 1993.

Ryan, John K. "The Wager in Pascal and Others." In *Gambling on God: Essays on Pascal's Wager*, ed. Jeff Jordan, 11–19. Lanham, MD: Rowman and Littlefield, 1994.

Said, Edward W. *The Question of Palestine*. New York: Vintage Books, 1992.

Sartre, Jean-Paul. *The Words*. Trans. Bernard Frechtman. New York: Random House, 1981.

Schuurman, Paul. "Willem Jacob 's Gravesande's Philosophical Defence of Newtonian Physics: On the Various Uses of Locke." In *The Philosophy of John Locke: New Perspectives*, ed. Peter Anstey, 43–57. London: Routledge, 2003.

Scott, Clive. *Vers Libre: The Emergence of Free Verse in France, 1886–1914*. Oxford: Oxford University Press, 1990.

Screech, M. A. *Montaigne and Melancholy: The Wisdom of the Essays*. London: Duckworth, 1983.

Secord, James A. *Victorian Sensation: The Extraordinary Publication, Reception and Secret Authorship of "Vestiges of the Natural History of Creation."* Chicago: University of Chicago Press, 2000.

Seidel, Michael. "The Man Who Came to Dinner: Ian Watt and the Theory of Formal Realism." *Eighteenth-Century Fiction* 12, nos. 2–3 (2000): 193–212.

Shapiro, Marianne. "An Old French Source for Ugolino?" *Dante Studies* 92 (1974): 129–48.

Shaw, Prudence. "*Paradiso XXX.*" In *Cambridge Readings in Dante's Comedy.* Ed. Kenelm Foster and Patrick Boyde, 191–213. Cambridge: Cambridge University Press, 1981.

Shklar, Judith N. *Ordinary Vices.* Cambridge, MA: Harvard University Press, 1984.

Shuger, Debora. *Habits of Thought in the English Renaissance: Religion, Politics, and the Dominant Culture.* Berkeley: University of California Press, 1990.

Shuttleworth, Sally. *George Eliot and Nineteenth-Century Science: The Make-Believe of a Beginning.* Cambridge: Cambridge University Press, 1984.

Sim, Stuart. "'All That Exist Are "Islands of Determinism"': Shandean Sentiment and the Dilemma of Postmodern Physics." In *Laurence Sterne in Modernism and Postmodernism,* ed. David Pierce and Peter de Voogd, 109–21. Amsterdam: Rodopi, 1996.

Siskin, Clifford. *The Work of Writing: Literature and Social Change in Britain, 1700–1830.* Baltimore: Johns Hopkins University Press, 1998.

Sorabji, Richard. *Necessity, Cause, and Blame: Perspectives on Aristotle's Theory.* Ithaca: Cornell University Press, 1980.

Starobinski, Jean. *Jean-Jacques Rousseau: Transparency and Obstruction.* Trans. Arthur Goldhammer. Chicago: University of Chicago Press, 1988.

Starobinski, Jean. *Montaigne in Motion.* Trans. Arthur Goldhammer. Chicago: University of Chicago Press, 1985.

Steen, Francis F. "'The Time of Unrememberable Being': Wordsworth's Autobiography of the Imagination." *Auto/Biography Studies* 13, no. 1 (Spring 1998): 7–38.

Stephens, W. P. *The Theology of Huldrych Zwingli.* Oxford: Clarendon Press, 1986.

Stern, J. P. *The Dear Purchase: A Theme in German Modernism.* Cambridge: Cambridge University Press, 1995.

Stock, Brian. *Augustine the Reader: Meditation, Self-Knowledge, and the Ethics of Interpretation.* Cambridge, MA: Harvard University Press, 1996.

Stoddard, Eve Walsh. "Flashes of the Invisible World: Reading *The Prelude* in the Context of the Kantian Sublime." *Wordsworth Circle* 16, no. 1 (Winter 1985): 32–37.

Stott, Rebecca. *Darwin and the Barnacle.* New York: Norton, 2003.

Sylla, Edith Dudley. "Business Ethics, Commercial Mathematics, and the Origins of Mathematical Probability." In *Oeconomies in the Age of Newton,* ed. Margaret Schabas and Neil DeMarchi, 309–37. Raleigh: Duke University Press, 2003.

Tayler, Edward W. "The First Individual." In *Soundings of Things Done: Essays in Early Modern Literature in Honor of S. K. Heninger, Jr.,* ed. Peter E. Medine and Joseph Wittreich, 251–59. Newark: University of Delaware Press, 1997.

Taylor, Charles. *Sources of the Self: The Making of the Modern Identity.* Cambridge, MA: Harvard University Press, 1989.

Terrasse, Jean. "Aspects de l'espace-temps dans *Jacques le fataliste.*" *Eighteenth-Century Fiction* 6, no. 3 (1994): 243–57.

Thomas, Keith. *Religion and the Decline of Magic.* New York: Scribner, 1971.

Tierney, Richard. "On the Senses of '*Symbebekos*' in Aristotle." *Oxford Studies in Ancient Philosophy* 21 (2001): 61–82.

Trahir, Lisa. "Short-Circuiting the Dialectic: Narrative and Slapstick in the Cinema of Buster Keaton." *Narrative* 10, no. 3 (October 2002): 307–25.

Trahir, Lisa. "The Ghost in the Machine: The Comedy of Technology in the Cinema of Buster Keaton." *South Atlantic Quarterly* 101, no. 3 (Summer 2002): 573–90.

Traugott, John. *Tristram Shandy's World: Sterne's Philosophical Rhetoric.* New York: Russell and Russell, 1954.

Tromp, Marlene. *The Private Rod: Marital Violence, Sensation, and the Law in Victorian Britain.* Charlottesville: University Press of Virginia, 2000.

Trotter, David. *Cooking with Mud: The Idea of Mess in Nineteenth-Century Art and Fiction.* Oxford: Oxford University Press, 2000.

Turnovsky, Geoffrey. "The Enlightenment Literary Market: Rousseau, Authorship, and the Book Trade." *Eighteenth-Century Studies* 36, no. 3 (2003): 387–410.

Van Steenberghen, Fernand. *Aristotle in the West: The Origins of Latin Aristotelianism.* Trans. Leonard Johnston. Louvain: Nauwelaerts, 1970.

Vernant, Jean-Pierre. "The Individual within the City-State." In *Mortals and Immortals: Collected Essays,* ed. Froma I. Zeitlin, 318–33. Princeton: Princeton University Press, 1991.

Vickers, Ilse. *Defoe and the New Sciences.* Cambridge: Cambridge University Press, 1996.

Vidal, Kathryn Simpson. "Diderot and Reader-Response Criticism: The Case of *Jacques le Fataliste.*" *Studies in Eighteenth-Century Culture* 15 (1986): 33–45.

Virilio, Paul. *The Information Bomb.* Trans. Chris Turner. London: Verso, 2000.

Virilio, Paul. *A Landscape of Events.* Trans. Julie Rose. Cambridge, MA: MIT Press, 2000.

Virilio, Paul. *Negative Horizon.* Trans. Michael Degener. London: Continuum, 2005.

Virilio, Paul. *Unknown Quantity.* Trans. Chris Turner. London: Thames and Hudson, 2003.

Wahrman, Dror. *The Making of the Modern Self: Identity and Culture in Eighteenth-Century England.* New Haven: Yale University Press, 2004.

Walker, William. *Locke, Literary Criticism, and Philosophy.* Cambridge: Cambridge University Press, 1994.

Warminski, Andrzej, and Cynthia Chase, eds. "Wordsworth and the Production of Poetry." Special issue, *Diacritics* 17, no. 4 (1987).

Warren, Howard C. *A History of Association Psychology from Hartley to Lewes.* New York: Charles Scribner, 1921.

Wedin, Michael. *Aristotle's Theory of Substance: The Categories and Metaphysics Zeta.* Oxford: Oxford University Press, 2000.

Whateley, Richard. "Review of *Northanger Abbey* and *Persuasion.*" In *Persuasion,* ed. Patricia Meyer Spacks, 196–205. New York: W. W. Norton, 1995.

Williams, Raymond. *Keywords: A Vocabulary of Culture and Society.* New York: Oxford University Press, 1983.

Wind, Edgar. "The Four Elements in Raphael's Stanza." *Journal of the Warburg and Courtauld Institutes* 2 (1938–39). 75–79.

Winkler, Kenneth. "Lockean Logic." In *The Philosophy of John Locke: New Perspectives,* ed. Peter Anstey, 154–78. London: Routledge, 2003.

Wippel, John F. *The Metaphysical Thought of Thomas Aquinas.* Washington, DC: Catholic University of America Press, 2000.

Witmore, Michael. *The Culture of Accidents: Unexpected Knowledges in Early Modern England.* Stanford: Stanford University Press, 2001.

Wittkower, Rudolf. *Architectural Principles in the Age of Humanism.* 3rd ed. London: Alec Tiranti, 1962.

Wolfson, Susan. *Formal Charges: The Shaping of Poetry in British Romanticism.* Stanford: Stanford University Press, 1997.

Woloch, Alex. *The One vs. the Many: Minor Characters in the Space of the Protagonist in the Novel.* Princeton: Princeton University Press, 2003.

Wordsworth, Jonathan, and Stephen Gill. "The *Two-Part Prelude* of 1798–99." *JEGP* 62 (1973): 503–25.

Wu, Duncan. "Tautology and Imaginative Vision in Wordsworth." *Charles Lamb Bulletin,* n.s., 96 (October 1996): 174–84.

Wu, Duncan. *Wordsworth's Reading, 1770–1799*. Cambridge: Cambridge University Press, 1993.

Yates, Frances A. *The Art of Memory*, Chicago: Chicago University Press, 1966.

Yolton, John. *The Two Intellectual Worlds of John Locke: Man, Person, and Spirits in the "Essay."* Ithaca: Cornell University Press, 2004.

Žižek, Slavoj. *The Sublime Object of Ideology*. London: Verso, 1989.

Žižek, Slavoj. *The Ticklish Subject: The Absent Centre of Political Ontology*. London: Verso, 1999.

INDEX